Henry William Dulcken

The World's Explorers

Or, travels and adventures

Henry William Dulcken

The World's Explorers
Or, travels and adventures

ISBN/EAN: 9783337212636

Printed in Europe, USA, Canada, Australia, Japan

Cover: Foto ©Andreas Hilbeck / pixelio.de

More available books at **www.hansebooks.com**

THE

WORLD'S EXPLORERS;

OR,

TRAVELS AND ADVENTURES.

BY H. W. DULCKEN, PH. DR.

ILLUSTRATED WITH

MANY ENGRAVINGS FROM DESIGNS BY EMINENT ARTISTS.

LONDON:
WARD, LOCK, AND TYLER,
WARWICK HOUSE, PATERNOSTER ROW.

CONTENTS.

BRUCE AND ABYSSINIA.

I.—Truth Stranger than Fiction. Critics of the Last Century: their Ignorance and Injustice. Bruce the Traveller. His Birth and Early Life. Indian Scheme. Study of Oriental Languages. Consulship at Algiers. Bruce Departs on his Travels. Lions and Lion-eaters. Ruins of Ancient Cities. Caravan. Shipwreck at Bengazi. Arrival at Alexandria. Cairo *Page* 1

II.—Cairo in the Last Century. Ali Bey and his Favourites. Bruce as an Astrologer. Trying a Prescription. Bruce's Voyage up the Nile. The Nile Boat. Crocodiles. Kenne. The Caravan. Quarrel with the Leader. Cosseir. Fable of the Emerald Mountain. A Boat without Nails. Arrival at Jidda. Curious Adventure. Eastern Method of Trading. Voyage towards Massuah. Arrival in Abyssinia 11

III.—Description of Abyssinia. Political State of the Country. Ras Michael's Usurpation. Ozoro Esther. Spirited Conduct of Bruce. Advance to Gondar. Adventure with the Cow. Beefsteaks off the Living Animal. "Yagoube" at Court. Abyssinian Banquets. Bruce Continues his Journey. Cataract of Alata. Fazil, the Robber Chief. His Submission and Second Revolt. Difficulties Encountered by Bruce. He Reaches the Source of the Nile. Conclusion 21

THE ASTORIANS.

I.—Vast Extent of North America. Extensive Emigration from Europe. The Mormons and their Progress. The Rocky Mountains. Jacob Astor. His Early Life. His Progress in America. Great Scheme of Colonisation and Commerce. The Fur Trade. The Various Great Companies. Details of Mr. Astor's Plan 37

II.—The Two Expeditions. The Tonquin and her Commander. Quarrels on Board. Ill-humour of the Captain. Opposition of the Partners. The Captain's Complaints to Mr. Astor. Arrival at the Sandwich Islands. Unappreciated Botanists and Explorers. Arrival at the Columbia River. Difficulty of Landing. Loss of a Boat's Crew. Foundation of Astoria. Description of the Red Indians 45

CONTENTS.

III.—Astoria. Departure of the Tonquin. Anxiety respecting Mr. Hunt and his Party. Bad News concerning the Tonquin. Tragical Fate of that Vessel and her Crew. Gloom in the Settlement. Mr. Macdougal's Stratagem to Frighten the Indians. Post Founded at Okinagan. New Year's Eve Celebrated under Difficulties . . . . . Page 53

IV.—Expedition of Mr. Hunt. Character of Hunt. His Extensive Preparations. The Missouri Fur Company and Mr. Manuel Lisa. Pierre Dorion, the Half-breed Interpreter. John Day, the Hunter. Account of Blackbird, the Omahaw Chief. Mr. Bradbury's Adventure with the Indians 59

V.—Encounter with the Sioux. Manuel Lisa and his Schemes. Buffalo Plains. Antelopes. Aricaras and Cheyennes. Difficulties of the March. William Cannon and the Grizzly Bear. The Pilot Knobs. Pierre Dorion's Squaw. Her Patient Endurance and Courage. Arrival at Astoria. New Expeditions Planned. 65

VI.—Mr. Astor's Plans. The Beaver Fitted Out and Despatched. War between Great Britain and the United States. Mr. Macdougal's Marriage with the Daughter of Comcomly. His Equivocal Conduct. Arrival of Mr. Hunt at Astoria. Macdougal Sells the Settlement to the British North-American Fur Company. Surprise and Regret of Mr. Astor. The British Take Possession of Astoria. Macdougal Joins the Fur Company. Renewed Efforts of Mr. Astor. His Further Career. Conclusion . 69

MARCO POLO.

I.—A Remarkable Arrival. The Three Travellers. The Banquet. Surprise of the Guests. Marco Polo and his Works. First Journey of the Elder Poli. The Tartar Empire. Jenghis Khan and his Conquests. Kublai Khan. His Wish to Open Communications with Europe. His Commission to the Brothers. Their Second Journey, in Company with Marco. Panic of their Monkish Companions. Marco's Account of Cashmere. Journey Across the Great Desert of Gobi 75

II.—Arrival at the Confines of China. Reception by Kublai Khan. Account of the Alligator. Elephants and Rhinoceroses. Talent and Energy of Marco. The Poli Promoted by Kublai Khan. Account of China. Desire of the Poli to Return Home. Refusal of the Khan. Opportunity Afforded by the Proposed Marriage of the Khan's Granddaughter. Proposal to Reach the Borders of Persia by Sea. The Khan's Parting Injunctions 84

III.—Homeward Voyage of the Poli. Java. Description of Sumatra. Counterfeit Mummies of Diminutive Men. Account of Zeilan, or Ceylon. Summary Judicial Practice. Madagascar. Account of the Roc, or Rukh. The Island of Socotra. Description of Various Animals. Accurate Particulars concerning the Giraffe, or Camelopard. Intelligence of King Arghun's Death. Arrival of the Poli in Venice 89

CONTENTS.

COMMODORE ANSON'S VOYAGE ROUND THE WORLD.

I.—Heroism of British Sailors. War with Spain in 1739. The Right of Search. Captain Jenkins and his Grievances. The Manilla Galleon. Anson's Squadron Fitted Out. Embarkation of Chelsea Pensioners. Crowded State of the Ships. Disease and Death on Board the Ships. The Trial's Disaster. Arrival at Port St. Julian, on the Patagonian Coast. Departure of the Squadron for Strait-le-Maire. Intelligence of the Spanish Squadron . . . . *Page* 97

II.—Stormy Weather in the South Atlantic. Difficulty in Rounding Cape Horn. Frightful Increase of the Scurvy on Board. Frequent Deaths. Arrival at the Island of Juan Fernandez. Effect of Fresh Vegetables on the Crew. Seal's Flesh. Description of Juan Fernandez. Alexander Selkirk. The Goats. Arrival of the Gloucester. Her Deplorable Condition. The Trial and the Anna. The Severn and Pearl Put Back. Wreck of the Wager and Sufferings of the Captain and Crew . . 104

III.—Brighter Prospects. Capture of Spanish Merchantmen. Information respecting the Spanish Squadron. The Trial's Prize. Intelligence concerning a Treasure at Paita. The Ships Sail Thither. Attack on the Town. An Easy Capture. Cowardice of the Spaniards. The Town Burnt. Two more Prizes Taken by the Gloucester. Losses of the Paita Merchants 113

IV.—Anxiety of Anson to Take the Spanish Galleon. The Island of Quibo. Monkeys as an Article of Food. Parrots and Turtle. Disappointment concerning the Treasure Ship. The Gloucester Abandoned and Sunk. Renewed Sickness on Board the Centurion. Vain Attempts to Land at Anatacan and Deringan. The Island of Tinian. Providential Arrival there. Fertility of the Island. Abundance of Fresh Vegetables and Cattle. The Sick Carried Ashore. Causes of the Sickness on Board 121

V.—The Centurion Driven to Sea. Trying Position of the Commodore. Anson's Resolution. Construction of a Ship. Return of the Centurion. Flying Proas of the Islanders. The Centurion proceeds to Macao. The Ship Refitted. Determination to Take the Acapulco Galleon. Anson's Address to the Crew. Cheerfulness of the Men. Warlike Exercises and Preparations on Board. Suspense and Expectation 129

VI.—Appearance of the Spanish Galleon. Anson's Judicious Arrangements. Method of Fighting the Centurion. Confusion on Board the Galleon. Capture of the Spaniard. Sufferings of the Prisoners on Board the Centurion. Anson's Return to Macao. Chinese Duplicity. A Faithful Interpreter. Return to England by the Cape of Good Hope. War between England and France. Anson's Fortunate Escape. Importance of his Voyage 136

CONTENTS.

Captain Cook and his Discoveries.

I. Importance of Cook's Voyages. Early Life of James Cook. His Practical Seamanship. Voyages at the Beginning of the Reign of George III. The expected Transit of Venus over the Sun. Expedition Fitted Out under Cook's Command. Madeira. The Portuguese in Rio. Passage round Cape Horn. Patagonia. Arrival at Otaheite. Character of the Natives. Judicious and Humane Conduct of Cook . . . . . *Page* 143

II.—Surf-swimming at Otaheite. Thievish Propensities of the Natives. Tupia the Otaheitan accompanies Cook. Singular Customs in Otaheite. Cook's Arrival at New Zealand. Circumnavigation of the Islands. Cook's Strait. Account of the Natives. Cook's Exploration of the Coast of New Holland. Narrow Escape of the Endeavour. Natives of New Holland. Cook Takes Possession of New South Wales. Voyage to Batavia 152

III.—Pestilential Climate of Java. Death of Tayeto and Tupia. Mortality among the Crew. Running a Muck. Cape Town and St. Helena. Return to England. Determination to Send a Second Expedition. Cook Undertakes the Command. Question concerning a Southern Continent. Fitting-out of the Ships. Precautions against Scurvy 161

IV.—Voyage to the South. Punctiliousness of Cook. The Southern Ocean. Danger from Ice Islands. Existence of a Southern Continent Disproved. Dusky Bay, New Zealand. Queen Charlotte's Sound. Cannibalism of the New Zealanders. Otaheite. Danger of Shipwreck. King Otoo. Huaheine. Omai, the South Sea Islander. The Friendly Islands. The Two Ships Part Company. Thievish Propensities of the New Zealanders. Fresh Proofs of Cannibalism 167

V.—Second Run to the South. Hardships and Dangers. The Ships obliged to turn Northward. Cook's Design of Exploring the Pacific. Easter Island. Curious Statues. Otaheite. Barter with Red Parrots' Feathers. Oree, the Chief. New Zealand. Tragical Occurrence to Captain Furneaux's Crew. Details of the Massacre. Rounding the Horn. Survey of Staten Island and Southern Coast of America. Return to England. Brilliant Success of the Voyage 176

VI.—Preparations for a Third Voyage. Question concerning the North-West Passage. The Resolution and Discovery Fitted Out. Kerguelen's Land. Island of Desolation. Van Diemen's Land. Passage to New Zealand. The Friendly Islands. Taboo. Human Sacrifices at Otaheite. Visit to Eimeo and Bolabola. Christmas Island. Nootka Sound. The Natives: their Shrewdness and Rapacity 185

VII.—New Attempt to Penetrate Northward. Stopped by the Ice. Further Exploration of the Sandwich Group. Discovery of Owyhee. Karakakooa Bay. Return of the Ships. Fatal Attack. Death of Cook. Further Proceedings of Captain Clerke. Return to the North. Fur Trade at Canton. Death of Clerke. Return of the Ships in 1779 . . . 193

CONTENTS.

FERNAND MENDEZ PINTO.

I.—Achievements of Eminent Men and their Fame. Kepler and Galileo. Calumnies Attached to Certain Names. Bacon and Walton. Slander Promulgated by Cervantes concerning Pinto. Repeated by Congreve. Figuier's Translation of Pinto's Travels. Their Value. Pinto's First Voyage. His Capture and Slavery. His Voyage to India. He is Despatched from Malacca to Sumatra. The King of the Battas . *Page* 201

II.—Pinto's Mission to the King of Aaru. Hostilities against the Acheens. Pinto's Shipwreck. He is Employed by a Mussulman Merchant. Antonio de Faria turns Pirate, and is Joined by Pinto. Captures and Adventures. Shipwreck. The Chinamen Tricked 210

III.—Another Piratical Cruise. Meeting with a Chinese Pirate Junk. Treaty of Alliance. Encounter with Coja Acem. Victory of Antonio de Faria, and Death of Coja Acem and his Crew. Triumphal Reception of the Victors at Ningpo. Further Adventures. Plunder of the Tombs. Disastrous Shipwreck, and Death of Antonio de Faria 219

IV.—Pinto in Trouble. Kindness of the Bonzes. Retribution. Harsh Captivity. Travels in China. Improved Circumstances. Singular Affray among the Portuguese. Their Punishment. Attack on Pekin by the Tartars. Taking of Quangsay by the Tartars. The Portuguese Enter the Service of the Tartar King 225

V.—Portuguese Boasting. Raising of the Siege of Pekin. Magniloquent Descriptions of Pinto. George Mendez and his Talents. Departure of the Portuguese. Renewed Quarrels among them. Piracy and Shipwreck. Events at Tanixumaa. The King of Bungo. Great Reputation of Fernand Mendez Pinto 233

VI.—Accident to the King's Son. The Portuguese Depart for Liampoo. Great Expedition Prepared for Japan. Disastrous Events. Pinto Shipwrecked on the Loochoo Islands. Condemned to Death. Pardoned through the Intercession of the Women. Pinto Advocates the Conquest of the Loochoo Islands. Return to Liampoo and Malacca. Pinto's Embassy to the King of Martaban. Treachery of the Portuguese. Martaban Taken by the Burmese. Procession of the Vanquished. Lamentable Fate of the Royal Family 238

VII.—Description of Siam and Ava. Former Magnificence of the Cities. Effects of Revolutions. New Calamities of Pinto. A Portuguese Renegade. Another Shipwreck. Dreadful Sufferings and Cannibalism. Father Francis Xavier, the Missionary. Pinto's Further Adventures. His Final Return to Goa. His return to Portugal, Disappointment, and Neglect. Conclusion of his Chronicle 249

CONTENTS.

THE VOYAGE OF LA PÉROUSE.

I.—La Pérouse and his Merits. Importance of his Voyage. Its Origin. Its Political Intention. Early Life of La Pérouse. His Gallantry and Humanity. His Conduct towards the English. Plan of his Voyage. Its Exaggerated Extent. Departure from Brest. Remarkable Appearance of St. Elmo's Lights . . . . *Page* 257

II.—Successful Precautions against Disease on the Boussole and Astrolabe. Congregation of Whales in Strait Lemaire. Easter Island. Remarkable Monuments. State of Cultivation. Pilfering Propensities of the Natives. Run to the North. Port des Français. Its Capabilities as a Trading Settlement. Lamentable Accident and Loss of Twenty Lives. Climate of Port des Français compared with that of Labrador. Voyage to Monterey 265

III.—The Portuguese Settlement of Macao. The Philippine Islands. Manilla. The Coast of Tartary. Bay of Castries. The Tartar Inhabitants. Their Honesty and Friendliness. Survey of the Coasts of Sagalien. Kamtschatka. The Russians and their Government 275

IV.—La Pérouse's Memorial to Captain Clerke. The Kamtschadale Nation. Ravages of Small-Pox. Intermarriages with the Russians. De Lesseps Travels to Europe Overland. His Account of his Travels. Return to the Southern Hemisphere. The Island of Maouna. Architectural Pretensions of Native Buildings. Appearance of the Natives. Death of M. de Langle 282

V.—Voyage Across the Pacific. Vavao, in the Friendly Islands. Norfolk Island. Run to Botany Bay. La Pérouse's Last Letters. Departure from Australia. Long Doubt concerning the Fate of the Expedition. Voyage of Admiral D'Entrecasteaux in Search of La Pérouse. Unfortunate Issue of D'Entrecasteaux's Voyage. Rumours concerning Relics of the Expedition. Voyage of Captain Dillon, and its Results 289

ALEXANDER VON HUMBOLDT AND HIS TRAVELS.

I.—Humboldt's Long and Arduous Career. His First Work. His Pursuit of Geology. His Appointment as Inspector of Mines. He Resolves to Travel. Verifies the Experiments of Galvani. Designs to Join Captain Baudin's Expedition to the Southern Hemisphere. On the Failure of that Expedition Resolves to Pass the Winter in Spain . . 300

II.—Humboldt Receives Permission to Visit the Spanish Colonies in South America. Resolves to Travel to New Spain. Writes to Ask his Friend Bonpland to Join Him. Embarks for the West Indies on a Spanish Frigate. Visits the Peak of Teneriffe. The Dragon-Tree at Orotava. Humboldt's Interesting Views and Researches regarding the Age of Trees 306

CONTENTS.

III.—Various Zones of Vegetation in the Island of Teneriffe. Passage to the West Indies. Observations on Atlantic and other Ocean Currents. Great Beds of Seaweed. The Sargasso Sea. Arrival in the West Indies. A Doctor Sangrado. Earthquakes and Eruptions of Volcanoes. Connection of the Phenomena. Humboldt's Views on Volcanic Action . *Page* 314

IV.—Theatment of Slaves. The Marshes of Araya. Salt Works. A Castilian Shoemaker. Cheap Immortality. Manners and Customs of the Natives of Araya. Effect of the Dominion of the Priests. The Capuchins of Caripe. Cavern of the Guacharo. Nocturnal Birds. Singular Method of Procuring Oil. Abundant and Varied Flora of Caripe. The Vultures of Cumana. Their Lazy Habits 321

V.—Adventure with a "Zambo." Narrow Escape of Bonpland. Eclipse of the Sun. Earthquake Shocks from the Volcano of Pinchinca. Phosphorescence of the Sea. The Hangman of Cumana. La Guayra. A Zealous Physician. Ascent of the Saddle Mountain. The Difference between Promise and Performance. Harmless Bees . . . 329

VI.—Journey across the Llanos, or Great Plains. Aspect of the Llanos. Steppes in Various Parts of the World. Animal Life in the Llanos. The Horse and Ox Tribe and Cereal Plants. The Dry Season and the Rainy Season. The Gymnotus, or Electric Eel. Method of Capture. The Apure and Orinoko. Canoe Voyage. Nocturnal Life of Animals. Savage Tribes of America 335

VII.—Land Journey across the Cordilleras. Disappointment of Humboldt. Volcanic Agency. Singular Method of Travelling. The Great Volcanic Peaks of the Andes. Their Height, &c. Public Works of the Old Peruvians. Roads and Palaces. Conquest of Peru, &c. 348

VIII.—Nature of Volcanic Agencies in the Andes. Cotopaxi. The Quina or Cinchona Bark. Architectural Remains in Peru. The Inca Roads. Aqueducts and Fortifications. Destruction of Public Works in Peru by Spanish Conquerors. Caxamarca. Remains of the Palace. "Baths of the Inca." Pizarro and Atahuallpa. The descendants of Atahuallpa. A Peruvian Aladdin's Garden 353

CAPTAIN FLINDERS.

I.—Flinders' only Memorial. His Early Predilections for Exploring. The Tom Thumb: its Crew and First Voyage. Mr. Bass Penetrates as far as Port Philip. Discovery of Bass's Strait. Lieutenant Flinders is Entrusted with the Command of an Exploring Expedition. The Investigator Commences her Great Work. The French Expedition. Grand Preparations. Interview between Captain Flinders and the French Commander. The Two Expeditions Separate. Hospitality to the French at Sydney. The Investigator Proceeds along the North Coast. Departure for England. Wreck of the Porpoise and Cato 360

CONTENTS.

II.—Want of Assistance in the Captain of the Bridgewater. The Bridgewater Deserts the Two Wrecks. The Crews of the Porpoise and Cato reach an Adjacent Sandbank. Captain Flinders Starts for Sydney and Rescues his Companions. Leaves again for England in the Cumberland. Puts in for Repairs at Mauritius. The Governor Accuses Him as a Spy. Filthy Lodgings. The French Government's Passport Repudiated. Appearance of the Record of the French Expedition. Public Feeling in France. The Emperor Signs the Order for his Release. De Caen's Behaviour. Flinders Returns to England. His Death . . . . . . *Page* 366

EYRE: GOVERNOR AND EXPLORER.

I.—Overlanders. Wealth of the Colonists. Scarcity of Water in the Interior of Australia. The Australian Explorer. Services of the Explorers. Social Position of the Overlanders. Magnitude of their Operations. Demand for New Pastures. Country round Adelaide. Application to Mr. Eyre. He Accepts the Command of the Expedition. Departure of the Explorers. Repeated Failures in Attempting to go Northwards. Eyre Determines to go Westward. The Expedition is Sent Back. The Exploring Party. The Coast Line of South Australia. Want of Water . . - 372

II.—The Water-bags Empty. The Horses Give Way. The Sandhills. A Well Made. No Water but at the Various Sandhills. Superior Endurance of Man above other Animals. Half the Distance Accomplished. Restlessness of the Horses. Mr. Eyre and his Overseer Watch Them. Murder of the Overseer. Escape and Recapture of the Horses. The Adelaide Natives Steal the Provisions. The Horses Killed for Food. A Whaling Barque Sighted. Return to Adelaide. Quarrels between the Aborigines and Colonists. Mr. Eyre appointed Black Protector, Governor of Wellington, N. Z. Lieutenant-Governor of Jamaica. Full Governor. Respect for Mr. Eyre in Australia 378

LIST OF ILLUSTRATIONS.

	PAGE
Duck-bill, The	4
Egyptian Dancing Girls	5
Lion, Lioness, and Cubs	8
Crete	9
Baalbec, The Great Gate at	10
On the Nile	12
Egyptian Female Costumes	13
Sphinx, The, and the Great Pyramid	16
Ruined City of the East	17
Smyrna	19
Egyptian Woman	20
Hyenas and Leopard	24
Buffaloes	29
Abyssinian Wedding Sports	33
Mormon City of Utah, The	37
Mormon Encampment	40
A Beaver Village	41
Indian Weapons and Ornaments	48
A Mandan Chief	49
Chippewa	52
Indian Burying Place	57
Buffalo Hunting on the Prairie	61
Blackbird and his Favourite Squaw	64
The Elk and the Red Deer	69
Dacotah Chief	73
Leopards and Panther	76
Pekin	80
Pisa	81
The Rhinoceros	85
The Hippopotamus	89
Condor and Vultures	92
Giraffes	93
Cabul	96
Spearing Turtle off the Island of Tinian	101
Tailpiece	103

	PAGE
Seals and Walrus	105
Goats	109
Tailpiece	112
Tailpiece	120
Breadfruit Trees at Tinian	121
Parrots	124
Proa Laden with Breadfruit	125
Savage Weapons	127
Tailpiece	128
Terns or Sea Swallows	133
Schooner	135
A Street in Canton	139
The Koodoo and Nylghan	141
Dance of the Australian Aborigines	143
Sea Birds of the Southern Ocean	148
Stormy Petrel—Wandering Albatross	149
Surf Swimming	153
Opossums	157
A Native Home	159
Tattooed Head	160
Cape of Good Hope	164
St. Helena	165
Tailpiece	166
Iceberg	168
Flying Fish	169
Banyan Tree	173
Australian Native	175
Tropical Birds	180
Eagles	184
South African	185
Canoeing in the Pacific	189
Esquimaux of Nootka Sound	192
Polynesian Huts	193
Tiger	197
Fejee Man	200
Wine-Making in Portugal	204

LIST OF ILLUSTRATIONS.

	PAGE
Great Apes, Baboon, &c.	208
Goenong Api—Banda Isles	209
View in Siam	213
Bats	217
Tailpiece	224
Camels	229
Tailpiece	232
Tropical Animals	233
Zebras	237
Tailpiece	241
Chinese	248
Elephant	253
Savage Weapons	267
Polar Bears	269
Song Birds	273
Russian Peasants	275
Pelicans	277
Kamtschadale Sledge	282
Barbadoes from the Sea	288
The Tapir	292
Scene in the Friendly Islands	293
Republicans Escorting Louis XVI. to Paris	297
Tailpiece	299
Humboldt	301
A Silver Mine	304
Reindeer	305
The Capybara or Cavy	308
Tortoise	313
Ibex	314
Scene in the Andes	316
Jaguar, Puma, and Lynx	317
Tailpiece	320
Mountain Region	325
Madrid	329
Scarborough	332
Armadillos and Pangolins	337
Capturing Wild Cattle in the Llanos	340
Humming-birds	344
Sapagous and Viverræ	345
Tailpiece	347
Hippopotamus	348
Llamas	357
An Australian Native	361
Australian Fishermen	364
An Australian Duel	369
Map of Coast Line from Adelaide to King George's Sound	372
Hurling the Spear	376
Throwing the Boomerang	381

LIST OF SEPARATE ILLUSTRATIONS.

	PAGE.
BRUCE AND ABYSSINIA—BRUCE FIRES A TALLOW CANDLE THROUGH THREE SHIELDS	1
A HERD OF BISONS	37
VENICE	75
AMERICAN MONKEYS	97
THE KANGAROO	143
THE WALRUS	176
OSTRICH, EMU, AND CASSOWARY	201
CHINESE COMMERCIAL JUNKS	238
SOUTH SEA WHALE FISHERY	257
LA GUAYRA, NEAR CARACCAS	300
TOUCANS	352
CAPTAIN FLINDERS—GOVERNOR EYRE	360

THE WORLD'S EXPLORERS.

BRUCE AND ABYSSINIA.

I.

Truth Stranger than Fiction—Critics of the Last Century: their Ignorance and Injustice—Bruce the Traveller—His Birth and Early Life—Indian Scheme—Study of Oriental Languages—Consulship at Algiers—Bruce Departs on his Travels—Lions and Lion-eaters—Ruins of Ancient Cities—Caravan—Shipwreck at Bengazi—Arrival at Alexandria—Cairo.

IN one of Captain Marryat's clever books there is an amusing story of an English sailor, who, strongly urged to tell a tale for the delectation of a Turkish pasha, proceeds to spin one of the most wonderful "yarns" ever perpetrated by nautical adventurer. The dangers and escapes of Sindbad the Sailor are as nothing compared with the perils and adventures of this modern mariner. He relates how in a gale the crew of his ship were compelled to "station two men to hold the captain's hair on his head," how "a little boy was carried up into the air by the force of the gale, and then slid back on a moonbeam unharmed to the deck of the ship," with many other particulars equally marvellous and strange. The pasha listens to all with an air of imperturbable gravity. Each extravagant fiction gains ready and undoubting credence with him; and, however "tough" the English Jack's yarn may be, the Turkish dignitary is ready for fresh marvels. But amid all this mass of absurdity there happens to be just one little grain of truth. Jack mentions by chance in the course of his marvellous narrative that in his travels he has met with an animal which has a bill like a duck, and four webbed feet—he is alluding, in fact, to the well-known "duckbill" of New Holland. At this the pasha's patience is exhausted: he who has contentedly submitted to the barefaced demands Jack has been all along making on his credulity, cannot bring himself to believe in the existence of a duck-billed quadruped; and by the mouth of his vizier and interpreter, he indignantly admonishes the narrator to refrain from telling him such impudent lies. Whereupon honest Jack departs, marvelling greatly that the pasha should have pitched upon the only piece of truth in the whole yarn as the subject of his indignant protest.

This little anecdote furnishes no unapt illustration of the behaviour of a number of British and foreign critics at the close of the last century with regard to an enterprising and persevering traveller. Not that the British public of the latter part of the eighteenth century was wanting in credulity. When a rumour was spread of the appearance of a ghost in Cock-lane, Smithfield, a multitude of the curious flocked to hear the spectre's knockings, and returned with a full conviction of the reality of their supernatural host; the impudent quack, Dr. Graham, never lacked dupes to listen to his preposterous stories of cures he had effected, or to pay the unconscionable fees he demanded for pretended services; but when a brave, honest gentleman, who had perilled his life and sacrificed his fortune in the cause of science, came home from his travels with a plain account of what he had seen and experienced in distant lands, he was assailed with sneers by the malevolent, and with open denial by the incredulous; and the public, taking its tone from sundry ignorant and self-elected critics, refused to the veracious narrative of James Bruce the credence it had given to the fictitious pretensions of a score of earlier writers. Dr. Johnson, himself the very reverse of a traveller, pronounced in a few turgid sentences a dictum adverse to the Abyssinian pilgrim's credibility; a graceless German, named Raspé, wrote a marvellous farrago of impossible achievements, which he dubbed *The Adventures of Baron Munchausen*, and sarcastically dedicated to Bruce; and presently there appeared a certain Baron de Tott, who, emboldened by the storm of ridicule he saw pouring down on the devoted head of the traveller, boldly declared his belief that Bruce had not been in Abyssinia at all. And preposterous as this assertion might seem, there were many who believed it, until the well-known Daines Barrington wrote an elaborate vindication of his friend, and silenced the baron and his followers.

It will be our task, in these pages, briefly to recount the labours of the Abyssinian traveller, and to show how those labours were requited.

James Bruce, the discoverer of the sources of the "Blue Nile," was born on the 14th December, 1730, at the seat of a long line of ancestors, Kinnaird House, in the county of Stirling, in Scotland. His family was one of considerable antiquity, and could trace back its annals to a younger son of the heroic Robert Bruce. James was the elder of two sons, and the heir-apparent to the estate of Kinnaird; his father, naturally and wisely anxious to give him an education commensurate with the position he would one day be called to occupy, sent him first to a good school in the neighbourhood of London, and then to Harrow. At the latter school, where he remained four years, he appears to have acquired a considerable knowledge of the ancient languages, and to have made himself popular and beloved. At the age of seventeen he returned to his native country, in order to commence the study of the law at the University of Edinburgh.

But the study of the law presented little to gratify his ardent imagination, while the close application it demanded proved too heavy a tax on a frame which, slender and delicate, gave little promise of the athletic strength to which it attained in after days. Mr. Bruce was soon obliged by ill-health to abandon his legal studies, and he looked around in search of a new field for his energies. India was then, as it has ever since been, the country towards which many a restless and enterprising spirit looked ardently as a field where fame and fortune could be won, and to India James Bruce resolved to proceed. He was too old to be sent out as a writer in the East India Company's service, and determined, therefore, to seek permission to settle in Hindostan as a free trader, under the patronage of the court of directors. Bent on obtaining this privilege he repaired to London in July, 1753, when he was twenty-three.

His Indian scheme, however, was destined to remain unfulfilled In London he made the acquaintance of the family of a Mrs. Allan, the widow of a wealthy wine-merchant, to whose daughter he was married in February, 1754; whereupon he gave up the idea of proceeding to India. Perhaps this was a fortunate resolve; for in 1756 occurred the taking of Calcutta by the infamous Surajah Dowlah, an event followed by the massacre of the Black Hole, in which Mr. Bruce might have perished with the other hapless victims of the wretched despot, soon himself to meet his reward at the hands of the victors of Plassey, led by the young and intrepid Clive.

A few short months saw Bruce a widower. His young wife fell a victim to consumption, and Bruce returned almost heartbroken to London. For some years he devoted himself to the study of Oriental languages; for, as the depression of spirits produced by his great grief yielded insensibly to the natural effect of time on a character singularly energetic and active, Bruce conceived the idea of a new career in which difficulties and dangers were to be overcome and fame was to be gained. The death of his father in 1758 put him in possession of the paternal estate, and the idea of Eastern travel and exploration took a firmer hold on his imagination in proportion as his

THE DUCK-BILL.

unwearied industry gave him a greater insight into the Ghees, or Ethiopic, and the Arabic languages, the objects of his diligent study during some years.

In 1762 the consulship at Algiers was offered to Mr. Bruce, who eagerly accepted it, as an official position could not fail to be a stepping-stone to the enterprise he had determined to prosecute. This was nothing less than the discovery of the source of the Nile, a problem that had perplexed the learned of various ages, and which even kings at the head of victorious armies had failed to solve. After holding the consulship for a year, during which time he displayed eminent firmness and resolution in the course of a quarrel with the savage Dey, Bruce applied for leave of absence to travel in the interior, and then for permission to resign his appointment. Though he had steadfastly

EGYPTIAN DANCING GIRLS.

advocated the interests of his own government in opposition to those of the Dey, his uniform honesty and singleness of purpose so gained the good opinion of that barbaric potentate, that he was furnished with valuable letters of recommendation to the governors of the places he intended to visit in Algiers, and to the Beys of Tunis and Tripoli.

And now, attended by ten spahis or dragoons, excellent good horsemen, but exceedingly cowardly, Bruce set out on his journey, the primary object of which was to explore the various towns in the Barbary States where ruins of ancient temples and other buildings might be found, and to make drawings and write descriptions of these antiquities. He had hired an Italian artist named Balungani to assist him with his drawings; but the poor draughtsman died of dysentery long before the travels of Bruce came to an end.

Our hero was a model traveller in many respects. He had prepared himself for his enterprise by a long and arduous course of study, and was able to speak in the modern Greek, the Arabic, and the Ethiopic languages. He had devoted much attention to mathematics and astronomy, and was thus enabled to take observations and determine longitudes and latitudes with an accuracy to which his detractors themselves have borne unwilling witness. He knew enough of the principles of surgery and medicine to make himself valued and respected by many a wild tribe, and, moreover, he stood six feet four inches in height without his stockings, and was possessed of courage and determination at least proportionate to his bodily stature. Such was the traveller who sallied forth to explore the then almost unknown districts of the Barbary States.

On the frontiers between Algiers and Tunis, he stopped at Hydra, the Thunodrudum of the ancients. Here he found a tribe of Arabs, called the *Welled Sidi Boogannim*—the sons of the father of flocks. They are a very rich tribe; they pay no tribute, form a kind of half-military, half-religious order, and are bound by a vow to eat lion's flesh as their daily food. They are naturally expert hunters, and are exempted from tribute in consideration of the services they perform in ridding the country of lions. Bruce himself ate lion's flesh with the Welled Sidi Boogannim, and describes the flesh of the male lion as tough, lean, musky in flavour, and altogether resembling what he could fancy would be the taste of old horseflesh. The flesh of the she-lion he describes as fatter and less disagreeable; but the meat of a whelp of six or seven months was the most nauseous of all.

In reference to this fact of lion-eating, which has been abundantly verified by later travellers, Bruce tells an anecdote strongly illustrative of the hardness of belief of the learned in those times, and of the difficulty with which a traveller gained credence who had to teach some new thing. A Dr. Shaw, of Oxford, who had travelled among the Arabs, and under whose notice this custom of lion-eating had come, very naturally mentioned the circumstance on his return to England but this would not do for the Oxford common-room. That lions ate men everybody knew; but a man eat a lion—preposterous! So the doctor, a peaceable man, anxious to propitiate his critics, discreetly omitted the fact of the lion-eating in his narrative, and merely hinted at it in his appendix. Our traveller was not the man to take a similar course. When he had once asserted a thing as a fact, he considered it a point of honour to maintain his assertion, and contradiction only made him cling the firmer to his position, on the good old principle that, however wide a scope there might be in matters of theory for difference of opinion, facts were not to be suppressed or explained away, inasmuch as, if once true, they were true always.

As he travelled from place to place, diligently drawing every remarkable relic of antiquity that came in his way, noticing at Lambessa the sculptured standard of a legion with the proud old inscription "Legio Tertia Augusta," and at Kisser, the Colonia Assuras of the ancients, a small square temple with instruments of sacrifice carved upon it, the explorer could not fail to meet with stirring adventures, more especially as the country was in a state of war. In the ruins of Spaitla, the ancient Suffetula, his studies were unpleasantly interrupted by a visit from a lawless tribe, the Welled Omram. These marauders blockaded Bruce and his party, who fortified themselves within the high walls of the ruined temples of Spaitla, and kept the besiegers at bay with their guns. The arrival of a friendly tribe rescued the besieged garrison, who were reduced to a state of semi-starvation when the relieving force freed them from their tormentors. At Feriana, the ancient Thala, which Metellus destroyed in his pursuit of Jugurtha, King of Numidia, he found fishes like gudgeons swimming merrily in baths of very warm water. Near Tripoli he met the Emir al Hadj, or commander of the annual caravan conducting the yearly throng of pilgrims who journey from Fez and Zuz, in Morocco, to Mecca. A disorderly rabble rout these hadji proved to be—about three thousand in number, with some fourteen thousand camels. They mistook Bruce and his horsemen for mounted banditti, and showed a disposition to run, but plucked up courage, which soon changed to insolence when they found that the travellers were peaceable men, and had no confederates lurking in the neighbourhood.

At Ras Sem Bruce visited the petrified city, respecting which it had been asserted, and, indeed, extensively believed in Africa, that the Divine vengeance had overtaken the inhabitants, and suddenly transformed them to stone, as they were engaged in their daily employment. A French consul had once offered a considerable sum to the Arabs for a specimen of petrified humanity, and had been rewarded by becoming the possessor of a very rudely sculptured statue. As may be supposed, our enthusiastic investigator found no stony inhabitants at Ras Sem, but he had an opportunity, for the first time, of observing the habits of

LION, LIONESS, AND CUBS.

the jerboa, a curious long-legged mouse, remarkably long-limbed and agile. Soon after this Bruce was shipwrecked in a Greek vessel, near the harbour of Bengazi, and very narrowly escaped with his life. His account of his escape reads like a passage from *Robinson Crusoe*:—

The vessel, he says, was very ill accoutred. She had enough of sail, but no ballast. A crowd of passengers fleeing from the famine were taken on board. The commander was not accustomed to those seas. A light, steady breeze, promising a short and agreeable voyage, soon became violent and cold. A storm of hail followed, and the gathering of the clouds seemed to threaten thunder. The captain was preparing, on Mr. Bruce's persuasion, to put into the harbour of

CRETE.

Bengazi, when the vessel unexpectedly struck on a sunken rock in the entrance to the harbour, and at no great distance from the shore. Mr. Bruce and his two servants, one of whom, Roger M'Cormack, was an old man-of-war's man, went down into one of two boats that were towing astern, trusting to their own skill to get ashore. Before they could get clear of the ship, a crowd of passengers rushed in after them. They had not got twice their boat's length from the ship when they were drenched by a wave which nearly filled their frail craft, and drew a howl of despair from the wretched passengers. Bruce had fortunately stripped himself for a swim, retaining only his waistcoat and drawers. A silk sash was wrapped round him. In his breast-pocket he had a pencil, a small pocket-book, and a watch. The next wave was to determine the fate of those in the boat; he, therefore, called his servants to follow him if they could swim, and instantly let himself down in the face of the wave. With all his strength and activity a swimming, he could not withstand the force of the surf. From the ebbing wave he received a violent blow on the breast, which threw him upon his back, and occasioned him to swallow a considerable quantity of water. He dipped his head while the next wave passed over. He was now breathless, weary, and exhausted, but almost on land. A large wave floated him up; but he was again struck on the face and breast, and involuntarily twisted about by the violence of the ebbing wave. As a last effort, he tried to feel the bottom, and happily reached the sand with his feet, although the water was still over his mouth. This success inspired him with new vigour. He floated on with the influx of the wave, and, by sinking and touching the ground, withstood the ebb. At last, finding his hands and knees upon the sand, he fixed his fingers in it, crawled forward a few paces when the sea retired, and, having got beyond its reach, he sank insensible on the ground.

The Arabs, in the meantime, came down to plunder the vessel. The persons in the boat had perished. One boat was thrown ashore; the Arabs had several others. In these they made their way to the ship to plunder the wreck, and brought the people safe to land. A blow on the neck with the butt-end of a lance was what first awakened Bruce from the senseless state in which he lay, after escaping the violence of the waves. The Arabs, believing him, from his dress, to be a Turk, after beating, kicking, and cursing him, stripped him of

THE GREAT GATE AT BAALBEC.

the scanty clothing yet upon him; and, after treating the rest in the same manner, went to their boats, to seek the bodies of those who had been drowned. On its appearing, however, that the shipwrecked wayfarer was not a Turk, but a poor Christian physician, the swarthy wreckers somewhat relented towards him, and threw around his bruised and wearied form a tattered baraca. The sheikh of the tribe ordered him a supper, and he afterwards procured a passage to Canen, in Crete, in the ship of a French captain, who happened to be at Bengazi. Thence, after recovering from a dangerous illness, Bruce proceeded to Sidon, Baalbec, and Palmyra, everywhere making drawings, examining hieroglyphics, seeking to decipher doubtful or obscure inscriptions, and bearing hardships, fatigues, and occasionally sickness, with unfailing buoyancy of spirit. At length he arrived at Alexandria, and thence proceeded to Cairo. He had now received some scientific instruments from Europe, and was bent on making every preparation for the expedition from which he justly hoped to earn credit and fame—the project which had been present to his mind for years, and to which he had clung through discouragement and dissuasions which would have shaken a less vigorous resolution—the attempt to discover the sources of the Nile.

II.

Cairo in the Last Century—Ali Bey and his Favourites—Bruce as an Astrologer—Trying a Proscription—Bruce's Voyage up the Nile—The Nile Boat—Crocodiles—Kenne—The Caravan—Quarrel with the Leader—Cosseir—Fable of the Emerald Mountain—A Boat without Nails—Arrival at Jidda—Curious Adventure—Eastern Method of Trading—Voyage towards Massuah—Arrival in Abyssinia.

A VERY different place was the Cairo whence James Bruce started on his voyage up the Nile from the bustling city through which thousands of travellers now stream every month; bound for the presidencies of our Indian Empire. The overland route had not yet been dreamt of, and the camel, horse, and mule were the only means of transport where now the iron steed and the iron road have established themselves—a type of modern progress and civilisation amid the stagnation of the East. The voyage up the Nile, now a favourite trip with luxurious "howadji;" who, as the author of the *Nile Notes* observes, are accustomed to "suffer and be strong" on a luxurious sofa, surrounded by all the means and appliances of comfort, was at that time a dangerous undertaking, not to be achieved without much negotiation and entreaty, and much propitiation of various men in power. It was a Cairo without donkeys for hire and sellers of jewellery—

A NILE CARAVAN.

a Cairo hostile to strangers and intolerant of exploring zeal—that Bruce entered at the end of the year 1768.

Fortunately, however, one circumstance was in his favour. Ali Bey, Pasha of Egypt, was entirely swayed in his counsels by three advisers—a Jew, a Greek, and a Coptic Egyptian—and the third of these men, Risk by name, possessed the greatest share of the Bey's confidence. Risk was greatly impressed at sight of the astronomical and scientific instruments Bruce had brought with him, and looked upon the gigantic British traveller as a great necromancer and magician, to whom, accordingly, he applied for prophecies concerning future events, especially touching the issue of a certain expedition to Mecca which was shortly to be undertaken. In a country where the bastinado or death by impalement might be the consequence of a mistake, it was a serious thing to meddle with astrology; but Bruce judiciously contrived to give an oracular ambiguity to his prophecies. He had, moreover, the satisfaction of knowing that he should be far beyond the territories of the pasha before the issue proved their correctness or their fallacy; and Risk, whose respect for a prophet that had such manifold and complicated appliances was unbounded, recommended Bruce in warm terms to his master. The Bey also happened to be unwell, and Bruce, suspecting that the illness arose from excess at table, prescribed a very simple remedy, which was first tried, on the principle, "Fiat

EGYPTIAN FEMALE COSTUMES.

experimentum in corpore vili," on an unfortunate monk of the Greek convent, and then used by the Bey with complete success. This proof of profound medical science completed the favourable impression Bruce had already made, and he departed on his journey well provided with letters of recommendation from the bey himself, and from the janissaries, to the principal authorities, political, military, and ecclesiastical, with whom he might expect to be brought in contact.

And now, on the 12th of December, 1768, Bruce started on the voyage up the Nile. He travelled in a boat a hundred feet long, provided with two tall masts and enormous lateen sails, the greater of them a hundred and twenty feet in length. He passed the famous pyramids of Ghizeh, concerning which he surmised that they were hewn out of the solid rock—an opinion disputed by later travellers.

After some delay, the rais, or captain of the boat—a hadji who had made the voyage to Mecca, and never tasted fermented liquor—made his appearance with his son, very completely intoxicated. When this worthy follower of the prophet had slept himself sober, the voyage commenced in real earnest, and day after day the great boat worked its way up the broad current of the Nile, between the flat banks studded with palm trees, beneath whose scanty shade crouched poverty-stricken villages—past magnificent ruins, telling of the mighty Roman people, who left their mark in stone and sculpture wherever their vast yoke had been placed on the necks of the nations—past fishermen, on triangular wooden rafts supported on jars, floating down the stream to sell their pottery in the market-place at Cairo—past Comaicedy, where the Nile inclines to the westward, and Nizelet el Aral, consisting of miserable huts, where the people wove boats with sugar-canes for a voyage down stream to Cairo. At Rhoda, where Bruce attempted to land to make drawings of some ruins, he was attacked by the natives, who stole the turban of his servant Mahomet, but were put to precipitate flight when a blunderbuss full of pistol-bullets was fired over their heads. Christmas Day, ninety-and-nine years ago, brought them to the ruins of Dendera, and here they saw the first crocodile. We are told that hundreds of these animals were afterwards seen lying upon every island of the river, like herds of cattle; yet the inhabitants of Dendera drive their beasts of every kind into the water, and they stand there for hours. Girls and women, too, who come to fetch water in jars, stand up to their knees in the water for a considerable time, and, if we may guess by what happens, their danger is full as little as their fear, for none of them that Bruce ever heard of had been bitten by a crocodile. Further on he tells us that the ancient notion recorded in the fable of Æsop, that the dogs run along the banks of the Nile, lapping the water as they go, lest the crocodile should seize them if they tarried, is a fiction, for he himself saw many dogs quenching their thirst, standing quietly in the river without showing any of the apprehension of danger attributed to them in the ancient story.

After a voyage of sixty-four days, Bruce quitted the Nile. During his passage up the river he had diligently taken observations of the longitude and latitude of every important place, and subsequent researches have testified to the accuracy of these labours. That they might not be lost, in case of fatal accident to himself, Bruce took care, before leaving the Nile, to "write up his journal," and send his various manuscripts to friends at Cairo, to remain with them till the issue of his enterprise should be known. And now he joined the caravan for Kenne, the ancient Cæne Emporium, and the really perilous part of his journey commenced; for, of the two hundred mounted guards who accompanied the caravan for its protection, it might truly be asked, "Quis custodiet ipsos custodes?" Not only were they arrant thieves, but Bruce shrewdly suspected discretion with them was considered decidedly the better part of valour, and before a few attacking Arabs they would run, like Falstaff, upon "instinct." Subsequent observation convinced him that his opinion was not ill-founded.

An attempt to steal a portmanteau confided by some Turks to Bruce, and the severe chastisement inflicted on the offender by the proprietors, had nearly involved our traveller in a serious quarrel with Sidi Hassan, the leader of the caravan, and the rabble rout under his command. Hassan found fault with Bruce for patronising the Turks, and further declared that the whole camp was in disturbance on account of the beating of the man, and that it was as much as he could do to prevent his followers and servants from falling upon and exterminating Bruce and his followers. With characteristic intrepidity, our undaunted traveller laughed this covert threat to scorn. "With regard to your preventing people from murdering me," he said, "it is a boast so ridiculous that I only laugh at it Those pale-faced fellows who are about you, muffled up in burnouses for fear of cold this morning, are they capable of looking janissaries like mine in the face? Speak low, and in Arabic, when you talk at this rate, or it may not, perhaps, be in my power to return the compliment you paid me last night, or hinder them from killing you on the spot." On this a man behind exclaimed, "Were ever such words spoken? Tell us, master, are you a king?" "If Sidi Hassan is your master," replied Mr. Bruce, "and you speak to me on this occasion, you are a wretch! Get out of my sight!" By a display of resolution, not unmixed, perhaps, with a little occasional bluster, to maintain "prestige," the traveller managed to preserve his position among the doubtful characters into whose company he was continually brought.

Bruce especially mentions the quantity of jasper, granite, and marble of various colours seen by the travellers on their way from Terfoowey to Cosseir, and he conjectures that hence the ancients must have drawn the stores of stone with which the ornamental parts of their cities were built. He declares that he passed in four days more porphyry, marble, and jasper than would have built Rome, Athens. Corinth, Memphis, Syracuse, Alexandria, and, as he vaguely adds, "half-a-dozen such cities." At Cosseir, a mud-walled village on the Red Sea, Bruce heard a strange story of a mountain of emeralds, said to be at no great distance, and while waiting for the return of a ship that was to convey him from Cosseir down the Red Sea towards Abyssinia, he made an excursion thither; but he found that Eastern romance had been at work here; the substance called emerald turned out to be nothing more nor less than a kind of green granite; some brittle green crystal was the nearest approach to an emerald to be

THE SPHINX AND THE GREAT PYRAMID.

found. The craft in which Bruce now navigated the Red Sea was curiously constructed. It had but one sail, like a straw mattress, made of the leaves of a kind of palm-tree, which the natives call "doom." This sail was fixed above, and could be drawn up like a curtain, but did not lower with a yard, like an ordinary sail, so that, upon stress of weather, if the sail was furled, it was so topheavy that the ship must founder, or the mast be carried away. The planks of the vessel, however, were sewn together, and there was not a nail nor a piece of iron in the whole ship, so that when it struck on a rock—a casualty that happened more than once in the course of the voyage—no great damage was done.

By the time our traveller reached Jidda, a port of considerable note, he presented a very woebegone appearance. He had been suffering for some time from ague, and the anxieties and dangers of his journey had told upon him to such an extent that the Emir Bahar, a captain of the port, could scarcely believe that he was an Englishman, but took him for a Galiongy, or Turkish sailor. At the house frequented by the Bengal merchants he was also looked upon as an impostor; but a certain benevolent Captain Thornhill, looking upon him as a countryman in distress, procured him immediate succour and a passage to India, and sent him into a sort of warehouse where the merchants were accustomed to show samples of their goods.

RUINED CITY OF THE EAST.

Feeling himself safe here, Bruce, after taking some refreshment, stretched himself on the ground to enjoy the first quiet sleep he had been able to indulge in for many days, and as he lay dozing he could hear several English sailors, who sauntered down from the quay to take a look at him, discussing his appearance among themselves, and they all seemed to decide that he was a particularly ill-looking fellow, and beyond all question a Turk. In the meantime, however, Jousef Cubil, governor of Jidda, a person of an inquisitive, or rather acquisitive, turn, began inspecting the traveller's trunks with a general view to plunder, by the ingenious process of taking off the hinges, and thus opening them at the back, without disturbing the locks, and greatly was this dignitary disturbed on finding a firman of the Grand Seignior, a white satin bag addressed to the Khan of Tartary, a green and gold silk bag with letters for the Sherriffe of Mecca, a plain crimson satin bag with letters for Metical Aga, and, lastly, a letter to himself from Ali Bey, peremptorily commanding him to advance the bearer's views by every means in his power. Jousef at once proceeded to where Bruce sat contentedly on a mat at the Bengal house, solacing himself with coffee, and when matters had been explained, strong letters of recommendation were procured for him to the Prince of Massuah, the King of Abyssinia, Michael the prime minister, and the King of Sennaar, and in addition to this Mahomet Gibberti, an Abyssinian, was sent with Bruce to Massuah (Massouah) to witness and report on his reception there.

Bruce was greatly astonished at the manner in which trade was carried on at Jidda, and at the confidence with which cargoes are disposed of on credit to Arab and Turkish merchants. He says, "Nine ships may be there from India, some worth perhaps two hundred thousand pounds. One merchant, a Turk living at Mecca, some thirty hours' journey off, where no Christian dares venture, whilst the whole continent is open to the Turk for escape, offers to purchase the cargoes of four out of these nine ships himself; another of the same caste comes and says he will buy none unless he has them all. The samples are shown, and the cargoes of the whole nine ships are carried into the wildest parts of Arabia by men with whom you would not willingly trust yourself alone in the field. This is not all. Two Indian brokers come into the room to settle the price—one on the part of the Indian captain, the other on that of the buyer, the Turk. They are neither Mahometans nor Christians, but have credit with both. They sit down on the carpet, and take an Indian shawl, which they carry on their shoulders like a napkin, and spread it over their hands. They talk in the meantime on different subjects—of the arrival of ships from India, or of the news of the day, as if they were employed on no serious business whatever. After about twenty minutes spent in handling each other's fingers under the shawl, the bargain is concluded—say for nine ships—without one word ever having been spoken on the subject, or pen or ink used in any shape whatever. There was never one instance of a dispute happening on these sales." It is difficult to read this account without a latent idea that the traveller's imagination or credulity must have betrayed him into a little exaggeration.

It would be wrong to pass from this part of Bruce's adventures without noticing the very valuable nature of his observations of longitude and latitude, which, in spite of fatigue, anxiety, danger, and occasional ill-health, he carried on with indefatigable perseverance

SMYRNA.

throughout his voyage in the Red Sea from Cosseir to the Strait of Babelmandeb. It reads somewhat oddly side by side with the sneering detraction of Lord Valentia and Mr. Salt, who travelled over the same ground many years afterwards, apparently with the view of disproving as much as possible of Bruce's narrative, to find an English naval captain who accompanied his lordship telling us how he "made use of Mr. Bruce's observations, which he found exceedingly accurate." As an instance of the spirit in which these late travellers spoke of Bruce, it may be here noted that because he had mentioned a predilection for *blue* cloth and *blue* beads among the females of Abyssinia in his day, they take occasion, on finding that no such preference existed in their time (forty years later), to lament that Mr. Bruce should have misled them by his inaccurate statement, and induce them to bring merchandise of a colour which they found unsaleable, as though Fashion—that proverbially fickle goddess—were bound to change her nature in Abyssinia, and to abdicate her functions for half a century.

With ready good-humour, Bruce laughed the rais or captain of his primitive vessel out of the superstitious fears that beset him from the rumour that the ghost of an Abyssinian who had died on board had been seen on several occasions riding on the bowsprit.

"My good rais," said Mr. Bruce gravely to the commander, who had come aft in hot haste to consult him upon this prodigy, and urgently requested him to come forward and speak to this supernatural intruder, "I am exceedingly tired, and my head aches much with the sun, which hath been very violent to-day. You know the Abyssinian paid for his passage, and if he does not overload the ship (and I apprehend he should be lighter than when we took him on board), I do not think that, in justice or equity, either you or I can hinder the ghost from continuing his voyage to Abyssinia, as we cannot judge what serious business he may have there."

The rais, who must have more than half suspected that his distinguished passenger was quizzing him, declared that he did not care for his life more than another man, but still insisted that Bruce, as a learned man, ought to speak to this contumelious spectre. Bruce thereupon suggested that the rais should go forward and invite the ghost aft into the cabin, but as neither the rais nor any of his men dared carry the message, the matter blew over for the time. At length, after a long and tedious voyage, Bruce landed in the harbour of the Island of Massuah, and now he would soon enter the ancient Empire of Abyssinia.

III.

Description of Abyssinia—Political State of the Country—Ras Michael's Usurpation—Ozoro Esther—Spirited Conduct of Bruce—Advance to Gondar—Adventure with the Cow—Beefsteaks off the Living Animal—"Yagoube" at Court—Abyssinian Banquets—Bruce Continues his Journey—Cataract of Alata—Fazil, the Robber Chief—His Submission and Second Revolt—Difficulties Encountered by Bruce—He Reaches the Source of the Nile—Conclusion.

IN Bruce's time the realm of Abyssinia was divided into three great portions, but the continual disturbances and frequent political revolutions rendered these boundaries liable to frequent change—in fact, their condition was like that of the sprung topmast in Marryat's novel, which the magniloquent carpenter described as "precarious, and not at all permanent." Between the Red Sea and the River Tecazze extended the Tigré district; while from the Tecazze westward to the Nile was the province of Amhara. To the south of these two provinces lay the country of the Galla tribes. From the sea to some distance inland extends a plain, very hot and unhealthy. Then begin three successive ranges of mountains, each presenting a separate elevation and its peculiar climate, the heat naturally decreasing as a greater height is attained; the Abbo Jared, the highest of the Abyssinian mountains, rises to a height of 15,200 feet. In some parts of the country Bruce describes the climate as delightful, the hills covered with cattle, and the fields with verdure; in others, naked plains and dreary wildernesses extended for many miles before the tired wanderer.

At the time when Bruce arrived, a revolution had just taken place in the country. Ras Michael, the crafty and astute governor of the Tigré district, had put the king to death, and raised in his place a youth, a species of *roi fainéant*, in whose name he governed with a sway as independent as the authority exercised by the *maires du palais* at the court of the later Carlovingians. To strengthen his influence, he had married the beautiful Ozoro Esther, daughter of the Iteghe, or queen-mother, and established himself at Gondar, the capital of the country. Bruce was well provided with recommendations to some of the principal persons in Gondar, and in his intercourse with them showed an admirable amount of tact and self-reliance. No man better understood the art of "being all things to all men," and he became equally popular with the stern and fierce old Ras, the weak young king, the beautiful Ozoro Esther, and the melancholy Iteghe, in whom a queenship of thirty years had but produced the conviction of the vanity of all earthly things.

His first difficulty was with the naybe, or governor, of Massuah, the port where he landed. This officer considered the chance of plundering a stranger in the light of a golden opportunity not to be carelessly thrown away. But Bruce understood his position and privileges as a British subject too well to be intimidated, and haughtily said that he would visit the naybe no more. "Whatever happens to me," he said to the officers of the divan, "must befall me in my own house. Consider the figure a few naked men will make *the day my countrymen ask the reason of this, either here or in Arabia.*" And with this he turned his back on the assembly, and departed without further ceremony. No wonder that as he departed he heard a voice behind him exclaim, "A brave man! *Wallah Englese!* A true Englishman, by Heaven!" Resolution and an undaunted bearing had the desired effect, and the naybe, considering that, after all, it would not be safe to drive such a man to extremity, permitted him at length'to go his way in peace.

After crossing the Taranta Mountain, our traveller entered upon an exceedingly fertile range of country. On the road the *cortége* was frequently disturbed by the prowling hyenas, who would come forth from their haunts among the bushes, and slink round the travellers at a little distance, greedily eyeing the asses and mules. In one instance, when five asses were to be brought up Taranta, they congregated in such numbers that the four Moors who were driving the asses became seriously alarmed for their own safety—indeed, the villainous plunderers, grown bold by numbers, seized an ass, and dragged it down; but one of the Moors, who was armed with a musket, fired it among them, whereupon they fled. Great herds of antelopes were also seen; and so devoid of fear were they that they allowed the travelling party to pass through the midst of them, only moving slightly to the right and left, like a herd of grazing cows in a meadow.

As the success of Ras Michael, and the fear in which that crafty ruler was personally held, had produced a kind of calm in Abyssinia, Bruce determined to take advantage of this period of tranquillity, and push forward at once for Goudar. He encouraged his drooping companions by hopes of reward and preferment, and as much by his own cheery example as by his promises prevailed on them to proceed. On his way to Gondar he was witness of an incident the relation of which in Europe was received with a general shout of incredulity, though the accounts of subsequent travellers have completely verified the existence of the custom which it illustrates. He had just lost sight of the ruins of Axum, the ancient capital of Abyssinia, when his party overtook three travellers driving a cow before them. They had black goatskins upon their shoulders, and lances and shields in their hands; in other respects they were but thinly clothed; they appeared to be soldiers. He says, "The cow did not appear to have been fatted for killing, and it occurred to us that she had been stolen. This, however, was no business of ours; nor was such an occurrence at all remarkable in a country so long engaged in war." Bruce's attendants had some conversation with the drivers. Soon after one of the latter "tripped up the cow so as to throw her roughly on the ground, which was but the beginning of her sufferings. One of them sat across her neck, holding down her head by the horns; the other twisted the halter about her fore-feet; while the third, who had a knife in his hand, in place of taking her by the throat, got astride upon her body before her hind-legs, and gave her a very great wound in the upper part of her buttock." Mr. Bruce, who, from the time when he saw the cow thrown on the ground, naturally concluded she was to be killed, was completely astounded to see the man with the knife deliberately cutting two large pieces of flesh out of the wretched animal, and these steaks were afterwards spread on one of the shields. The men now proceeded to cure the wound. The skin, which had not been separated completely, was flapped over the wound, and fastened at the edges with small wooden pins; a plaster of clay was further spread over the place, and then the unhappy cow was compelled to rise, and was driven away, as Bruce tells us, "to furnish a fuller meal when they should meet their companions in the evening."

The shouts of incredulity with which the relation of this incident was received in England seem to have arisen from a misconception. The hearers and readers seem to have jumped to the conclusion that Bruce meant to represent this cutting of flesh from the living animal as an everyday occurrence, and that he wished them to believe the cow was to be kept alive for an indefinite time after the operation. But the written narrative conveys nothing of the kind. The very expression, "to furnish a fuller meal when they should meet their companions in the evening," indicates that the cow was then to be slaughtered, and that unusual hunger or greediness induced the drivers to commit a cruel act, one which Bruce, during all his residence in

HYENAS AND LEOPARD.

Abyssinia, never saw repeated, although the native manner of slaughtering cattle was almost equally cruel. But the incident was quite a windfall to the critics and satirists, who, with Peter Pindar at their head, fell upon it quite as greedily as the Abyssinians upon the tortured cow; and having demonstrated, to their own satisfaction, that the cutting of flesh from the living animal was a fiction, they proceeded to deny the now well-known fact that the Abyssinians ate raw meat, though the experience of travellers abounds with instances of their use of diet still more disgusting to Europeans. The "beef-steak" anecdote was supposed to furnish a case against Bruce, whose critics worked it against him with malignant perseverance.

As Bruce approached Gondar the country became more and more fruitful in appearance; luxuriant wheat-fields and groves of sugar-cane gave evidence of the fertility of the soil; but the bad government and the ravages of continual war kept the inhabitants poor in spite of the bounty of Nature. But it is rare in Eastern countries to find the mass of the population rising above the most abject poverty.

Bruce's acquaintance with the Tigré language, and his elementary knowledge of medicine, were of great importance to him in making his way in Abyssinia. It happened, moreover, that at the time of his arrival the children of the fair Ozoro Esther were suffering from an attack of small-pox, a disease greatly dreaded in Abyssinia, where it had made great ravages, especially at Massuah. Bruce, or "Yagoube," as he was called, was immediately requested to show his skill; he prescribed plenty of fresh air and cleanliness, with a few simple remedies; his patients quickly recovered; and the influence of Yagoube, the Englishman, was firmly established at court. The young king took evident pleasure in his society, and admitted him to frequent interviews; with the Iteghe he stood exceedingly well; Ozoro Esther, who considered she owed the lives of her children to him, became his firm friend; and even the stern and taciturn Ras Michael would occasionally unbend in his society. Bruce gives us the following description of the Ras:—"He was an old man with white hair, dressed in many short curls; his face was lean; his eyes were quick and vivid, but seemed a little sore from exposure to the weather; he seemed about six feet high, though his lameness made it difficult to guess with accuracy; his air was perfectly free from constraint. They must have been bad physiognomists that did not discern his understanding and capacity by his countenance; every look conveyed a sentiment with it; he seemed to have no occasion for other languages, and, indeed, he spoke but little."

The favour Bruce had gained at court naturally excited a certain amount of jealousy, and raised up enemies against him. Foremost among these was Guebra Mascal, a nephew of Ras Michael, a bold and determined soldier, but a very ill-conditioned fellow, much given to boasting, and valuing himself especially on his skill with the firelock. An altercation into which Bruce was betrayed with Guebra at a banquet, nearly led to bloodshed; and on this occasion Bruce seems to have displayed more courage than discretion; but he afterwards completely re-established his position by performing the feat of piercing three shields with a tallow-candle fired from a gun—an exhibition that filled the king and the whole court with unbounded astonishment and admiration. The banquets in Abyssinia, at which raw meat formed the *pièce de résistance*, are described as degenerating towards their close into drunken and brutal orgies; and as Bruce was obliged, in his capacity of courtier, to be present at many of them, his health suffered considerably. He thus became doubly anxious to prosecute his journey and make his way to the source of the Nile, and begged to be allowed to depart. The king and the ladies tried all in their power to dissuade him from his enterprise; they represented the dangers of the route, and the hostility of the Galla tribes among whom Bruce would have to make his way. The Iteghe was especially emphatic in her dissuasions. "See," said she, "how every day furnishes us with proofs of the contradiction and folly of human nature. You are come from Jerusalem through vile Turkish governments, and hot unwholesome climates, to see a river and a bog, no part of which you can carry away, were it ever so valuable, and of which you have in your own country a thousand larger, better, and cleaner, and you take it ill when I discourage you from the pursuit of this fancy, in which you are likely to perish, without your friends at home ever hearing when or where the accident happened: while I, on the other hand, the mother of kings, who have sat upon the throne of the country more than thirty years, have for my only wish, night and day, that after giving up everything in the world, I could be conveyed to the Church of the Holy Sepulchre in Jerusalem, and beg alms for my subsistence all my life after, if I could only be buried at last within sight of the gate of that temple where our blessed Saviour once lay.' So different are the aspects in which the same things are viewed by various natures. The enterprise which our traveller fondly hoped should immortalise his name and give him a place in the glorious catalogue of British worthies, appeared to the Abyssinian princess but as " a visit to a bog, no part of which he could carry away."

There was, however, a reason with which Bruce was not at that time fully acquainted for the depressed tone of the Iteghe's spirits. Fazil, the rival chief, who disputed the supremacy of Ras Michael in Abyssinia, had collected a numerous army, and the old captain had gone forth to oppose him, and wage what at best must be a dangerous and doubtful conflict. Ras Michael marched with his army to defend his usurped authority, carrying with him the king, the Iteghe, Ozoro Esther, and his whole court; and Bruce was free to continue his journey. On the 21st of May, 1770, he came to a magnificent cataract of the Nile, whose height he estimates from a rough measurement made with poles and sticks at about forty feet. He describes the swollen river as pouring over the rock in an unbroken sheet half-a-mile in width. Jerome Lobo, the Jesuit, had described this cataract of Alata as one in which it was possible to sit down behind the fall between the rock and the projecting deluge of water; but Bruce denies the possibility of this. It is probable, however, that in the many years which intervened between the visits of Lobo and Bruce, the bed of the river above the cataract may have changed so as to render a feat which was perfectly practicable in Lobo's day an impossibility in the year 1770.

The war appears to have been carried on with great ferocity; Ras Michael's soldiers plundered and set fire to the villages on both sides of their route, and their enemies rivalled them in ferocity. A certain Woodage Asahel, a chief whose hatred to Ras Michael was implacable, showed considerable talent in guerilla warfare, appearing when least expected to make a dash at some part of Michael's army, and disappearing as suddenly as he had come. Woodage Asahel's men hovered on the outskirts of the Abyssinian army, like the Cossacks on the wings of Napoleon's force, in the campaign of 1812; and their leader was allowed on all hands to be "the most merciless robber the age had produced in all Abyssinia."

A feigned submission of Fazil put an end to the expedition of the king, and before commencing his retreat towards Gondar he made a grant to Bruce of the village of Gresh, and the district of the source of the Nile, that the traveller might have a right to draw supplies of provisions and necessaries thence for himself and his servants. Indeed, throughout all their intercourse, the king, with whom Yagoube was a prime favourite, treated Bruce with exceeding kindness and condescension, and was unfeignedly sorry to part with him, especially as he considered Bruce's project as alike harebrained in character and frivolous as regarded the object in view.

The king's troubles soon began afresh; Ras Michael's cruelties had exasperated a great part of the population of Abyssinia, who rose in revolt against him. Fazil renounced his allegiance on the first opportunity, and Bruce saw that it would be impossible to continue his journey without first conciliating the goodwill and obtaining the permission of this dangerous chief. With equal resolution and tact he visited Fazil in his quarters, where he found the formidable chief seated in barbaric fashion in a tent, on a cushion with a lion's skin upon it. He had a cotton cloth, "like a dirty towel," wrapped round his head. His upper garment or cloak was drawn far over his hands; so that when Bruce came forward, bowing, to kiss one of them, he could not get at it, and was obliged to salute Fazil's sleeve. Our traveller shrewdly suspected that this covering up of the hands was intended as a mark of disrespect; for Fazil's manner, during their first interview, was the reverse of friendly. He affected to ridicule Bruce's design of visiting the source of the Abaye; he declared that the region was inhabited by the wild Galla, a ferocious and terrible people, and that Bruce must be raving to think of trusting himself among them. It seems that Abba Salama, a priest, who detested Bruce, had been endeavouring to persuade him to bar our traveller's further progress. Fazil endeavoured to excite his visitor's wrath by an affectation of contempt. "I would have you to consider," he was pleased to say, "that the men of this country are not like yours; a boy of these Galla would think nothing of killing a man of your country. You white people are all effeminate; you are like so many women; you are not fit for going into a province where all is war, and inhabited by men warriors from their cradle."

In general, Bruce had his temper, which was naturally fiery, under proper control; but the insults of Fazil stung him to the quick, and he threw judgment and discretion to the winds. He roundly told the savage that, in all the barbarous nations among whom he had passed, he had found none who would insult a defenceless stranger as he had been insulted that day. He protested against the name of Frank, by which Fazil had called him, and in reference to the chief's disparaging remarks concerning white men, boldly declared that there were soldiers among his countrymen who, with five hundred men, would trample all Fazil's Galla savages, "who had been warriors from

BUFFALOES.

their cradle," in the dust; and that he himself, mounted on horseback, and armed in his usual way, would think little of encountering and vanquishing the two best horsemen and soldiers from among these famous men ; and hereupon they parted, mutually dissatisfied.

A little reflection, however, calmed both the disputants ; and in the morning Fazil was evidently in a better temper, for he invited Bruce to a great breakfast, where he offered his guest "honey and butter, and raw beef in abundance, as also some stewed dishes that were very good." The sight of the presents Bruce had brought completely mollified him, and he now showed himself as ready to advance his visitor's designs as he had been eager, the day before, to oppose them. He introduced him to seven Galla chiefs, whom he had summoned, "the most thief-looking fellows," Bruce declares, "I had ever seen in my life," and caused these savage warriors to swear that they would help and protect Yagoube. He moreover invested him with the government of the Agow Gresh, where the head of the Nile is situated, gave him a reliable guide, and, as a crowning token of goodwill, caused a very handsome grey horse to be brought to the door of the tent as Bruce was bidding him farewell. " Take this horse," said Fazil, " as a present from me. It is not so good as your own ; but, depend upon it, it is the horse which I rode upon yesterday when I came here to encamp. But do not mount it yourself ; drive it before you bridled and saddled as it is ; no man of Maitsha will touch you when he sees that horse ; it is the people of Maitsha, whose houses Michael has burnt, whom you have to fear, and not our friends the Galla."

Protected by the powerful Fazil, Bruce encountered no annoyance from the natives ; but Woldo, the guide provided by that chief, proved a very slippery customer. This amiable personage pretended to fall violently ill, magnified the distances that still remained to be crossed, and at last declared that he could proceed no farther. Bruce met this imposture with characteristic firmness. He told Woldo that any trick played upon him would turn out very much to the disadvantage of the perpetrator ; and that he, as a physician, was perfectly competent to distinguish a real from a feigned sickness. "Look you," he said, when Woldo talked piteously of the " great hill" yet to be overcome before they could arrived at Gresh, " lying is to no purpose. I know where Gresh is as well as you do, and that we have no more mountains or bad places to pass through, therefore if you choose to stay behind you may ; but to-morrow I shall inform your master, Welletor Yasous, of your behaviour." Woldo hereupon recovered his health with miraculous swiftness, and being propitiated by the gift of a silken sash, on which he had set his heart, proved perfectly tractable and compliant. The "big hill" he had described so pathetically proved to have no existence save in his own imagination; when they had gone a little distance farther he said—"Look at that hillock of green sod in the midst of that watery spot; it is in that the two fountains of the Nile are to be found; Gresh is on the face of the rock where two green trees are; if you go the length of the fountains, pull off your shoes, as you did the other day; for these people are all pagans, worse than those that were at the ford" (he alluded to a tribe who would not let our traveller's party cross the river without pulling off their shoes in token of respect towards a stream they held sacred), "and they believe in nothing that you believe, but only in this river, to which they pray every day, as if it were God; but this perhaps you may do likewise." And now Bruce, rushing precipitately down the hill in the direction pointed out by Woldo, regardless of two severe falls among the prickly bushes in his headlong course, found himself at last at the goal of which he had dreamed through so many anxious days and sleepless nights. Before him rose an island of green turf in the form of an altar, apparently the work of art, and he stood in rapture over the principal fountain which rises in the middle of it—at last he had reached the source of the Nile.

* * * * *

And here, in the moment of his triumph, we leave our enterprising traveller. He had not, indeed, solved the whole problem that had puzzled geographers and kings for ages; for it was only the source of the Blue Nile, whose waters he now quaffed exultantly with his Greek servant Stratos; the White Nile still hid his head far to the south, and it was reserved for two travellers of our own day to drink the waters of the discovered Nile at the spring-head of the mighty stream.

The travels and researches of Bruce were worthy of a better reward than he received when, after many years, he returned, first to England, and then to his own country. The incredulity which the narrative of his travels excited embittered his last years. That he was sometimes careless about names and dates, and that the account of his travels, written long after the events they describe, are not free from inaccuracies, is certain; but the general tone, though here and there disfigured by bombast, is one of eminent candour and honesty, and would, to any but an ignorant and carping critic, carry with it a conviction of trustworthiness.

Bruce died from the effects of an accidental fall, in his own house, at Kinnaird, in April, 1794.

The following particulars of the country into which a British force advanced towards the end of 1867 are, with immaterial changes, drawn from Consul Plowden:—

The ancient form of government in Abyssinia was a despotic monarchy, with many Persian forms and Jewish institutions. This, while powerful, was preferable to the present state of lawless violence, and afforded an appearance of unity, however ill the law may have been executed, as appears by their records. Long before its fall, the inroads of Mahomedans on the coast of the Red Sea, and of the Gallas on the southern and eastern boundaries, had much reduced the ancient limits of the empire; and the royal family had ceased to be regarded with respect or fear, even in the few provinces that their arms could still defend.

This monarchy was finally overthrown by Ras Michael of Tigré shortly after the visit of Bruce to Gondar; and that Ras was next attacked and defeated by the Gallas, under pretence of avenging the emperor. The son of Ras Michael having been afterwards slain in battle by the Mahomedans from Edjo and Worrahaimano, in the general confusion that ensued, a young man of no note from the former province, named Gooksa, seized the province of Begemder, and received from the deposed but still recognised "Ahtiee," or emperor, the title of Ras. Here the power of the Church was felt, and though by the aid of Mussulman sabres he had overthrown Christian forces, and felt himself strong enough to portion out the country amongst his followers, and to contemn the royal shadow at Gondar, he was obliged to profess the Christian faith, not daring to risk the holy war that would otherwise have been kindled by the priests.

He then became virtual ruler of Abyssinia, as far as subtlety and force could confirm his title; but in the north, Tigré, or, as Plowden writes, Teegray, acknowledged only its native princes, and Godjam, in the south, kept him occupied in constant wars with various fortune. For nearly seventy years this Galla dynasty held Begemder, and if not acknowledged sovereigns were most powerful pretenders. It is owing to this revolution, and the consequent number of claimants for power, none of whom succeeded in establishing a permanent and hereditary authority, that relations with Abyssinia have been since so difficult and fruitless.

Ras Ali, the grandson of Gooksa, having received tribute and a professed allegiance from the other chiefs, including him of Tigré, became the sole Ras. Nevertheless, all men having arms in their hands and many leaders heading large armies, the whole period of his twenty-two

ABYSSINIAN WEDDING SPORTS.

years' reign the Ras was in the saddle, and his palace was his tent; being engaged in pursuing those who fled into impregnable mountain strongholds or pathless wildernesses, or in striking down others who withstood his arms in open fight. During his reign he overcame three powerful cabals of the northern and southern chiefs combined. During the government of Ras Gooksa, the Ras Welda Selasee, in Tigré (to whom an embassy was sent by England), and Ras Gibree, in Semen, were independent. Oubieh (Plowden writes Oobeay), the grandson of Ras Gibree, slew Dejaj—or Dejaz—Sabagardis, the successor of Ras Welda Salasee, who also contemplated a strict alliance with us; and after that victory conquered Tigré, which he held for twenty years. Although Dejaj Oubieh became, by this acquisition of territory, a formidable rival, he was, after several severe struggles, forced to recognise Ras Ali as his chief, to pay him tribute yearly, and to send a quota of troops as feudal service. All rivals being apparently vanquished, the Chief of Godjam, Dejaj Birro, alone held out unconquered through the whole period of Ras Ali's power. After repeated victories over the troops sent against him, an overwhelming force, headed by the Ras in person, drove him for refuge to his mountain, where he remained shut up for five years. During this period was Plowden's mission, while the Ras Ali might be said to be, in one way or the other, complete master of Abyssinia. But this mastery, however proud a position for himself, secured by a turbulent and licentious army, was necessarily factitious; and the numerous bands of Gallas, his relatives, brought by him to sustain his precarious power, with the difficulty of feeding the immense army he kept up, in no way added to the security of property and the tranquillity of the land. Indeed, he had many troubles even in his camp; for the great chiefs, though from fear they rendered him feudal service, yet, chafing at the obligation, still asserted almost sovereign rights in their several provinces. Many of them, who claimed descent from the royal family of Gondar, or whose ancestors had held high offices under the Empire, considered themselves with some reason his equals. Others, again, of inferior pretensions, plundered the country, or exacted contributions in proportion to their force. The Ras, could all his vassals be united, might have mustered at one time 50,000 men of all arms; and his rival, Oubieh, 30,000; yet many a petty adventurer, their equal in birth perhaps, with only 500 or 1,000 followers, trusting to the strength of his mountains or valleys and his local influence, continually braved these rulers; and though, after much bloodshed, many of them were reduced to obedience, enough were always under arms to render the roads unsafe without a military force, or the escort of a strong caravan of merchants. It may easily be conceived that each chief, in proportion to his importance, dealt pretty much as he pleased with travellers or merchants on his own ground; and in these matters the Ras was powerless, or too careless, to interfere, inasmuch as he knew it easy to provoke a rebellion amongst a soldiery that regarded inaction as a penalty and war as a delight. Little vigour was shown in suppressing these outbreaks, the Ras generally caring little if his own supplies were not cut off, or his revenues seriously diminished. He generally made terms with his rebellious vassals, preferring policy to force.

The feudal sovereignty of the Ras having been established by the sword, and depending any time on the issue of a battle, he was obliged, in appointing a "Dejajmatch," or governor of a province, to be attentive to the claims of the great families, who, from their hereditary influence, must be either rulers or rebels in their respective districts; the doubtful alternative of destroying them he was always too merciful to adopt. These chiefs followed him to war, and gave him a portion of their revenues; they bestowed on their retainers districts and villages as they pleased; and the pay of each was the revenue he could extract from these allotments.

The Ras reserved for himself a number of provinces, to provide for his household officers and troops. The soldiers were paid an uncertain sum of money occasionally, and had a monthly allowance of corn. This corn was sometimes measured out from the Ras's granaries; but more often a half-plundering licence to quarter themselves in the reserved provinces was given. This was not always patiently acquiesced in, and bloody struggles ensued, in which the peasantry sometimes succeeded in expelling the soldiery; the weakness of the Ras generally obliging him to overlook such an affair.

The petty household of a chief who has three or four villages is an exact imitation, on a ludicrous scale, of that of one who musters at a word 5,000 horse. He has all officers, and no servants; his "king's mouth," his major-domo, his grand butler, his chief of commissariat, his jester, his master of the horse, and so forth; this with an establishment of perhaps thirty persons, each system revolving round its sun or candle. Yet, as every military man who is courageous or well connected may hope with reason to reach the highest grade, they practise state without thinking themselves absurd. The Ras is, truly, only the most powerful of a number of competitors; several of those who acknowledged him as feudal superior maintaining their right to judge without appeal. It is one favourable trait in this long rivalry, that poison, or assassination, has rarely, if ever, been resorted to; their warfare being open, often chivalrous.

Such was the state of Abyssinia in Consul Plowden's time, and such it has remained with not great variation till now. The advent of King

Theodore gave the Abyssinians an Emperor, King, or Negus again. But although he put his foot on the neck of his enemies more firmly than any Abyssinian ruler of modern times, and repressed many acts of brigandage and oppression, he has not had it, any more than any one else, entirely his own way.

The Abyssinian Expedition undertaken under the command of Sir Robert Napier, in 1867, leads to the consideration of many difficult questions. The future of Abyssinia, the position of the Turks and Egyptians, and our own stations and possessions in the Red Sea, are all involved in the issue of the policy which has led us to the land of the Negus Theodore. Here is not the proper place to discuss that policy. Considerable rivalry has often been displayed between the English representatives and French emissaries in the lands bordering the Red Sea—the passage to India. In Persia we have intrigued against them, whilst they have not been slow to return the compliment. In India we are supreme at present; but it was stated by eminent authorities in the House that, for the sake of our prestige there, it was necessary to take active measures to release Consul Cameron. The French and other continental governments are watching our proceedings narrowly; they would by no means be sorry to hear of our ill-success, for it is in human nature that we take a little comfort from the troubles of our friends and associates. Whether, therefore, the reasons were sufficiently weighty to commit the nation to such an enterprise as the Abyssinian Expedition, we have yet to learn; but the Expedition being a fact, then we must all wish it success, if not a speedy return.

A HERD OF BISONS.

THE ASTORIANS.

THE MORMON CITY OF UTAH.

I.

Vast Extent of North America—Extensive Emigration from Europe—The Mormons and their Progress—The Rocky Mountains—Jacob Astor—His Early Life—His Progress in America—Great Scheme of Colonisation and Commerce—The Fur Trade—The Various Great Companies—Details of Mr. Astor's Plan.

IF any ten persons of ordinary education were desired to indicate on a map of the world the part whose manifold natural resources have been least developed by the industry of man, nine out of the ten would probably point to the great North American continent. And in this case the verdict of the majority would be the true one. The stream of emigration has, indeed, for a long time been flowing towards the West, deepening and widening year by year, and absorbing in its current men from all parts of the Old World, and especially from Europe. Peasants from the Black Forest have floated their frail boats of fir-planks down the Neckar and the Rhine, to embark on the broad ocean, and carry their labour to a region where, as one of their own poets has said, "He who ploughs the land shall reap." Political fugitives hurrying from the dangerous lands of despotism, artisans in quest of a new market for their various crafts, enterprising and speculative traders and merchants, have sought "fresh fields and pastures new" in the regions of the Far West. Not the least among the reasons that have contributed to people the Western wilds, and raise cities as if by enchantment in regions where the bear and the buffalo had roamed in undisputed sovereignty, has been the rise and progress of that wonderful sect the Mormons, who, uniting to a strange and ludicrous fanaticism a remarkable amount of perseverance and courage, have formed and consolidated an empire on the shores around the Great Salt Lake. In spite of all this various activity, millions of acres that might laugh with harvests still lie unclaimed and untouched by the hand of man, lonely and deserted, save for the occasional passage through them of some trading caravan, or some party of painted Indians on the war-trail or on a hunting expedition. The vast extent of the country, the various barriers interposed by ranges of mountains, and still more effectually by desert plains, the rigour of the climate in some parts, and the absence of means of communication in others, long prevented the regions around the Rocky Mountains from being included in the regular track of emigration. But already these barriers are disappearing before the magic of science. The iron road is forcing its way through hitherto deserted tracts, superseding the heavy waggon that painfully creaked across the boundless prairies; already the great republic has stretched forth its arm to the Pacific, and included within its jurisdiction all the land to distant San Francisco.

The discovery, made some twenty years ago, that gold existed in large quantities in California, has resulted in planting many a thriving community in spots which might otherwise have been left for many years to wandering herds of buffaloes, solitary grisly bears, and tribes of "Redskins" equally solitary and nomadic; and it may truly be said that an amount of colonisation and progress which would require centuries for its achievement under ordinary circumstances, has been accomplished in the "Far West" within fifty years.

Our readers will do well to bear these facts in mind if they would form a just estimate of the condition of the western and north-western portion of the great North American continent at the beginning of the present century. No gold-fields had yet been discovered; no farms had been established in the fruitful spots by the banks of great rivers, to be the nuclei of thriving villages and towns; the Rocky Mountains had indeed been crossed by explorers, but no idea yet existed of establishing a regular route. It was at this period, when Western North America was indeed a wilderness, pathless, deserted, and in a great measure unexplored, that a scheme of colonisation and trade remarkable alike for the boldness of its conception, the originality of its plan, the soundness of the views on which it was founded, and the extensive range of its operations, was conceived and executed through the energy and perseverance of one man. This scheme was the foundation of a settlement on the Pacific, at the mouth of the Columbia river, and it was originated and accomplished under the auspices of John Jacob Astor.

This remarkable man, who by his own exertions throughout a long life of industry and probity, gained for himself a foremost place among the merchant princes of the world, was born of poor parents, in the little town of Walldorf, near Heidelberg, in Germany, on the 17th of July, 1763. His father carried on the trade of a butcher in the place, and John Jacob was the last of four sons of a first marriage. On the death of his wife, the elder Astor took to himself a second helpmate; and this new marriage, which produced a second family, seems to have lessened the comfort and narrowed the means of subsistence of the elder children. Accordingly, as the Astor lads grew up, they began to turn their thoughts to the remedy which seems naturally to suggest itself to the imagination of the German peasant, when pinched by poverty or roused by tyranny into anger. The youths emigrated one after another; and in due time John Jacob, or "Nobbele," as he was called at home, strapped his knapsack on his shoulders, took staff in hand, and stepped into the little market boat that was to carry him down the Neckar and the Rhine to the port of embarkation—whence he hoped first to reach England, and ultimately America, the "land of promise" in the imagination of the German peasant of the Black Forest and the Palatinate.

It was in the winter of 1783 that Astor, who had been living for some time in London, embarked for America. The season was unusually severe, and the ship was for a long time blocked up by the ice in Chesapeake Bay. During the period of enforced idleness, Astor made the acquaintance of a countryman, who earned a good income by buying furs at the frontier stations, and carrying them across the ocean to England for sale when he had amassed a sufficient number.

MORMON ENCAMPMENT.

The account given of the condition and future prospects of the fur trade by the dealer determined the future plans of the enterprising young traveller. He would learn all that was to be learnt about furs; he would be a furrier—in time a fur-merchant; and this should be his road to independence and wealth. This resolution he carried out with unswerving industry and untiring perseverance. It is told of him how, soon after this time, while success and prosperity had not yet begun to loom in his future, he one day passed along the Broadway of New York, celebrated already in those days for its magnificent houses. "Ah," said the young German, looking coolly up to the lofty buildings

THE ASTORIANS. 41

on each side, "I'll build a finer house than any of these some day—and in this very street too;"—and he lived to found in New York, not only

A BEAVER VILLAGE.

a house for himself, but more than one institution to perpetuate his memory.

Mr. Astor had been many years in New York, and the penniless

German immigrant had become one of the wealthiest and most respected men in the city, when in the year 1810 he set about the execution of the great scheme of colonisation and commerce the outlines of which we have now to present to our readers. The idea originated in the following circumstances:—

As in the discovery of Central and Southern America the one object of the colonising Spaniards and Portuguese had been the acquisition of gold, so in the cold and bleak regions of Northern America the English and French settlers and traders had confined their attention and their hopes to the traffic in furs. Already in the reign of Charles II. a vast tract of British America had been conceded to the Hudson's Bay Company, who had established their forts and stations at various points in the wilderness, and carried on a twofold trade. They trafficked with the Indian tribes, to whom they gave beads, iron and steel ornaments and implements, guns of coarse manufacture, blankets, kettles, and not unfrequently ardent spirits, in exchange for furs. They, moreover, maintained a number of hunters and trappers in their own service;—men accustomed to live for months together in the wilderness, trapping beaver by the great lakes—hunting the wild animals of the forest, and themselves not unfrequently hunted by parties of hostile Indians. The company, possessing a huge monopoly in the sole right of hunting over thousands of square miles, had amassed great wealth. The French, during their occupation of Canada, had not been unmindful of the benefits to be derived from the trade in peltries; and licences had been frequently granted to certain merchants, and sometimes to the widows or other representatives of deceased officers, empowering them to fit out expeditions to traffic with the Indians for furs. On such occasions large boats, manned by sturdy rowers called "voyageurs," and by adepts in woodcraft who bore the appropriate name of "coureurs des bois," would push their way up the great Canadian rivers, with whose every bend and reach these experienced travellers were well acquainted. At various places the Indian tribes, and sometimes solitary trappers who had for years been pursuing their lonely industry in the silent woods, came down to trade; and frequently an expedition of the kind returned to its starting-place with a cargo of furs whose value was sufficient amply to repay all outlay and risk, though the lion's share was absorbed by the projectors and proprietors, and the hardy men who had borne the peril and suffering obtained but a trifling share of the profit. They are described as a strange race these coureurs des bois and voyageurs, sprightly, mercurial, somewhat given to bragging of their exploits and of their "hairbreadth 'scapes by flood and field," active and hard-working, fond of singing and dancing, but, on the other hand, subject to fits of sudden depression, and easily led for evil as for good. After Canada came into the possession of the British, the old system was changed. Merchants made ventures on their own account, no licences being required. The two rival centres of the fur trade, Michilimackinac and Montreal, sent out expeditions, and by endeavouring to outbid each other brought the trade into confusion. In 1787 a number of merchants, chiefly at Montreal, amalgamated with some of their rivals, and formed "The North-West Fur Company." This corporation for a time engrossed almost the whole of the Canadian fur trade, conveying merchandise for traffic up the great lakes and rivers, and bringing back valuable cargoes of furs from the high northern latitudes, even as far as the Great Slave Lake. Another British company was soon started to work the trade of the west and south-west, which the North-West Fur Company had left almost untouched. This second association had its headquarters at Michilimackinac, or Mackinaw, and was hence known as the Mackinaw Company.

We could scarcely suppose that the government of the United States looked with favour upon this concentration of the fur trade in the hands of the British: it could hardly fail to see the vast profits that accrued from the traffic, and some feeble attempts were made to establish trading houses at various points; but these desultory efforts were powerless to withstand the concentrated action of the companies. Mr. Astor now offered, if the government would countenance and assist him, to turn the American fur trade into the hands of American citizens; and was encouraged by the expressions of favour bestowed on his scheme by the government to hope for a substantial co-operation which he never received. Under a charter from the State of New York he organised the "American Fur Company," with a capital of a million of dollars, the whole of which he provided; then, in 1811, he bought out the Mackinaw Fur Company, amalgamating that association with his own under the name of the "South-West Company." Before this amalgamation was carried out he had already set on foot two expeditions;—and it is the history of these expeditions we have now to describe.

The plan which Mr. Astor laid before the United States Government, and the execution of which he pursued unaided and alone, comprised two main points—first, to form a settlement, and secondly, to organise direct and permanent communication with that settlement both by sea and land. The locality for the new trading town was to be a spot selected at the mouth of the Columbia river, which pours its waters into the great Pacific Ocean in 47° north latitude. Here the company was to establish its headquarters, and here was to be the grand fur depot; minor stations at suitable distances from each other, and in localities frequented by the native tribes, were to be established successively as necessity or convenience suggested. Mr. Astor admitted four gentlemen into partnership with himself. Three of these had been clerks in the North-West Company and had abandoned that association, by which they considered themselves ill-treated. Their names were Mackay, Macdougal, and Mackenzie. The fourth of Mr. Astor's partners was Mr. Wilson Price Hunt, of New Jersey, an American gentleman of great experience and worth.

Anxious, if possible, to avoid the hostility of the North-Western Company, as he was already certain of the rivalry of the Hudson's Bay association, Mr. Astor made overtures to the directors at Montreal, offering to give them a share in his enterprise. They not only refused to co-operate with him, but endeavoured, by despatching an expedition of their own towards the mouth of the Columbia, to forestal the coming of Mr. Astor, and spoil his market with the natives. Finding that nothing was to be effected by negotiation, the spirited merchant now determined to try what he could achieve in the fair and open field of competition.

The chief articles of agreement between Mr. Astor and his partners were these:—Mr. Astor was to be at the head of the company, to manage its affairs in New York, to furnish vessels, goods, ammunition, and to pay all charges up to 400,000 dollars; in return he was to have half the profits, the remaining half to be divided among the other partners. If successful, the association was to continue for twenty years; an agent was to reside for a term of five years at the settlement on the Pacific, and Mr. Hunt was to be the first to undertake this duty.

II.

The Two Expeditions—The Tonquin and her Commander—Quarrels on Board—Ill-humour of the Captain—Opposition of the Partners—The Captain's Complaints to Mr. Astor—Arrival at the Sandwich Islands—Unappreciated Botanists and Explorers—Arrival at the Columbia River—Difficulty of Landing—Loss of a Boat's Crew—Foundation of Astoria—Description of the Red Indians.

AND now, preliminaries having thus been settled, Mr. Astor determined that one party of the new colonists should proceed to their destination by sea, and another by land. The land expedition was to travel up the Missouri, across the Rocky Mountains, and down the Columbia river, exploring the country, and noting the points where trading stations could be established. Mr. Hunt, the American partner, was appointed leader. For the expedition to proceed by sea round Cape Horn, and thence to the Columbia river, up the Pacific, a fine ship called the Tonquin had been provided, and furnished with every requisite for the new colony; even to a little schooner to be used in trading up the river. The vessel was well armed, moreover, and placed under the command of Captain Jonathan Thorn, of New York, who had been a lieutenant in the United States Navy. Some artisans went in her, and also thirteen Canadian voyageurs. The partners Messrs. Mackay and Macdougal were among the passengers, and several young men went out as clerks.

It was on the 8th of September, 1810, that the Tonquin started on her voyage; and she had not been at sea many hours before unmistakeable symptoms appeared, foreboding difficulties of various kinds between Captain Thorn and his passengers. The honest captain was the most single-minded of men. He knew that Mr. Astor, the originator of the expedition, had himself borne the whole expense; and the captain accordingly bent all his energy towards saving Mr. Astor's purse, and consulting Mr. Astor's interest in every possible way. His one object, like that of an honest letter-carrier, was to convey his cargo to the destined port in the very shortest time; and, educated in the strict discipline of the navy, he considered himself entitled to carry out a despotic system of rule on his own quarterdeck. On the other hand, among his heterogeneous passengers there were many causes of discord. Macdougal and Mackay, and two junior partners, an uncle and a nephew of the name of Stuart, looked upon themselves as part proprietors of the ship and cargo, and accordingly as entitled to command Captain Thorn. The Canadian voyageurs, unsurpassed in skill and resource on their own rivers and lakes, became peevish and morose under the influence of sea-sickness; and when they got well they complained of the man-of-war fare offered to them on board, requiring delicacies the very mention of which filled Captain Thorn with unmitigated disgust. "And these," he writes indignantly to Mr. Astor, "are the fellows who boasted that they could eat dog!" The young clerks, too, showed an aptitude at forgetting the main object of the voyage and a levity which was an abomination to Captain Thorn. Naturally enough, they kept journals in which they recorded many matters new and curious to them, though to the old sailor everyday occurrences; this the captain considered waste of time. The partners murmured at and disobeyed his "man-of-war" order to put out all candles at eight o'clock every night. He threatened to put the chief partner, Macdougal, in irons, and Macdougal swore that on such a thing being attempted he would shoot the captain through the head. Peace was only restored by the intervention of some quieter spirits. At one of the Falkland Islands the captain hove to, and sent a boat on shore for water. Messrs. Mackay and Macdougal took the opportunity to go on a hunting excursion, and were very nearly left behind; the indignant captain setting sail without waiting for the boat when his signals of recall were disregarded. Another time, on a similar occasion, he compelled Macdougal and the elder Stuart, with the boat's crew, to follow the ship for many hours, tugging hard at the oars; and even then, in spite of the threats of the younger Stuart, who feared his uncle's life would be sacrificed, he would hardly have given in, but that fortunately the wind came ahead, and the ship's way was stopped. In a letter written a day or two afterwards to Mr. Astor, the bluff captain says—"Had the wind *unfortunately* not hauled ahead soon after leaving the harbour's mouth, I should positively have left them; and indeed I cannot but think it an unfortunate circumstance for you that it so happened, for the first loss in this instance would, in my opinion, have proved the best, as they seem to have no idea of the value of property, nor any apparent regard for your interest, although interwoven with their own."

Thus, amid much jarring and wrangling, the voyage proceeded uncomfortably enough. Especially between Macdougal and the captain there existed a kind of chronic feud. Mr. Macdougal considered himself, reasonably enough, as the proxy and representative of Mr. Astor during the absence of Mr. Wilson Hunt, while the captain was bent on arrogating all authority to himself. Occasionally Mr. Macdougal required that some packages of the cargo should be opened to supply the men with new clothing and other necessaries; and on such occasions the wrath of the captain was sure to break forth at a proceeding which he stigmatised as contrary to all custom and precedent, and subversive of discipline and authority.

Early in February, 1811, the Tonquin reached the Sandwich Islands, and anchored at Owyhee, the island where the enterprising and humane navigator, Captain Cook, had been murdered not many years before. Captain Thorn's object was to obtain provisions, especially a supply of pork and fresh vegetables, and then to sail away at the earliest moment; the travellers, on the other hand, were rather inclined to protract their stay to the utmost possible limits; for the partners wished to cultivate the friendship of the chiefs with a view to future trade, and even to the formation of a settlement, in connection with their enterprise; the voyagers who were of a scientific and botanical turn were delighted with the new genera of plants they found in these favoured regions; and the younger clerks were vehemently disposed to cultivate the acquaintance of the dusky beauties, by whose smiles several of them were fairly captivated. All this was a weariness and vexation of spirit to gallant Captain Thorn, who inveighed against everything that could cause delay, and whose letters to Mr. Astor show an increasing bitterness of spirit as the voyage "dragged its slow length along;" at length the partners seriously threatened to deprive him of the command, and the prospect of a mutiny was added to his other vexations. This effectually soured his temper, and increased his impatience at anything that seemed to him like interference or contradiction; and matters were in this unsatisfactory condition when the Tonquin arrived opposite the mouth of the Columbia river on the 22nd of March.

For many miles from the point where it pours its waters into the Pacific Ocean the Columbia river forms a broad estuary, whose navigation is exceedingly intricate by reason of many banks and shoals. The weather had been stormy during the last days before the Tonquin's arrival, and the voyagers beheld a surf tumbling angrily on the shore or leaping high into the air, where it encountered the impediment of a rock, so that the whole mouth of the river was masked by a broad belt of foam. Accordingly the captain, not deeming it prudent to bring the ship near shore until a channel should be found, ordered Mr. Fox, the first mate, to take with him in a boat three Sandwich Islanders, who had embarked with our voyagers at Owyhee, and Martin, an old and experienced sailor, who had been in those regions before. The mate demurred; he represented that in a service of such danger he ought at least to have his boat manned by part of the regular crew, and appealed to the partners, who sided with him and remonstrated with the captain. But this interference only made Captain Thorn more determined than ever to be obeyed to the very letter: and poor Fox put off with tears in his eyes, and with dark forebodings that he was going to his death. Very sadly were those forebodings verified; the crew and passengers gazed after the little boat so long as it remained in sight; after awhile the waves hid it from view. All that day, and during the restless and anxious night which followed, they waited for the return of the boat and her crew, but nothing more was ever heard of either. After several attempts to land in the pinnace, another boat was despatched, manned by three sailors and two Sandwich Islanders; this was swamped, and two out of the three

INDIAN WEAPONS AND ORNAMENTS.

THE ASTORIANS. 49

sailors perished in the waves. The remaining sailor, Stephen Weekes, with the two Sandwich men, succeeded in reaching the shore; but one of the latter died the same night from exhaustion and cold; and thus, when at length the Tonquin was able to stand in for the mouth of the

A MANDAN CHIEF.

river and make her way up the channel, eight of her company had already perished, and the natural feeling of sorrow at their loss was embittered by the unavoidable thought that some of these lives had been sacrificed through the obstinacy of Captain Thorn.

The gloom which this calamity naturally cast over the colonists was in some measure dispelled by the necessity for immediate exertion. For the next few weeks there was much to be done in exploring the region round the mouth of the Columbia river, and fixing on a site for the new settlement. Mr. Macdougal was especially anxious to cultivate friendly relations with the Indians, especially with Comcomly, a wary old one-eyed chief of the Chinooks. Macdougal seems to have been somewhat too anxious to exhibit his importance as the representative of the head partner in the enterprise; and his activity, though generally laudable and useful, occasionally degenerated into mere fussiness and an inveterate tendency to meddle. Captain Thorn, on the other hand, held the whole Indian race in unmitigated contempt, and stigmatised them on every occasion as a fraternity of the greatest rogues unhung. Utterly despising them as ignorant savages, he considered himself and his disciplined crew a match for any number of them, and neglected many precautions which had been especially impressed upon him by Mr. Astor; and fatally did the consequences of this neglect recoil upon himself and his ship.

The Red Indian, as he is described in such books as *The Last of the Mohicans*, and the various other tales of the American novelist Cooper, and other highly-coloured narratives of the kind, differs almost as much from the Indian of actual life, as the theatrical sailor and peasant differ from the tar of the naval and the merchant service, and the ploughman of Sussex or Dorsetshire. No delusion has been more completely dispelled by authentic information than the imaginary picture which, drawn from hearsay by writers who in many instances had never so much as beheld a Redskin, professed to portray how " wild in woods the noble savage ran." Wild enough was the savage, in all conscience; and, moreover, he had a great tendency to *run*, and even to skulk in the woods, preferring ambush to open attack, and treachery to fair fighting; but the nobility of his character was an hallucination sure to be very quickly abandoned by all who had personal dealings with him. As the various Indian tribes, those of the Pacific coast as well as the nations who inhabited the interior of the vast regions between the Missouri and the mouth of the Columbia river, played a great part in the history of the Astorians, it may be well here to give a few general characteristics of their mode of life and government. They were divided into many separate nations, each having its own chiefs, and originally possessing its own territory; but the predatory and warlike nature of the race, their universal dislike to settled dwelling-places and peaceful labour, had shown itself in constant and cruel wars. In these contests some of the weaker tribes had been driven from their country and completely ruined; so that of many once powerful tribes there remained only a scattered remnant, hiding from their foes in thickets and deserts, and dragging out a miserable, starved existence in constant peril and fear. Some tribes, like that of the Sioux, were especially noted for ferocity and for a delight in carnage; others, who dwelt on the banks of the great rivers, and lived principally on fish, were less enterprising and warlike than the hunter tribes, who, from being continually on horseback, and living chiefly on the flesh of the buffalo and bear, became sinewy and lithe in appearance, and fierce in character. Those nations who had been brought most into contact with the white men became wonderfully versed in the chicanery and wiles of traffic; while treachery and fraud, though allowed sometimes to remain in abeyance on ordinary occasions, were employed as an *ultima ratio* alike by all. In a case where blood had been shed, "life for life" was the maxim of Indian honour. The death of a slain Indian was only to be atoned for by the death of one or more white men. But even this rule was not immutable; and at least one instance occurred in the experience of our adventurers, in which the death of an Indian was atoned for, and the hand of revenge stayed, by a judicious distribution of blankets and tobacco. Of forgiveness to be given without a "consideration," or from other motives than policy, they had no notion; and one of their most dangerous characteristics was the quiet and deep dissimulation with which they would hide their meditated revenge until the moment came when it could be safely indulged. Their power of enduring hardship throughout a long period was, to a great extent, an effect of early training and of the vicissitudes attending their unsettled life, in which periods of want and plenty would alternate sometimes in a very unexpected manner. Some of the hunting parties were known to live for weeks, and to make long marches, upon a pittance of food which would hardly have been sufficient to support life in a white man; but on discovering an unexpected supply of food, they gorged themselves to an extent that caused them to remain for days in an almost torpid state. Of honesty and fair dealing, as a matter of principle, they knew nothing. On one occasion when Mr. Hunt, the American partner, wished to buy a number of horses of a chief for purposes of transport, that worthy replied that he could undertake to furnish Mr. Hunt with the number required; for if he happened not to have so many in camp, his people could easily steal more. They showed great aptitude in bargaining, and soon became adepts in the art of raising the price of an article in exact proportion to the necessity or the eagerness of the intending purchaser. Generally, where skins were to be the objects of traffic, the market rate was fixed by an experienced chief, to whose tariff all the rest conformed. In many instances they showed tokens of boast-

CHIPPEWA.

fulness and a love of parade, and often carried the scalps of slain enemies in triumph through their villages on their return from a warlike expedition. When driven to frenzy by long-continued ill-success on their warlike forays, a party of braves would sometimes devote their clothes to the medicine. They would cast away all their garments, and sally forth armed with their weapons to try and charm fortune back by some desperate deed of valour. All hard work, except hunting and fighting, was done by the squaws, who, indeed, would have despised their lords as weak and womanish, had the dusky warriors shown any inclination to derogate from their position by doing anything useful.

Such were the people with whom the trading operations of the colonists had to be carried on. Mr. Astor had obtained a good practical knowledge of Indian character in the course of many journeys he had made during the earlier part of his career. He had given very definite instructions to his representatives, and especially to Captain Thorn, concerning the method of dealing with the red men. The judicious advice he gave may be thus summarised :—" Treat the Indians kindly but firmly. If they proffer friendship, accept their overtures, without believing too readily in their sincerity ; avoid offending their prejudices or their pride, and admit only a few of them on board the ship at the same time."

III.

Astoria—Departure of the Tonquin—Anxiety respecting Mr. Hunt and his Party—Bad News concerning the Tonquin—Tragical Fate of that Vessel and her Crew—Gloom in the Settlement—Mr. Macdougal's Stratagem to Frighten the Indians—Post Founded at Okinagan—New Year's Eve Celebrated under Difficulties.

IT was in the spring-time that the expedition reached the Columbia river ; and all its members were speedily employed in preparing to establish their new settlement. A spot near the entrance of the bay was fixed upon, and in honour of the originator of the enterprise the new city received the name of Astoria. The first business was to build storehouses for the reception of that part of the Tonquin's cargo which was to be left for the use of the settlement; and this naturally consumed much time, though Captain Thorn's anxiety to "get on," and sail away towards the north, where he was to trade for furs at various parts, increased day by day. Comcomly and his men, it appeared, had no furs to dispose of,—whereupon the captain, in great dudgeon, refused to admit any one of them on board his ship. He severely censured Mr. Macdougal, who tried to conciliate the Indians,—and day by day his contempt for the "ragamuffins" became more open and undisguised. At last, early in June, the last bale of goods had been landed, and the Tonquin sailed out of the bay with the captain and crew on the last voyage she was ever to undertake. Soon after, Mr. Stuart left them with a small party on a reconnoitring expedition into the interior, with the especial view of fixing on spots for trading ports. The Astorians, thus reduced in number, began to look anxiously for the arrival of Mr. Hunt with the party he was to lead overland to Astoria, and their anxiety was increased by the suspicious attitude of the Indians, who disappeared from the settlement, and were supposed to be planning a combined attack upon the settlers. Even Comcomly, who had at first been so friendly, was now hardly ever to be seen.

To guard against the impending danger, Astoria was fortified as far as the means at hand would permit, and with four small cannon upon their battlements, and a stockade as an outwork of defence, the colonists waited for tidings of the Tonquin and of Mr. Hunt's expedition.

In August a party of Indians arrived at the settlement. They brought alarming accounts concerning the Tonquin, which they declared had been entirely destroyed. The report, at first discredited as an idle rumour, was repeated by a second set of Indian visitors; and at last there came an Indian who, in consequence of his knowledge of the coast and his partial acquaintance with the English language, had been engaged as interpreter on board the Tonquin. His narrative unhappily put an end to all doubts concerning the fate of the unfortunate ship and her crew.

On leaving Astoria the Tonquin had borne away to the northward, and soon arrived in a bay in Vancouver's Island, where she cast anchor opposite an Indian village. Presently some of the Indians came on board, and Mr. Mackay, the partner, with several companions, was received on shore with much honour by the chief Wicananish. Mr. Mackay remained on shore all night, a few Indians being detained on board the Tonquin as hostages; and the next morning packages of cloth, blankets, fishhooks, knives, and the various other articles which form the staple of trade with Indians, were spread out in tempting profusion on the ship's deck, in sight of the natives. They, on their part, brought plenty of sea-otters' skins, and there seemed every prospect that a brisk trade would be done. But the Indians were not inexpert in the wiles of traffic. They had been accustomed to buy and sell with the white men, and were under the influence of a cunning old chief named Nookamis, whose dictum settled the market price. Captain Thorn was not a man who would brook contradiction, even from his own countrymen. The habit of command, working on a temper naturally despotic, had made him hard and unyielding; and great was his disgust when Nookamis and the Redskins treated his proffered price for an otter-skin with scorn, and demanded more than double the amount. Not an inch would he budge from the position he had once taken up, and he totally disregarded the arguments and persuasions of old Nookamis, who followed him about the deck, holding out an otter-skin and pestering him with his importunity. At last the old chief began to change his tone, and attempted to banter Captain Thorn upon the shabby price he had offered;—whereupon the choleric commander suddenly turned round in a rage, snatched the skin from Nookamis, and rubbed it over his face, and then sent him away by the application of sundry vigorous kicks, equally hurtful to the chief's corporal and mental sensibilities. Old Nookamis went ashore vowing vengeance, and his followers were as angry and indignant as he. All trading chances had been destroyed by this outbreak—and the interpreter, who knew the revengeful character of his own people, strongly urged Captain Thorn to leave the harbour. Mr. Mackay and Mr. Lewis warmly seconded the interpreter's arguments; but the captain, trusting to the arms and ammunition with which he was plentifully provided, and to the prowess of himself and his crew, refused to listen to them.

Next morning at daybreak a large canoe was seen approaching the ship. The Indians in the canoe, who appeared to be unarmed, held up otter-skins, and asked to be allowed to come on board and trade. They were admitted; the wares brought by the Tonquin were once more spread out; and a brisk trade commenced. The savages showed especial eagerness to buy knives in exchange for their peltries; presently other canoes appeared, and around the sides of the ship other canoes came paddling up, whose occupants were soon scrambling on deck. Again the wary interpreter became alarmed, especially as he suspected the savages were secretly armed; he repeated his warning of the previous day, and urged the necessity of caution. At length Captain Thorn himself became uneasy. Seven men were sent aloft to make sail; others of the crew were commanded to heave up the anchor, and preparations were made to clear the ship of the crowd that encumbered the deck. But now the Indians offered to trade on the captain's own terms. More and more of them came swarming up the sides, and at length, when a determined effort was made to get rid of them, they suddenly gave a general yell and rushed upon the devoted captain and crew. Mr. Mackay was among the first victims; he was killed with many stabs and flung overboard. Mr. Lewis, mortally wounded by a knife-thrust in the back, fell down the hatchway. Captain Thorn fought desperately, but was despatched after killing several of his enemies; and the rest of the crew, who defended themselves bravely with handspikes, axes, and any weapon they could catch up, were massacred and thrown into the sea. The seven men who were aloft unfurling the sails, stared down in horror upon the scene of blood below. They then slid down the ropes and endeavoured to gain the cabin. Three of them were stabbed to death as they touched the deck, but the four others rushed down the companion-way and barricaded themselves, with the wounded Mr. Lewis, in the cabin. Here they found guns and ammunition, and opened a fire through some holes in the cabin stairs, which soon cleared the deck, the Indians paddling off in their canoes to the shore. A consultation was now held. Mr. Lewis advised his companions in misfortune to slip the cable, and endeavour to escape with the ship. But they declared that the wind set so strongly into the bay that the ship would infallibly be driven ashore, and avowed their intention of endeavouring to reach Astoria by coasting in their boat. Mr. Lewis, desperately wounded as he was, refused to accompany them, and they launched their boat and departed. These particulars were obtained by the interpreter in a subsequent interview with the four unfortunate men, who afterwards fell into the hands of the Indians, and were cruelly put to death. All that day none of the savages ventured to approach the Tonquin; but early next morning some canoes were seen cautiously approaching to reconnoitre. Mr. Lewis had determined upon taking a terrible revenge for the massacre of the crew. He appeared on deck, made friendly signs to the Indians, and invited them on board. When he found they were preparing to accept his invitation, he disappeared down the ladder into the cabin. On came the savages, intent on plunder, and suspecting no snare. Great was their glee when they found the rich bales of goods on deck, abandoned, as it seemed, to their rapacity. They commenced the work of rifling the ship with shouts of savage joy, and soon the decks of the Tonquin were covered with dancing, howling savages, while hundreds more hovered round in their canoes, waiting their opportunity to join in the work of spoliation. Suddenly the ship blew up with a tremendous explosion! Mr. Lewis, sternly resolved in his purpose of revenge, had set fire to the powder-magazine;—and with the fragments of the unfortunate Tonquin more than a hundred of the ruthless plunderers were buried in the waves.

The interpreter, who had been standing in the main chains, was blown into the water, and managed to scramble into one of the canoes, whose crews, frantic with fear, were hastening ashore. For some time he was detained in a sort of captivity, that he might not carry to the Astorians the intelligence of their companions' tragic fate. But he managed to escape, and brought the terrible news to the settlement, where it occasioned a general gloom. When, long afterwards, the sad story reached New York, Mr. Astor rightly characterised it as a calamity the consequences of which could not be estimated; but with characteristic energy he refused to be daunted by the disaster, and set about repairing it by the fitting out, at great trouble and cost, of

INDIAN BURYING PLACE.

another vessel to take the place of the unfortunate Tonquin. In Astoria the intelligence, which seemed to the Indian tribes an evidence of the weakness of the settlers, could not fail to produce a bad impression. The natives began at once to be suspicious and insolent, and seemed to meditate a treacherous attack. Mr. Macdougal, however, managed to avert the danger by ingeniously practising upon the superstition of the Indians. Knowing the dread they had of the ravages of the small-pox, he exhibited to Comcomly and the other chiefs a corked bottle, which he declared contained that deadly disease. He assured them that he could, by merely opening the bottle, set the terrible stranger free to work havoc among them, their wives and children; and threatened that the cork should fly from the bottle upon the slightest indication of treachery or hostility on their part. Whereupon the panic-stricken

Indians, fully persuaded that Macdougal could execute his threat, begged the "great small-pox chief" to let the cork remain where it was, promising on their part the utmost loyalty and devotion to the white settlers. The combined force of terror and self-interest kept them faithful to their word; and the settlement had cause to rejoice in the successful strategy of the "small-pox chief." As the season advanced, the intelligence of the presence of purchasers of furs at the mouth of the Columbia river brought not a few beaver-trappers and other wanderers of the wilderness to the settlement; and early in October a portion of Mr. David Stuart's party came back from the port on the Okinagan, accompanied by a Canadian creole named Regis Brugiere, one of those hunters called freemen in the fur trade—hardy men who have served their time in one of the fur companies, and then continue their profession on their own account, setting their beaver-traps in the great wilderness beside rivers and lakes, and frequently sojourning in complete solitude for months, and even years, until their stock of peltries has so far accumulated that they consider it worth selling at some frontier post.

As the autumn advanced and the rains set in, the Indians began to break up their camps and retire into the woods. The excursions of the little "Dolly" up the river for provisions were not always successful, and the settlers began to look forward with much anxiety for the appearance of Mr. Hunt and his party, who were to make the journey to Astoria overland. The winter came on, and in spite of the disquieting aspect of affairs, the Astorians contrived to usher in the year 1812 with something like festivity. The Canadian voyageurs especially distinguished themselves in celebrating New Year's Eve with all due honours. Flour and rum had been liberally served out for the preparation of cakes and punch. A ball was improvised, in which, for want of lady partners, the voyageurs stood up to dance with each other, and with the proverbial gaiety of Frenchmen forgot all their dangers and troubles in the festivity of the moment.

But still the overland party came not; and not the least among the anxieties of the band of hardy adventurers, who began a new year under such dangerous and difficult auspices, must have been the thought that perhaps they would never come at all; that their bones were perhaps already whitening on the inhospitable slopes of the Rocky Mountains, or in the pathless deserts between the foot of that great range and the Pacific coasts; that Mr. Hunt and his brave comrades might have furnished new members to the vast army of the martyrs of exploration, and that his expedition might be chronicled among the many that are recorded in the history of travel as having set out on their journey in high hope and joyful expectation, whose path has been traced to a certain point in their adventurous route, and who then have been heard of no more!

IV.

Expedition of Mr. Hunt—Character of Hunt—His Extensive Preparations—The Missouri Fur Company and Mr. Manuel Lisa—Pierre Dorion, the Half-breed Interpreter—John Day, the Hunter—Account of Blackbird, the Omahaw Chief—Mr. Bradbury's Adventure with the Indians.

LEAVING the little community at Astoria, we have now to follow the fortunes of that overland expedition whose arrival was so anxiously expected. If Mr. Astor had been somewhat mistaken in the nautical leader he had chosen, in the person of Captain Thorn, to command the enterprise by sea, his selection of the commander of the land expedition was, at any rate, eminently judicious. Mr. Wilson Hunt possessed all the courage and the singleness of purpose evinced by the ill-starred commander of the Tonquin, together with a discretion, an equanimity, and a mastery over himself in which poor Captain Thorn had shown himself lamentably deficient. During all the perils and dangers of his adventurous journey, harassed as he was frequently alike by the treachery and cunning of the red men with whom he came in contact, the intrigues of a rival company, and the insubordination and unfaithfulness of some of his own followers, he showed himself from beginning to end as a man of unswerving courage, inexhaustible resource, and rigid justice and equity. In many respects his task was far harder than Thorn's; and but for the rare qualities he displayed, the overland expedition could scarcely have escaped a conclusion as disastrous and tragical as that of the Tonquin's voyage.

The first care of the leader was to recruit boatmen, or "voyageurs," from Mackinaw. After considerable trouble he obtained a sufficient number, among whom, however, were some rather "hard bargains," men either worn out by a life of toil or insufferably lazy, and far more ready to disembark and boil the great camp-kettles than to urge the canoe up the Missouri. A valuable addition to the party was found in a new partner, Mr. Ramsay Crooks, who had already made journeys in the service of the North-West Company, and who especially warned

Mr. Hunt against the hostilities to be apprehended from the Sioux Indians, who had compelled him to abandon a former journey, in which he and his followers had, indeed, hardly escaped with their lives from the lurking foes who fired at them, on every opportunity, from the banks of the river. After numberless delays the expedition, consisting of about sixty persons, started from St. Louis on their voyage up the Missouri river. Mr. Hunt was well aware that he could not accomplish the whole of his journey before the winter, for it was already September. He had therefore determined to go as far as he could before the river became unnavigable through ice, and then to winter in some convenient spot. The voyageurs laboured, on the whole, patiently and well, and the three heavy boats toiled on against such obstacles as sandbanks, an adverse current, piles of driftwood, sunken trunks of trees, called sawyers, and various other impediments, until, on the 16th of November, the travellers came to the mouth of the Nodowa river, where, in a good hunting country, they were to pass the winter. Mr. Hunt here met with another partner, a Mr. McClellan, an energetic and enterprising man, who afterwards proved very useful. Mr. Hunt, however, found that his force was not strong enough to proceed through the hostile countries he should have to traverse; for the Canadians, excellent rowers though they might be, had given various indications that they cared very little for fighting. He therefore returned to St. Louis with a few followers to obtain further reinforcements; and, indeed, such an accession of strength was especially desirable, as besides the expected dangers from Sioux and Blackfeet Indians, Mr. Hunt plainly saw that he would find it difficult to combat the hostility of a rival expedition sent out by the Missouri Fur Company, under an enterprising partner, Mr. Manuel Lisa.

This gentleman was just about to lead an expedition in the same direction that Mr. Hunt's company intended taking. His primary object was to obtain intelligence of a partner named Henry, who had started with a company the year before, and had not since been heard of. The setting out of two expeditions at the same time naturally rendered it more difficult for Mr. Hunt to procure either voyageurs or hunters, as the rival company was bidding high for the services of such men, and in spite of great perseverance and judgment, Mr. Hunt only succeeded in procuring a few men, and those not of the best class. The one thing indispensable was to procure the services of an interpreter who knew the language of the Sioux, and could negotiate, if necessary, with that warlike tribe; and this necessary article was found in the person of Pierre Dorion, a half-breed, a wonderful vagabond of mingled Indian and Canadian extraction. This remarkable gentleman had lived much among the Indians, and, it was rumoured, possessed a

BUFFALO HUNTING ON THE PRAIRIE.

squaw and a family among every tribe; but his chief wife, who permanently accompanied him, was a Sioux woman. He was a clever fellow in his own way, and useful and tolerably trustworthy when sober; but then he was so often drunk. At times, whatever might be the work in hand, the fascination of the whiskey-bottle would be too strong for Pierre Dorion, and, indeed, it was this unfortunate predilection for "firewater" that had embroiled him with the Missouri company, in whose service he had been, and procured Mr. Hunt the opportunity of engaging him. It appeared that, in the previous year, at a frontier fort belonging to the company where Pierre had been staying, the whiskey mania seized upon this erratic son of the woods. He had been supplied with the means of gratifying his propensity, four quarts of whiskey having been supplied to him out of the company's stores; but this whiskey had been charged to his account at ten dollars the quart. Now, strong drink at half-a-sovereign for half-a-pint was too strong even for Pierre Dorion, who in a fit of indignation quitted his masters and took service with Mr. Hunt. Nor would his sense of justice permit him to discharge the extortionate demand before he went. Mr. Manuel Lisa, with the manifest object of hampering his rival's proceedings, took measures for arresting Pierre at St. Louis, and thus detaining him for the debt. But the wily half-breed, on receiving intelligence of this intention, quietly left the boat, and marched away into the woods with his wife, his two babies or papooses, and all his worldly wealth. He promised to rejoin the company some distance above St. Louis, and was as good as his word. Meanwhile the travellers had been reinforced by John Day, a famous hunter, whose name is immortalised in the John Day's River, a small tributary of the Columbia; by Mr. Bradbury and Mr. Nuttall, two naturalists; and by a few stalwart hunters, and once more the adventurous party worked up the Missouri.

In due time they reached the chief town of the Omahaws, at that period a numerous and powerful tribe, the exploits of whose great chief, the Blackbird, were still fresh in the mouths of men. This famous savage had been noted for his daring and sagacity, and for the mighty influence he possessed over his tribe; but not a little of that influence had been due to a strange, and, as it appeared, a supernatural power possessed by the gloomy chief. When any man offended the leader of the Omahaws, the Blackbird would prophesy the death of the offender within a certain time, *and the prophecy was always fulfilled.* Before the allotted period had passed, the victim of the chieftain's wrath wasted away in an unaccountable manner, in a dread and mysterious disease that had but one termination. The truth was that an unscrupulous trader had imparted to the Blackbird a knowledge of the deadly qualities of arsenic, and the wily savage employed this dangerous knowledge as a means at once of revenge, and of maintaining his power over his simple and superstitious subjects.

The only person who had any real power over the gloomy chief was a young and beautiful wife, who had originally been sent to him to sue for peace, when her tribe had been reduced to extremity by Blackbird's attacks. And even her influence was ephemeral; for he slew her in a fit of anger.

When the travellers had gone some distance beyond the country of the Omahaws, their real dangers began. The Sioux Tetons, a ruthless tribe, who had earned for themselves the title of the Pirates of the Missouri—these were the people who had stopped the progress of an expedition under Crooks and McClellan the year before, it was said at the instigation of Mr. Manuel Lisa, of the Missouri Fur Company, against whom, consequently, Mr. McClellan entertained the most bitter hostility. When, therefore, two Indians gave notice that the Sioux Tetons were in the neighbourhood, the hardy hunters and trappers felt uneasy, while something very like panic spread among the Canadian voyageurs. Mr. Bradbury, the naturalist, was in the habit of filling his shot-pouch with corn, and starting in the morning on a botanising expedition up the banks of the river, rejoining his companions at the close of the day. One morning he had thus set forth, full of ardour for science, and utterly oblivious of Sioux Tetons and all dangerous savages generally. In the afternoon, as he stood waiting for the boat, a hand was suddenly laid upon his shoulder. "Starting and turning round," says the biographer of the expedition, "he beheld a naked savage, with a bow bent, and the arrow pointed at his breast. In an instant his gun was levelled, and his hand upon the lock. The Indian drew his bow still farther, but forbore to launch the shaft. Mr. Bradbury, with admirable presence of mind, reflected that the savage, if hostile in his intent, would have shot him without giving him a chance of defence; he paused therefore, and held out his hand. The other took it in sign of friendship, and demanded, in the Osage language, whether he was a Big-Knife (American). He answered in the affirmative, and inquired whether the other was a Sioux. To his great relief, he found that he was a Ponca. By this time two other Indians came running up, and all three laid hold of Mr. Bradbury, and seemed disposed to compel him to go off with them among the hills. He resisted, and sitting down on a sand-hill, contrived to amuse them with a pocket compass. When the novelty of this was exhausted, they again seized him, but he now produced a small microscope. This new wonder again fixed the attention of the savages, who have far more curiosity than it has been the custom to allow them. While thus engaged, one of them suddenly leaped up, and gave a war-whoop. The hand of the hardy naturalist was again on his gun, and he was prepared to give battle, when the Indian pointed

BLACKBIRD AND HIS FAVOURITE SQUAW.

down the river, and revealed the true cause of his yell. It was the mast of one of the boats appearing above the low willows which bordered the stream. Mr. Bradbury felt infinitely relieved at the sight."

V.

Encounter with the Sioux—Manuel Lisa and his Schemes—Buffalo Plains—
Antelopes—Aricaras and Cheyennes—Difficulties of the March—William
Cannon and the Grizzly Bear—The Pilot Knobs—Pierre Dorion's Squaw—
Her patient Endurance and Courage—Arrival at Astoria—New Expeditions
Planned.

THREE hardy hunters were now picked up in the woods, and induced to join the expedition; and very opportune was this meeting for our travellers, for soon afterwards a large war party of the dreaded Sioux was encountered, numbering about six hundred warriors. These ranged themselves at a point of the river somewhat above the boats, and were evidently determined to dispute the passage. Mr. Hunt, on his part, was not disposed to turn back, and prepared for a fight. On seeing this, the savages held a parley; and in the end the calumet of peace was smoked, and the opposition of the Sioux was overcome by a judicious present of tobacco and corn.

The ingenious Mr. Manuel Lisa, who had already made overtures for a junction of the two expeditions for purposes of mutual defence, now came up with his party; and a sort of alliance, though by no means a cordial one, was made. It soon appeared, however, that Lisa was endeavouring to detach some of Mr. Hunt's men from their allegiance. An attempt made to tamper with the redoubtable Pierre Dorion put that worthy personage into a fury, an allusion having been indiscreetly made to that ancient grievance the whiskey debt; a quarrel occurred which almost led to bloodshed, and McClellan openly declared that he would shoot Lisa dead on the least appearance of treachery.

All confidence between the two sides being now at an end, the rival parties coasted on opposite sides of the river, Mr. Hunt taking especial care to keep slightly in advance, that Lisa might not get the start of him, and work upon the Indians to his prejudice. And now they entered the pathless wastes in which the great herds of buffalo, the chief source of support to some of the Indian tribes, were roaming in unchecked freedom. We are told, "At one place the shores seemed absolutely lined with buffaloes; many were making their way across the stream, snorting, and blowing, and floundering. Numbers, in spite of every effort, were borne by the rapid current within shot of the boat, and several were killed. At another place a number were descried on the beach of a small island, under the shade of the trees, or standing in the water like cattle, to avoid the flies and the heat of the day. * * *. Besides the buffaloes, we saw abundance of deer, and frequent gangs of stately elks, together with light troops of sprightly antelopes, the fleetest and most beautiful inhabitants of the prairies."

There are two kinds of antelopes in these regions: one nearly the size of the common deer, the other not much larger than a goat. Their colour is a light grey, or rather dun, spotted with white, and they have small horns, like those of a deer, which they never shed. Nothing can surpass the delicate and elegant finish of their limbs, in which lightness, elasticity, and strength are wonderfully combined. All the attitudes and movements of this beautiful animal are graceful and picturesque; and it is altogether a fit subject for the fanciful uses of the poet, as the oft-sung gazelle of the East. John Day, the hunter, was very successful in shooting these beautiful animals. He used to attract them by fastening a handkerchief to the end of a ramrod, and waving it in the air, while he lay concealed among the long grass; the antelopes, coming up to inspect the novel sight, were shot down as they came within the range of the marksman.

At a village of the Aricara Indians, the travellers had an opportunity of seeing the excellent horsemanship of the Indians. They seemed almost to live on horseback, and even the smallest children were fastened on the backs of shaggy ponies. Their skill in horse-breaking and horse-stealing was remarkable. The Cheyenne Indians rival the Aricaras in their skill as riders.

The march across the prairies towards the west was far more toilsome and harassing than the navigation of the river. Sometimes the travellers were in great straits for provisions, at others they were menaced with Indian attacks. It was very difficult to procure horses for the transport of the baggage and goods; and it was amid difficulty of every kind that they slowly made their way westward towards the Rocky Mountains. Some alarm was created more than once in the camp by the discovery of tracks of the grizzly bear. William Cannon, one of the hunters attached to the expedition, had a narrow escape from one of these formidable animals. Cannon had been bantered somewhat freely by his companions on his ill-success in hunting, and his inaccuracy as a marksman. He one day sallied forth alone, determined to bring home game of some kind. He was fortunate enough to shoot a buffalo, and we are told, "As he was at a considerable distance from the camp, he cut out the tongue and some of the choice bits, made them into a parcel, and slinging them on his shoulders by a strap passed round his forehead, as the voyageurs carry packages of goods, set out all glorious for the camp, anticipating a triumph over his brother hunters." But poor Cannon had not calculated on the bad company he might meet by the way. In a narrow ravine a grizzly bear came trotting after him. Cannon dropped the buffalo meat, and ran for his life. The grizzly did not seem to care for eating buffalo when there was a chance of eating hunter; he passed the place where the meat lay without even stopping to sniff at it, and kept steadily on after the affrighted hunter. Cannon, almost breathless with haste and fright, managed to reach a tree, into which he scrambled. Bruin established a blockade at the foot of the tree, and waited with a methodical patience extremely irksome to the hunter until night came on, and Cannon was left to conjecture whether the bear had abandoned his post or was still "on duty." The morning dawn, however, showed that he had betaken himself away; and the baffled hunter was glad to make his way back to the camp, without thinking it worth while, under the circumstances, to make any search for his dropped parcel of buffalo meat.

An important point in the journey was reached when the travellers came near to the Pilot Knobs, three peaks of the Rocky Mountains which serve as landmarks to companies crossing the range. In the desert region they had to traverse on the western side of the range they suffered terribly from hunger, thirst, and cold. It was necessary to leave almost all the goods behind in pits, or, as they are called by the backwoodsmen, "caches," made to receive them. Mr. Crooks and some of the party who were unable to proceed with the rest were left behind in the wilderness; and the gloomiest apprehensions for the future took possession of nearly all the wanderers. Through danger, toil, and hardship, the poor squaw, the wife of Pierre Dorion, trudged uncomplainingly on. She became the mother of a poor little papoose, which lived but a short time after its birth. Even this event did not hinder her from keeping up with the rest, and the poor woman's example was of infinite service in restraining the petulance of the voyageurs, who, however much disposed they might be to lament their fate, could not well give way to despondency while a woman was so patiently enduring hardship and want in their company.

At length after trials and sufferings innumerable, after losing several of their number, and more than once almost despairing of their

68   THE WORLD'S EXPLORERS.

own chance of safety, the adventurers reached the settlement of Astoria on the 15th of February, 1812. They had traversed a distance of

THE ELK AND THE RED DEER.

3,500 miles from St. Louis, and considering the difficulties and dangers of their route, their preservation seems little short of miraculous.

With the return of spring the Indian tribes who had abandoned the coast in the autumn reappeared to commence their fishing. When the mild season had fairly set in, various expeditions were sent out from the settlement. One was to carry a supply of goods to Mr. Stuart's post on the Oakinagan; another to search for Mr. Crooks and John Day, who had been perforce left behind in the wilderness when they could proceed no farther; thirdly, it was requisite that the "cache" or hiding-pit in which a great quantity of goods had been concealed should be visited, and the goods, if they still remained in safety, carried away. One of these objects, at least, was successfully accomplished. Mr. Crooks and John Day were discovered in the last extremity of misery and destitution. They had fallen into the hands of marauding Indians, who had literally stripped them naked, and taken from them all they possessed, not leaving them so much as a flint and steel wherewith to kindle a fire. John Day afterwards became insane, and put an end to his own life. The hardships of that dreadful time had unsettled the poor hunter's brain. The cache was found plundered of its contents. The most important expedition was to proceed overland to New York, carrying despatches to Mr. Astor. The leader of this party was a clerk, Mr. John Reed, who unfortunately chose to inclose the valuable papers in a shining tin case, an object especially likely to attract the notice and raise the cupidity of the Indians, who could scarcely fail to covet the glittering box as a "great medicine." In the sequel the tin case was carried off by Indians, and almost caused the death of many of the travellers.

VI.

Mr. Astor's Plans—The Beaver Fitted Out and Despatched—War between Great Britain and the United States—Mr. Macdougal's Marriage with the Daughter of Comcomly—His Equivocal Conduct—Arrival of Mr. Hunt at Astoria—Macdougal Sells the Settlement to the British North-American Fur Company—Surprise and Regret of Mr. Astor—The British Take Possession of Astoria—Macdougal Joins the Fur Company—Renewed Efforts of Mr. Astor—His Further Career—Conclusion.

MEANWHILE Mr. Astor, whose master mind had planned the enterprise, was determined to carry out his project of establishing a trade with the Russian settlements for peltries, which should be carried to China for sale. The Beaver, a fine ship of nearly 500 tons, was despatched by Mr. Astor, who made an arrangement with the Russian

Fur Company, trading in the north-east, to supply them with stores in return for peltries. The Beaver started on her voyage, and in due time arrived at Astoria, from whence she sailed to the Russian settlements, and collected a valuable stock of furs, which Mr. Astor destined to supply the market in China. Partly through various delays on the voyage, partly also through the mismanagement of those to whom the affair had been intrusted, this part of the enterprise resulted, like the rest, in a heavy loss to the projector.

But the event which contributed more than any other to the failure of the Astorian enterprise was the breaking out of the war which now began between the United States and Great Britain. This rendered communication by sea with the settlement hazardous and difficult, and exposed the little community at the mouth of the Columbia river to the chance of a visit from a hostile ship of war. Though all probabilities pointed to a speedy restoration of peace between the two countries, the worthy Mr. Macdougal, who occupied the place of command in the settlement, felt, or affected to feel, that the fate of the enterprise was sealed, and gave way to an unnecessary despondency that violently contrasted with the fussy and consequential airs he had formerly assumed. He had, indeed, strengthened himself by cultivating friendly relations with the Indians, and had actually married a daughter of the old chief Comcomly; vastly to the satisfaction of that astute personage, who glorified himself greatly on the strength of having as his son-in-law a white man of such exalted position, and who sent his daughter to her expectant bridegroom so thoroughly painted and anointed, according to Indian notions of a complete marriage toilette, that immediate and copious ablutions were considered necessary before the bride could be presented to a community whose notions of adornment were of a very different kind.

Comcomly's alliance was of material use to the settlement. A man of considerable weight and authority among his own people, he interposed sometimes as a mediator, sometimes as a guard, between the Astorians and Indian tribes less friendly than his own. A valuable stock of furs had, moreover, been collected; the settlement began to get into what may be considered as "working order," when the conduct of Macdougal gave the final blow to the whole enterprise.

Whether his action was really inspired by fear and distrust, and by the natural timidity of a mind at once restless and weak, or whether the accusations afterwards made against him were well founded, and he sold the interests of Astoria to promote his own with the North American Fur Company, will always remain a matter of conjecture. Certain it is that he did not clear his character in the eyes of Mr. Astor, who attributed the final failure of the enterprise to him, and did not believe that he had acted in good faith.

Macdougal, in fact, resolved to take the extreme measure of abandoning the settlement. He openly expressed his conviction that all the chances pointed towards failure, and declared that it would be far better to dispose of the stock of furs for what they would fetch, to the British North American Fur Company, than to let the whole fall into the hands of the enemies of the United States as a prize of war. He spoke openly in the settlement of his gloomy apprehensions and anticipations of evil.

> "And fear, admitted into public councils,
> Betrays like treason."

Even old Comcomly at last became disgusted, and declared in confidence to various of his own friends that his daughter had married a squaw.

The active and intelligent Mr. Hunt, who arrived at Astoria shortly after Macdougal had publicly announced his resolution, testified great surprise at the extreme course proposed, the necessity for which he could not at all see; but he failed to shake the determination of Macdougal. It is a noteworthy circumstance, moreover, that just at this time three clerks, British subjects, passed with Macdougal's consent from Mr. Astor's service into that of the North-Western Fur Company; and immediately afterwards a negotiation was opened by Macdougal for a sale of the whole Astorian stock of furs to the company before mentioned, and for a transfer to them of the settlement itself. This transaction appears the more equivocal when we consider the relative positions of the contracting parties at the time when it was effected. Macdougal was in possession of a strong fort well supplied with provisions and garrisoned by sixty men; the North-Western Company, on the other hand, was in so destitute a condition that he was obliged actually to feed them while the negotiations were being carried on; and yet he allowed them to dictate the terms of the transfer, as if the whole matter had been in their hands. The stock of furs passed out of the hands of the Americans at a ruinous sacrifice—parcels of otter-skins worth 500 dollars were disposed of for 50, and the more valuable peltries were transferred at a proportionate reduction. This part of the transaction seems to have affected Mr. Astor more painfully than all the rest; and, indeed, there was so large a portion of the stock for which nothing at all was allowed, that that gentleman was quite justified in considering his property as virtually given away. He soon afterwards wrote to Mr. Hunt—" Had our place and our property been fairly captured, I should have preferred it. I should not have felt as if I were disgraced."

Washington Irving, who gives what appears to be a most impartial and moderate account of these transactions, concludes the account of them in the following significant words:—" All these may be unmerited suspicions; but it certainly is a circumstance strongly corroborative of them that Mr. Macdougal, shortly after concluding this agreement, became a member of the North-West Company, and received a share productive of a handsome income."

The rest of the history of Astoria is soon told. On the 12th of December in the same year, the Racoon, a British sloop of war, arrived at the mouth of the Columbia river, the visit having been undertaken at the instigation of the North-Western Fur Company, whose managers pointed out that a great advantage would accrue from the value of the property in the hands of the Pacific Fur Company, represented by Mr. Astor. Great was the indignation of the captain of the Racoon when he found that the whole stock had already been purchased and removed by the very people who had counselled the enterprise, and in his first indignation he swore that the North-West Company should refund their gains to the British government. On calmer reflection, however, he was obliged to content himself with formally taking possession of the settlement in the name of his Britannic majesty, changing the name of the place from Astoria to Fort St. George, and consoled himself as best he might for the loss of the prize-money he and his officers had confidently expected to gain. Mr. Hunt, who had been absent on the affairs of the settlement, arrived soon after, and great was his indignation when he heard of the forced sale that had taken place. Mr. Macdougal, now a partner in the North-West Company, suggested that probably the goods might be repurchased at an advance of 50 per cent., a proposition not calculated to appease the wrath of the energetic and faithful guardian of his principal's interests.

Nothing more remained to be done but to embark with the remainder of the settlers, and thus for a time Astoria became British territory. At the conclusion of the short war it was restored to the

THE ASTORIANS. 73

United States, and it is a remarkable proof of the unwearied perseverance of Mr. Astor, and of his wonderful tenacity of purpose, that in spite of his immense losses, and the heavy and repeated disappointments to which he had been subjected, he was even now ready to renew

DACOTAH CHIEF.

the enterprise, if only he could obtain what ought to have been extended to him from the first—the protection and support of the government. To procure this he made an application to the President of the United States, pointing out the obvious advantages to be gained by keeping the fur trade in the hands of Americans, and the amount of revenue that would be lost should the British succeed in re-establishing and extending their monopoly. But the Columbia river with its tributary streams was now in the hands of the British, and then, as now, possession was considered as "nine points of the law." The American government was not prepared to risk the chances of a serious quarrel, and perhaps the rupture of a lately-concluded peace, for the sake of an enterprise which it persisted in looking upon as a private trading venture, and the opportunity was again lost.

For many years the liberal-minded merchant continued his career of enterprise and usefulness in New York, and when at length that career was closed, the testamentary disposition of his property showed that he had been alike mindful of the claims of the land that gave him birth and of the adopted country which had opened to him a career leading to wealth and honour. Alike in the village whence he had gone forth a penniless lad, and in the great city where he had achieved affluence, rose institutions that perpetuate his memory, and render a nation participators in his good fortune; but those friends who, received into his most intimate confidence, were best able to tell how far higher than private emolument he valued public usefulness, were accustomed to say how to the last day of his life Jacob Astor never ceased to regret the splendid opportunity that had been thrown away in the premature abandonment of the outwork of civilisation and commerce, founded with so much toil, and danger, and suffering on the shores of the mighty Pacific, at the mouth of the Columbia river.

VENICE.

MARCO POLO.

I.

A Remarkable Arrival—The Three Travellers—The Banquet—Surprise of the Guests—Marco Polo and his Works—First Journey of the Elder Poli—The Tartar Empire—Jenghis Khan and his Conquests—Kublai Khan—His Wish to Open Communications with Europe—His Commission to the Brothers—Their Second Journey, in Company with Marco—Panic of their Monkish Companions—Marco's Account of Cashmere—Journey Across the Great Desert of Gobi.

IN the year of grace 1295 there arrived in the splendid and wealthy city of Venice three travellers, whose appearance may well have excited some attention even in that place, then the emporium of commerce of the Western world, and thronged not only with travellers from all parts of Christendom, but with visitors also from the lands of "Heathenesse"—grave Moors, keen-eyed Copts, and many a swarthy visitor from the lands that lie beneath the tropic sun. Two of our travellers were men already past the prime of life, while the third had not yet reached the age of forty years. Their faces were tanned and weather-stained; their threadbare garments, of a shape and make unknown in Venice, proclaimed them newly arrived from some distant land; and even their speech, though Italian for the greater part, was mingled with many strange words which none but themselves could understand. Great was the astonishment, and equally great the doubt and incredulity in Venice, when one of the sunburnt strangers announced himself as Maffeo Polo, the head of a patrician family of Venetian merchants, and declared his two companions to be Niccolo Polo, his brother, and Marco, the son of Niccolo, just returned to their native city, after an absence of no less than twenty-four years, spent in travels to the farthest corners of the world.

So long a time had elapsed, indeed, since the departure of the persons who had been known under these names in Venice, that the city was loath to accept the statement of the travellers; the more so, perhaps, as the claims of these men to be acknowledged as the Poli involved the overturning of some existing and long-established arrangements. That three Poli had actually left Venice nearly a quarter of a century before was remembered by many of the older inhabitants, but the absent ones had long been given up as dead, and the handsome palace belonging to the family in the Strada San Giovanni Chrisostomo

LEOPARDS AND PANTHER.

had for years been in the possession of one of their kindred; and admittance was at first refused them, and only at length reluctantly granted when various circumstances combined to prove that these poorly-clad personages were indeed the long-forgotten Poli, and that their marvellous tale of a long residence as honoured guests and trusted ministers at the court of a great Asiatic potentate was not the fable it at first appeared. Soon it became manifest, also, that the pecuniary circumstances of the returned wanderers were not to be accurately judged by the lowliness of their apparel. They were evidently wealthy, and their biographer, Ramusio, relates the manner in which they contrived to place this important fact altogether beyond dispute.

After obtaining possession of their own house it seems they invited their numerous relatives and connections to a grand banquet. This mediæval house-warming was arranged on a scale that throws the most splendid of modern festivities into the shade. The three travellers issued from their apartments to meet their guests in the dining-hall habited in long flowing robes of crimson satin. After the washing of hands, the preliminary ceremony at grand entertainments in those days, the hosts exchanged their satin robes for similar dresses of damask, the suits in which they had entered the banqueting-hall being given as "largesse" to the attendants. After the first course they appeared in new garments more costly than the last, the material in this instance being crimson velvet, and in due sequence the damask and the velvet garments were given to the servants, the hosts now habiting themselves in plain suits, such as were worn by their guests. And now came a surprise which completely eclipsed the magnificence of these preliminaries.

After the servants had retired from the room, Marco Polo brought in the three patched, threadbare suits which had produced so unfavourable an impression in Venice upon the return of the travellers. One of these suits he handed to his father, and another to his uncle, retaining the remaining one for himself; and then they all three began to rip up the seams and patches in the unsightly garments with their knives; then, even as the toad, "ugly and venomous," is said, in poetical parlance, to wear "a precious jewel in its head," so did these tattered and unsightly shells disclose kernels of inestimable worth. Carbuncles, sapphires, emeralds, and diamonds, cunningly sewn up in the despised garments, were displayed in magnificent profusion before the dazzled eyes of the guests. The travellers, it appeared, had chosen this method of conveying home the bounty of the great Asiatic prince whom they served; and all doubts as to their identity, and as to the fact of their voyaging, were at once set at rest by the display of this very tangible result.

It is with the name of Marco Polo, the youngest of the three travellers, that the history of the voyages they made in company has been associated; indeed, there seems to be a fitness in this, as Marco underwent the greatest perils, and was, moreover, the only one of the three who left a detailed account of his wanderings. He may justly be considered the Herodotus of the Middle Ages, and though he certainly did not sift the information he gathered during his various pilgrimages with the careful reticence of a modern traveller, he is entitled to the merit of telling truly and honestly, so far as his memory will serve him, what he has witnessed in various lands; and though marvellous tales, wherein the figure hyperbole is much employed, are of frequent occurrence during his work, he takes care to distinguish between hearsay and actual experience, and prefixes a cautious "They say," or I have heard," to each of these tales of marvel. On the other hand, the accuracy of his general statements, and the exactness of many of his descriptions, have been corroborated by many subsequent travellers, and though his travels were not published till long after his death, they must have thrown what in those days appeared a flood of light on many countries, each of which had been a *terra incognita* until then.

The father and uncle of Marco were, as we have mentioned, Venetian merchants. Shortly before the birth of our hero, Niccolo and Maffeo Polo quitted Venice on a commercial journey to the East. They disposed of the goods they carried with them at Constantinople, and here the idea seems to have struck them that a new market for their industry, and one yielding a handsome profit, might be found still farther in the East, among the Tartars on the borders of the Caspian. Accordingly, they invested in jewels the money they had received for their goods, crossed the Euxine to the Crimea, and thence made their way eastward to the shores of the mighty Caspian.

The Tartar empire has more than once had a great influence on the history and destinies of European nations. Already, in the fifth century, Attila, the "Scourge of God," had poured his vast hordes of hideous warriors over the affrighted West—the moody savage king of whom the affrighted nations said that where his horse's hoof had trodden the grass would grow no more, and whose hideous followers the terrified imagination of the Gothic tribes, among whom they first appeared, painted as the offspring of witches and demons. The very nation and city to which the Poli belonged owed its origin in some sort to the invasion of this savage chief, for it was an affrighted community of Italy, flying from the advance of the conqueror, after the destruction of the fair and ancient city of Aquileja, who took refuge among the islands and lagoons of the Adriatic, and there, on the island of Rialto, laid the foundation of what afterwards became the lordly and opulent Venice. In the very century in which the Poli undertook their voyage, another conqueror had arisen among the Tartar race, whose achievements threw those of Attila into the shade, and who was destined to found an empire far more wide-spread and more enduring than that of the Scourge of God, whose career had been arrested by the stroke of sudden death while his work was yet unfinished. Jenghis Khan, the great Tartar chief, had once more made the name of the Tartar a spell with which to alarm the nations, and now his grandson, Kublai Khan, was strengthening and indefinitely extending the power his great ancestor had founded. Once more, in the thirteenth century, had the Tartars broken forth from the deserts of Asia, and poured over the plains of the West in a flood which the best efforts of the armies of Europe were unable to stem; and it had even been feared that Western civilisation and Christianity itself would perish beneath the fierce onslaught of the invaders, when the death of a Khan providentially called back the leader of the host that had invaded Europe, and for a time averted the danger. Such were the circumstances under which the Poli began their enterprising travels among a nation as much dreaded as it was imperfectly known.

In its commercial aspect, the journey of the brothers was eminently successful. They disposed of their jewels to good advantage, and were about to take leave of the friendly Tartar chief who ruled the part of the country into which they had penetrated, when the breaking out of hostilities between him and some Western tribes cut off the road to Constantinople. Accordingly, they turned their faces once more to the East, and were soon after persuaded by an ambassador of the Grand Khan, whom they met in the city of Bokhara, to extend their travels still farther, and seek an interview with Kublai Khan himself, and after a long and tedious journey through snowy deserts and across barren plains, they arrived at the conqueror's court.

Kublai Khan received his visitors very graciously. They were the first Italians who had arrived at his court, and he evidently appreciated their zeal and perseverance, and showed every desire to do them all honour. He expressed an anxiety to enter into relations of friendship and alliance with the papal power, and intrusted his visitors with a royal letter to the Pope, wherein he requested that a certain number of learned men might be sent to him, with a view of converting his people to the Christian faith, and to teach them the principles of the sciences. He also furnished them with a most convenient and useful passport, in the shape of a golden tablet displaying the imperial sign manual, or "grand chop," the possession of which warrant frequently procured for the travellers gratuitous food and lodging, besides all necessary

PEKIN.

protection on their journey for themselves and their suite. Much has been said concerning the advantages of a British Foreign Office passport to travellers journeying on the continent, but they sink into insignificance compared with the merits of a document which absolves the bearer from paying hotel bills.

This first voyage of the Poli has here been indicated in a very summary manner, but its accomplishment occupied a long time. The brothers had been many years absent from Venice, though the dates in the narrative are so confused that it is almost impossible to fix the precise period. The wife of Niccolo Polo had long been dead, but shortly after the departure of her husband from Venice she had given birth to a son, Marco.

This Marco was now a well-grown youth, inheriting to the full the enterprise and energy of his father and uncle, and gifted with the mingled determination and caution which form the chief qualification of the explorer. The Pope to whom the Khan's letter had been addressed was, however, dead, and a considerable time elapsed before the college of cardinals appointed his successor. The choice at length fell upon a bishop who knew the Poli, and who was strongly interested in their cause. Trebaldo, the former legate at Acre, was raised to the papal throne as Gregory X., and furnished by him with presents to the Khan, and accompanied by two Dominican friars, to whom ample authority had been given in such matters ecclesiastic as the ordination

PISA.

of priests and the consecration of bishops, the two elder Poli once more set out for the dominions of the Grand Khan, with young Marco in their company. This was at the end of 1271 or the beginning of 1272.

Contrary to the general rule of their order, whose monks were in those days among the most zealous and self-sacrificing of missionaries, the two friars quickly gave up the enterprise. They were alarmed at an invasion of Armenia which had been undertaken shortly before by the Sultan of Babylon, and hastened to deliver up their credentials to the Poli, and to place themselves under the protection of the Knights Templars. But the enterprise of the combined merchant and traveller, characteristic of the Poli family, would not allow our three Venetians to give up their enterprise in this its earliest stage. They had started with the idea of visiting Kublai Khan's coast, and to Kublai Khan's coast they were determined to penetrate; therefore bidding farewell to the recreant friars, they pushed forward to the north-west, trading on their route whenever an opportunity offered. Their progress was slow. Thus in the country of Badakhshan, near the sources of the Oxus, they lingered for a whole year, and thence penetrated into the territory of "famed Cashmere."

Marco's description of this region shows that he was not free from the superstition of the thirteenth century regarding the practice of magic. The particulars he gives concerning the country have been abundantly verified by later travellers. In his chapter "On the Province of Kesmur" he tells us—"Its inhabitants have their peculiar language. They are adepts beyond all others in the arts of magic, insomuch that they can compel their idols, though by nature dumb and deaf, to speak: they can likewise obscure the day, and perform many other miracles. They are pre-eminent among the idolatrous nations, and from them the idols worshipped in other parts proceed. From this country there is a communication by water with the Indian Sea. The natives are of a dark complexion, but by no means black, and the women, although dark, are very comely. Their food is flesh, with rice and other grains, yet they are in general of a spare habit. The climate is moderately warm.   *   *   *   The natives of this country do not deprive any creature of life, nor shed blood, and if they are inclined to eat flesh meat, it is necessary that the Mahometans, who reside amongst them, should slay the animal. The article of coral, carried thither from Europe, is sold at a higher price than in any other part of the world."

From this favoured region the travellers pursued their journey through the present Afghanistan, where Marco especially notices the large-horned goat, and so on to Bucharia to the famed city of Kashgar. Our author does not entertain a high opinion of the inhabitants of the city and region of Kashgar. Though he does justice to their industry and ability, he describes them as a sordid and covetous race, eating badly, and, adds Messer Marco emphatically, "drinking worse." This latter must have been a serious defect in the eyes of the young Venetian.

One of the most toilsome events of the journey was the crossing the great desert of Gobi—the "Hungry Desert" or "Sea of Sand." The part of the account of this journey wherein our traveller details his personal experiences is accurate enough, but here, as elsewhere, he repeats with undoubting good faith the marvellous tales which he hears, so that the real dangers and discomfort of the journey across the desert of Gobi are here and there heightened by imaginary terrors. No doubt these wonderful tales arose in part from natural phenomena imperfectly understood, such as the mirage. Appearances of this kind, viewed by persons whose imaginations are rendered perhaps morbidly acute by fatigue and fear, naturally assume terrific shapes, and give rise to tales of wonder, and these tales our worthy Marco seems to have reproduced with much simplicity, giving them apparently to his readers for what they are worth. He speaks of the journey across the desert in its narrowest part as occupying a month. "During these thirty days," he says, "the journey is invariably over sandy plains or barren mountains, but at the end of each day's march you stop at a place where water is procurable—not, indeed, in sufficient quantity for large numbers, but enough to supply a hundred persons, together with their beasts of burden. At three or four of these halting-places the water is salt and bitter, but at the others, amounting to about twenty, it is sweet and good. In this tract neither beasts nor birds are met with, because there is no kind of food for them." Then he goes on to speak of the supernatural wonders of the great desert, of travellers belonging to caravans who, loitering behind their companions, have heard familiar voices calling to decoy them from their road; of phantom bodies of cavalry appearing to the startled traveller, and causing him to take to flight in terror of being plundered, so that he perishes miserably of hunger in the pathless waste; of spirits of the desert, who fill the air with the sounds of martial music and the clash of arms, to the dismay of the travellers, who expect an immediate attack. "Such," says Marco Polo, "are the excessive troubles and dangers that must unavoidably be encountered in the passage of this desert."

II.

Arrival at the Confines of China—Reception by Kublai Khan—Account of the Alligator—Elephants and Rhinoceroses—Talent and Energy of Marco—The Poli Promoted by Kublai Khan—Account of China—Desire of the Poli to Return Home—Refusal of the Khan—Opportunity Afforded by the Proposed Marriage of the Khan's Granddaughter—Proposal to Reach the Borders of Persia by Sea—The Khan's Parting Injunctions.

LONG journeyings succeeded the crossing of the desert of Gobi. During these Marco records many things then considered new and strange, but now "familiar as household words." Among others he describes the rhubarb-plant, and the cloth made from asbestos, "in the nature of a salamander." At length the party reached the confines of China, and here they were detained a whole year, for the Khan was absent on a distant expedition, and they and their mission seemed to have been forgotten. But at length they were admitted into the presence of the great Kublai, and performed the kotoo, or nine prostrations. The conqueror, who was at that time engaged in the conquest of China, from whence he expelled the Ming dynasty, received the travellers as graciously as before, and extended his especial favour to young Marco, whom he employed in many affairs of importance. At one time he made him governor of a province for three years, a period beyond which, according to the laws of the empire, no officer could hold authority in the same place.

Among the animals here met with, Marco Polo especially notices the yak and the musk animal, the account given of which is much more accurate than the particulars wherewith we are favoured concerning the alligator, which Marco describes as a huge serpent with two feet. His account, in another part of his work, of the rhinoceros, of which many wondrous fables had been reported, the shape of the creature being even altered to that of the graceful unicorn, is much more correct. He tells us—

"In this country" (he is speaking of Java) "are many wild elephants and rhinoceroses, which latter are much inferior in size to the elephant, but their feet are similar. Their hide resembles that of the buffalo. In the middle of the forehead they have a single horn, but with this weapon they do not injure those whom they attack, employing only for this purpose their tongue, which is armed with long sharp spines, and their knees or feet, their mode of assault being to trample upon the person, and then to lacerate him with the tongue. Their head is like that of a wild boar, and they carry it low towards the

THE RHINOCEROS.

ground. They take delight in muddy pools, and are filthy in their habits. They are not of that description of animals which suffer themselves to be taken by maidens, as some people suppose, but are quite of a contrary nature." He adds—"There are found in this district monkeys of various sorts, and vultures as black as crows, which are of a large size, and pursue the quarry in a good style."

Marco appears to have been in many respects a model traveller, sparing no pains to acquire the languages of the countries he visited, anxious to please the Khan by activity in business, and not neglectful of his private affairs when circumstances permitted him to make a journey on his own account. Like his father and uncle, he seems to have lived on the very best terms with Kublai Khan, and describes his position, speaking of himself in the third person, modestly, yet with a certain sense of dignity. He says—

"Marco, on his part, perceiving that the Grand Khan took a pleasure in hearing accounts of whatever was new to him respecting the customs and manners of people, and the peculiar circumstances of distant countries, endeavoured, wherever he went, to obtain correct information on these subjects, and made notes of all he saw and heard, in order to gratify the curiosity of his master. In short, during seventeen years that he continued in his service he rendered himself so useful that he was employed in confidential missions to every part of the empire and its dependencies, and sometimes also he travelled on his private account, but always with the consent, and sanctioned by the authority, of the Grand Khan. Under such circumstances it was that Marco Polo had the opportunity of acquiring a knowledge, either by his own observation or by what he collected from others, of so many things, until his time unknown, respecting the eastern parts of the world, and which he diligently and regularly committed to writing, as in the sequel will appear."

Our traveller here speaks truly. His position at the court of Kublai gave him peculiar and exceptional facilities, of which he availed himself to the utmost; and it may be added that what he saw "by his own observation" he generally describes with tolerable accuracy; it is in "what he collected from others" that the strong flavour of the marvellous and the supernatural is found. And, indeed, this credulity of our good Marco is not so wonderful as may at first appear. Here was a man surrounded with things which, familiar as they are to the children of this age, from their spelling-book days upward, were to him strange and new. In China he found cities and provinces whose population and extent far exceeded the population and extent of the famous Italian republics; he saw public works whose magnitude astonished him; where he had expected, according to the ideas of his countrymen, to find a savage and barbarous people, little advanced in civilisation beyond the state of nomadic tribes, he found a mighty and well-organised empire, full of industry and wealth, teeming with a vast population, and ruled by a prince of considerable power, enlightenment, and talent; and every day brought under his own observation things new and strange, of which till then he had had no conception. It is hardly to be wondered at, therefore, that he was ready to give ear to any new marvel the report of which might reach him; and that imaginative tellers of wondrous tales found in him a ready and willing listener. It must be remembered, moreover, that the travels of Marco Polo were written down long before the invention of printing; that there are many traces of interpolations in the work; and that very probably some of the most marvellous tales, and many of the most glaring inaccuracies, have been added long after the death of the original author of the travels by the transcribers who copied his work.

At length, after many years of residence, in wealth and honour, at the court of the great Kublai, our travellers began to think of turning their faces homewards. The two elder Poli were now advanced in years, and were naturally anxious to see their native land again, and after their many perils and wanderings to husband out life's taper at the close, and spend the evening of their days in the beautiful city of the Adriatic. But when the subject of their departure was mooted to the aged Kublai Khan, that gracious but despotic prince would in no wise grant them leave to go. If they wanted more wealth and honours, he said, he had enough to satisfy them to the utmost of their expectations; but they had become indispensable to him, and must remain where they were; nor did he seem to understand what attractions the distant city of Venice could have to compensate them for what they would lose in quitting his empire, or to warrant the long and perilous journey they must undertake to get there. Chance, however, not long afterwards came to their aid, and procured them the permission they had sought in vain. It happened that a certain Prince Arghun, a Tartar chief who ruled in Persia, and who was a relation of Kublai Khan, was in want of a wife, and despatched an embassy to the great emperor to solicit that a lady of the family of Kublai might be sent to him from China. Kublai accordingly determined to bestow on Arghun one of his grandchildren, a young princess of seventeen, who accordingly set forth with the ambassadors to go with them to Persia.

But the turbulent state of some of the intervening countries rendered it impossible to traverse them; and after vain efforts, during several months, the embassy and the princess were obliged to turn back, and made their appearance once more in China at the capital of Kublai. Now Marco had made more than one voyage on the Indian Ocean; and when, on returning from one of his voyages, he found the princess and the ambassadors, as it were, land-locked, and unable to depart, he boldly proposed to carry them to Persia by sea, declaring that, if he were furnished with a proper fleet, he would bring them to the Persian Gulf more cheaply and far more safely than they could travel by land. This was a welcome proposition to the ambassadors, who had been three years absent from their own country, and were naturally anxious to return home; and therefore Marco strongly urged them to use every endeavour to obtain the consent of Kublai Khan, without whose permission nothing could be done in the matter.

Marco says—" Should his majesty incline to give his consent, the ambassadors were then to urge him to suffer the three Europeans" (namely, himself and his father and uncle), "as being all persons skilled in the practice of navigation, to accompany them until they should reach the territory of King Arghun." The Grand Khan, upon receiving this application, showed by his countenance that it was exceedingly displeasing to him, averse as he was to parting with the Venetians. Feeling, nevertheless, that he could not with propriety do otherwise than consent, he yielded to their entreaty. Had it not been that he found himself constrained by the importance and urgency of this peculiar case, they would never have obtained permission to withdraw themselves from his service. He sent for them, however, and addressed them with much kindness and condescension, assuring them of his regard, and requiring of them a promise that when they should have resided some time in Europe, and with their own family, they would return to him once more. With this object in view he caused them to be furnished with the golden tablet, or imperial passport, which contained his order for their having free and safe conduct through every part of his dominions, with the needful supplies for themselves and their attendants. He likewise gave them authority to act in the capacity of his ambassadors to the Pope, the Kings of France and Spain, and the other Christian princes.

THE HIPPOPOTAMUS.

III.

Homeward Voyage of the Poli—Java—Description of Sumatra—Counterfeit Mummies of Diminutive Men—Account of Zeilan, or Ceylon—Summary Judicial Practice—Madagascar—Account of the Roc, or Rukh—The Island of Socotra—Description of Various Animals—Accurate Particulars concerning the Giraffe, or Camelopard—Intelligence of King Arghun's Death—Arrival of the Poli in Venice.

FURTHER enriched by the liberality of the Khan, the Poli departed, with a gallant fleet of fourteen large ships, from the land where they had acquired so much wealth and honour. And now commences a new chapter in the wanderings of these indefatigable voyagers. It was at the beginning of the year 1291 that they set sail from the Pekin river, touched at the present Amoy, then called Hia-muen, and steered along the coast of Cochin-China to Isiampa. The description given of Java is evidently derived from hearsay. Thence the travellers proceeded to the eastern entrance of Malacca Straits, and so on to Sumatra, where they stayed five months, till the season was favourable for crossing the Bay of Bengal, the most arduous stage of their journey.

In his chapter on Sumatra, which he calls "Java Minor," Marco gives an account of a curious imposture sometimes practised in Europe in those days, in the sale of so-called mummies of a diminutive race of men, whose existence in those days it was as heterodox to doubt as to express disbelief in the existence of mermaids. Marco Polo gives the following account of these monkey-mongers:—"It should be known that what is reported respecting the dried bodies of diminutive human creatures, or pigmies, brought from India, is an idle tale, such pretended men being manufactured in this island in the following manner:—The country produces a species of monkey of a tolerable size, and having a countenance resembling that of a man. Those persons who make it their business to catch them shave off the hair and tail, leaving the hair only about the chin, and where it grows on a man. They then dry and preserve them with camphor and other drugs, and having prepared them in such a mode that they have exactly the appearance of little men, they put them into wooden boxes, and sell them to trading people, who carry them to all parts of the world. But this is merely an imposition, the practice being such as we have described; and neither in India nor in any other country, however wild and little known, have pigmies been found of a form so dimnutive as these monkeys exhibit."

In a short chapter on the Angaman or Andaman Islands, our traveller speaks of the ferocity and cannibalism of the inhabitants—a fact abundantly corroborated by subsequent voyagers. He describes them as a most brutish and savage race, having heads, eyes, and teeth resembling those of the canine species. Then we are taken across to the island of Zeilan, or Ceylon, of which Marco gives an account that must have been looked upon as fabulous by those to whom it was first related, though Cordiner, many centuries afterwards, confirmed its accuracy in every important particular. The pearl fishery is very accurately described, even to the fact of the employment of enchanters or magicians to charm away the sharks—a precaution considered so necessary by the divers, that they will not venture to ply their submarine avocations unless one of these impostors is present to insure, as they fancy, their safety. He notices, also, the self-immolation practised by superstitious natives, and the practice of suttee, or the burning of the wife on the funeral pile of the dead husband. The

Cingalese mode of obtaining satisfaction from a debtor in Marco's time was so curious and summary that it may be given in the author's own words; it certainly seems a considerable improvement on the more lengthy and tedious practice of Western nations.

"Offences in this country," says Marco, "are punished with strict and exemplary justice, and with regard to debtors the following customs prevail:—If application for payment shall have been repeatedly made by a creditor, and the debtor puts him off from time to time with fallacious promises, the former may attach his person by drawing a circle round him, from whence he dares not depart until he has satisfied his creditor, either by payment or by giving adequate security. Should he attempt to make his escape, he renders himself liable to the punishment of death, as a violator of the rules of justice. Messer Marco, when he was in this country, on his return homeward, happened to be an eyewitness of a remarkable transaction of this nature. The king was indebted in a sum of money to a certain foreign merchant, and although frequently importuned for payment, amused him for a long time with vain assurances. One day, when the king was riding on horseback, the merchant took the opportunity of describing a circle round him and his horse. As soon as the king perceived what had been done, he immediately ceased to proceed, nor did he move from the spot until the demand of the merchant was fully satisfied. The bystanders beheld what passed with admiration, and pronounced that king to merit the title of most just who himself submitted to the laws of justice." Truly a summary way of procuring payment, but scarcely suited to modern times; for how many people might not find themselves suddenly and unexpectedly confined within the charmed circle?

Readers of the *Arabian Nights*—and who has not read that charming work?—must remember two celebrated episodes in the adventures of the indomitable Sindbad the Sailor—one tells of the valley of diamonds and the methods of obtaining those precious gems by throwing pieces of meat into the valley to be picked up by the eagles who frequented it, and who afterwards were compelled to drop the flesh, to which the stones were found adhering. The other relates to the gigantic bird called the roc or rukh, by whose means Sindbad was rescued from imminent death. Both these tales were told to Marco, who reproduces the first tale with his simple prefix, "Messer Marco was told," and evidently leaves it to the reader to believe or disbelieve, as their credulity or scepticism may prompt. The story concerning the marvellous bird he gives thus, among some hearsay intelligence he has collected concerning the island of Madagascar:—"The people of the

CONDOR AND VULTURES.

island assert that at a certain season of the year an extraordinary kind of bird, which they call a rukh, makes its appearance from the southern region. In form it is said to resemble the eagle, but it is incomparably greater in size, being so large and strong as to seize an elephant in its

GIRAFFES.

talons, and to lift it into the air, from whence it lets it fall to the ground, in order that when dead it may prey upon the carcass. Persons who have seen this bird assert that when the wings are spread they measure sixteen paces in extent, from point to point, and that the feathers are eight paces in length, and thick in proportion. Messer Marco Polo, conceiving that these creatures might be griffins, such as are represented in paintings, half bird and half lion, particularly questioned those who reported their having seen them as to this point, but they maintained that their shape was altogether that of a bird, or, as it may be said, of the eagle. The Grand Khan having heard this extraordinary relation, sent messengers to the island, on the pretext of demanding the release of one of his servants who had been detained there, but in truth to examine into the circumstances of the country and the truth of the wonderful things told of it. When they returned to the presence of his majesty, they brought with them (as I have heard) a feather of the rukh, positively affirmed to have measured ninety spans, and the quill part to have been two spans in circumference. This surprising exhibition afforded his majesty extreme pleasure, and upon those by whom it was presented he bestowed valuable gifts." We consider that they were bold men, these envoys of his majesty, for the penalty, had they been detected in hoaxing the Khan, could not have been a light one. Or did the hoax merely consist in the report made to the credulous Venetian?

That the stories of the rukh have their origin in tales originally told of large condors and vultures, and exaggerated as they passed into traditions, there can be little doubt; or perhaps geological traces of gigantic antediluvian birds, such as have been met with in New Zealand and elsewhere, may have something to do with the mystery.

In speaking of the island of Socotra, or, as he calls it, Soccoteraa, at the north-eastern extremity of Africa, Marco gives some particulars, correctly enough, concerning the whale fishery, and the obtaining of oil and ambergris. He explains how the whale is harpooned, and how, after the creature has been struck, he tells us that—"To the iron a long rope is fastened with a buoy at the end, for the purpose of discovering the place where the fish, when dead, is to be found." It is strange, however, that in all his wanderings our traveller makes no mention of the great wall of China, which he must, in the course of his travels, have seen more than once. On that stupendous piece of engineering, the Grand Canal, on the other hand, he bestows a warm tribute of well-deserved admiration. Some writers suppose, and indeed it seems reasonable, that as Marco's travels are written in short detailed chapters, some of these have been lost through the *laches* of certain of the transcribers. This is the more probable, as in the edition of the learned Ramusio there is evidently an omission of this kind, one chapter at least having been dropped out of Ramusio's book, though reference is made to it in a subsequent portion of the work.

The tiger is frequently mentioned in Marco's travels under the nobler name of the lion. In one passage reference is evidently made to the animal called the chetah, or hunting leopard. We are told that "The Grand Khan has many leopards and lynxes kept for the purpose of chasing deer, and also many *lions*, which are larger than the Babylonian lions, have good skins and of a handsome colour, being streaked lengthways with white, black, and red stripes. They are active in seizing boars, wild oxen and asses, bears, stags, roebucks, and other beasts that are the objects of sport. It is an admirable sight when the lion is let loose in pursuit of the animal to observe the savage eagerness and speed with which he overtakes it. His majesty has them conveyed for the purpose in cages placed upon cars, and along with them is confined a little dog, with which they become familiarised." The Khan, we are told, had also eagles trained to stoop at wolves.

A very correct account is given of the giraffe, or camelopard, which Marco describes as a handsome beast. He says—" Its body is well proportioned, the fore-legs long and high, the hind-legs short, the neck very long, the head small, and in its manners it is gentle. Its prevailing colour is light, with circular reddish spots." He also mentions the custom practised by some nations of making elephants encounter each other in mortal combat.

Eighteen months had elapsed from the sailing of the fleet when it reached Ormuz, on the Persian Gulf, the place of its destination. By this time the numbers of the voyagers had been woefully decreased by the vicissitudes and perils inseparable from a long voyage. Marco relates that no less than *six hundred* men had perished, while of the women who formed the suite of the princess there had died only one. After all, the object of the long sea voyage could not be accomplished, for at Ormuz the travellers received intelligence that King Arghun had been dead some time. His son, who was of tender age, had succeeded him, and during the minority of the young king the affairs of the nation were administered by the prime minister Kiakato. By the direction of the regent, the princess was handed over to the young prince, and thus the responsibility of the Poli with regard to her terminated. We are not told what was the further history of the granddaughter of Kublai Khan, who had come so far in quest of a husband.

Soon-after, while on their homeward journey, our travellers received the news of the death of their generous friend and patron, the aged Kublai Khan. They hastened onward with what speed they might to Trebizond and Constantinople, whence they proceeded to Venice, arriving in their native city, after an absence of nearly a quarter of a century, in the year 1295. Immediately after their arrival the famous banquet was given which has been already described.

CABUL.

AMERICAN MONKEYS.

COMMODORE ANSON'S VOYAGE ROUND THE WORLD.

I.

Heroism of British Sailors—War with Spain in 1739—The Right of Search—Captain Jenkins and his Grievances — The Manilla Galleon — Anson's Squadron Fitted Out—Embarkation of Chelsea Pensioners—Crowded State of the Ships—Disease and Death on Board the Ships—The Trial's Disaster—Arrival at Port St. Julian, on the Patagonian Coast—Departure of the Squadron for Strait-le-Maire—Intelligence of the Spanish Squadron.

STRICTLY speaking, the celebrated voyage of the squadron which started from England in 1740, under the command of the valiant Anson, cannot be classed among exploring expeditions. The equipment and the objects of the fleet were altogether warlike, and no scientific aim animated the brave men who were destined to undergo dismal suffering and hardship, and most of whom bade farewell to their country and friends for the last time when they embarked on that memorable voyage. But as the globe was circumnavigated by the gallant Centurion before she once more entered the Channel, years afterwards, a battered hulk, and as the result of the voyage increased the geographical knowledge of the time, as well as the warlike prestige of Great Britain on the ocean, an account of the sufferings and perils of Anson's crews may find a fitting place in a narrative of adventures of the World's Explorers. And, indeed, in few pages of our naval annals does the indomitable spirit of the British seaman appear in brighter colours than in the plain, unadorned narrative of the voyage of Anson, published in 1748 by the Rev. Mr. Walter, who accompanied the Centurion as chaplain. Peril, misfortune, and suffering in their most ghastly shapes hovered round the ill-fated ships from the beginning to the end of the enterprise. More than once, for months together, the most sanguine spirits must have been secretly calculating how long the crazy, storm-beaten planks that interposed between them and destruction could resist the death that raged around them, eager to force an entrance; or how many days would elapse before the pestilence that stalked in their midst should lay its ruthless hand upon the last of their number, and leave the shattered vessels, already scarcely under their control, to drift at random upon the long swell of the ocean, to be found by later navigators manned with corpses, like Sir Hugh Willoughby's ship two centuries before. Even the intrepid commander himself—bravest among the brave as he was—must sometimes have had a dark foreboding of the time when his crews, able to struggle no longer against wind and wave, and pestilence and blank disappointment, should give up the task in despair. But throughout all, that wonderful instinct of obedience—that sense of "doing his duty" to which he who had the best right to understand the nature of the British sailor appealed on the tremendous day of Trafalgar—maintained discipline and honour in the breast of each weary and toilworn mariner; and nobly did those brave men die with their officers in generous rivalry, anxious only to do their duty to kin and country so long as life should last.

It was in the year 1739 that the heartburnings and jealousies that had long existed between the maritime powers of Great Britain and Spain, after an abortive attempt at compromise, culminated in war. On the coast of America washed by the great Pacific, known in those parts as the Spanish Main, and in a lesser degree along the eastern coast-line of the great continent, the Spaniards arrogated to themselves certain rights and privileges against which the spirit of the British tars had long risen in sturdy rebellion, and which were scarcely less offensive to the British merchants whose ships navigated those distant seas. Foremost among these assumed privileges was the obnoxious right of search. The Spaniards were in the habit of boarding all foreign vessels they encountered to search for contraband goods; and this inquisitorial practice became additionally distasteful from the arrogant and oppressive manner in which the search was frequently carried on. Louder and fiercer grew the expressions of defiance and anger; the matter quickly assumed national importance; and at length an event occurred which blew the smouldering embers of discontent into a flame.

In 1738 there was examined at the bar of the House of Commons a man whose statement, even in those days of imperfect and hearsay reports of legislative proceedings, aroused a thrill of indignation throughout the British Empire. Captain Jenkins, a master of a merchant ship, being interrogated on the subject of the treatment he had undergone at the hands of the Spaniards, made a dismal report of their proceedings. His ship had been boarded by a revenue cutter, or *guarda costa*. The Spaniards had apparently expected to make a haul of contraband goods, and, disappointed in finding nothing to satisfy their cupidity, had vented their disappointment upon the unfortunate skipper. They assailed him with opprobrious epithets, they tortured him cruelly, threatened to kill him, and filled the measure of their iniquities by cutting off one of the unfortunate captain's ears, bidding him carry that to his king, whom they, moreover, promised to treat in the same manner if George II. ever fell into their hands—a somewhat improbable contingency, by the way. Poor Captain Jenkins carried home the memory of his grievances and his amputated ear to England, and produced them both before the indignant and sympathising House; but the chief effect of the sitting was made when, on being asked the somewhat irrelevant question, " What he had thought when subjected to these indignities?" Captain Jenkins replied, " I recommended my soul to God, and my cause to my country." After this there was nothing more to be said. War was decided on, and the government of Spain had in the sequel to pay a very considerable smart-money for Captain Jenkins's ear. That the captain was no poltroon was abundantly proved by his subsequent career; for the East India Company, sympathising with his misfortunes, afterwards employed him, and he highly distinguished himself in the operations against the Indian pirate Angria.

Among the warlike operations to be undertaken against the Spaniards, it was determined to despatch an expedition to the Pacific to operate against the enemy's commerce in the equatorial regions, and to capture or destroy their merchantmen. But the chief object of the enterprise was to make prize' of the rich treasure ship which sailed every year from Acapulco, in Mexico, to Manilla, in the Philippine Islands. It was known, moreover, that the Spaniards would despatch a squadron to operate in the equatorial seas, and thus it was hoped that the glory of a naval victory would be added to the substantial benefits expected to accrue from the expedition. Accordingly, in 1740, the ships which were to comprise the squadron were put into commission and prepared for the enterprise. They were the Centurion, Commodore Anson's ship, of 60 guns and 400 men ; the Gloucester, mounting 50 guns and carrying 300 men, Richard Norris commander ; the Severn, of like strength, commanded by the Hon. Edward Legg; the Pearl, of 40 guns and 250 men, commanded by Matthew Mitchell; the Wager frigate, 28 guns and 160 men, Dandy Kidd commander; the Trial sloop of 8 guus and 100 men, commanded by the Hon. John Murray; and 2 pinks, or victualling ships, carrying extra provisions, their cargo to be distributed among the various ships so soon as there should be room to receive it, after which the pinks were to be discharged. Such was the squadron which, after long and vexatious delays, left St. Helen's Roads to tide it down channel with a contrary wind, on the 18th of September, 1740.

There had been many vexatious delays in the fitting out of the vessels. The difficulty of procuring men was great, and for nine months the ships had been lying in port, waiting for their complement, which was at length made up by the strange expedient of shipping between four and five hundred invalids, out-pensioners of Chelsea Hospital, who were to do duty as marines and landsmen. This was a cruel, and at the same time a foolish expedient. The poor old men were totally unfit to endure the hardships and privations of a long sea voyage, amid the horrible discomforts which all men-of-war's crews had to endure in those days, when overcrowded ships, total want of ventilation, absence of cleanliness, and the distribution of mouldy and decayed provisions, were added to the inevitable discomforts that surround the seaman's life. These unhappy invalids were of no service beyond merely representing so many items in the ships' registers. They soon began to die off very fast, and in the sequel not one of them survived to see England again.

Surrounded by a gallant fleet of above a hundred and fifty sail of outward-bound merchant ships, the squadron made its way down the channel; then, parting from the traders when their course diverged, Anson's vessels made the best of their way to their first place of destination, the island of Madeira. But here already their distresses began. The ships were crowded with men unable to do sailor's duty; the wind was mostly contrary, and forty days elapsed before the island of Madeira was reached. This was a serious consideration; and the season was already far advanced, and the crews had every reason to dread the passage round Cape Horn in the stormy winter season. It was the 4th of November before the commodore left Madeira. He appointed the island of St. Catherine's, on the coast of Brazil, as the place of rendezvous for the vessels of the squadron, in case they should get separated from each other, and fail to meet at the Cape de Verde Islands; and thus, with a fresh supply of wine and water and provisions on board, and in sanguine expectation of being able soon to give a good account of the enemy, the squadron hoisted sail for the American coast, and bade farewell to the island of Madeira.

The foolishness of the policy that had made up the numbers of the expedition by crowding the vessels with old and infirm men now became apparent. We already find the captains reporting to the commodore

SPEARING TURTLE OFF THE ISLAND OF TINIAN.

on the 20th of November that their crews are in a very sickly condition, and suggesting the propriety of giving them more air between decks. Indeed, the wonder seems to be how men could have existed at all under the conditions amid which the man-of-war's men of the last century passed their lives. When, after a run of a month across the Atlantic, the ships brought up at St. Catherine's, eighty sick men, about a fourth of the crew, were landed from the Centurion, and the other ships of the squadron, we are told, had as many in proportion to their numbers. Numerous deaths had also occurred on the various ships during the passage to St. Catherine's. Commodore Anson seems to have taken every practicable measure for the health of his sailors. The spaces between decks, which the chaplain describes as "inexpressibly filthy and loathsome," were thoroughly cleansed; the ships were, moreover, fumigated from end to end, and the rigging of each was thoroughly overhauled, in anticipation of the rough weather which might be expected in the passage through high southern latitudes in the winter season. Various places of rendezvous for the ships were again appointed, and once more the squadron set sail for the southward.

The passage to Port St. Julian, at the northern extremity of Patagonia, gave the travellers a foretaste of what they might expect during their subsequent voyage. The Trial sloop, a vessel quite unfitted to attempt the passage round the Horn, lost her mainmast in a squall, and nearly all the remaining ships suffered damage in various ways. Mr. Walter speaks of the mishaps of the brave little Trial in the following terms:—

"Being come to an anchor in the bay of St. Julian, principally with a view of refitting the Trial, the carpenters were immediately employed in that business, and continued so during our whole stay at the place. The Trial's mainmast having been carried away about twelve feet from the cap, they contrived to make the remaining part of the mast serve again, and the Wager was ordered to supply her with a spare maintopmast, which the carpenters converted into a new foremast. And I cannot help observing that this accident to the Trial's mast, which gave us so much uneasiness at that time, on account of the delay it occasioned, was in all probability the means of preserving the sloop and all her crew, for before this her masts, how well soever proportioned to a better climate, were much too lofty for these high southern latitudes; so that, had they weathered the preceding storm, it would have been impossible for them to have stood against those seas and tempests we afterwards encountered in passing round Cape Horn."

On the 23rd of February, 1741, the squadron quitted Port St. Julian, and steered for Strait-le-Maire, between States Island and Tierra del Fuego. As the wind and tide hurried them through this passage, and the weather was bright and fair, the spirits of the crews rose rapidly. They considered that, once in the Pacific, and steering towards a milder clime, their course would be comparatively easy, and began to indulge in visions of victory over the squadron of Admiral Joseph Pizarro, of which they had obtained intelligence at Madeira, as having sailed to the American coast to frustrate their designs; and the prospect of prize-money came also to console these poor fellows among their perils and discomforts. "Animated by these delusions," says the chaplain, "we traversed these memorable straits, ignorant of the dreadful calamities that were then impending, and just ready to break upon us—ignorant that the time drew near when the squadron would be separated never to unite again, and that this day of our passage was the last cheerful day that the greater part of us would ever live to enjoy."

II.

Stormy Weather in the South Atlantic—Difficulty in Rounding Cape Horn—Frightful Increase of the Scurvy on Board—Frequent Deaths—Arrival at the Island of Juan Fernandez—Effect of Fresh Vegetables on the Crew—Seal's Flesh—Description of Juan Fernandez—Alexander Selkirk—The Goats—Arrival of the Gloucester—Her Deplorable Condition—The Trial and the Anna—The Severn and Pearl Put Back—Wreck of the Wager and Sufferings of the Captain and Crew.

THE weather now suddenly changed, and a period of unparalleled hardship and suffering for the travellers succeeded. Before the ships were well clear of the straits a violent gale arose from the northward, blowing them hither and thither, and tossing about the huge hull of the Centurion as if she had been a wherry. Snow and sleet blinded the mariners, and rendered the rigging and cordage of the vessels brittle and unmanageable; great waves washed over the deck, overturning and injuring the men, more than one of whom were carried overboard and drowned. The upper works of the Centurion were so loosened by her continual rolling and pitching that the water rushed into the officers' cabin in floods, and a night seldom elapsed during which some of them were not washed out of their beds; and the Gloucester and the Trial sloop were almost wrecked. It was only by means of the most unremitting exertions, and through the assistance rendered to the other ships by the Centurion, that the vessels were kept afloat during the terrible months that succeeded the departure from Port St. Julian. At length the ships lost sight of each other, and each had to struggle on separately to gain the next place of meeting, the island of Juan Fernandez.

As month after month went by, amid toil, and hardship, and privation, the scurvy, that terrible scourge of sailors in past times, but which has in modern days been entirely banished from our navy, and almost completely from the merchant service, by the use of a few simple remedies and preventives, broke out with terrible violence among the ill-fated crews. In the month of April forty-three men died of this disease on board the Centurion. In the month of May double that number perished; and by the time the Centurion reached land, in the middle of June, two hundred of her people had been buried, and the survivors were in such a state that not more than six men in each watch were capable of doing duty.

ANSON'S VOYAGE ROUND THE WORLD.   105

As might be expected, the poor old invalids who ought never to have been embarked on such a service as this, suffered most. Wounds

SEALS AND WALRUS.

that the veterans had received in past wars, and which were supposed to be long healed, reopened; and in one case an old man of seventy, who had been wounded fifty years before at the battle of the Boyne, found his long-healed hurts bursting out afresh under the influence of the terrible scurvy, as if they had never been cured; and even bones that had been once broken, parted again, to the horror of the agonised sufferers. Never has the sailor's scourge appeared in a more malignant form than it assumed on board the Centurion and her ill-starred companions. The chaplain tells us in his plain, straightforward way how the least depression of spirits following upon ill news was sure to produce a number of deaths; how many who, though confined to their hammocks, seemed yet to have a fair share of vigour left, expired on simply being removed from one part of the ship to another, in their hammocks; and how others who deceived themselves with the belief that they were recovering, fell down dead while making an effort to quit their beds. And all this terrible sickness occurred at a time when the stormy weather would have rendered the working of the ships a matter of difficulty even if every man on board had been well and fit for duty.

At length it became evident that the preservation of the remains of the crew on board the Centurion depended upon a speedy arrival at Juan Fernandez. So far from being able to attack the enemy, the most sanguine began to doubt the possibility of saving the ships; and, as the chaplain observes, time was extremely precious, the men dying four, five, and six in a day. It was under these deplorable circumstances that the enfeebled crew of the Centurion at length sighted the island of Juan Fernandez at daybreak on the 9th of June.

It was with the greatest difficulty that the few men capable of duty on board the Centurion contrived to bring their shattered vessel near the long-desired land. The beautiful aspect of the island, diversified with mountain and valley, green meadows and falling cascades, acted like a charm on the storm-tossed mariners. Even those among the sick who were not in the last stage of the terrible scurvy, crawled on deck to feast their eyes with the sight of the land; and so great was the eagerness for fresh vegetables, the natural remedy for scorbutic disease, that the first boat despatched on shore brought back a quantity of grass, which was eagerly devoured. The boat also brought back some seals, which the sailors looked upon as fresh meat. We are told these were not much admired, because, during the absence of the boat, the men on board had caught a quantity of excellent fish, but afterwards they were considered very wholesome and pleasant food.

The Centurion was scarcely at anchor before the Trial sloop came in. Her condition was as deplorable as that of the commodore's ship, and it was only by the assistance of some men sent on board from the Centurion that she was worked into the bay. Out of his small complement of men Captain Saunders had lost thirty-four, and the rest were so enfeebled by sickness that only himself, his lieutenant, and three men were able to stand by the sails. There must have been deplorable neglect and mismanagement in the berthing and victualling of our sailors in those days to have produced such mortality, even when all allowance has been made for the unavoidable loss produced by hardships and the dangers of the seas.

To many of the sufferers the relief came too late. Though the sick were conveyed on shore in their hammocks and at once deposited in tents constructed for them, a duty in which all the officers without distinction bore a part, they continued for some time to die at the rate of five or six each day. At last the rest and quiet, and still more the welcome change of diet, began to tell on the survivors, and those who were not in the last and most inveterate stage of the illness began to recover rapidly. And now the commodore, ever mindful of his duty, began to look anxiously for the arrival of the rest of the squadron; for he was determined with his diminished crews to meet the squadron of Don Pizarro at the first opportunity, and in every other respect to carry out to the minutest particular the instructions he had received on being appointed to his command.

Juan Fernandez, the island where the storm-beaten voyagers were resting from their labours, had been a famous resort of the ships of the buccaneers and pirates of the Spanish Main during the lawless times when the vessels of these rovers held the dominion of the seas in those parts. It was here that Alexander Selkirk, of Largo, in Scotland, had been left on shore at his own desire more than thirty years before; and here he lived that life of solitude during five years that has been immortalised in the poem of Cowper, and, it is said, in the pages of Defoe's immortal biography. Selkirk, in relating the adventures that befell him in the solitary kingdom where he was "monarch of all he surveyed," used to tell how he at last became sufficiently active to run down the goats that furnished him at once with food and the materials for clothing, and that when he caught more of these creatures than he wanted he used to mark their ears and let them go. As the very first goat caught by the Centurion's crew had its ears slit, it was conjectured to have been one of those which Selkirk had thus marked, especially as its long and venerable beard proclaimed it a patriarch of the herd, who might well have been a survivor of the period when the Scotch sailor roamed among the solitudes of those green hills and valleys. Other goats were afterwards found with their ears marked in the same manner, and all these had the appearance of extreme old age.

On the 19th of June a ship was seen on the horizon. As she neared the island it was observed that she had only her lower sails or courses set, and one topsail; and after a time she was supposed to be the Gloucester. She disappeared after a time, and as she did not reappear until the 26th, it was feared that she must have been so much weakened by sickness or other causes that her crew could no longer navigate her, and Commodore Anson sent off a boat's crew with a boat-load of fresh provisions and water to the help of the distressed vessel, and at last, after efforts in which several days were consumed, the ship was brought to an anchor. The unhappy Gloucester was, however, in a deplorable condition; scarcity of water had been added to the other embarrassments and perplexities of her crew, who for a long time had been reduced to an allowance of a pint a day per man. This circumstance, added to the ordinary hardships of that stormy voyage, had produced a frightful mortality on board. Two-thirds of the crew were dead, and the survivors were in such a state of misery and disease that the officers and their servants were almost the only men who remained fit for duty. But for the opportune assistance sent by the commodore, who on the following day despatched a second boat's crew to help the Gloucester, the storm-beaten ship could not have been brought to an anchor; even then this was not effected till after weeks of labour and anxiety, and not till the 23rd of July was the Gloucester safely anchored in the bay beside her consort. Death had made a still further clearance among her unhappy sailors, and before the sickness abated three-fourths of the Gloucester's crew had been buried.

One of the most remarkable features of the expedition was the perseverance and energy evinced by the crews of the various ships amid the greatest personal distresses and dangers. So soon as the sick were landed from the Centurion, the enfeebled crew had begun the labour of refitting the ship. Though they were reduced to such a condition by sickness that only a few of the most robust could undertake the labour of felling trees, and sawing the trunks into billets, the others were fain to carry these billets, one at a time, to the beach,

ANSON'S VOYAGE ROUND THE WORLD. 109

many of them absolutely hobbling on crutches to perform this duty. But there was no "giving up," even when things were at the worst;

COATS.

the patient, hardy sailors, officers and men alike, kept steadily in view the object for which the expedition had been fitted out; and their first anxiety was to put themselves in a position of defence, and avoid "the disgrace which must befall them if they had to fight their sixty-gun ship with thirty men," for to them the idea of striking their flag under any circumstances conveyed the idea of dishonour. Various appearances on the island denoted that vessels had been there lately; and as the Spanish merchantmen avoided Juan Fernandez as a place where the enemy's men-of-war were likely to look in, it was conjectured that the ships, which had left tokens of their presence in the shape of broken earthenware and other relics, must have belonged to Pizarro's squadron. After a time the gallant little sloop Trial came staggering into the bay, in a condition almost as destitute as that of the Gloucester when she made the island; and towards the end of August, when the crews were already on a short allowance of bread, and had made the unpleasant discovery that the late purser of the Centurion had neglected to ship many necessary stores which were supposed to be on board, and whose absence might produce the most serious consequences, the hearts of the brave soldiers were rejoiced by the arrival of their victualler, the Anna, pink.

On the whole, the Anna had been far more fortunate than any of the other ships. She had indeed run a great risk of being wrecked on a desolate coast, but at the very time when she was drifting fast towards a rocky lee-shore, and nothing but immediate destruction was expected, an opening was discovered that led into a most excellent harbour, where the crew had been able to rest from their labours, at the time when the Centurion, the Gloucester, and the little Trial were buffeted about in the stormy seas of the high southern latitudes. The Anna's men accordingly presented quite a favourable contrast, on their arrival at Juan Fernandez, to the crews of the other vessels, and greatly increased the efficiency of the squadron. Their healthy condition demonstrated the value of those only practical preventives of scurvy at sea—fresh provisions and good water.

The Anna was the last ship that joined the commodore. The fate of the three that were still missing was not ascertained till long afterwards. The Severn and the Pearl were unable, in spite of their utmost efforts, to get round Cape Horn, and were at last obliged to put back and steer for the Brazils, and thus ended their connection with the squadron. Far worse was the fortune that befell the frigate Wager. That ill-fated ship, to the command of which Lieutenant Cheap had succeeded, struck on a sunken rock at daybreak on the 15th of May, in latitude 47° south. Captain Cheap, who had been greatly exerting himself, had unfortunately dislocated his shoulder by a fall down the after-ladder, and, contrary to the usual custom among British seamen, much confusion occurred. Some of the crew became mutinous; they armed themselves with any weapons they could seize, and, worse than all, broke into the spirit-room, where many drank themselves into a state of helplessness. The captain seems, in his disabled condition, to have done everything he could to restore discipline and order, but in vain. The instinct of subordination was lost, and could not be restored. The men could not be induced to work perseveringly to save what could be obtained from the wreck, and the scarcity of provisions, augmented by this neglect, caused quarrels and heartburnings among them. When they were at length assembled on the island near which the ship had struck—and even this was not effected until several had been drowned, in consequence of their drunkenness—the majority differed from the captain in their opinion as to the course to be pursued. Captain Cheap, anxious to do his duty to the commodore, and to retrieve his ill-fortune, strongly urged that the ship's company, about a hundred and thirty in number, should embark in the frigate's boats, and make for the island of Juan Fernandez, there to rejoin the squadron. He represented that in their passage to that island they should be in the track of vessels, and could scarcely fail to fall in with some Spanish merchantman; that it would be an easy matter to take the trader, and convert her to their own use; and that thus they might obtain for themselves a better ship than the one they had lost wherewith to take a further share in the expedition. But the men, thoroughly weary of the enterprise, and of everything belonging to it, strongly disapproved of this proposition. They suggested, as the most feasible plan, that the long-boat should be lengthened, and that all should embark in her, and endeavour to make their way through the Straits of Magellan and round the coast to the Brazils; and they immediately set about preparing the long-boat to carry out this design. Quarrels and heartburnings continued during their enforced residence on "Wager Island," as they named their rock of refuge. A midshipman, who became especially mutinous, was shot dead by Captain Cheap, who appears to have acted with some precipitation in this matter; and though this instance of severity silenced the disaffected for a time, it increased the distrust and suspicion with which they already regarded the commander, on account of his open opposition to their plans. At length about eighty of the men departed southward in the long-boat. Desperate as their enterprise was, they succeeded at last in reaching the Brazils, woefully thinned in numbers. Death had meanwhile been busy at Wager Island, where only nineteen persons now remained. After many further misfortunes, Captain Cheap succeeded at last in reaching the island of Chiloe with the survivors of his party. He and his men were treated with much humanity by the Spaniards who held that island, and ultimately they were exchanged by cartel for some Spanish prisoners taken by the British, and returned to England. Such was the fate of the unfortunate ship Wager.

III.

Brighter Prospects—Capture of Spanish Merchantmen—Information respecting the Spanish Squadron—The Trial's Prize—Intelligence concerning a Treasure at Paita—The Ships Sail Thither—Attack on the Town—An Easy Capture —Cowardice of the Spaniards—The Town Burnt—Two more Prizes Taken by the Gloucester—Losses of the Paita Merchants.

THUS was the powerful squadron which had sailed from St. Helen's reduced to two ships of war—one of which, the Gloucester, was almost in a sinking state—to a small sloop and a victualling ship. But on the principle, perhaps, that when matters are at the worst they must mend, the fortunes of the expedition began to brighten from this period. On the 8th of September the spirits of the sailors were gladdened by the appearance of a strange sail bearing away to the north-east. The Centurion immediately got all her hands on board, and was towed out of the bay by all the boats to give chase. The ship, probably a Spanish merchantman, managed to give her pursuers the slip, and the disappointed Centurions had already put their vessel about to return to Juan Fernandez, when their spirits were gladdened by the sight of another sail between four and five leagues distant. The movements of this new stranger seemed to indicate that she was a ship of war belonging to Pizarro's squadron. This put the crew of the British ship into the highest spirits. By Commodore Anson's command the officers' cabins were at once pulled down and thrown overboard. The casks of provisions and water that stood between the guns were disposed of in the same summary manner; so the decks were soon clear, fore and aft, ready for a fight. These preparations, however, proved unnecessary, for the strange ship proved to be only a Spanish merchantman —"without so much as a single tier of guns," the worthy chaplain observes, with some appearance of bitterness. Four shots fired from the Centurion among the Spaniard's rigging were sufficient to make the crew of the good ship Nuestra Senora del Monte Carmelo lower their topsails in token of submission; and when Mr. Saumarez, the first-lieutenant, came on board, he found the ship's company in a horrible fright, in the expectation of being subjected to the worst of cruelty at the hands of their captors. It appeared on this and on many subsequent occasions, that Spanish agents, clerical and lay, had spread abroad among that nation the most horrifying tales of British cruelty and rapine ; and

I

the crews of the various prizes taken by Commodore Anson and his companions were agreeably disappointed at finding themselves treated with all proper humanity and consideration by an enemy who did not consider that a war between two great nations furnished an excuse for buccaneering atrocities. The Nuestra Senora had a valuable cargo. She belonged to Callao and was bound to the port of Valparaiso, in Chili. Her captors were chiefly gratified by the discovery of a considerable treasure on board in specie and silver plate; for as there were no facilities for disposing of the cargo, only that portion which could be removed to their own ships was of any practical value to them.

Very valuable information was furnished by the crew and passengers of the captured ship. The expedition of Don Pizarro had, it appeared, proved a complete failure. The terrific gales which had played such havoc with the English ships round the Horn had reduced the Spanish vessels to even greater distress; and Don Pizarro was moreover firmly persuaded that the English vessels had never rounded the Cape. Accordingly he had put back into the Rio de la Plata; but he sent an express overland to the Governor of Callao, to inform him that perhaps English cruisers might be navigating the seas. Hereupon the governor had despatched an armament, whose traces the English had discovered in Juan Fernandez; and had these ships met the Centurion and Gloucester in their crippled condition, the result might have been most disastrous to our arms.

The ships had actually been cruising in the neighbourhood of Juan Fernandez until within a few days of the arrival of the Centurion at that island; and the circumstance of their missing the land when first they endeavoured to make their port, which had been looked upon as a great misfortune by the toil-worn crew of the Centurion, had, in fact, proved the cause of their safety.

All toil, and peril, and suffering were now forgotten, in the exciting prospect of encountering the enemy, and in the pleasant prospect of fame and success. The little Trial sloop, whose appearance in the stormy southern latitudes was a source of continual surprise to the Spanish prisoners, who could hardly be made to believe that a vessel of such diminutive size had really rounded Cape Horn, was sent to cruise off Valparaiso, and to intercept some merchantmen which were expected to sail from that port. The Gloucester, patched up and strengthened as well as circumstances would allow, was sent to await the arrival of the commodore off the island off Paita, where the Spaniards had a fortified town; and at last, on the 18th of September, the Centurion, with her prize in company, sailed away from the island of Juan Fernandez, which had indeed been a haven of rest and safety to her exhausted and storm-beaten crew.

A few days after the Centurion's departure from Juan Fernandez her crew were delighted by the discovery of two ships at some distance. The Centurion at once made all sail towards the one nearest her, and the men were at their guns ready to pour a broadside into the stranger, when Commodore Anson caused her to be hailed in Spanish by the captain of the Nuestra Senora del Carmelo, who had been a prisoner on board the Centurion since the capture of his own ship. To his great surprise the answer came in English, and in the well-known voice of Lieutenant Hughes, of the Trial sloop. The strange ship had, it appeared, been captured by the Trial a few days before, and the other vessel was the sloop herself in a disabled condition. She had had a smart chase after the Spaniard, whose crew had screened all their lights when night came on, and attempted to escape in the darkness; but a crevice they had forgotten to stop had "prated of their whereabout" to the watchful foe, and caused their capture. They submitted at the first broadside fired by the Trial. The ship was a large merchantman, the Aranzazu, bound from Callao to Valparaiso with a valuable cargo, and silver to the amount of £5,000. This was the last service performed by the brave little Trial, which was now in a deplorable condition. Her masts were badly sprung; her timbers were in such a ricketty condition that they would hardly keep together; and so much was she strained that it was only by continual pumping she could be kept above water. Accordingly, upon a memorial being presented by her commander to Captain Anson, the commodore determined to take the crew out of the sloop and destroy her; and as the Spanish merchantman was strongly built, and, indeed, had already been used as a ship of war by the Viceroy of Peru, it was determined that she should be constituted a frigate in the service of his Britannic Majesty, under the name of the "Trial's prize." Commodore Anson accordingly made out new commissions for Captain Saunders, of the Trial, and his officers, and that commander received directions to scuttle and sink the sloop, after taking out of her all that could be obtained in the way of stores, whereupon he was to rejoin the commodore in his new ship. This was accordingly done, and for some time the ships cruised in the Pacific in hopes of taking merchantmen from Callao or Valparaiso. They, however, made prize of but one more ship, on board of which they found some lady passengers, who were treated by the commodore with great consideration and respect, to their great surprise, and especially to that of the Spanish crew, to whom the English had been represented as a set of buccaneers, wholly destitute of humanity and mercy ; and, as the historian of the expedition judiciously observes, this conduct of the commodore's had a very good effect in inspiring confidence and respect towards the English in the minds of the Spaniards. Mr. Walter observes, with a sly touch of humour, that a Jesuit priest who was on board was so completely astonished at the consideration shown by Commodore Anson to the Spanish ladies, that this admirable conduct of a generous enemy induced him to interpret in a loose and hypothetical way the doctrine of his Church that the souls of heretics cannot be saved.

And now the ships, having quitted the stormy southern latitudes, careered along before the pleasant trade winds of the tropics, the flying fish and bonitos frisking about her; and on the 10th of November the hearts of the crews were gladdened by the capture of another prize, among whose cargo is mentioned the singular item of "a number of Roman indulgences." Mr. Walter adds—"This cargo, under our present circumstances, was not of much value to us." Among the people on board this last prize there was, however, an Irishman named Williams, who had some valuable intelligence to offer. The governor of the Spanish town of Paita, it appeared, had been informed by a merchantman which put in at that harbour of the presence of an English squadron in those seas, and, justly alarmed by the intelligence, he had at once sent to inform the Governor of Lima, and had likewise commenced removing the treasure then deposited at Paita to Piura, an inland town, where it would be safe from the attacks of the enemy ; a considerable quantity of silver was also said to be lying at the custom-house at Paita, waiting to be conveyed away to a Mexican port in a ship which was rapidly preparing for sea, and was expected to be ready in a very few days. These considerations induced the commodore to determine on attacking the town of Paita, an enterprise by which he expected to inflict much damage on the enemy, and to obtain a reward in prize-money for his own crews. Moreover, the numerous Spanish prisoners on board his ships made very considerable inroads on the stock of provisions, and it was highly desirable at once to obtain a new supply, and to set on shore the extra consumers, who were very much in the way. To Paita accordingly the Centurion bent her course, with the two prizes in company, her crew highly elated with the double prospect of gaining prize-money and of having a brush with the Dons.

In order that the Spaniards might not have time to remove their valuables from Paita, it was necessary to conduct the attack on the place with the utmost despatch and secrecy. The commodore therefore determined to send an expedition of boats upon this duty, and intrusted the execution of the enterprise to Lieutenant Brett. Two of the Spanish pilots who had been taken in one of the prizes were ordered to guide the lieutenant first to the landing-place, and then along the narrow and tortuous streets of the town. The liberty of all the Spanish prisoners on board was promised in case of the success of the expedition; while on any appearance of treachery the pilots were to be instantly shot, and the Spanish prisoners would be conveyed as captives to England. Under these prospects of reward and punishment, no failure on the part of the pilots was apprehended, and the readiness with which the Spaniards had on every occasion yielded at sea did not point to the probability of their making a very terrific resistance on shore. By a strange coincidence, one of the pilots was the very man who, twenty years before, had been forced to act as guide to Captain Clipperton and his people at the taking of Truxillo.

It was ten o'clock at night when the ships made sail towards the town. At five leagues' distance the course of the ships was checked, and the boats put off, their object being to remain undiscovered as long as possible. They succeeded in escaping observation until they had reached the entrance of the bay, but then the crew of a vessel riding at anchor perceived them, and rowed off for the shore with all speed, shouting the alarming intelligence that "the English dogs" were coming. The whole place was instantly in alarm. Lights could be seen flashing to and fro, and the fort opened a fire upon the boats, whose crews bent vigorously to their oars, well aware that their safety lay in effecting a landing as soon as possible. A cannon-shot that whizzed close over their heads further quickened their motions, and upon landing they were conducted into a by-street by the pilot, where, in a sheltered position, they were formed into something like order, and marched forth to the open parade or square, on one side of which stood the fort, and on the other the governor's house.

The darkness of the night, the confusion arising from the suddenness of the attack, and the shouting and clamour of the excited sailors, who were mad with delight at the prospect of a fight and of subsequent pillage, all combined to give the enemy an exaggerated idea of their assailants' numbers, and very little resistance was made. The merchants who owned the treasure in the town made a faint demonstration of defending the governor's house, but retired after receiving a volley from the assailants; and as to the governor himself, that exemplary functionary was so anxious to get to a place of safety that he even forgot to take with him his wife, a young lady of seventeen, to whom he had only been married three or four days before; and the unfortunate lady was borne off in a most dishevelled and bewildered state by a couple of sentinels, barely in time to prevent her from falling into the victors' hands. In a quarter of an hour the town was in the hands of the English, with the loss of one man killed and two wounded. The fort and the governor's house were put under the control of a guard, and a number of sturdy negroes whom our men found in the place were pressed into the service to carry the chests of treasure found in the custom-house to the fort for safety. But for the precipitate flight of the governor, Mr. Brett would have been glad to treat for the ransom of the place, but the retreat of that prudent officer precluded any arrangement of the kind.

The sailors, who were in the highest spirits at the success of their enterprise, could not be restrained from plundering the houses, whose inhabitants had fled *en masse*. "The first things which occurred to them," says Mr. Walter, "being the clothes which the Spaniards in their flight had left behind them, and which, according to the custom of the country, were most of them either embroidered or laced, our people eagerly seized these glittering habits and put them on over their own dirty trousers and jackets, not forgetting, at the same time, the tye or bag-wig and laced hat which were generally found with the clothes; and when this practice was once begun, there was no preventing the whole detachment from imitating it. And those who came latest into the fashion not finding men's clothes sufficient to equip themselves, they were obliged to take up with women's gowns and petticoats, which (provided there was finery enough) they made no scruple of putting on, and blending with their own greasy dress; so that when a party of them, thus ridiculously metamorphosed, first appeared before Mr. Brett, he was extremely surprised at their appearance, and could not immediately be satisfied that they were his own people."

Meanwhile the Centurion had been approaching the bay under easy sail, and greatly rejoiced were officers and crew to behold the English colours hoisted on the flagstaff of the fort. At eleven the next morning the first fruits of the easy victory were brought on board, in the shape of a boatload of dollars and church plate. Mr. Brett prosecuted the business of removing the valuables with the utmost vigour, and the movements of his men were quickened by an appearance which threatened an attack from the enemy. The Spaniards, who were no doubt somewhat piqued at having been sent scampering out of their town by a force of sixty men, assembled on the neighbouring heights in something like military array, commanded by the redoubtable governor. Among them they had a body of two hundred horse from Piura, with kettledrums, standards, and all regimental appurtenances. The English had, however, formed such a moderate estimate of the enemy's powers, that they continued very calmly to load their boats with the valuables and coin to be found in the place, quite undismayed by the Spanish demonstration, which they were the less disposed to regard as serious, as they thought horse soldiers would hardly trust themselves in the narrow streets of the town. Lieutenant Brett was very anxious to treat with the governor for the ransom of the town, a measure which would have equally benefited both parties, as there were many valuable wares which the English could not carry away with them, and the destruction of which must have been ruinous to the Spanish merchants. Lieutenant Brett accordingly sent various messages to the governor by inhabitants of the town, declaring that he should not insist upon anything like a just equivalent, but that if no negotiations were opened he should certainly burn the town; but the governor was too much afraid or too sulky to send any kind of answer.

It seems difficult to account for the cowardice of the Spaniards on this occasion, when even regard for their own interest could not stimulate them to a display of courage or resolution. The only deed of daring enacted on their side was achieved by an Englishman resident among them. This worthy, who had been a ship carpenter at Portsmouth, probably wished to gain a reputation for courage among the community to which he now belonged. He accordingly came down unarmed to a sentinel, whom he deluded with overtures of submission, and then, rushing in upon him, deprived him of his pistol. He was, however, pursued by two of the Centurion's men, and paid for his foolhardiness with his life.

When all the specie in the town had been removed, Paita was set on fire in many places, and was soon in a blaze from end to end. When the English were seen to be retreating to their boats, the Spaniards made a show of coming down from the hills to attack them, but they took care to keep a considerable distance between themselves and their foes. It is, however, lamentable to reflect on the immense loss of property, and the consequent ruin of individuals, which this species of warfare involved. In the taking of Paita, as in the capture of their various prizes upon the high seas, the amount of spoil in gold and silver which fell into the victors' hands was a very small matter in comparison with the enormous quantity of valuable wares they were compelled to destroy for want of the means to carry them off. Just as they were quitting Paita they fell in with the Gloucester, which had taken two prizes, on board the smaller of which were found twelve thousand pounds' worth of doubloons, hidden in bales of cotton. This money, like the greater part of that found in the town, belonged to the unfortunate Paita merchants.

BREAD-FRUIT TREES AT TINIAN.

IV.

Anxiety of Anson to Take the Spanish Galleon—The Island of Quibo—Monkeys as an Article of Food—Parrots and Turtle—Disappointment concerning the Treasure Ship—The Gloucester Abandoned and Sunk—Renewed Sickness on Board the Centurion—Vain Attempts to Land at Anatacan and Deringan—The Island of Tinian—Providential Arrival there—Fertility of the Island—Abundance of Fresh Vegetables and Cattle—The Sick Carried Ashore—Causes of the Sickness on Board.

THE taking of Paita was an achievement of some importance, but the grand object of the voyage was yet to be accomplished. Commodore Anson had determined to capture the great galleon or treasure-ship that sailed annually from Acapulco in Mexico to Manilla in the Philippine Islands, and now the time drew near when this enterprise could be undertaken. It was now November, and the galleon was expected to sail from Acapulco early in January. Therefore the commodore determined to proceed first to the island of Quibo for a supply of fresh water, of which his people stood greatly in need.

At Quibo the ships' companies, who by this time had become most catholic in their freedom from prejudice as regarded any kind of fresh food, made many a meal off the monkeys with which the place abounded. The guanaco was also found there in abundance. The only birds to be seen were parrots. The torpedo, or sting-ray, whose powers of imparting an electric shock are well known, was also found in these regions. The ships' crews also luxuriated on turtle, with great benefit to their health; and it is mentioned as an unparalleled circumstance that, during a space of seven months, they buried only two men. This favourable state of things they attributed to the salubrity of the climate and the wholesomeness of the diet enjoyed by the men.

The next few months were passed in vain endeavours to intercept the galleon, which was supposed to be in the neighbourhood of Acapulco. For the time, however, the commander's hopes were disappointed, and the crew of the Centurion's cutter, which had been detached to cruise off Acapulco, with the hope of intercepting the galleon, were almost starved to death before they found means to rejoin their ship. It also became necessary to destroy the Trial's prizes, the Carmelo and Carmin, which had till now accompanied the captors. At last, as it became evident that no treasure-ship would be despatched that year, Commodore Anson resolved to run across the Pacific to the Ladrone or Marian Islands, where he might have an opportunity of overhauling his ships. The original number of the squadron was now reduced to two, the Centurion and the Gloucester; and of the large crews that had started from England, there remained not a sufficient number alive to navigate the two ships with anything like safety. And even this was not the worst, for heavy weather came on, with large rolling seas. The position of the Centurion became difficult and dangerous, but that of the Gloucester was most deplorable. The unhappy ship laboured so heavily that she could hardly be kept above water by the most strenuous exertions of the captain and crew, who laboured incessantly at the pumps, without being able to free her from the water which found its way through her gaping seams into the hold. Day after day men were detached from the enfeebled crew of the Centurion to help their brethren on board the Gloucester, and it became more and more apparent to all that this unfortunate ship would never see the completion of the voyage. Matters became worse with the weather, and at last reached a climax when a violent storm obliged the ships to lie-to for some days, and prevented the usual assistance being rendered by the Centurion to her unfortunate consort. When the weather moderated, a boat was sent on board the Gloucester by the Centurion; the report she brought back is best told in Mr. Walter's own words. He says:—

"Our boat soon returned with a representation of the state of the Gloucester, and of her several defects, signed by Captain Mitchell and all his officers, by which it appeared that she had sprung a leak by the stern-post being loose and working with every roll of the ship, and by two beams amidship being broken in the orlop, no part of which, the carpenters reported, was possible to be repaired at sea; that both officers and men had worked twenty-four hours at the pump without intermission, and were at length so fatigued that they could continue their labour no longer, but had been forced to desist with seven feet of water in the hold, which covered their cask so that they could neither come at fresh water nor provision; that they had no mast standing but the foremast, the mizenmast, and the mizen-topmast, nor had they any spare mast to get up in the room of those they had lost; that the ship was, besides, extremely decayed in every part, for her knees and clamps were all worked quite loose, and her upper works in general were so loose that the quarter-deck was ready to drop down, and that her crew was greatly reduced, for that there remained alive on board her not more than seventy-seven men, sixteen boys, and two prisoners, officers included, and that of this whole number only sixteen men and eleven boys were capable of keeping the deck, and several of these very infirm."

An examination made by the Centurion's carpenter, whom the commodore sent on board the Gloucester for the purpose, showed that this melancholy account was not exaggerated, and that it was merely a question of days how long the ill-fated ship could remain above water. Therefore, in the presence of this unavoidable necessity, the commander determined to take the survivors of the crew on board the Centurion, with whatever stores could be saved, and then to abandon the waterlogged ship to her fate. Captain Anson was especially desirous of saving two of the Gloucester's anchors, as his own ship was ill-furnished in this respect. But the Gloucester rolled and laboured so much that this was found impracticable. Nothing of importance could be transferred but the chests of specie, which were got on board the Centurion with considerable difficulty and danger. Five casks of flour were also secured, but three of these, it was afterwards discovered, had been spoilt by the salt water. The melancholy duty of bringing the sick on deck

PARROTS.

and transferring them to the Centurion had next to be performed; there were nearly seventy of these unfortunate men, and in spite of every care three or four of them died in the boats on being brought into the air. Then, lest by any chance the water-logged ship should continue to float, and should fall into the hands of the enemy, she was set on fire on the evening of the 15th of August, 1742. All night long she continued to burn fiercely. The explosion of her loaded guns, which went off one by one as the fire reached them, sounded like signals of distress, and must have struck mournfully upon the hearts of all on board the Centurion. At last, towards morning, the ship blew up, with a huge column of black smoke, but without much noise.

PROA LADEN WITH BREAD-FRUIT.

Indeed, her powder must have been thoroughly wetted by her leaky condition. The good chaplain ends his record of these events with the simple words, " Thus perished his Majesty's ship the Gloucester."

And now began a period of suffering and danger surpassing in horror anything the Centurion's crew had yet endured. The storm that proved fatal to the Gloucester had driven this, the last surviving ship of the squadron, far out of her course. Her own condition was hardly better than that of the gallant vessel that now lay buried beneath the waves, and an almost universal despondency had at last taken possession of the minds of the crew. Under the influence of this depression the number of the sick on board increased with fearful rapidity.

Every day saw eight, ten, or even twelve corpses lowered into the deep; and even those who had been healthy during the whole voyage now began to droop visibly. A dangerous leak was sprung in the gunner's storeroom, and only the fortunate occurrence of a few calm days enabled the carpenters to apply a partial remedy; to stop it entirely they declared to be impossible without getting at it from the outside, which could only be done when the ship was laid ashore. At length two islands, Anatacan and Deringan, were sighted; but it was impossible to obtain an anchorage, and the weather was so rough that the languishing crew dared not even send a boat on shore to obtain a supply of cocoanuts or bread-fruit for the sick, and as the island diminished in the distance, the last hope of the forlorn mariners seemed drifting from their sight. "Thus," writes Mr. Walter, "with the most gloomy persuasion of our approaching destruction, we stood from the island of Anatacan, having all of us the strongest apprehensions (and those not ill-founded) either of dying of the scurvy or perishing with the ship, which, for want of hands to work her pumps, might in a short time be expected to founder."

But it was not the will of God that these brave mariners should be added to the number of gallant men who have perished on the wide ocean without leaving a record of their heroism and sufferings. When matters had come to the very worst, and the only question seemed to be who should survive to witness the end, a merciful Providence brought the ship to the island of Tinian, one of the Ladrone group. On the morning of the 27th of August this island was sighted; and soon afterwards a proa was seen proceeding under sail to the southward. Immediately the instinct of duty was strong in the breast of the storm-tossed sailors. As it was known that the Spaniards kept a force at the island of Guam, and the presence of the proa seemed to infer that there were inhabitants on Tinian, it became advisable at once to obtain intelligence concerning the Spaniards, and to prevent them from ascertaining the lamentable condition of the Centurion, and learning how little she would be able to oppose an effectual resistance to an attack. Accordingly the Spanish colours were hoisted, with a red flag at the foretopmast-head; and the crew of the proa, deceived into the belief that the strange ship was their own galleon from Acapulco, approached near enough to be taken prisoners by the Centurion's cutter. There were four Indians under the command of a Spaniard. The account given by the Spaniard of the resources of the island filled the

Centurion's crew with joy. They were assured that the island not only afforded plenty of fresh water, but that cattle, poultry, and hogs were to be found running wild there in great numbers, so that it was used as a storehouse for the Spanish garrison at Guam, to which the captain of the proa belonged. He had, in fact, been sent to Tinian with some Indians to procure a cargo of jerked beef for the garrison at Guam, and a bark of about fifteen tons burden, which lay at anchor near the island, was destined to receive the cargo when enough beef had been prepared.

SAVAGE WEAPONS.

There was intelligence for the poor mariners, languishing for fresh provisions and wholesome air and rest! The contrary winds and currents which had been anathematised by the harassed voyagers had probably for the second time preserved them from capture, or perhaps destruction. The bark was at once secured, lest the Indians should escape in her and carry intelligence of the Centurion's arrival to the garrison at Guam. The anchor was let go, and under the stimulus of revived hope the feeble crew contrived after five hours of hard work to furl their sails, and preparations were made for once more landing the sick. It was, indeed, time; for such was the condition of the crew that out of the united survivors of the company of the Centurion, Trial, and Gloucester ships, that at their departure from England had mustered nearly a thousand men, only seventy-one men could be mustered capable of standing at a gun on the greatest emergency, and these included the boat's crew, and some Indians and negroes who had been made prisoners at various times.

The presence of the Indians on the island proved a fortunate event, for these men had erected a large hut, twenty yards long and fifteen broad, as a storehouse for their beef. This was at once cleared and converted into an hospital for the sick, who could thus be transported on shore without waiting for the erection of tents.

In the duty of carrying the sick ashore, every one, to the commander himself, took part. A melancholy procession they were—one hundred and twenty-eight persons, few of whom could hobble on crutches to the great hospital-hut. But so entirely was the lamentable state of these poor fellows attributable to preventible causes, that, though twenty-one were buried on that day and the preceding one, during the two months of their subsequent stay on the island not above ten men were lost. Fresh air and wholesome food, and especially acid fruits, were an infallible specific against the horrible scurvy, and hardly ever failed to cure those who were not absolutely in a dying state when they landed. It seems incredible that long after this period our navy continued to be annually decimated by this terrible scourge, and yet no effectual measures for the health of the men were introduced into the code of our maritime regulations.

V.

The Centurion Driven to Sea—Trying Position of the Commodore—Anson's Resolution—Construction of a Ship—Return of the Centurion—Flying Proas of the Islanders—The Centurion proceeds to Macao—The Ship Refitted—Determination to Take the Acapulco Galleon—Anson's Address to the Crew —Cheerfulness of the Men—Warlike Exercises and Preparations on Board—Suspense and Expectation.

AT the earliest possible moment, those of the sick who had partially recovered were sent back on board the Centurion, and the process of watering the ship began. The anchors were also weighed, that the cables might be examined and strengthened as far as possible, for it was apprehended that the time of the new moon would bring violent gales. But in spite of every precaution, the worn cables were not sufficient to bear the strain. On the 22nd of September a furious gale was blowing. The great majority of the crew, to the number of a hundred and thirteen, including Commodore Anson himself, were on shore. All communication with the ship was cut off, for no boat could live in such a sea. As evening came on many were the anxious glances cast towards the ship; for the few men on board were manifestly insufficient to carry her out to sea, and it was very doubtful if she would ride out the gale at her anchors. As the night wore on the gale increased. At midnight signals of distress were sent up in the shape of blue-lights, and guns were fired from the ship, but it was too dark for these to be seen or heard. The storm continued to rage; and when the morning dawned, and the watchers on the island looked out anxiously over the wild waste of tumbling waters, they gazed on one another in blank dismay, and the hearts of the boldest stood still, for the Centurion had disappeared!

The position in which Commodore Anson now found himself was one of the most trying in which a commanding officer could be placed. The men had scarcely recovered from the despondency that naturally accompanies the grievous sickness from which they had so long suffered, and now there had suddenly come upon them the most terrible calamity of all.

No one could tell whether the Centurion had foundered, or had only been driven off the land; but even in the latter and more favourable

K

contingency it was very improbable that the few men on board her would be able to do anything but let the ship run whithersoever the gale should drive her. Their present place of refuge was so entirely out of the track of ships that the island was quite unknown to the generality of Europeans; it was not likely, therefore, that they would be rescued by a chance vessel. Added to this, there was the danger that the Spaniards might come from Guam, and, in the absence of any documents to prove the rank of the officers and the status of the men, might treat them as pirates, and put them to an ignominious death. The sailors knew all this, and the commander must secretly have felt bitterly disquieted, but, to all outward appearance, he remained calm and unmoved. With ready common sense, while he professed his unhesitating belief that the Centurion had only been driven off the coast by the gale and would quickly return, he represented to the men that they must provide against every chance that might prevent the Centurion's return by themselves preparing the means of quitting the island. The small bark of fifteen tons, intended to receive the cargo of jerked beef, might be lengthened twelve feet, and thus made fit to carry them all to China. The carpenter said that this could be accomplished by the united efforts of the crew; therefore, he argued, it behoved them to set to work at once. For himself he would not require from any of them more than he, their commander, would be willing himself to do, nor should they make any exertion in which he would not take his share. Thus, if the Centurion should not return, they would be able to extricate themselves from their dilemma, and if she reappeared, they would only have lost a few days', or at most a few weeks', labour.

In the presence of such sterling counsel it was impossible to despair. The British sailor is not generally the man to leave his officer to work alone, and in a short time all was activity and labour. The work of enlarging the bark was begun under great difficulties; many of the most necessary tools had to be made before anything else could be done, and even the smith's bellows were ingeniously constructed with some hides which the ship's company themselves tanned, and a gun-barrel for a pipe. A dry-dock was dug for the bark, and she was brought into it with infinite labour and difficulty, and day after day found the shipwrecked mariners hard at work upon the preparation of their ark of safety.

The 9th of October saw the work so far advanced that they calculated they should launch their little ship by the 5th of the next month.

On the 11th, however, one of the Gloucester's men, a man who had been on a hill in the centre of the island, came rushing down frantically to his comrades, waving his hands and shouting, "The ship! the ship!" Mr. Gordon, a lieutenant of marines, ran with the good news to the captain, and Commodore Anson, throwing down the axe with which he had been hard at work, for the first time lost his composure, and gave way to an outburst of thankful joy. It was true: there, in the offing, slowly but surely nearing the island, was the old Centurion herself. A boatful of provisions for the refreshment of her crew was at once despatched, and the next afternoon she came to an anchor amid the acclamations of all. She had been away nineteen days, and it was only by the persevering and incessant exertions of the few brave men on board that she had been brought back to the island.

The business of watering the ship was now carried on with great vigour, but before it was completed the ship was driven once more off the shore. This time, however, the admiral and most of the crew were on board, and as the weather was more favourable the rest managed to come off in the ship's boats, with the exception of about thirty, who were away in the woods, and were consequently left behind. When, five days afterwards, the Centurion stood in again for the island, these indefatigable men had already begun to shorten the "fifteen ton" bark, and prepare her for sea. At last, late in October, the Centurion sailed away, well furnished with water, provisions, and fruits, from an island that had been in every sense a place of safety and refreshment to her crew, and that well deserved its Spanish name of Buenavista.

Mr. Walter was especially struck with the appearance of the flying proas or canoes, of which several were seen at the island of Tinian. He describes their construction in the following manner:—

"The construction of this proa is a direct contradiction to the practice of all the rest of mankind, for as the rest of the world make the head of their vessels different from the stern, but the two sides alike, the proa, on the contrary, has her head and stern exactly alike, but her two sides very different; the side intended to be always the lee side being flat, and the windward side made rounding in the manner of other vessels; and, to prevent her oversetting, which, from her small breadth and the straight run of her leeward side, would, without this precaution, infallibly happen, there is a frame laid out from her to windward, to the end of which is fastened a log, fashioned into the shape of a small boat, and made hollow; the weight of the frame is intended to balance the proa, and the small boat is by its buoyancy (as it is always in the water) to prevent her oversetting to windward, and this frame is usually called an outrigger. The body of the proa (at least of that we took) is made of two pieces joined endways, and sewed together with bark, for there is no iron used about her. She is about two inches thick at the bottom, which at the gunwale is reduced to less than one." These craft will sail before the trade winds at the rate of twenty miles an hour, and have been justly called flying proas.

Through all danger and difficulty Commodore Anson never lost sight of the object he had proposed to himself, and which he was determined to carry out at all hazards. He had set his heart upon taking the Manilla galleon, and every obstacle and every delay he encountered only made him more firmly resolved to carry out this part of the intention of the Government whose servant he was. Before he could combat the great Spanish ship with any chance of success, it was necessary that the Centurion should be put into fighting condition. The stores and fittings necessary to put the ship into condition could not be procured nearer than China; and accordingly the Centurion's course was shaped for Macao by way of the island of Formosa. At Macao, a Portuguese settlement, he was received in a friendly manner by the governor, who, however, told him plainly that he could not furnish him with the required stores and provisions without an order from the Chinese Government, and the procuring of this permission was attended with a great many difficulties and delays. The Chinese merchants made all sorts of promises, declaring that they would use their utmost influence with the viceroy; and after a great deal of shuffling on their part, during which they caused the loss of much valuable time, they at length coolly informed Captain Anson that they could do nothing in the matter, for that the viceroy was by far too great a man to be approached by them.

Nothing daunted, the commodore determined to proceed himself to Canton, and partly by liberal offers, partly by judicious firmness, he succeeded, after some months, in having his ship hove down and thoroughly overhauled. The dangerous leak which for many months had kept the ship in hourly danger of foundering, was permanently stopped; the vessel was thoroughly victualled and furnished with all necessary stores; and at last, in the spring of 1743, the Centurion sailed away from Macao in a very different condition from that in which she had entered the roads some months before. Her crew was, moreover, recruited by some twenty new men and boys, and

TERNS OR SEA SWALLOWS.

mustered two hundred and twenty-seven hands, a small complement still for a ship of her size, but yet sufficient, under a brave and judicious commander, to make her a match for any Spaniard that sailed the seas.

Commodore Anson was aware that by cruising off Acapulco the preceding year he had prevented the usual galleon from putting to sea for the Philippine Islands, and therefore he had reason to expect that there would this year be two of these ships despatched, instead of one. Accordingly he resolved to shape his course for Samal, the first of the Philippine Islands usually visited by the Acapulco ship, and then to cruise off a point called Espiritu Santo, and await the arrival of the galleon; and as it was the middle of April when the Centurion left Macao, and the time for the arrival of the galleon at the Philippines was early in June, he had every prospect of being in time. He had studiously concealed his intentions while the ship was refitting; but now that she was fairly at sea, he summoned all hands to the quarter-deck, and told the crew he purposed fighting the galleons. At the same time he cautioned them against crediting the absurd stories they had heard concerning the immense strength of the enemy's ships, and their reputed "shot-proof sides," promising them to lay the Centurion so close to the enemy that the shot should go, not through one of the Spaniard's sides, but through both. This speech, which was exactly to the taste of the sailors, was received with three "strenuous cheers," and nothing was now talked of but the taking of the galleons. Of the issue of the combat the men had not the least doubt. They talked of the galleons as if one or both had been already captured, and the ship's butcher asked and received permission to keep the two last of the sheep brought from Canton "for the entertainment of the general of the galleon."

Every measure was taken to bring the crew into an efficient state. Frequent exercise at the great guns, and incessant practice in firing at a mark, the commodore giving small prizes to the best shots, soon made them very expert, and their dexterity in the use of small-arms was of great importance in the fight which was to ensue.

It was the end of May when the Centurion arrived at her station off Cape Espiritu Santo. The eagerness of all on board to meet the enemy is well illustrated in the journal kept by one of the officers on board, and of which Mr. Walter gives some extracts. The officer in question writes:—

"May 31. Exercising our men at their quarters, in great expectation of meeting with the galleons very soon, this being the 11th of June their style."

"June 3. Keeping in our stations, and looking out for the galleons."

"June 5. Begin now to be in great expectation, this being the middle of June their style."

"June 11. Begin to grow impatient at not seeing the galleons."

"June 13. The wind having blown fresh easterly for the forty-eight hours past, gives us great expectations of seeing the galleons soon."

"June 15. Cruising on and off, and looking out strictly."

"June 19. This being the last day of June N.S., the galleons, if they arrive at all, must appear soon."

VI.

Appearance of the Spanish Galleon—Anson's Judicious Arrangements—Method of Fighting the Centurion—Confusion on Board the Galleon—Capture of the Spaniard—Sufferings of the Prisoners on Board the Centurion—Anson's Return to Macao—Chinese Duplicity—A Faithful Interpreter—Return to England by the Cape of Good Hope—War between England and France—Anson's Fortunate Escape—Importance of his Voyage.

THIS state of suspense had lasted just a month, when it was ended by the discovery, one morning at sunrise, of a sail bearing down upon them from the south-east. The stranger came steadily on, and after a time it became evident that she was the long-looked-for galleon. On perceiving the Centurion she did not alter her course, for it appeared that her commander, trusting to the size of his ship, and the considerable numbers of his crew, was resolved to fight the enemy, well knowing the comparative inferiority in size and strength of Commodore Anson's ship.

With great alacrity and joyous zeal the Centurion's men prepared for the long-expected combat. Their judicious commander had taken precautions to insure quickness and promptitude in the preparations for battle, while all confusion and hurry were avoided. Thirty picked marksmen were posted in the tops, where they did good service. With admirable judgment Anson had appointed two men to each gun, to be solely employed in loading it; while the rest of the men, divided into gangs of ten or twelve, moved about the decks, firing each gun as it was got ready; thus harassing the Spaniards much more than if the guns had been discharged in broadsides, in which case it was their custom to lie down and let the shot pass over them, taking advantage of the time to retaliate during the necessary interval whilst the guns were being reloaded. The Spaniards, on their part, lay-to, to await the coming up of the Centurion. They had delayed the duty of clearing their decks till the last moment, and the Centurion's men, as they came up, could see their adversaries throwing cattle overboard, and making great efforts to regain the time they had wasted. Thereupon the commodore ordered his people to open fire upon them with the bow-chasers, to embarrass their motions, and increase the confusion on board the galleon.

The galleon replied briskly enough to this attack with her stern-chasers; and when the Centurion came up with her, a fair pounding hammer-and-tongs fight began. The Spaniards fought well, and were right valiantly commanded by their general; but they lacked the seamanship of the British, who at the outset obtained the advantage in station, and kept it almost to the end of the battle. Mr. Walter tells us:—

"And now the engagement began in earnest, and for the first half-hour Mr. Anson overreached the galleon and lay on her bow, where, by the great wideness of his ports, he could traverse nearly all his guns upon the enemy, whilst the galleon could only bring a part of hers to bear. Immediately on the commencement of the action the mats with which the galleon had stuffed her netting took fire and burnt violently, blazing up half as high as the mizen-top. This accident—supposed to be caused by the Centurion's wads—threw the enemy into great confusion, and at the same time alarmed the commodore, for he feared lest the galleon should be burnt, and lest he himself too might suffer by her driving on board him; but the Spaniards at last freed themselves from the fire by cutting away the netting, and tumbling the whole mass which was in flames into the sea. But still the Centurion, keeping her first advantageous position, firing her cannon with great regularity and briskness, whilst at the same time the galleon's decks lay open to her topmen, who having at their first volley driven the Spaniards from their tops, made prodigious havoc with their small arms, killing or wounding every officer but one that ever appeared on the quarter-deck, and wounding in particular the general of the galleon himself. And though the Centurion after the first half-hour lost her original situation, and was close alongside the galleon, and the enemy continued to fire briskly for near an hour longer, yet at last the commodore's grapeshot swept their decks so effectually, and the number of their slain and wounded was so considerable, that they began to fall into great disorder, especially as the general, who was the life of the action, was no longer capable of exerting himself. Their embarrassment was visible from on board the Centurion, for the ships were running so near that some of the Spanish officers were seen running about with great assiduity to prevent the desertion of their men from their quarters. But all their endeavours were in vain, for after having as a last effort fired five or six guns with more judgment than usual, they gave up the contest, and the galleon's colours being singed off the ensign-staff in the beginning of the engagement, she struck the standard at her topgallant-masthead, the person who was employed to do it having been in imminent peril of being killed, had not the commodore, who perceived what he was about, given express orders to his people to desist from firing. But the danger was not over when the Spaniard struck her colours. Immediately afterwards the commodore was informed that the Centurion was dangerously on fire near the powder-room. The conflagration was, however, happily extinguished before the alarm had been allowed to spread, and all were soon busily employed in the task of transferring the prisoners from their own ships to the Centurion, with the exception of a few who were retained on board to assist in working the galleon."

The Spaniards had suffered severely in the action, the crowded state of their vessel and the confusion on board contributing, no doubt, to their loss. Sixty-seven had been killed, and more than eighty wounded, while the English list of casualties showed only two men killed, and seventeen men and one officer wounded; " of so little consequence," observes Mr. Walter, "are the most destructive arms in untutored and unpractised hands." The prisoners were greatly chagrined when they found that the Centurion's crew did not amount to half their own number, and some of them loudly expressed their indignation at "being beaten by a handful of boys." The fear of a mutiny among them was now added to the other anxieties of Commodore Anson, who was obliged to confine his captives in the Centurion's hold under a strong guard; while swivel-guns, loaded with grapeshot, were kept on deck, pointed at the hatchways, ready to fire down among them at the first outbreak. The poor wretches suffered fearfully in this marine "black hole," and their woes were aggravated by want of water, for the supply on board was so short that it was necessary to restrict them to a pint a day, a fearful hardship in a torrid climate. They were kept alive, indeed; but when they at length emerged from their loathsome prison they are described as looking more like ghosts and spectres than real men.

The silver in bars and coins—of which there was a great quantity on board the galleon—was at once transferred to her conqueror, and victors and vanquished made sail in company for Canton River. On their arrival at the Bocca Tigris, a narrow channel at the mouth of the river, the evident strength and the warlike aspect of the two vessels excited considerable alarm, and the pilots of the place received secret instructions from the mandarin forbidding them to guide the stranger ships past the forts. Anson, however, compelled the pilot he had taken on board to bring him past these threatening castles, which proved on observation formidable only in appearance, and made no attempt to dispute the passage. The poor pilot was threatened with hanging at the yardarm if the ships struck, and under the mingled influence of the fear of punishment and hope of reward performed his task efficiently enough. The Chinese mandarin, indeed, caused the poor fellow to be beaten for disregarding his command; but the commodore, to whom the pilot came piteously exhibiting the marks of the punishment he had received, gave him a sum of money that sent him away rejoicing.

A STREET IN CANTON.

Anson proposed to stay in the Canton River till the shifting of the monsoon, and meanwhile to obtain a supply of provisions for his homeward voyage. The Spanish prisoners were sent down the river in two junks, and set at liberty at the Portuguese settlement of Macao. And now began a series of tedious and intricate negotiations with the viceroy at Canton, considerably complicated by the duplicity and bad faith of the mandarins. Attempts were made to extort from the Centurion the duties paid by merchantmen. Every obstacle was thrown in the commodore's way in his attempts to obtain provisions, and it was only at length, by a very significant hint at the strength of his ships and their fighting capabilities, that he brought the Chinese officials to anything like reasonable terms. One of the officers who went on shore to walk was beaten and plundered, and it appeared that the authorities, though profuse in their promises to punish the delinquents, had more than connived at the outrage. A topmast that had been towing astern of the Centurion was one night cut loose and carried off. The commodore, who considered that this was not a very portable article, or a thing easily hidden, thought fit to offer a reward of fifty dollars to a mandarin for the recovery of the spar, which accordingly reappeared in a few days, whereupon Commodore Anson gave fifty dollars to an interpreter or linguist through whom he transacted his business with the mandarins, to be paid over to the official through whose means the spar had been recovered. The worthy interpreter, however, thought fit quietly to retain the cash. The wily mandarin indirectly questioned the commodore, and elicited the fact that the interpreter had received the money, whereupon that unfortunate embezzler was stripped not only of his plunder, but of all his legitimate earnings in the commodore's service, and beaten within an inch of his life. Afterwards the poor wretch came crawling to Anson in a state of abject misery, begging for help. The commodore, naturally enough, upbraided him with the folly that had made him risk losing a couple of thousand dollars on the chance of an illicit gain of fifty. The interpreter's reply was characteristic—" Chinese man very great rogue, truly!" said this model of incorruptibility, "but have fashion—no can help."

How widely this agreeable fashion was diffused among the celestials the commodore and his crew soon had good reason to know. Never was known such a community of cheats as these worthies of the Canton River. No provisions, living or dead, that were sold by Chinese dealers escaped the plague of adulteration. On finding that carcasses of hogs were bought by weight, they managed to fill them with water; when live hogs were purchased they crammed the unhappy brutes with salt, to induce them to drink largely just before bringing them on board. Live fowls were crammed in like manner with gravel, so that the weight was in some instances increased ten ounces by this honest device. And inasmuch as they were quite free from any prejudice against eating animals that had died a natural death, they managed to mutilate the last batch of hogs and poultry they delivered on board

ANSON'S VOYAGE ROUND THE WORLD.   141

the Centurion in such a manner that two-thirds of the hogs and all the fowls died before the ship was out of sight of land; and many Chinese

THE KOODOO AND NYLGHAU.

boats followed in the Centurion's wake to pick up the carcasses as they were flung overboard by the disgusted crew. At the last they were anxious to impress the barbarian strangers with an idea of their forts, by drawing out the garrisons on the ramparts; and one man of unusual stature was seen marching to and fro in an especially conspicuous manner. This paladin was clothed in complete armour; but from certain appearances the crew shrewdly suspected that the redoubtable warrior's panoply was formed, not of vulgar iron, but of a peculiar kind of glittering paper.

As the crew of the Centurion was far too weak in numbers to take both their own ship and the galleon to Europe, the latter was sold to the merchants of Macao at a price far below her value. It was, moreover, of the highest importance that the Centurion should return to England as quickly as possible; for her rich freight would have rendered her a most valuable prize, if any project could be formed to intercept her on her homeward voyage. At last, on the 15th of December, 1743, the Centurion finally set sail from China, to return to England round the Cape of Good Hope. A short stay at the Cape, then in the possession of the Dutch, retarded the passage to England; and it was not till the 10th of June, 1744, when they were not far from the Lizard, that a British ship from Amsterdam brought our voyagers intelligence of the war that was being carried on between England and France. This was startling news. The French could scarcely fail to have a fleet cruising in the Channel, and the weather-beaten Centurion, with her weary storm-tossed crew, was not in the best fighting condition.

But for the third time the commodore's good fortune clung to him. A thick fog came on; and, hidden by its friendly veil, the Centurion passed through the midst of a large French fleet, who thus lost the chance of a prize of rare value. Not till he anchored at Spithead on the 15th did Anson know how great had been his peril. He had been absent from England three years and nine months. The narrative of his voyage round the world stands brilliantly forth amid the tales of naval adventure as a proof of what the courage, fortitude, and endurance of British sailors can effect, when guided by a commander who unites cool judgment to quick resource and unflinching resolution.

THE KANGAROO.

CAPTAIN COOK AND HIS DISCOVERIES.

DANCE OF THE AUSTRALIAN ABORIGINES.

I.

Importance of Cook's Voyages—Early Life of James Cook—His Practical Seamanship—Voyages at the Beginning of the Reign of George III.—The expected Transit of Venus over the Sun—Expedition Fitted Out under Cook's Command—Madeira—The Portuguese at Rio—Passage round Cape Horn—Patagonia—Arrival at Otaheite—Character of the Natives—Judicious and Humane Conduct of Cook.

THE voyages of Captain Cook in many respects form a contrast to the celebrated expedition of Commodore Anson, from which they differ alike in the object for which they were undertaken, the means by which they were carried out, and the results that have been derived from them. The gallant commander of the Centurion was essentially a man of war, who, employed in a warlike cause, fulfilled his duty in a brilliant manner; Cook, on the other hand, sailed in the interests of peace, science, and civilisation. Anson went forth to fight against his country's enemies, Cook to explore unknown seas, and enrich the world with the peaceful triumphs of navigation and research. The one, in the stern pursuit of his duty, destroyed to the value of above a million of "enemy's property;" the other enriched his country and the world with knowledge that has already been worth many millions, and whose value has not yet been exhausted, or even fully appreciated.

Captain James Cook was born of humble parents, at Marton, in Yorkshire, in the year 1728. His father belonged to the labouring class, and, like his illustrious son, rose by his own exertions from his original station. He became under-steward on the estate on which he had long and honestly laboured. James, one of a family of nine, received a very rudimentary education, and was apprenticed to a shopkeeper; but soon exchanged the drudgery of the shop for the more congenial career of a seaman. He served for seven years as apprentice to the owner of a fleet of colliers, and the dangerous coasting service proved to him a most valuable school of practical navigation. Active, eager, and industrious, he mastered the details of his profession in an unusually short time; and at the expiration of his apprenticeship was promoted to the post of mate on board a collier. In 1755 he volunteered on board the Eagle, a sixty-gun ship, and soon afterwards his efficicucy and good conduct, backed by the interest of friends of his family, raised him from before the mast. The Mercury, a small vessel, was to accompany the squadron of Sir Charles Saunders, bound to the Gulf of St. Lawrence; and young James Cook was appointed master of this vessel.

The English were at this time occupied in the task of wresting Canada from the French, and a British fleet was sent to strengthen the army of General Wolfe. The difficult and perilous task of taking soundings before the ships proceeded to their stations was intrusted to Cook, who fulfilled his duty in the most efficient manner, and in doing so narrowly escaped capture by the enemy. On one occasion he only saved himself by stepping out of his boat at the bow as some Indians who were in pursuit of him rushed in at the stern. He afterwards made a survey of the coast of Newfoundland and Labrador, a service of especial utility from the importance of the former settlement as a fishing station. Thus, step by step, by repeated services unobtrusively rendered, but rich in practical worth, the young mathematician won his way to distinction and honour.

With the reign of George III. began an age of exploration and discovery in the distant regions of the Pacific, and in those parts of the Atlantic that had hitherto escaped the investigation of mariners. In 1764, Commodore Byron started on his memorable voyage round the world in the Dolphin, following in some measure the track pursued by Anson's squadron nearly a quarter of a century before. In 1766 a second voyage round the world in the Dolphin was undertaken by Captain Wallis, and further discoveries were made; while in the meantime Captain Carteret achieved a similar enterprise in the sloop Swallow, a miserable old tub quite unfit for the important service on which she was despatched. But a still more arduous work was now to be intrusted to the energy and skill of Cook.

In the year 1716 the illustrious astronomer Halley, himself a great voyager in the cause of science, had pointed out the advantages to be obtained by an accurate observation of a transit of the planet Venus over the sun's disc. The parallax of the sun and the dimensions of the solar system, with the distance of the sun from the earth, could be determined with an accuracy yet unattained by an accurate observation of this phenomenon. The transit of Venus over the sun only occurs once in more than a century. It had happened in 1639, and was to be expected again in 1769; and Halley exhorted those who should come after him not to let this grand opportunity for scientific observation pass without making due use of it. His admonitions were not forgotten, and in 1766 the Admiralty prepared to send out an expedition to the southern seas to take the necessary observations.

It had been originally intended to put the enterprise under the direction of Dalrymple, the eminent astronomer, with whom was to be associated a naval officer who should undertake the practical command; for former experience in the case of Halley himself had shown that a purely scientific commander cannot always secure the necessary subordination and respect among his crew. Dalrymple, however, refused to have anything to do with the enterprise unless he had the entire command; and in this dilemma Cook was mentioned as a proper man to undertake the responsible duty. Accordingly he received a lieutenant's rank and a commission appointing him commander of the

L

enterprise. With him were associated Mr. Green, an astronomer, Dr. Solander, a Swedish botanist of considerable attainments, and Mr. Banks, a young gentleman of large fortune, who zealously devoted himself to science, and afterwards made for himself a celebrated name as Sir Joseph Banks, President of the Royal Society. He survived till 1820.

With rare judgment Lieutenant Cook selected for his enterprise a stout, strongly-built collier, the Endeavour, well knowing that a ship built for the coasting trade would be easier to navigate in intricate and dangerous channels than a frigate or line-of-battle ship, and would, moreover, contain much more room for stores. Thus, on the 26th of August, 1768, Cook sailed from Plymouth on a voyage destined to be recorded as one of the most remarkable in the annals of maritime discovery.

The first and most important object of the expedition was to note the transit of Venus over the sun's disc; and by the advice of Captain Wallis, who had returned from a voyage of discovery round the world while the preparations of Cook's expedition were in active progress, it was decided that King George the Third's Island in the South Sea, now more generally known by its native name of Otaheite, should be the point where the astronomers were to make their observations.

Accordingly, Cook steered for the Pacific, following the usual route of vessels in those days—namely, by way of Madeira to the Brazils, and thence to Strait le Maire, the scene of such terrible discomfort and danger to the ships of Anson's squadron. Cook gives a few interesting particulars concerning Madeira, and graphically and truly describes it as a place for which Nature had done everything and art and industry nothing. He speaks of the negligent and imperfect cultivation of the splendid vines with almost a prophetic foreknowledge of the results this carelessness would produce in the deterioration of the grapes, and consequently of the famous vines of the island. The good commander's ideas of artistic taste and fitness were moreover outraged by the pictured saints to be found in numbers on the walls of the convents, *and many of whom were attired in laced coats.*

Coasting southward along Brazil, the Endeavour reached Rio Janeiro. The Portuguese authorities seem to have looked with considerable suspicion upon the strange ship, especially as the governor of Rio, whose scientific knowledge was probably of a very elementary kind, could not at all be made to understand the object of the voyage.

That a ship should be sent thousands of miles for the sake of astronomical observations was to him a great and unfathomable mystery, and the transit of Venus itself was a thing he could by no means be made to comprehend. At last, however, he became impressed with a vague notion that the phenomenon in question was "the passing of the North Star through the South Pole;" and, sorely harassed in his mind with all manner of doubts as to the real intentions of his visitors, the worthy viceroy caused them to be strictly watched. To the last he seems to have been persuaded that the true object of the voyage was rather political than scientific, and was connected with some sinister design on his Portuguese Majesty's town of Rio.

On the coast of Patagonia immense flocks of sea birds were observed, from the stately albatross to the stupid penguin. The scientific gentlemen on board were also astonished at the appearance of the *Fucus giganteus*, an enormous sea-weed, whose stalks were hundreds of feet in length, growing up and spreading over the surface of the water, where there was a perpendicular depth of eighty-four feet. This is the same plant which has been described by Alexander von Humboldt in his *Views of Nature*.

The gigantic inhabitants of Patagonia, with whom the voyagers held some intercourse, were very degraded specimens of the "noble savage," and appeared destitute, not only of intelligence, but even of curiosity. Some of them came on board, but did not appear at all impressed by the multitude of new and strange objects they saw. They gazed around them with looks of vacant indifference; nor on their landing and rejoining their companions was any anxiety exhibited by the latter to hear what they had seen. A tragic adventure happened to a party consisting of Mr. Banks, Dr. Solander, and other gentlemen, with some servants and sailors, who ascended a mountain on a botanising expedition. They had secured their plants and were returning to the ship when violent snowstorms retarded their progress, and it became apparent that they must pass the night on shore. This was a hard and even a dangerous prospect, and they determined to make what speed they could to the shelter of a wood, and there pass the night by a fire. Dr. Solander, who in his native country had crossed the Kolen range of mountains between Norway and Sweden, knew of the fatal drowsiness that frequently seizes the weary traveller, and of the effects of indulging in the inclination to rest, and implored his companions to keep moving, whatever pain the effort might cost them. "Whoever sits down," he said, "will sleep, and whoever sleeps will wake no more." Thus urged, the travellers pushed sturdily onward; but as night came

SEA BIRDS OF THE SOUTHERN OCEAN.

on, the cold became more and more severe. Dr. Solander himself was the first to feel the approach of the fatal lethargy against whose insidious attacks he had warned his companions; and, "recking not his own rede," he piteously begged to be allowed to lie down and sleep, though

STORMY PETREL—WANDERING ALBATROSS.

he had emphatically declared that to sleep was to die. Richmond, a black servant, felt the same inclination, and began to linger behind;

and in a short time, in spite of the entreaties of Mr. Banks and the other gentlemen, the two half-stupefied men lay down on the ground. Mr. Banks, with admirable forethought, had sent some men on to kindle a fire when Dr. Solander and Richmond began to flag. With great difficulty the doctor was conveyed to this fire and revived; but Richmond and another man perished from the terrible cold.

Cook was fortunate in the weather in rounding Cape Horn. The albatross now appeared larger than ever, and our travellers certainly laid themselves open many times to the penalties and sorrows that befell Coleridge's Ancient Mariner, for they not only "shot the albatross" whenever they could find him, but ate him too, without the slightest scruple. "The albatrosses we skinned," says Dr. Hawksworth's account, taken from the journals of the commanders and gentlemen, "and having soaked them in salt water till the morning, we parboiled them; then having thrown away the liquor, stewed them in a very little fresh water till they were tender, and had them served up with savoury sauce; thus dressed the dish was universally commended, and we ate of it very heartily even when there was fresh pork on the table." Throughout all this part of the voyage the remarks of Cook on the navigation of the seas around Cape Horn exhibit him as a true practical sailor; and the comparative ease with which he found his way around the boisterous Horn must be partly attributed to his excellent seamanship, and to the unceasing vigilance he exercised in every period of danger and difficulty.

Thus the most perilous part of the voyage was passed without serious loss or damage; and the Endeavour entered the Pacific, steering for the appointed harbour in Matavai Bay.

Otaheite, or King George the Third's Island, as it had been termed by Captain Wallis, has always claimed more attention, both on religious and political grounds, than any other island in the Pacific groups. It has long been a favourite field for missionary enterprise, Roman Catholics and various Protestant denominations having vied with each other in their efforts to convert the inhabitants; and not quite a quarter of a century has elapsed since the forcible establishment of a French "protectorate" on the island, and certain insults offered to Mr. Prichard, the British consul, who tried to defend the unfortunate native queen Pomaré, nearly led to a rupture of amicable relations between England and France. But, as Hermann Melville acutely observes in his amusing book *Omoo*—the best account, by the way, that has been written of the island in our own times—"Saint George and Saint Denis were not going to cross swords about Tahiti," and the difficulty was amicably adjusted. In our own days, Papetee Bay, the principal harbour of the island, has become a calling place for ships, chiefly American, engaged in the South Sea whale fishery; and it may be safely affirmed that the intercourse with the crews of these vessels, and with other visitors to the island, has wrought most lamentable effects upon the character and prospects of the inhabitants. In Cook's time the people of Otaheite were a handsome race, tall, strong, and well made, and many among the women had considerable pretensions to beauty. They had already made acquaintance with Europeans, Captain Wallis and former voyagers having touched at Otaheite, and in their behaviour they were generally exceedingly friendly and obliging. In many points of their character they resembled children; easily excited to laughter or tears, they seemed incapable of long preserving the memory either of joy or sorrow, and every passing feeling of their minds was plainly expressed in their faces. They were exceedingly fond of approbation, and of an affectionate disposition, eager to show friendship to their visitors, and quickly forgetting any cause of complaint or quarrel that might arise. Simple and unsuspicious, they allowed their visitors to land and build a fort, and never seem to have imagined that the power of the strangers who had come over the great sea to visit them could be used otherwise than for their benefit. On the other hand, they were arrant thieves, and in this particular the only difference between chiefs and people appeared to be that the chiefs showed something like shame when caught in the fact, and the people did not. They were very ingenious in various ways, especially in the manufacturing of tappa, or native cloth, from the fibres of the bark of trees. The commander, immediately upon landing, drew up a set of "Regulations to be observed by every person in or belonging to his Majesty's bark the Endeavour," in the cultivation of intercourse and trade with the natives. These regulations especially enjoined that the natives should be treated with justice and humanity; and as Cook himself took care to see that they were not infringed with impunity, the effect was satisfactory to all, and perfect confidence was soon established between the natives of Otaheite and their visitors. The commander's judicious conduct in rigidly punishing the first offender who attempted to wrong the natives had the best effect. The ship's butcher received a sound flogging for threatening to cut the throat of a chief's wife who refused to sell him a stone hatchet. The natives, when they saw the punishment begun, earnestly tried to procure pardon for the offender, and the whole transaction impressed them with a respect alike for the power and for the justice of Cook.

The chief object of the voyage, the observation of the transit of Venus, was successfully accomplished. The sun rose on the important day without a cloud, and the time of the transit was very accurately noted by Mr. Green, the astronomer, and the other scientific gentlemen attached to the expedition. A second set of observations, taken at the neighbouring island of Eimeo, were equally satisfactory with those at Otaheite.

II.

Surf-swimming at Otaheite—Thievish Propensities of the Natives—Tupia the Otaheitan accompanies Cook—Singular Customs in Otaheite—Cook's Arrival at New Zealand—Circumnavigation of the Islands—Cook's Strait—Account of the Natives—Cook's Exploration of the Coast of New Holland—Narrow Escape of the Endeavour—Natives of New Holland—Cook takes Possession of New South Wales—Voyage to Batavia.

NONE of the customs of the Otaheitans seem to have excited so much surprise in their visitors as the practice of surf-swimming, of which the following account is given:—"We came," says the commander, "to one of the few places where access to the island is not guarded by a reef, and consequently a high surf breaks upon the shore; a more dreadful one, indeed, I had seldom seen. It was impossible for any European boat to have lived in it, and if the best swimmer in Europe had by any chance been exposed to its fury, I am confident that he would not have been able to preserve himself from drowning, especially as the shore was covered with pebbles and large stones. Yet in the midst of these breakers were ten or twelve Indians swimming for their amusement. Whenever a surf broke near them they dived under it, and, to all appearance with infinite facility, rose again on the other side. This diversion was greatly improved by the stern of an old canoe, which they happened to find upon the spot. They took this before them, and swam out with it as far as the outermost breach; then, two or three of them getting into it and turning the square end to the breaking wave, they were driven in to the shore with incredible rapidity, sometimes almost to the beach; but generally the wave broke over them before they got half way, in which case they

CAPTAIN COOK AND HIS DISCOVERIES. 153

dived, and rose on the other side with the canoe in their hands. They then swam out with it again, and were again driven back, just as our holiday youth climb the hill in Greenwich Park for the pleasure of rolling down it. At this wonderful scene we stood gazing for more than half-an-hour, during which time none of the swimmers attempted to come on shore, but all seemed to enjoy the sport in the highest degree."

SURF-SWIMMING.

The incurable propensity of the natives to steal was the cause of frequent petty disputes and misunderstandings. Never did a nation seem so universally afflicted with kleptomania as these islanders appeared to be. Everything on which they could lay felonious hands disappeared as if by magic. At one time the quadrant with which the observation of Venus was to be taken was carried off; at another, almost all the clothes of some of the gentlemen disappeared mysteriously while the owners were sleeping in a friendly tent; and the discovery of each theft was but the prelude to the commission of the next. On the other hand they were quite free from the vindictiveness and malice that characterised the inhabitants of many other islands. The offences occasionally committed against them by the ship's crew were never remembered with anything like rancour or a desire for revenge. On the whole, Cook formed a most favourable opinion of the Otaheitans, and declared that, except for their inveterate propensity to thieve, they would bear comparison with any people he had ever seen.

The chiefs and nobles were a taller and finer set of men than the common people; they were, moreover, lighter in colour, so that Captain Wallis had imagined there were two distinct races on the island, the one subject to the other. The difference, however, seems attributable to the easier and more luxurious life of the chiefs. One of these nobles, a man named Tupia, with his boy Tayeot, determined to accompany the expedition; and as it was supposed that his knowledge of the language and customs of the inhabitants of various islands might be turned to good account, his offer was accepted. Tupia was a man of some science; he had a certain knowledge of astronomy, and during any part of the subsequent voyage could always point out the position of Otaheite by a reference to the stars.

After a stay of about three months at Otaheite, Cook set sail, with the knowledge that the grand object of the voyage had been achieved. He gave to the group of islands of which Otaheite formed the principal one the name of the Society Islands. On passing Bora-bora, an island whose people had been lately at war with Otaheite, Tupia was exceedingly urgent in requesting Cook to fire great guns at the hostile coast, that the warriors of Bora-bora might see what powerful allies his people had gained. His whim was gratified; but as the Endeavour did not touch at Bora-bora the effect of this diplomatic proceeding on the islanders could not be ascertained. Not the least curious among the customs of Otaheite was the practice of considering the new-born son of a chief or king as the immediate inheritor of his father's rank and wealth, the father, during the rest of his life, acting only as regent during the minority of the son. Thus Oberea, the Queen of Otaheite, who during the time of Captain Wallis's visit enjoyed undisputed sway and the highest consideration in the island, had already lost much of her position and influence at the time of Cook's first landing; for a son had been born to her, and this child was considered as the king of the island.

CAPTAIN COOK AND HIS DISCOVERIES. 155

After passing several other islands Cook made his way to New Zealand, which had been discovered by Tasman, the Dutch navigator, about a century and a quarter before. The people here could understand the language spoken by Tupia; but they were very hostile and fierce, and no presents or blandishments could conciliate them. They came boldly out of the woods to attack the voyagers with long pikes and lances; and at the very first meeting four of them made so hostile a demonstration against a boat's crew that to save their own lives Cook's people were obliged to shoot one of their assailants dead. It was now thought advisable to capture some of these savage islanders, and by subsequent kind treatment to disarm their resentment; but this plan likewise failed. An attempt was made to cut off two canoes in the bay, and capture the crews. One party escaped by paddling; but the other, which consisted of seven persons, finding retreat impossible, determined to fight, and attacked Cook's men so furiously with sticks, stones, and other weapons, that it was necessary to fire upon them, and four were unhappily killed at the first discharge. The three survivors, who were mere youths, expected nothing less than instant death at the hands of their captors, and were accordingly greatly delighted when they found themselves kindly treated and loaded with presents. They seemed intelligent and impressionable, and sang a native song with a taste that surprised the English. They were afterwards set on shore, where the presents they displayed were looked upon with indifference; and the questionable expedient of their capture seems, like most questionable expedients, to have turned out a failure, for the natives continued fierce and distrustful to the last. At length a party of them made a very determined attempt to capture Tayeto, Tupia's boy, and very nearly succeeded in their enterprise; so at last Cook, seeing that nothing was to be done with these savages, sailed away to the northward, after giving to the place where his ship had spent time so unprofitably the name of Poverty Bay.

True to his conscientious and methodical habits, the commander made an accurate survey of the coast of New Zealand. He discovered a broad river to which he gave the name of the Thames, and was particularly struck with the appearance of the Heppahs, or fortified villages, of the inhabitants, who, with all their ferocity, and, as was afterwards ascertained, their cannibalism, were remarkably intelligent and ingenious, and possessed arts and a religion of their own. New Zealand had until then been considered a part of the almost unknown Terra Australis;

but Cook proved it to consist of two separate islands divided by a strait, through which he passed, and to which his name has very properly been given. The circumnavigation of New Zealand was an achievement of much importance; and now Cook, who had great doubts as to the existence of the Terra Australis incognita of Tasman, a continent supposed to stretch to the South Pole, sailed away from New Zealand on the 31st of March, 1770, determined to set this question at rest. Three weeks' sailing brought him to the east coast of Australia. He landed at the place which afterwards obtained an unenviable notoriety in the annals of transportation under the name of Botany Bay, an appellation first given to it on account of the rich plant-stores found there by the indefatigable Mr. Banks and Dr. Solander. The persevering industry with which the coast here, as elsewhere, was examined, proved of the utmost use to subsequent navigators; and, indeed, there seems to have been hardly one of our great navigators who possessed the attribute of thoroughness in so great a degree as it was shown by Cook. In surveying, taking soundings, and making observations, he was indefatigable.

The natives were seldom seen, and in many respects appeared far below the New Zealanders in intelligence and activity. On one occasion, we are told, "The people who were left on board the ship said that while we were in the woods about twenty of the natives came down to the beach abreast of her, and having looked at her some time, went away; but we that were ashore, though we saw smoke in many places, saw no people. The smoke was at places too distant for us to get to them by land, except one, to which we repaired. We found ten small fires still burning within a few paces of each other, but the people were gone; we saw near them several vessels of bark, which we supposed to have contained water, and some shells and fishbones, the remainder of a recent meal. We saw also, lying upon the ground, several pieces of soft bark, about the length and breadth of a man, which we imagined might be their beds; and on the windward side of the fire, a small shade, about a foot and a-half high, of the same substance. The whole was in a thicket of close trees, which afforded good shelter from the wind. The place seemed to be much trodden, and as we saw no house, nor any remains of a house, we were inclined to believe that as these people had no clothes they had no dwellings, but spent the nights, among the other commoners of Nature, in the open air; and Tupia himself, with an air of superiority and compassion, shook

CAPTAIN COOK AND HIS DISCOVERIES. 157

his head and said that they were Taata Enos—'poor wretches.'" In this instance Cook was mistaken. The natives of New Holland have

OPOSSUMS.

their rude huts, or Gunyon; and the strips of bark found by the exploring party were probably the materials of which these rude dwellings had been built. Here our travellers also, for the first time, saw that singular animal the kangaroo.

A terrible and well-nigh fatal accident now befell the Endeavour. The coast along which the explorations were carried on was an eminently dangerous one; the sea was full of sudden and unexpected shoals, and of rocks rising abruptly from the bottom. Amid all these perils the Endeavour had threaded her way unharmed; but one memorable night, at eleven o'clock, she suddenly struck upon some coral rocks at about eight leagues from the land. So violent was the shock that some of the planks that formed the sheathing, and part of the false keel, could be seen in the moonlight floating away from the vessel. The ship grated violently against the rock, and the water rushed into the hold. The crew, under the captain's direction, did everything that could be done under the circumstances. All heavy stores were thrown overboard, to lighten the ship. The fresh water was started in the hold, and pumped out; the guns and the iron and stone ballast were got rid of immediately. Fortunately, the weather was calm, and a sail, wadded with oakum, was got over the ship's side, and made fast over the part where the water was rushing in. The men laboured resolutely at the pumps, and at length the tide lifted the ship off the rock. With a less able commander than Cook, the Endeavour must inevitably have been lost; but with consummate seamanship he navigated her across the perilous eight leagues to the shore, and ultimately brought her safely into a small cove at the mouth of a stream, which afterwards was named Endeavour River; while the cape near which the disaster to the ship occurred was aptly designated Cape Tribulation. "Upon this occasion," says Cook, "I must observe, both in justice and gratitude to the ship's company and the gentlemen on board, that although, in the midst of our distress, every one seemed to have a just sense of his danger, yet no passionate exclamations or frantic gestures were to be heard or seen. Every one appeared to have the perfect possession of his mind, and every one exerted himself to the uttermost, with a quiet and patient perseverance equally distant from the tumultuous violence of terror and the gloomy inactivity of despair."

It was not until the Endeavour was emptied and thoroughly examined that the full amount of the late peril was recognised. A large fragment of coral rock, after forcing its way through four planks, had been broken off, and remained sticking in the wound it had made, and acting as a stopper. Had the leak not been thus plugged, eight pumps—instead of the four which the Endeavour possessed—would not have been sufficient to keep the ship above water. The expedient of the sail, too, had done signal service, for the oakum with which the inner surface of the sail had been strewn had forced its way into the interstices between the fragment of rock and the edges of the hole it had bored.

The natives here were more sociable than those of Botany Bay, and

A NATIVE HOME.

would probably have been pronounced by Tupia not quite such poor wretches. They were certainly entirely destitute of clothing, but they by no means despised ornaments, rejoicing in bracelets and necklaces of hair and shells. Their chief pride seemed to be in the piece of bone, five or six inches in length, which they thrust through the pierced cartilage of the nose. The sailors of the Endeavour made very merry over these singular ornaments, which they likened to spritsail-yards. Nothing would induce these people to part with any of their ornaments, nor had they any idea of traffic or barter. The only thing in the possession of their visitors which excited their cupidity was a turtle,

160   THE WORLD'S EXPLORERS.

which they endeavoured to appropriate by force, and things that were given them they left lying about upon the beach, as children would fling away toys when the charm of novelty was gone.

Once more the ship was entangled among the reefs, and in imminent danger of being lost; she was saved by being steered through a small opening, which Cook appropriately named Providential Channel. Before quitting the eastern coast of New Holland, he solemnly took possession of the whole stretch he had explored, from 38° to 10° south lat., in the name of his Majesty King George III., giving it the name of New South Wales, and the island upon which the ceremony took place was called Possession Island.

The length of the voyage and the occasional scarcity of fresh provisions had now begun to tell in a very marked manner upon the health of the ship's company. Poor Tupia, the Otaheitan, had several times been ill with the scurvy, and many of the crew were in a very weak state. Cook therefore resolved to abandon his intention of surveying the coasts of New Guinea, and made the best of his way to the Dutch settlement of Batavia on the island of Java, in the hope that a short residence on shore would recruit the strength of the sick.

III.

Pestilential Climate of Java—Death of Tayeto and Tupia—Mortality among the Crew—Running a Muck—Cape Town and St. Helena—Return to England—Determination to Send a Second Expedition—Cook Undertakes the Command—Question concerning a Southern Continent—Fitting-out of the Ships—Precautions against Scurvy.

BUT the remedy proved worse than the disease. The pestilential climate of Java told fatally upon the enfeebled voyagers. The low swampy position of Batavia, and the numerous canals by which it is ntersected, produced malaria and intermittent fever, and one after another of the ship's company was attacked by the insidious foe, until there were not ten men left in the ship fit for duty. Among the first victims was the surgeon of the ship, Mr. Monkhouse, "a sensible, skilful man," says Cook, who, like Nelson, was always anxious to give all possible praise to his officers. Next died Tayeto, Tupia's boy, and then poor Tupia himself, who had been long ailing, and who sank rapidly on hearing of the lad's death. The loss of this simple islander was much regretted by the whole ship's company. He had several times been eminently useful as an interpreter in New Zealand and elsewhere, and had always shown himself as an amiable, worthy man, not without shrewdness and good sense, and perfectly amenable to discipline.

The condition of the ship necessitated a stay of some time in the pestiferous climate of Batavia. When the keel came to be examined a very alarming state of things was discovered. "How much misery did we escape," exclaims the narrator, "by being ignorant that a considerable part of the bottom of the vessel was thinner than the sole of a shoe, and that every life on board depended on so fragile a barrier between us and the roaring ocean!" The ship was accordingly "hove down," and the necessary repairs were pushed forward with all possible despatch. But the progress of the disease among the voyagers was more rapid still. Dr. Solander and Mr. Banks barely escaped with their lives, after being removed to a house in the country. Seven men were buried before the ship finally sailed out of Batavia roads, and when the Endeavour at last left the deadly shore behind her she had forty sick on board, and all the rest were languid and feeble, with one notable exception. The sailmaker, a jovial old salt, more than seventy years of age, had never been unwell since their arrival at Batavia, "and it is very remarkable," says the narrative, " that this old man during our stay at this place was constantly drunk every day." The anti-temperance veteran, however, died before the end of the voyage.

The horrible practice of *mock*, or, as it is generally called, running a muck, is noticed by Cook. The man who designs to run a muck first madly intoxicates himself with opium, and then rushes through the streets with a naked weapon in his hand, cutting down every one whom he meets, until he himself is slain or captured. The motive is always revenge, and thus the man who runs a muck is in most cases a slave who has been rendered frantic by some real or supposed wrong, for which he can obtain no legal redress. Any man who captured an amock, or, as the name was corruptly called, a mohawk, alive, was entitled to a considerable reward. The punishment for running a muck was death by breaking on the wheel. The evil effects of the climate of Batavia continued to show themselves among the crew for a long time after the departure of the Endeavour from that fatal shore. Dysentery and fever raged in the ship, and nearly every evening the body of a sailor was committed to the deep. Mr. Green, the astronomer, Mr. Parkinson, the naturalist, and the boatswain and his mate were among those who perished. The ship was thoroughly washed with vinegar between decks, and the drinking water was purified with lime; but in spite of all curative and preventive measures twenty-three deaths occurred within a few weeks of the Endeavour's departure from Batavia.

A short stay at the Cape restored the survivors to comparative health. Among the animals at the Cape, Cook and his companions especially remaked the koodoo, or, as it is called in the journal of the voyage, the coe doe, a creature of the deer kind, as large as a horse, and with fine spiral horns. The country at the back of the Cape at that time contained very few settlers, and these were thinly scattered over a great extent of territory, living at enormous distances from each other. While the Endeavour was at the Cape, a man came to Cape Town, a fifteen days' journey, bringing his children with him. When our voyagers, surprised that the man should travel with such an incumbrance, suggested that he might have left his children with his next neighbour, he replied that his next neighbour resided at a distance of five days' journey from him. Fortunately the bushmen, or plunderers, who infested these outposts of civilisation, never attacked the settlers openly, but made stealthy forays to carry off the cattle, generally by night. This had given rise to a strange custom among the other natives of training bulls to attack the thieves, just as watch-dogs might be used in this country, and these horned guardians of the settlements wandered about the town at night, just as a mastiff might be let loose to patrol a farmyard.

The volcanic nature of the island of St. Helena, where the ship touched on her way from the Cape, is especially noticed. The account says, "It appeared, as we approached it on the windward side, like a rude heap of rocks, bounded by precipices of amazing height, and consisting of a kind of half-friable stone which shows not the least sign of vegetation, nor is it more promising upon a nearer view. In sailing along the shore, we came so near the huge cliffs, that they seemed to overhang the ship, and the tremendous effect of their giving way made us almost fear the event; at length we opened at a valley, called Chapel Valley, and in this valley we discovered the town. The bottom of it is slightly covered with herbage, but the sides are as naked as the cliffs that are next the sea. Such is the first appearance of the island in its present cultivated state; and the first hills must be passed before the valleys look green, or the country displays any other mark of fertility."

It was at the beginning of May, 1771, that Cook left St. Helena; on the 12th of July he landed at Deal, having completed his first voyage round the world in the space of two years and eleven months. In various ways the voyage had been a brilliant success. The survey of the eastern coast of Australia, which the commander had prosecuted under circumstances of great difficulty and danger, drew attention to the capabilities of New Holland for colonising purposes. The circumnavigation of New Zealand was also important; for until then the two islands of which it is composed had been considered as a part of Tasmania; and the scientific objects of the voyage had been very completely carried out. It was time, however, that the voyage should terminate. In spite of constant patching and splicing, the rigging and sails were so worn that on the passage from St. Helena to England something was giving way every day. By a strange coincidence, the long-wished-for land was discovered by the sharp eyes of the same lad who had been the first to discern New Zealand.

The successful results of Cook's first voyage stimulated the British Government to persevere in the path of discovery; and before the enterprising navigator had been home a year we find him embarking on a second voyage. On this occasion two vessels were despatched; and again, according to the judicious advice of Cook, ships were purchased

Cape of Good Hope.

that had been employed in the coal trade. Cook had already pointed out that the chief requisites for discovery-ships were stoutness of construction, that they might receive the least possible injury if by any chance they should run aground; roominess of construction, to enable them to carry the necessary provisions for the crew, and a cargo of miscellaneous articles for traffic with the natives; a moderate draught of water, that they might be navigated on unknown and dangerous coasts; and such limited burden as should not prevent their being laid ashore for repairs, if necessary. All these qualities were found combined in two Whitby ships, which were accordingly purchased of a Hull shipowner. They were called the Resolution and the Adventure.

ST. HELENA.

The former was of four hundred and sixty-two tons burden, the latter of three hundred and thirty-six.

On the equipment and fitting out of these vessels much judicious care was spent. Many of the officers had been with Cook during his former voyage, and Lieutenant Furneaux, to whom the command of the second ship was intrusted, had accompanied Wallis in his voyage round the world. Almost for the first time in the history of an expedition of this kind, it was considered necessary to adopt precautions to prevent disease among the crews. A quantity of salted cabbage, sour-krout, and other anti-scorbutic stores were placed on board each ship, and sundry articles, such as inspissated juice of wort, and a curious preparation called marmalade of carrots, were added by way of experiment. These judicious measures, supplemented by the care and vigilance of Cook himself, who exercised a rigid supervision in all matters affecting the health of his sailors, were crowned with such complete success as to establish the fact that scurvy is not by any means, as it had till then been considered, a necessary concomitant of long voyages, but that, like most other diseases, it arises from definite and preventible causes. As a further measure of convenience and safety, each ship carried on her deck the framework of a small vessel of twenty tons burthen, large enough to serve as a pink or victualler in distant islands, or to carry the crew in case of shipwreck. Two noted mathematicians, Messrs. Wales and Bayley, were engaged by the Admiralty to conduct the astronomical observations necessary during the voyage; and Mr. John Reinhold Forster and his son accompanied the expedition in the capacity so ably filled in Cook's first voyage by Mr. Banks and Dr. Solander. The fitting out of the expedition altogether reflected much credit on Lord Sandwich, the First Lord of the Admiralty, who fully appreciated its importance, and gave it the most energetic support and aid.

For a long time there had been a theory of the existence of a great southern continent. This belief was chiefly based upon the idea that as there was a great mass of land around the pole in the northern hemisphere, there must necessarily be a corresponding mass to balance it in the south. The testimony of Cook's first voyage had rendered this theory very doubtful; but it was considered desirable to have further proof before the idea of a southern continent should be definitely abandoned. Accordingly, Cook was directed in the first instance to sail to the southward, and settle this disputed point by observation, and then to prosecute investigations among the islands of he Pacific.

IV.

Voyage to the South—Punctiliousness of Cook—The Southern Ocean—Danger from Ice Islands—Existence of a Southern Continent Disproved—Dusky Bay, New Zealand—Queen Charlotte's Sound—Cannibalism of the New Zealanders—Otaheite—Danger of Shipwreck—King Otoo—Huaheine—Omai, the South Sea Islander—The Friendly Islands—The Two Ships Part Company—Thievish Proponsities of the New Zealanders—Fresh Proofs of Cannibalism.

AFTER some delays, Cook sailed from Plymouth on the 13th of July, 1772, just a year after his return from his first voyage. His course, as on the first occasion, was by way of Madeira, where the two ships arrived on the 29th. Water, wine, and fresh provisions having been procured at Funchal, the ships sailed away towards the Canary Islands, and on the way a portion of the inspissated juice of malt, which had been taken on board experimentally, was used in the manufacture of three puncheons of beer, to the great satisfaction of the ship's company on board each vessel.

Cook was punctilious in matters where he considered the honour of the British flag to be involved. He especially notices in his journal at Porta Praya, in the island of St. Jago, where he cast anchor to obtain a supply of fresh provisions, he saluted the fort with eleven guns, on a promise that the compliment should be returned with an equal number. Either by accident or design, the salute was, however, returned with only nine guns; but the governor apologised next day for the irregularity. The captain speaks with a very natural complacency of the healthy condition of his men at a time when the weather had been very bad. He says—"On the 27th, spoke with Captain Furneaux, who informed us that one of his petty officers was dead. At this time *we* had not one sick on board, although we had every kind of this thing to fear 'from the rain we had had, which is a great promoter of sickness in hot climates. To prevent this, and agreeably to some hints I had from Sir Hugh Palliser, and from Captain Campbell, I took every necessary precaution, by airing and drying the ship with fires made between the decks, smoking, &c., and by obliging the people to air their bedding, and wash and dry their clothes, whenever there was an opportunity. A neglect of these things," the captain judiciously adds, "causeth a disagreeable smell below, affects the air, and seldom fails to bring on sickness, but more especially in hot and wet weather."

After a short call at that noted half-way house for ships the Cape of Good Hope, the ships were steered southwards, in search of the great Antarctic continent. The weather suddenly became very cold, so that almost all the live stock procured at the Cape died; and a violent gale drove the voyagers far to the westward of their intended course. In latitude 50° South they first met with huge islands of ice, on one of which they nearly ran, in a thick fog. A number of stormy

ICEBERG.

petrels were here seen flying about the ships, and also many albatrosses, some of which the sailors caught with a hook and line. As they proceeded these ice islands increased in number, and penguins, the indigenous sea-birds of cold climates, made their appearance. On one day, no less than eighteen ice islands were passed, a circumstance which kept the crews on the alert; "for a ship that got to the westward of one of these islands when the sea runs high," says the captain, "would be dashed to pieces in a moment." The weather became so severe that the sails and rigging were all hung with icicles; and at last the further progress of the ships was stopped by an immense field of ice stretching towards the pole as far as the eye could reach. For many days the ships skirted this barrier, in the vain endeavour to find an opening in the ice to the southward; they were enabled, however, to get a good supply of fresh water from the floating blocks around the large ice islands, which were collected in the boats and melted on board the ships.

At length, after they had definitely disproved the existence of the supposed southern continent, the two captains bore up for New Zealand. Before they arrived there, however, the ships were separated from each other; and on the 26th of March, 1773, after beating about for four months in the stormy Southern Ocean, the Resolution cast anchor in Dusky Bay. On his passage Cook had been greatly struck with the

FLYING FISH.

appearance of the Aurora Australis, an atmospheric phenomenon corresponding to the Aurora Borealis of the Arctic Seas, and arising from the same causes; and now again Cook had reason to congratulate himself on the healthy condition of his crew. In spite of the continual hardships to which the crew had been exposed for months, the three great physicians, Cleanliness, Ventilation, and Diet, had kept the good ship Resolution clear of disease, an immunity which no ship under similar circumstances had yet enjoyed.

From Dusky Bay the Resolution proceeded to Queen Charlotte's Sound, the place of rendezvous appointed with Captain Furneaux in case the ships became separated. On the way they saw several waterspouts, which Cook rightly conjectured to have been caused by whirlwinds, as during their continuance the wind blew in puffs from all points of the compass. Of some of these waterspouts he gives the following account:—"Four rose and spent themselves between us and the land—that is, to the south-west of us; the fifth was without us; the sixth first appeared in the south-west at the distance of two or three miles at least from us. Its progressive motion was to the north-east, not in a straight but in a crooked line, and passed within fifty yards of our stern, without our feeling any of its effects. The diameter of the base of this spout I judged to be about fifty or sixty feet—that is, the sea within this space was much agitated, and foamed up to a great height. From this a tube, or round-body, was formed, by which the water, or air, or both, was carried in a spiral stream up to the clouds. Some of our people said they saw a bird in the one near us, which was whirled round like the fly of a jack as it was carried upwards. . . . . The weather continued thick and hazy for some hours after, with variable light breezes of wind. On reaching Queen Charlotte's Sound, Captain Cook found that the Adventure had been there for six weeks already, Captain Furneaux, her commander, had had several interviews with the natives, one tribe of whom proved to be the same people Cook had seen in his first voyage. They inquired very particularly after Tupia, and on hearing of his death seemed much concerned, particularly wishing to know, moreover, if he had been killed, or had died a natural death. Very decided proofs of their cannibalism had been obtained by Captain Furneaux's people. The Adventure was not so free from sickness as the Endeavour. At one time twenty of her people were sick of scorbutic disease; this may be attributed to a certain laxity on board with respect to sanitary precautions, and to the neglect of vegetable diet by the crew in Queen Charlotte's Sound. Cook justly observes that it requires both the authority and example of a commander to induce sailors to adopt a new article of diet, let it be ever so much for their benefit. On quitting New Zealand Cook left the natives some practical proofs of his goodwill, in the shape of a ram and ewe and some goats. He also caused a garden to be dug, and sown with useful culinary vegetables. From this time dates the introduction, among other plants, of the potato, which afterwards became a staple article of food with the inhabitants.

The Resolution now steered for Otaheite, with the Adventure in her company. On their way the two ships passed several of the low islands which the French navigator, De Bougainville, had aptly named the Dangerous Archipelago. Cook determined on this occasion to put into Oatipiha, or, as it is now called, Papetee Bay, at the S.E. of the island.

In carrying out this intention both vessels had a very narrow escape from shipwreck on the dangerous coral reefs at the entrance of the bay. The breeze which should have kept the ships off the reef fell to a calm, and the current set in strongly towards the rocks. An attempt made with the boats to tow the ships off the reef failed entirely. "As the calm continued," says Cook, "our situation became still more dangerous. We were not, however, without hopes of getting round the western point of the reef and into the bay, till about two o'clock in the afternoon, when we came before an opening or break in the reef, through which I hoped to get with the ships. But on sending to examine it I found there was not a sufficient depth of water, though it caused such an indraught of the tide through it as was very near proving fatal to the Resolution, for as soon as the ships got into the stream they were carried with great impetuosity towards the reef. The moment I perceived this I ordered one of the warping machines which we had in readiness to be carried out with about four hundred fathoms of rope, but it had not the least effect. The horrors of shipwreck now stared us in the face. We were not more than two cables' length from the breakers, and yet we could find no bottom to anchor, the only probable means we had left to save the ships. We, however, dropped an anchor, but before it took hold and brought us up the ship was in less than three fathoms water, and struck at every fall of the sea, which broke close under our stern in a dreadful surf, and threatened us every moment with shipwreck. The Adventure, luckily, brought up close upon our bow without striking." By great exertions they managed to get the ship afloat, and presently a providential land-breeze carried both ships out of the reach of danger. Had they been frigates, or the large heavy ships used at that period in the navy, there is no probability but that they would have been wrecked. During all this time many of the natives were on board, but they had no idea of the danger, and did not manifest any sense of uneasiness even when the ship struck. The natives in general behaved well, though as a matter of course they began pilfering; but a little judicious display of force on the part of Cook put them on their best behaviour, and matters went on amicably enough. Many inquiries were made after Mr. Banks, but very few asked concerning poor Tupia—an illustration of the fact that no man is a prophet in his own country, even in a small island in the South Seas. There was, however, a difficulty in getting provisions, and this determined Cook to proceed at once to Matavai.

Otoo, the king, was at Matavai when Cook arrived, but he seems to have been a somewhat timid potentate, and for a long while could not be persuaded to come on board the Resolution, frankly avowing that he was *mataou nu te paupoue*—that is, afraid of the guns. This warlike potentate was, however, treated with great respect by his subjects, of whom, according to the Otaheitan custom, his father was one. All appeared before him with uncovered head and shoulders. King Otoo caused his visitors to be entertained with a *heava*, or native dramatic representation, in which dancing had a great part. Some portions of the play seemed to refer to the visit of the strangers, but they did not know enough of the language to catch its meaning.

From Otaheite the ships proceeded to the neighbouring island of Huaheine. Orco, the chief of this island, had made the commander's acquaintance during Cook's first voyage, and came out with unfeigned pleasure to meet him. He showed great alacrity in keeping Cook's table supplied with the best vegetables, and presented him with several hogs; a great many of these animals were also offered by the natives for sale; so that the victualling of the ships went on briskly. Though small, the island of Huaheine was very fertile, and during the short stay of the ships no fewer than three hundred hogs were procured.

Captain Furneaux received on board at Huaheine a native of the island of Ulietea, named Omai. This Omai did not belong to the highest rank among the natives, but he proved quite an acquisition during the subsequent part of the voyage, and was even more useful than poor Tupia had been. He was brought to England by Captain Furneaux, and excited so much attention and interest that he was inveterately "lionised" during the two years of his stay. Even the king himself honoured Omai with an audience at Kew. The islander showed considerable tact and much good sense. Cook, who was a shrewd observer, had a high opinion of him, and said—

"Omai has most certainly a very good understanding, quick parts, and honest principles; he has a natural good behaviour, which rendered him acceptable to the best company, and a proper degree of pride, which taught him to avoid the society of persons of inferior rank. . . . . He was very watchful into the manners and conduct of the persons of rank who honoured him with their protection; he was sober and modest; and I never heard that, during the whole time of his stay in England, which was two years, he ever once was disguised with wine, or ever showed an inclination to exceed."

CAPTAIN COOK AND HIS DISCOVERIES. 173

Omai was ultimately taken back to his own country by Cook, in his third voyage, and carried with him so many tokens of the goodwill of the English, in the shape of presents of various kinds, that he was looked upon by his countrymen as a kind of millionaire, and became a living example that the old Latin Grammar quotation, "*Donec eris felix, multos,*" &c., holds good even in the uncivilised Society Islands no less than in civilised society. Captain Cook also took with him in the Resolution a youth of Ulietea named Oididee, or, as the natives called the name, Hete-hete.

From Ulietea Cook proceeded to the Friendly Islands, as he wished

BANYAN TREE.

to land at one of them, Middelburgh, before returning to New Zealand. At Middelburgh, a chief named Tioong at once came on board the Resolution, and entered into amicable relations with his visitors, and on landing Cook found the shore thronged with an immense unarmed multitude, who welcomed him to their country with acclamations. They were profuse in their gifts of cloth matting, fruits, and such other articles as they possessed, and seemed, says our commander, "more anxious to give than to receive." The position of the harbour where the boats had landed was charming, with rich tropical verdure.

Fine undulating lawns were skirted by groves of cocoa-nut trees, and with shaddock-trees heavy with their bright yellow fruit. The floor of Tioong's house was laid with mats, and gave a delightful view over the harbour. The air of the whole island was loaded with the fragrance of the fruit-trees. The chief possessed some well-ordered plantations, and the visitors noticed hogs and fowls running about the island. In the trafficking which soon commenced between the crews of the two ships and the natives, the greatest harmony and good-humour were preserved. The people showed themselves extremely anxious to oblige their visitors, and did honour to the discernment which had given to their group the designation of the Friendly Islands. At the island of Amsterdam, to which the two ships next bent their course, the visitors were received with similar demonstrations of goodwill, and the king of the island proposed to our commander, as a sign of friendship and alliance, that they should exchange names. This strange custom had already been found prevalent at the Society Islands, and at Huaheine, where the venerable Oree ruled, Captain Cook had been induced to take the name of Oree during his stay on the island, while his majesty was called Cookee. Amsterdam Island was still more highly cultivated than Middelburgh; the whole place being laid out in plantations, and the very hedges consisting of fruit-trees. The people paid implicit obedience to their chief, and it was noticed that though their curiosity regarding their visitors was great, they immediately ranged themselves in a circle at some distance, upon the command of their chief, and did not attempt to molest their visitors by crowding round and mobbing them—an example of politeness towards illustrious guests which might be commended to the attention of far more civilised communities. They expressed their thanks on receiving a present by placing the article on their heads. A most singular custom among them was the practice of cutting off one or both of the little fingers.

New Zealand was now visited by the two ships, and Cook, ever mindful of the interests of the people whose land he came to explore, gave to one of the chiefs some pigs and poultry, and a number of useful garden seeds; the chief was enraptured with his new acquisitions, and promised not to kill any of the animals, but to keep them to stock the island, and he went away rejoicing, the envied of all observers. In a great gale which occurred soon after, the Adventure, Captain Furneaux's ship, parted company with the Resolution, and was never able to rejoin her. Cook proceeded in the Resolution to Queen Charlotte's Sound, and was much mortified to find that the animals he had left with the natives on his former visit had mostly been killed by them. But the gardens his benevolent care had planted had fared better, and the potatoes in particular had thriven exceedingly. The tone of commercial morality among the natives in Queen Charlotte's

CAPTAIN COOK AND HIS DISCOVERIES. 175

Sound was decidedly low. Cook relates how he and his people purchased a large quantity of fish from them, and he says—" While we were upon this traffic they showed a great inclination to pick my pockets, and to take away the fish with one hand which they had just given me with the other. This evil one of the chiefs undertook to remove, and with fury in his eyes made a show of keeping his people at a proper distance. I applauded his conduct, but at the same time kept so good a look-out as to detect him in picking my pocket of a handkerchief, which I suffered him to put in his bosom before I seemed to know anything of the matter, and then told him what I had lost. He seemed quite ignorant and innocent till I took it from him, and then he put it off with a laugh, acting his part with so much address that it was hardly possible for me to be angry with him, so that we remained good friends, and he accompanied me on board to dinner."

Fresh proof was now obtained of the prevalence of cannibalism among these people; one of them absolutely brought a piece of human flesh on board the Resolution, and cooked and devoured it in the presence of the officers and crew, to the horror and disgust of all, and especially of Oedidee, the Otaheitan, who expressed the utmost indignation against the perpetrators of the savage act, telling them that they were vile men, and that henceforth he would never again be their friend. But the savages argued that there could be no harm in eating enemies whom they had killed in battle, and who, had the fortune of war been reversed, would have done the same to them; and they laughed at the expostulations of the more scrupulous Oedidee.

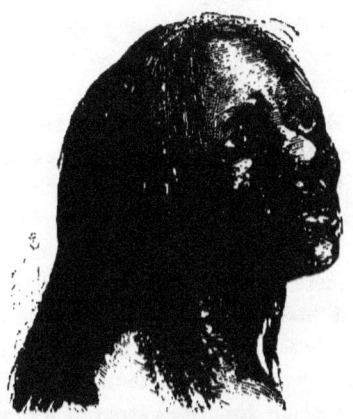

AUSTRALIAN NATIVE.

V.

Second Run to the South—Hardships and Dangers—The Ships obliged to turn Northward—Cook's Design of Exploring the Pacific—Easter Island—Curious Statues—Otaheite—Barter with Red Parrots' Feathers—Oree, the Chief—New Zealand—Tragical Occurrence to Captain Furneaux's Crew—Details of the Massacre—Rounding the Horn—Survey of Staten Island and Southern Coast of America—Return to England—Brilliant Success of the Voyage.

AS there appeared no prospect of the speedy arrival of the Adventure, and Cook was determined to go once more in search of the reputed southern continent, he left New Zealand on the 26th of November, and steered south towards the icy region of the Antarctic Circle. Again the ship was exposed to all the dangers of striking upon ice islands, or of being entangled among the pack or field ice; and the further the Adventure pushed her way towards the Southern Pole, the more convinced did her commander become, from the swell that rolled continually northwards, and from other signs which his practical judgment knew well how to appreciate, that there could be no great extent of land except in close proximity to the Southern Pole; and subsequent investigations have proved the correctness of his conclusions. The ship several times narrowly escaped running on ice islands, and had frequently been embayed among fields of ice; and day by day the navigation became more intricate and dangerous. At one time twenty-three of these floating islands were seen from the deck, while more than double the number could be counted from the masthead. Strong gales brought with them blinding showers of sleet and snow, which froze to the rigging, making the ropes stiff as wire, and the sails as hard as sheets of metal, so that at last the hoisting or lowering of a sail became a matter of the greatest difficulty; while thick fogs increased the difficulties and troubles of the mariners by adding a "horror of darkness" to the many dangers which beset their adventurous path through these unexplored seas. But not until the ice to the south stretched away, far as the eye could reach, in a thick impenetrable field, did the brave commander determine to turn the ship's prow once more to the north, and even then Cook was not satisfied with what had been done. He had certainly solved the problem for whose solution the expedition had been fitted out, and had ascertained beyond a doubt that no southern continent existed that was not wholly inaccessible from the barrier of ice by which it must be

THE WALRUS, OR SEAHORSE.

surrounded; but there appeared something yet to be done, and while this was the case Cook was not the man to steer for England. "To have quitted the Southern Pacific Ocean," he says, "with a good ship expressly sent out on discoveries, a healthy crew, and not in want either of stores or of provisions, would have been betraying not only a want of perseverance, but of judgment, in supposing the South Pacific Ocean to have been so well explored that nothing remained to be done in it. This, however, was not my opinion, for though I had proved that there was no continent but what must lie far to the south, there remained, nevertheless, room for very large islands in places wholly unexamined; and many of those which were formerly discovered are but imperfectly explored, and their situations as imperfectly known. I was, besides, of opinion that my remaining in this sea some time longer would be productive of improvements in navigation and geography, as well as in other sciences."

Accordingly, Cook communicated to his officers and crew his design of thoroughly exploring the Pacific, a course which would prolong the voyage for another year; and by both the intelligence was received with cheerfulness and satisfaction. No quality in this indefatigable man was more remarkable than the hold he gained over the affections of those he commanded, and this he owed chiefly to his sense of justice and his plain practical good sense. The men knew that he had their welfare and comfort always in view, and where he found it necessary to punish there was never any trace of vindictiveness or malice towards the offender.

The first result of Cook's resolve to continue his explorations in the South Sea was the discovery that the southern land, said to have been seen by Juan Fernandez, did not exist. Cook next rediscovered Easter Island, where, to his surprise, he found the inhabitants speaking a language closely resembling that of Otaheite; the names of the numbers, especially, were identical. The good people of Easter Island had elevated thieving to the state of a fine art. The travellers could scarcely keep their hats on their heads; their pockets were picked with a dexterity which the worthy Mr. Fagin's pupils might have envied, and so dexterously were the thefts managed, that the same article was in some instances sold to the travellers two or three times over, and then stolen from them after all. During the passage to Easter Island, the captain, whose health was in general excellent, fell seriously ill; and he mentions, as an example of the axiom that "circumstances alter

N

cases," how a favourite dog of one of the gentlemen on board was killed and cooked, that he might have broth and fresh meat during his convalescence; and how this fare, from which he would have turned with loathing in Europe, was eaten by him not only with great benefit, but with positive relish.

At Easter Island they found the gigantic statues and stone platforms mentioned by earlier travellers. These structures were monuments of ingenuity and perseverance, and evinced some knowledge of art; but the inhabitants could give no account of them, and they were evidently the work of a former race. Cook took them, from several indications, to be the burial-places of chiefs. The Marquesas Islands, originally discovered by Mendana, were next visited by Cook, who gives an almost enthusiastic account of the handsome features and stalwart frames of the natives. Here, again, a great affinity was noticed between the language of the natives and that of Otaheite. They had very little clothing, but were fond of ornaments, and wore elaborate headdresses made of the fibre of the cocoa-nut husk, adorned with pieces of mother-of-pearl and tortoiseshell. After discovering a few small islands, which he named after his friend Sir Hugh Palliser, Cook returned to Otaheite, which must by this time have been regarded quite as a South Sea home by his companions. They were received with joy by the natives in their old quarters at Matavai Bay, and treated as honoured guests with every demonstration of affectionate regard.

Here the useful discovery was made that the natives of all the Pacific Islands set a high value on red parrots' feathers, of which Cook's people had procured a large stock at the island of Amsterdam; and these proved never-failing means of barter when the original stock of goods was exhausted. Otoo, the king, treated his visitors to the spectacle of a grand naval review, and they were not a little astonished at the number and size of his Otaheitan majesty's vessels. A great crowd of people flocked to see the show, and our travellers conceived an erroneous idea of the magnitude of the population of the island, the natives having assured them, with an idea of increasing their own importance in the eyes of their guests, that the fleet exhibited was only the division belonging to one of the twenty portions into which the island was parcelled out. The people also showed considerable talent in dramatic representations. Several plays were acted for the amusement of the visitors. At Huaheine, in the Society Islands, Cook paid a visit to the venerable Oree, who manifested a strange curiosity to know the name of his guest's "Matai," or burying-place. Cook had no resource but to mention Stepney, the parish in which he stayed in London during the intervals between his voyages; and old Oree, quite satisfied with the answer, gravely repeated several times, " Tepnee matai no Tootee"—Stepney is the burial-place of Cook. Mr. Foster, of whom the same question was asked, replied more appropriately that a man who passed his life sailing about the world could not tell where he should be buried. At Ulietea they left Oedidee, who had been their useful companion for some months. Cook now fulfilled a very arduous and important duty by exploring various parts of the Pacific, which till then had been almost unknown. Among other regions thus explored was that of the Terra Australis del Espirito Santo of Quiros. He also discovered the Shepherd's Isles, a small group, Erromanga (afterwards celebrated by the martyrdom of Mr. Williams, the zealous missionary), Tanna, and many other islands, thoroughly exploring the coasts of these islands, which had till then been considered as portions of a great southern continent. To this group Cook gave the name of the New Hebrides. Norfolk Island, afterwards notorious as a penal settlement, was discovered by Cook at this time.

Once more the Resolution steered for New Zealand, and on the 18th of October Queen Charlotte's Sound was reached. The Adventure had certainly been there since the last departure of the Resolution; for a bottle containing the particulars of the visit, and instructions for Captain Furneaux, had been dug up and taken away. As the ships did not join company again during the voyage, it was not until after his return to England that Cook was made acquainted with the tragical event which occurred here. It seems that on finding the letter which informed him of the commander's arrival at Queen Charlotte's Sound and his subsequent departure, Captain Furneaux and his crew made every exertion to get their ship ready for sea as soon as possible, and when they were ready to sail a boat was sent on shore, with a crew of nine men, under the charge of a midshipman named Rowe, to procure a stock of wild celery for the voyage, as that vegetable grew in abundance in some of the bays. Some uneasiness was occasioned in the ship by the boat failing to return in the evening; but as Mr. Rowe, the midshipman, had been very anxious to start in the morning, it was supposed that either he had proceeded farther than was at first intended in exploring one or other of the bays and coves, or that the boat, left in charge of a careless boatkeeper.

180   THE WORLD'S EXPLORERS.

had been stove against a rock and could not be launched. In pursuance of this latter conjecture, when the missing crew failed to

TROPICAL BIRDS.

make their appearance next morning, a second boat was despatched commanded by Lieutenant Burney, and carrying some armed marines.

CAPTAIN COOK AND HIS DISCOVERIES. 181

The natives at first menaced the crew to prevent their landing, and their behaviour was doubtful, as though they meditated hostilities, but were deterred from any overt demonstration by the presence of the marines. For some time nothing suspicious was found; but at length, in a sequestered cove, the searching party came upon a number of baskets filled with meat, packed together with the fern-root which the natives use for bread. What this meat was they soon discovered to their horror; for presently one of the party picked up a human hand, and by the letters "T. H." tattooed on it in the Otaheitan fashion, the hand was identified as belonging to Thomas Hill, a forecastle man. In the next cove a number of mutilated remains were found, on some of which a party of native dogs were greedily feasting. A broken oar, stuck in the ground, to which the canoes had been fastened, showed that the attack on the boat's crew had been made here; and at some distance off a number of natives were observed watching the movements of the English, and inviting them by signs to land. Some volleys of musketry fired among them by the enraged marines sent them scrambling away into the woods, and it was not deemed prudent to follow them into their hiding-places for the doubtful satisfaction of killing some more of them. Therefore, after collecting for interment what mournful relics they could find strewn along the shore, Lieutenant Burney and his party returned on board, to report the miserable fate that had befallen ten of the best men in their ship. It was conjectured, and subsequent inquiries during Cook's third voyage proved the correctness of the idea, that the tragical occurrence had not been premeditated, but was the result of a sudden quarrel between the sailors and some of the natives. The English had trusted too much to the effect which they supposed their firearms would have in intimidating the natives; while the New Zealanders were quite cunning enough to know that when a musket has been discharged it must be reloaded before it can do them any further damage; and they knew how to take advantage of this interval to make a renewed charge. After this misfortune the Adventure made the best of her way back to England.

From New Zealand Cook purposed to return home round Cape Horn; and with his accustomed activity and zeal he examined that stormy region, and especially the coasts of Staten Island and Cape le Maire, much more closely than any former navigator had done. Such numbers of seals and sea-lions were found on the little islands near the

Horn that it was a very easy matter to kill scores of them. There was no danger in this sport, except in the chance of being run down by the seal in its endeavour to escape into the sea, whither they always fled for refuge when attacked. Cook says—"Sometimes when we came suddenly upon them, or woke them out of their sleep (for they are a sluggish, sleepy animal), they would raise up their heads, snort and snarl, and look as fierce as if they meant to devour us; but as we advanced upon them they always ran away, so that they are downright bullies." Sea birds were also found in these regions in vast numbers, and among land birds were noticed eagles, hawks, bald-headed vultures, the American turkey buzzard, and some thrushes and small birds.

In the far south Cook discovered another island, to which he gave the name of Georgia. It was a wild, desolate region of which Cook now took possession, with hoisting of colours and firing of muskets, in the name of King George; and, as the commander himself says, it did not seem probable that any one would ever be benefited by the discovery. Of the place where he landed Cook gives the following account:— "The head of the bay, as well as two places on each side, was terminated by perpendicular ice-cliffs of considerable height. Pieces were continually breaking off and floating out to sea; and a great fall happened while we were in the bay, which made a noise like cannon. The inner parts of the country were not less savage and horrible. The wild rocks raised their summits till they were lost in the clouds, and the valleys lay covered with everlasting snow. Not a tree was to be seen, nor a shrub even big enough to make a toothpick. The only vegetation we met was a coarse, strong-bladed grass growing in tufts, wild burnet, and a plant like moss, which sprang from the rocks. From various appearances, Cook made a conjecture, which subsequent observations have verified, concerning the existence of land round the South Pole. "It is true, however," he says, "that the greatest part of this southern continent (supposing there is one) must be within the polar circle, where the sea is so pestered with ice that the land is thereby inaccessible. The risk one runs in exploring a coast in these unknown and icy seas is so very great, that I can be bold enough to say that no man will ever venture farther than I have done, and that the lands which may lie to the south will never be explored. Thick fogs, snow-storms, intense cold, and everything that can render navigation dangerous must be encountered; and these difficulties are greatly heightened by the inexpressibly horrid aspect of the country—a country doomed by Nature never once to feel the warmth of the sun's rays, but to be buried in everlasting snow and ice. The ports which may be on the coast are in a manner wholly filled up with frozen snow of vast thickness, but if any should be so far open as to invite a ship into it, she would run a risk of being fixed there for ever, or of coming out in an ice island. The islands and floats on the coast, the great falls from the ice-cliffs in the port, or a heavy snowstorm attended with a sharp frost, would be equally fatal."

From the Horn the Resolute ran to Fayal, a port in the Azores, where a short stay was made; and thence Cook returned to England, completing this, his second voyage, in three years and eighteen days. During this long period he had lost only one man by sickness; and it was noticed that his men, when they returned to England, presented an appearance of robust health very different from the sickly look former crews had worn on their return from similar voyages. This immunity from such scourges as wrought havoc with the crews of Anson's squadron is to be attributed almost entirely to the practical good sense of the commander. Cook was not content to look upon sickness and misery as necessary adjuncts to a seaman's existence, or to regard the mortality produced by ignorance, indifference, and a systematic neglect of all sanitary rules and precautions as a visitation. One of the most important results of this second voyage is to be found in the plain, straightforward sentences in which the kind-hearted commander describes what he did to keep his men in health, and the effect of his expedients and precautions; and like the company in the story of Columbus and the egg, many captains and merchants who read Cook's journal must have been surprised to find how simple were the means by which such an important result as the keeping 118 men in health during a three years' voyage through every variety of climate had been attained. They may be briefly summed up as follow:—Care, in the selection of provisions, to enforce the use of anti-scorbutic vegetables, the much-maligned preparation called sour-krout being especially recommended when fresh vegetables cannot be procured; the frequent changing of the drinking water, the old store that had remained in the ship for some time being poured away whenever a fresh supply from the shore could be obtained; a rigid attention to the rules of cleanliness, and a thorough and frequent ventilation of every part of the ship, fires being kindled when it was necessary to produce a draught of air, and

184   THE WORLD'S EXPLORERS.

fumigation being also frequently resorted to; finally, special attention to the comfort and well-being of the crew, who were divided into three

EAGLES.

watches instead of two, an arrangement which gave them longer periods of unbroken rest than they could otherwise have enjoyed, and who were provided with a sufficient stock of clothing, so that they were not obliged to remain in wet clothes for want of a change. To these means may be added the example of the commander, who from the beginning to the end of the voyage ruled with gentle firmness the little community intrusted to his charge, careful in all things that affected their welfare, doing his duty thoroughly, and trusting in God.

SOUTH AFRICAN.

VI.

Preparations for a Third Voyage—Question concerning the North-West Passage—The Resolution and Discovery Fitted Out—Kerguelen's Land—Island of Desolation—Van Diemen's Land—Passage to New Zealand—The Friendly Islands—Taboo—Human Sacrifices at Otaheite—Visit to Eimeo and Bolabola—Christmas Island—Nootka Sound—The Natives: their Shrewdness and Rapacity.

COOK'S second voyage had thus been brilliantly successful, and our commander was rewarded with post rank in the navy and an appointment as one of the captains of Greenwich Hospital, a nomination to which a sufficient pension was attached. The Earl of Sandwich, under whose patronage the late voyage had been undertaken, was delighted with its result. The public interest in voyages had been stimulated by the discoveries and explorations of the Resolution and Adventure, and there was a general desire that further efforts should be made to obtain an accurate knowledge of distant shores.

A question, moreover, which was as old as the Elizabethan period, now began to be discussed and debated with renewed interest and vigour. The idea of a north-west passage to India through Hudson's Bay, across the north of America to Behring's Strait, had occupied the attention of the scientific world for more than a century and a half, and the boldness with which Cook had pushed forward towards the icy regions of the south seemed to suggest that the same measures would in the north be crowned with equal success, and that the question of the existence of a north-west passage might be set at rest as that of the existence of a southern continent had been. Defective knowledge concerning the climate, and the length and severity of winter in the Arctic regions, also left room for a hope which was afterwards dispelled long before the main question of the existence of a north-west passage had, in our own times, been settled in the affirmative. It was thought that the discovery of the passage would produce important commercial results, and that the route across the northern ocean could be made available for ordinary trading ships; whereas subsequent experience showed that a peculiar construction and equipment are necessary for the very existence of a ship in those wild seas. But in 1775 these facts were not known, the public attention and interest had been thoroughly awakened, and it was determined that the course of discovery, so gloriously begun, should be prosecuted with diligence to the end.

It might well be supposed that Cook, who had twice circumnavigated the globe and had borne the burden and heat of the day, might enjoy the repose he had so thoroughly earned, and leave to others the task of concluding the exploration of the Pacific by a survey of its northern coasts. But it happened that, early in 1776, a few months after his return to England, he was a guest at Lord Sandwich's house, and the feasibility of exploring a north-west passage by entering through Behring's Strait instead of Hudson's Bay was fully discussed. Cook, who had every right to give an opinion on such a subject, entered into the discussion with avidity, and when it appeared that Lord Sandwich had determined to send an expedition to the North Pacific, zealously offered to take the command himself. This so exactly coincided with Lord Sandwich's wishes that the offer was accepted as soon as made. It was quickly decided that two ships should be despatched as early in the year as they could be got ready, and the preparations for this, the third voyage of Cook, were pushed forward with all speed. The zeal of the sailors was further stimulated by the extension to ships of his majesty's navy of the reward of £20,000 that had been offered by Act of Parliament some thirty years before to any private English ship that should sail through the north-west passage, and whereas the old Act had defined that the route should be through Baffin's Bay and Davis's Strait, the terms were extended to ships sailing in any direction. Under such favourable auspices did the good captain sail, in July, 1776, from Plymouth Bay on the expedition from which he was never to return. He was in his old ship the Resolution, and among the company were many of his old men. A second ship, the Discovery, was put under the command of Captain Clerke; and as some unavoidable delay occurred in fitting her out, it was determined that she should join the Resolution at the Cape of Good Hope.

Cook's instructions were to proceed to the north-west coast of America, and to begin his explorations in 65 degrees north latitude; if possible, he was to make his way across the north of the American continent in an easterly direction to Davis's Strait. In the first instance he proposed to call at Otaheite and other islands of the Pacific groups, and took on board at the Cape several bulls and heifers, goats and horses, with the view of leaving them in those islands as a valuable gift to the inhabitants. Omai, the South Sea Islander, also took this opportunity of returning to his own people. He had been treated with great kindness and distinction during his stay in England, and parted from his new friends with evident sorrow, declaring that nothing but the certainty that this was the only opportunity he should ever have of returning to his own country would have induced him to quit them so soon.

Steering, as before, towards the Southern Pole, Cook came in sight of an icy shore that had been discovered a short time before by Kerguelen, a French navigator, and had by him been considered as a southern continent; but Cook, whose practical mind was not satisfied with mere conjecture, ascertained by exploration of the coast that Kerguelen's Land, or, as it is generally called on the maps, the Land of Desolation, is an island. From these southern latitudes the voyagers proceeded to Van Diemen's Land, which Cook, relying upon the account given by Captain Furneaux, held to be a portion of Australia. The natives are described as a degraded race, destitute of the ordinary curiosity and intelligence of savages. The only weapon observed among them was a kind of stick, and even this they used very unskilfully, failing several times to hit a block of wood set up by them as a mark; whereupon Omai, burning to exhibit the superiority of the weapons of his friends the English, and his own skill, fired off a musket which he held in his hand. The report set all the natives scampering into the woods, in spite of the reassuring exclamations of the travellers, and so great was their terror that one of them dropped an axe and several other presents he had received just before. From Van Diemen's Land the ships steered for the former harbour of the Resolution and the Adventure, Queen Charlotte's Sound, in New Zealand.

It was manifest that the natives here looked upon the arrival of the ships with no very cordial feeling of welcome, or even of security. They recognised Omai and several officers and men who had been on board the Adventure when the unfortunate affray happened that terminated in the death of Mr. Rowe, the midshipman, and his unfortunate boat's crew, and evidently expected that Cook had returned to take vengeance upon them for that atrocity. Their apprehensions were speedily quieted by the assurance that no further notice would be taken of an event that had happened long ago, but that any attempt to molest their visitors would be visited with condign punishment. On receiving this assurance they laid aside their fear, and many families took up their residence in the bay, close to the place where the ships had anchored. Cook now learned the particulars of the fray, which had originated in the attempt of some natives to snatch bread and fish from the English sailors, who were at dinner. The Englishmen resented this, and beat the thieves; whereupon, with the sudden vindictiveness of savages, the New Zealanders made an unexpected onslaught on the boat's crew, who were all killed in a few moments. Happy would it have been for the kind-hearted commander had he remembered this incident, and learned caution in his dealings with such men as these; but there was no place in his open, honest heart for suspicion; and, scrupulously careful where the interests and safety of others were concerned, he continued careless of his own, till that mournful day when his valuable life was sacrificed through just such a sudden burst of savage fury as that which had proved fatal to the boat's crew of the Adventure.

CAPTAIN COOK AND HIS DISCOVERIES.

Several fresh islands were discovered, and upon one of these, at a distance of two hundred leagues from the Society Islands, Omai met with four of his own countrymen, who had been driven to the island by a storm, in one of their frail canoes. Events of this kind had more than once happened in the Pacific Ocean. One notable instance s recorded, which occurred in 1696, when two canoes, with no less han thirty persons of both sexes on board, were tossed about at sea for seventy days, and finally cast on one of the Philippine Islands, after having performed a voyage of three hundred leagues. The island

CANOEING IN THE PACIFIC.

on which these Otaheitan castaways were found was called by the natives Wateeo. A trip to the Friendly Islands formed the next stage of the voyage, and the travellers were received with the same demonstrations of goodwill as on their first visit. A certain Feenou, who was first represented to Cook and his companions as the king of the whole group of islands, was evidently a very great personage. The very highest respect was shown him by all his countrymen, who implicitly obeyed his commands; but he proved to be only a kind of police commissioner, invested with extraordinary powers. They were afterwards introduced to the real king, who proved to be a very benign potentate, and received them in a manner worthy of the name they had given to his island realm. Here Cook noticed the use of the word "taboo," which was used in a very extended acceptation to signify "forbidden," and which has since found its way to our own vocabulary, a subject or an institution being often spoken of as "tabooed."

From the Friendly Islands Cook proceeded to Otaheite, and the ships were brought to an anchor in the familiar Matavai Bay. Otoo, the King of Otaheite, had been visited shortly before by two Spanish ships from Lima, and a bull and other animals had been left on the island. The live stock brought by the Resolution and Discovery was very acceptable to the king and chiefs, who did not, however, seem to realise the full value of the gift, and were inclined to give the preference to red feathers, which were a never-failing article of traffic among them. There was a great political difficulty in progress at the time when the travellers arrived. The neighbouring island of Eimeo had been for a long time in a state of revolt, and a great fleet sent out to reduce it to subjection had effected little. A new armament was, therefore, to be despatched; and now Cook obtained ocular certainty respecting the practice of offering human sacrifices which had long been rumoured to exist among the Otaheitans, a proof how superstition can produce cruelty even in mild and gentle natures. Towha, a chief of part of the island, who had commanded the former expedition, sent to Otoo one morning to inform him that he had killed a man to be sacrificed to the Ea tooa, or god, that the deity might be propitiated and give his assistance against Eimeo. Cook proposed to accompany Otoo to the Matai, or burying-place, where the poor islander's corpse was to be offered. Otoo readily consented to take the captain with him, and several other Englishmen joined the party. The ceremonies on the occasion were elaborate and numerous, and Otoo was particularly anxious that his visitors should take off their hats as soon as they entered the Matai.

It was customary not to give the unfortunate men selected for these sacrifices any notice of their fate, but to fall upon them suddenly and put them to death with blows of a club or with stones. "The unhappy victim offered up as the object of their worship upon this occasion," says Cook, "seemed to be a middle-aged man, and, as we were told, was a *toutou*—that is, one of the lowest class of the people. But after all my inquiries I could not learn that he had been pitched upon on account of any particular crime committed by him meriting death. It is certain, however, that they generally make choice of such guilty persons for their sacrifices, or else of common, low fellows who stroll about from place to place, and from island to island, without having any fixed abode, or any visible way of getting an honest livelihood, of which description of men enough are to be met with at these islands. Having had an opportunity of examining the appearance of the body of the poor sufferer now offered up, I could observe that it was bloody about the head and face, and a good deal bruised about the right temple, which marked the manner of his being killed, and we were told that he had been privately knocked on the head with a stone."

After visiting Eimeo and Bolabola (the island at which Omai had persuaded Cook to "fire great guns" on the former voyage) the prows of the ships were pointed north, and the Resolution and Discovery sailed to prosecute the main object of the voyage, the endeavour to find a passage through Behring's Strait across the continent of North America to Davis's Strait and Baffin's Bay. On his way northward Cook discovered Christmas Island, where they obtained a number of turtles. The island obtained its name from the fact that it was first seen on Christmas Eve of the year 1777. Some other islands were soon afterwards seen, the natives of which, to the surprise of Cook and his companions, spoke the language of Otaheite. They were very friendly and communicative, anxious to trade with their visitors, and exceedingly respectful withal, but thieves every man of them, like the other islanders of the Pacific. Among the articles they offered for barter their visitors especially remarked some cloaks and caps of feathers sewn upon a groundwork of netting, and so skilfully arranged as to form and colour, that, according to the commander's journal, "even in countries where dress is more particularly attended to, they might be reckoned elegant." The islanders were rich in pigs, poultry, and various vegetables. The predilection for red feathers noticed in the other groups extended to these islands, where an especial value was set upon the plumage of a bird resembling the bird of paradise. That cannibalism was practised among them was soon ascertained beyond doubt. To this group, of which he is the undoubted discoverer, the captain gave the name of the Sandwich Islands, in honour of his patron the Earl of Sandwich.

In March 1778, the ships, after a stormy passage to the north, arrived at Nootka Sound, on the North American coast, in latitude 44 degrees north. The natives, who had evidently before been in communication with Europeans, immediately opened a trade, offering valuable furs for a very moderate equivalent. They understood the use of iron, but put a higher value on brass; accordingly the sailors cut the buttons off their jackets, and bartered them away for the furs which the natives continued to offer in great abundance. They were very anxious to keep the market to themselves, and to prevent other tribes from communicating with the ships. Though peaceable and friendly, they considered that the strangers ought to pay for everything they wished to take, and even the right of cutting grass had to be purchased; and when the captain began to pay for this privilege in beads, it seemed as if every square inch of grass had a separate owner, so many pressed forward and asserted a right to a share in the purchase-money. But when they found that Cook's stock of beads was really exhausted, and that no more were to be had, these exclusive claims were abandoned, and the crews were allowed to cut wherever they wished. The natives were very ingenious in catching fish, large quantities of which they preserved. While the ships were at Nootka Sound visitors of a stranger tribe appeared in three canoes. One of them exhibited two silver tablespoons of Spanish manufacture, which he wore round his neck as an ornament.

ESQUIMAUX OF NOOTKA SOUND.

VII.

New Attempt to Penetrate Northward—Stopped by the Ice—Farther Exploration of the Sandwich Group—Discovery of Owyhee—Karakakooa Bay—Return of the Ships—Fatal Attack—Death of Cook—Further Proceedings of Captain Clerke—Return to the North—Fur Trade at Canton—Death of Clerke—Return of the Ships in 1779.

AFTER a short stay in Nootka Sound, Cook proceeded northward, and doubled the great promontory of Alashka, the most westerly point of the North American continent. He also ascertained the width of Behring's Strait, which he entered; and he pushed on to the northward, according to his custom surveying the coast wherever this was

POLYNESIAN HUTS.

practicable. He had advanced as far as 70 degrees north latitude when it became evident that the attempt to penetrate farther to the north must be abandoned. As far as the eye could reach extended a barrier of ice six feet in height, covered with walruses and seals, and it was evident that for months this barrier must remain unbroken. Accordingly Captain Cook determined to turn southward and defer the exploration of the northern sea till the following summer, consoling himself and his crew for the disappointment of the delay by the reflection that they would have time in the interval to explore the group of the Sandwich Islands, with which they had as yet only made a very cursory acquaintance. Corporal Ledyard, of the marines, who afterwards became distinguished as an African explorer, here distinguished himself by undertaking a perilous journey in an Esquimaux kajak, or covered canoe, to a Russian settlement, the commander of which had sent a present of fish and a Russian letter, which no one could read, to the captain.

Cook's perseverance in returning to the Sandwich group was rewarded by the discovery of a larger and more important island than any he had seen in those regions. It was called by the natives Owyhee, and seemed of sufficient importance to warrant the commander in spending several weeks in surveying it. The natives made very friendly demonstrations, brought abundance of provisions to the ships, and flocked to visit their guests in such numbers, that many who could not procure admission on board were continually swimming round the ships like fishes. They seemed to have the most profound respect for Captain Cook, to whom they did homage by throwing themselves flat on their faces before him, as if worshipping a being of supernatural power. They were, moreover, thoroughly under the control of their chiefs, whose friendship the kindness of the commander quickly secured, and thus a very friendly intercourse was established, which the petty thefts, which the English had now learned to look upon as unavoidable incidents in their dealing with islanders, were not suffered to interrupt. At Karakakooa Bay, on the west side of the island, the ships were brought to an anchor. The natives made great demonstrations of joy at this evidence of the intention of their visitors to make some stay among them, and all day long men and boys were swimming out to have a nearer view of them, splashing and frisking round the ship like shoals of porpoises. Kaoo, an influential chief, and Terreeoboo, the king of the island, were pleased to give their countenance and support to the visitors, and the king paid a ceremonious visit to the captain, which the latter returned in due form. A company of priests, established in the island, were also very generous in making presents of hogs and vegetables. When the time came for the departure of the ships, great regret was manifested by the natives, who had taken an especial fancy to Lieutenant King, and strongly importuned him to remain among them. At last farewells were exchanged, with every expression of mutual goodwill; and Captain Cook sailed away, with the Discovery in company, with the object of further exploring the coasts of the various islands. Soon afterwards, however, the Resolution sprang her mainmast in so serious a manner that it was considered requisite to return at once to Karakakooa Bay, there to effect the necessary repairs; and thither accordingly the mariners proceeded, little anticipating the fatal misfortune which was soon to give to the names of Karakakooa and Owyhee a mournful celebrity in the history of discovery.

When the ships arrived for the second time in the bay, it was found almost deserted. The people began soon to assemble, but the chiefs did not appear. Whether the return of the travellers with one of the ships in something like distress weakened the belief of the islanders in the power of their visitors, or whether the absence of their own chiefs removed a salutary check from them, certain it is that their conduct soon began to be turbulent and insubordinate, though the outward appearance of friendship was kept up, and they prostrated themselves before Captain Cook as readily as ever. But the pilfering which had been merely an annoyance on the former visit now increased to serious and positive theft, and at length two acts of depredation too grave to be overlooked were simultaneously committed. The pinnace of the Discovery was plundered, and the Resolution's cutter was detached from the buoy at which she rode, and carried off by the natives. In the Society Islands, when acts of this nature had been committed, the expedient of keeping one or more chiefs as hostages had frequently been adopted with success; and on this occasion Captain Cook determined to carry the king himself on board the Resolution, feeling sure that the detention of their king would induce the people to deliver up the cutter and the articles plundered from the pinnace. Accordingly Captain Cook came on shore in the pinnace, accompanied by a strong guard of marines. He had given orders that other boats should guard the entrance to the bay, and prevent any canoes from passing out, and had the launch in readiness to support him in case of need. Captain Clerke was in a small boat, and was left in command of one side of the bay, the last instructions he received from his superior officer being " to quiet the minds of the natives on his side of the bay by assuring them they should not be hurt, to keep his people together, and be on his guard." These instructions he implicitly carried out, ordering the marines to load with ball, and to remain within the tent, and explaining to Kaoo and the priests that no harm would be done to the people or to their king, but that the captain was resolved to recover the cutter, and to punish the thieves who had stolen it.

Meanwhile Cook landed with nine marines and a lieutenant. In the village the usual respect was shown him; and on his inquiring for the King Terreeoboo and his two sons, the lads were at once brought to him, and he was conducted to a house where he found the old king, who had just awoke from sleep. Terreeoboo made no objection on being invited to spend the day, with his two sons, on board the Resolution. He rose up readily and prepared to accompany his friend Cook; but his favourite wife, who seems to have suspected some design against the king, passionately dissuaded him from proceeding. Terror and suspicion quickly spread among the bystanders, and a hundred eager voices were joined to hers, frantically imploring the king not to trust himself on board the ship. Presently Terreeoboo himself became alarmed, and sat down on the ground with a troubled countenance, evidently undecided what to do. Captain Cook quickly perceived that he would not be able to get the king on board if the natives chose to unite in resistance. At the same time the lieutenant of marines proposed that his men should be drawn up along the shore, as they could then act better in case of need than when they were huddled together among the crowd; and accordingly the marines were stationed along the beach, and Cook and the lieutenant were left alone among the throng. The chiefs had now taken the alarm, and showed themselves prepared to resist by force any attempt to remove their king from among them. They were in the excited, turbulent state in which any untoward incident would suffice to turn their defiance into open attack; and at the critical moment the news of an incident of this kind was brought, and spread like lightning among them. A chief of the first rank had been killed by a shot fired from one of the boats to prevent a canoe from leaving the bay, and this news was brought just as Cook, having given up the idea of taking the king and his sons on board, was walking slowly towards the shore. The intelligence of their chief's death roused the natives to fury. They sent away the women and children, put on their war-mats, and armed themselves with their spears and with stones. A man advanced towards the captain brandishing an iron spike in one hand and a stone in the other, threatening by his gestures to fling the stone and to stab Cook with the spike. The captain desired him to desist, and at length, when the man persisted in advancing, fired at him with small shot. The charge failed to penetrate the thick war-mat worn by the savage, and this apparent harmlessness of our weapons increased the insolence of the islanders. A rush forward was made; and when the marines at length fired, the natives were very little intimidated. Indeed, the crowd was now so great that those in front were pressed onward by the rest, and the whole roaring,

CAPTAIN COOK AND HIS DISCOVERIES. 197

frantic mass rushed upon the thin line of marines drawn up on the beach, and on the unfortunate commander. The marines were unable

TIGER.

to stand against the shock. They were at once forced into the water; four of them were killed, and three others wounded. The lieutenant, severely stabbed with an iron dagger, barely escaped with his life. Fortunately he had reserved his fire, and was enabled to shoot a savage dead who rushed forward to despatch him after inflicting the first wound. The crews in the boats now began firing at the assailants, but amid the confusion of getting the wounded marines into the boats, and the horror and excitement of the moment, they could effect little.

Cook, meanwhile, was pursuing his dangerous way towards the nearest boat. What happened next is thus told in the journal of Captain Clerke:—" Our unfortunate commander, the last time he was seen distinctly, was standing at the water's edge, and calling out to the boats to cease firing and to pull in. If it be true, as some of those who were present have imagined, that the marines and boatmen had fired without his orders, and that he was desirous of preventing any further bloodshed, it is not improbable that his humanity on this occasion proved fatal to him; for it was remarked that, whilst he faced the natives, none of them had offered him any violence, but that having turned about to give his orders to the boats, he was stabbed in the back, and fell with his face in the water. On seeing him fall, the islanders set up a great shout, and his body was immediately dragged on shore, and surrounded by the enemy, who, snatching the dagger out of each other's hands, showed a savage eagerness to have a share in his destruction."

Another account, which agrees with Captain Clerke's report in the main features, gives a few additional particulars. It tells us of the gallant Cook—" He was observed making for the pinnace, holding his left hand against the back of his head to guard it from the stones, and carrying his musket under the other arm. An Indian was seen following him, but with caution and timidity, as if undetermined how to proceed. At last he advanced upon him unawares, gave him a blow on the back of the head with a large club, and then precipitately retreated. The stroke seemed to stun Captain Cook. He staggered a few paces, then fell on his hand and one knee, and dropped his musket. As he was rising, and before he could recover his feet, another Indian stabbed him in the back of the neck with an iron dagger. He then fell into the water about knee-deep, where others crowded upon him, and endeavoured to keep him under; but, struggling very strongly with them, he got his head up, and casting his eyes towards the pinnace, seemed to solicit assistance. Though the boat was not above five or six yards distant from him, yet, from the crowded and confused state of the crew, it seems it was not in their power to save him. The Indians got him under again, but in deeper water. He was, however, able to get his head up once more, and being almost spent in the struggle, he naturally turned to the rock, and was endeavouring to support himself by it, when a savage gave him a blow with a club, and he was seen alive no more."

Thus, by a sudden outburst of suspicious rage among a nation of fickle savages, perished this truly great and useful man. It seems strange that the lieutenant who commanded the launch should have returned to his ship without making an attempt to recover the mutilated body of his unfortunate commander, which lay for some time abandoned upon the beach. He seems, however, to have been bewildered, and not unreasonably, at the suddenness and violence of the attack, and did not consider himself justified in exposing the men under his command to the chance of the return of the savages in mass, flushed with victory. Captain Clerke was obliged to open a negotiation with the people for the recovery of the commander's remains. At length this was effected, and the bones of the great navigator were committed to the deep in the bay he himself had discovered, amid the sincere lamentations of the sailors, whose respect and affection he had nobly gained. He had not quite completed his fiftieth year, and had spent nearly a quarter of a century in the service of his country.

On the death of the lamented Cook, Captain Clerke succeeded to the command of the Resolution, and Lieutenant King was appointed to the Discovery. The intention of the late commander was carried out, and the ships were once more steered to the icy regions of Russian America. But, for the second time, the impenetrable barrier of ice arrested the progress of the navigators, and after a sojourn of some time among the Esquimaux tribes, and making acquaintance with some Russian traders, it was decided that the ships should return to England. This resolution was received with great rejoicing by the crews, who, we are told, were as glad as if they had already been in the British Channel. First, however, it was necessary to proceed to Canton for some indispensable repairs, and here the sailors were agreeably surprised to find an excellent market for the furs they had obtained by barter among the Esquimaux. One man made 800 dollars by his stock, and this was the more surprising, as the majority of the furs were not in good condition, the sailors having taken no care of them on the passage to Canton, and having frequently used them for bedding and

200 THE WORLD'S EXPLORERS.

other purposes. With the proverbial fickleness of sailors, the men, who had been all for a speedy return, now almost broke out into mutiny because they were not permitted to return to the North American coast for a fresh supply of peltries. The lesson, however, was not lost either on Britain or America, and from that time the trade in furs to China assumed very important proportions.

On the 4th of October, 1779, the ships anchored at the Nore, after an absence of more than four years. Captain Clerke had not long survived his beloved commander. He had long been in bad health, and died of a decline in the far North. The health of the crews had been as exceptionally good as on Cook's second voyage, and from the same reasons. On board the Resolution only five men had died, and three of these left England in bad health. The crew of the Discovery had had no fatal case of sickness during the whole voyage.

FEJEE MAN.

OSTRICH, EMU, AND CASSOWARY.

FERNAND MENDEZ PINTO.

I.

Achievements of Eminent Men and their Fame—Kepler and Galileo—Calumnies Attached to Certain Names—Bacon and Walton—Slander Promulgated by Cervantes concerning Pinto—Repeated by Congreve—Figuier's Translation of Pinto's Travels—Their Value—Pinto's First Voyage—His Capture and Slavery—His Voyage to India—He is Despatched from Malacca to Sumatra—The King of the Battas.

THE disproportion that too often exists between a man's actual achievements and the fame, honour, and emolument he derives from his actions, has been a fertile theme of comment in all times among biographers and historians. An accidental occurrence or circumstance, a witty saying, or a telling anecdote, will often make or mar the fame which should attach to the work of a lifetime. Thus the persecution of Galileo gave to the name of the Italian astronomer a wide-spread popularity which entirely eclipsed the glory of another great worker of his time, his correspondent and fellow-astronomer, Johann Kepler. Among a hundred persons who have heard the story how Galileo was compelled by an intolerant priesthood publicly to abjure the theory he knew to be true, and how by the famous "Por se muove" he protested against the tyranny to which he was being subjected, there is scarcely one who has heard of the "laws" of Kepler, or who can appreciate the mighty value of those laws, in which lay concealed the essence of the doctrine of gravitation, that was to be so magnificently demonstrated, in the next century, by the genius of Newton. On the other hand, how many are there not, who, totally unacquainted with the career of Francis Lord Bacon, have based their estimate of the great Lord Chancellor's character simply on that one line of paradox-loving Pope, who in his own flippant way describes a man whose genius he could not comprehend as "the greatest, wisest, meanest of mankind?" And how many, again, who, never having read a line of the kindly philosophy to be found in Izaak Walton's delightful book, are content to set down as a "cruel coxcomb" one of the gentlest men who ever loved the green fields, and in a greedy, self-seeking age preached the doctrine of contentment and thankfulness for common mercies, merely on the strength of a cynical couplet of Byron's? Nothing like a "smart" saying to mar the character of a man. It is so easily learned, and remains so well impressed in the memory.

Among travellers who have borne injustice from the incredulity of contemporaries and the flippant criticism of later writers, none have suffered more glaring wrong than the celebrated Portuguese traveller, Fernand Mendez Pinto. Cervantes, who "laughed Spain's chivalry away," very nearly succeeded in doing the same bad office for the fame of poor Pinto. Actuated, it would appear, partly by the national jealousy which existed in his time between his own nation and Portugal, and partly urged, perhaps, by the temptation which so few authors of the satirical turn of mind can resist, that of saying a "good thing," he dubbed the enterprising traveller *Mendax* Pinto, and the prince of liars; and in later times, Congreve, who very probably knew nothing about Pinto and his travels, except through the sneering allusion of the author of *Don Quixote*, perpetuated the slander by an oft-quoted line in one of his comedies, in which a foolish old astrologer is thus addressed: "Fernando Mendez Pinto was but a type of thee, thou liar of the first magnitude."

Thus was fixed upon poor Fernand Mendez a character which he by no means deserved. The strictures of Cervantes may have been prompted by the natural spirit of rivalry at the beginning of the sixteenth century between the Spaniards and Portuguese, keen competitors in the race of discovery, between whom Pope Alexander so conveniently divided the world. But if we allow for a certain looseness with regard to numerals, in which particular he may be classed with Marco Polo and the majority of mediæval travellers, there seems really no ground for the opprobrious epithets heaped upon him. Credulity and superstition were universal in his day, and from these weaknesses he is not free; but in general he describes the things he saw and the dangers he encountered in all good faith and sober seriousness; and for picturesqueness of narrative and quaint simplicity of style few books of his period will bear comparison with the account which he, a wayworn, travel-broken man, in his latter years indited concerning the wanderings and pilgrimages in which the greater part of his stormy existence had been passed.

In the year 1645 there was published in Paris a somewhat remarkable volume. It was entitled, *Les Voyages Avantureux de Fernand Mendez Pinto, fidèlement traduits de Portugais en François par le Sieur Bernard Figuier, gentilhomme Portugais;* and the work was dedicated to no less a personage than Monseigneur le Cardinal de Richelieu. No hasty compilation is this production of the Sieur Figuier, but a goodly quarto volume of more than a thousand pages, divided into many short chapters, and representing, as the translator states in his dedicatory essay to the cardinal, the labour of no less than eight years. Figuier makes a telling allusion to the critics, " who condemn as false what the feebleness of their minds prevents them from understanding." He concludes his epistle with these words:—" What has moved me to translate the book into French has been the desire to make public many singular matters on which other historians have not touched in their works, and to show by the same means the great things that the Portuguese have done in the East Indies, though the revolution of time has since deprived them of the fruit thereof, and to-day the Spaniards arrogate all the glory to themselves."

One of the chief sources of the value of Pinto's book of travels is in the vivid picture it presents of the character and spirit of travel in those days. Remarkable must have been the contradictions between the profession and practice of the Spanish and Portuguese adventurers of the sixteenth century. Sometimes it is very difficult to draw the distinction between their doings and actual piracy. In executing vengeance upon their enemies they manifested a truly Draconic severity; concerning the ordinary rights of nations they maintained a grand and lordly indifference; and yet they were not without the feeling of religion, deeply tinctured, however, with the utter intolerance and savage harshness of the time. Thus Pinto, a man of many sorrows and cares, an enthusiastic admirer of the missionaries whom he encountered in his Indian and Chinese travels, and especially of St. Francis Xavier, the most devoted of them all, speaks with perfect gravity of Mahometans thrown into the sea "for the glory of God," and evidently considers that to deprive an unbeliever of his goods and possessions is a perfectly justifiable spoiling of the Egyptians. Strange compounds of enthusiasm, heroism, and endurance with dense bigotry and utter intolerance were the Spaniards and Portuguese of three hundred years ago; and Pinto, a true "Portugal," exhibited in his narrative each of these characteristics.

Fernand Mendez Pinto appears to have been the very Jonah of travel.

From beginning to end his career was one long series of misfortunes, intermingled, indeed, with transient gleams of sunshine, which seem but to deepen the prevailing gloom of misfortune in which he was almost continually enshrouded. He was born at the beginning of the sixteenth century, in a little town in Portugal, and began life at the age of eleven or twelve years, at Lisbon, as the servant of a lady to whom he had been recommended by an uncle, "who," says Pinto, "was

WINE-MAKING IN PORTUGAL.

desirous of advancing my fortunes and of withdrawing me from the caresses and the spoiling of my mother." This was in 1521. A year and a half later young Pinto was involved in some scrape, on the nature of which he observes a discreet silence; he merely says—"An adventure happened to me which put me in manifest peril of my life. Consequently, to escape from death, I was obliged to abandon her dwelling with all the speed I could make." Accordingly, Pinto embarked on board a caravel laden with the horses and goods of a lord who was proceeding to Setuval. And here poor Pinto's misfortunes began. The caravel was captured by French pirates, who first designed to sell their prisoners at La Roche, in Barbary, but abandoned this design on taking a more valuable vessel a few days afterwards; whereupon they resolved to proceed at once to France, carrying with them only such of the captured crews as were able to help them in navigating their vessels, and the rest were landed at night at a place called Melides. They were in a very deplorable condition, "covered only," says Pinto, "with the wounds we had on our bodies, caused by the great number of lashes which we had received the preceding days." The wretched men managed to crawl to a neighbouring town, where they were kindly relieved by the inhabitants; and especially a certain Donna Beatrix de Pantoja, wife of the commander and grand provost of the town, played the part of a good Samaritan towards them. After this preliminary taste of the amenities of travel, young Pinto made his way to Setuval, where he remained in service for some years; but at last the spirit of adventure awoke in him, and he determined to embark on a voyage. "Inasmuch," he tells us, "as the wages that were then given in the houses of princes were not sufficient to maintain one, necessity constrained me to quit my master with the design of advancing myself by his favour, and to try and embark for the Indies. For that was my principal design at that time, and the most favourable method I could find for getting rid of my poverty. And although at that period I had very few commodities, I did not refrain from embarking, trusting myself to fortune, good or evil, in whatever form she might come to me in those distant countries."

It was on the 11th of March, 1537, that Mendez Pinto set out on his voyage in a vessel that sailed in company with four others. The ship in which Mendez was, first proceeded to round the Cape and up the Mozambique Channel to the Red Sea, and touched at an Abyssinian port. Soon after, the young traveller was persuaded to embark on one of two trading ships, or foists, to proceed on an expedition to Mecca. The captain of one of these foists was his very good friend; and, says Pinto, "the good hope he gave me concerning the voyage he was about to undertake was the cause that I embarked with him to accompany him, whereunto I was induced by the assurance he gave me of his friendship, joined to the promise that by his favour I might become rich easily and in a short time, which was the thing in the world I desired most. Trusting, therefore, in the promises this captain made me, and allowing myself to be deceived by my own hopes, I imagined myself already the possessor of great riches and of infinite treasures; not remembering how bitter and uncertain are the promises of men, and that I might not gain much fruit from the voyage I was about to undertake, because it was dangerous, and not the season for navigating in those countries." In this sober, straightforward style, the narrative of Fernand Pinto is written throughout. Here and there, indeed, his imagination or his credulity runs away with him in a description of what he has heard; but in describing his own feelings, motives, and actions, his writing is uniformly modest, frank, and tinged with a certain grave melancholy that is not without its charm.

Pinto's visions of wealth were soon dissipated in the rudest manner. His ship was attacked and taken by three piratical Turkish galleys, and thus our traveller was for a second time a prisoner. The Christian captives were carried to Mocha and paraded through the town amid the execrations and insults of the inhabitants, by whom, as well as by their captors, they were very brutally treated. Miserably beaten, half starved, and covered with wounds and bruises, the survivors were sold to whoever would purchase such damaged wares. Pinto fell into the hands of a Greek, and had a very bad time of it indeed. Afterwards he was purchased by a Jew, who carried him to Ormuz, on the Persian Gulf, and here he was delivered from slavery by two Portuguese gentlemen; and he ends the seventh chapter of his travels with pious thanksgivings for his liberty.

Finding a ship ready to sail to Goa, in the East Indies, Pinto embarked, with courage undiminished by past mishaps, and towards the end of the year 1538 he arrived safely at that port. Here he joined the captain of a foist who was going to visit the Queen of Onoro, on the Malabar coast, and afterwards intended to cruise against the Turks; and in this expedition he saw some rough work and reaped very small profit. Indeed, this part of his narrative reminds us of the letter of the French recruit, who, writing to his friend, says—"Nous avons eu de grands avantages; la mitraille m'a brisé les os; nous avons pris armes et bagages—et moi, j'ai deux balles dans le dos." And, indeed, it was with two wounds for his share of the profits that poor Mendez Pinto returned to Goa. But here better fortunes seemed about to smile on him. Don Pedro de Faria, captain-general of Malacca, took the disconsolate traveller into his service; and now Pinto had an opportunity of seeing and describing a country till then almost unknown even to the most adventurous of voyagers.

An embassy soon came to Don Pedro de Faria from the King of

Batta, in Sumatra, requesting help against the Acheens, another nation inhabiting the same island, and with whom his majesty was at war. Five nations then held sway in the land, and among them that of the Acheens seems to have been the most powerful. Mendez Pinto gives a vivid description of the country; and allowing for such inaccuracies as may be expected in the record of a traveller describing many things by hearsay, and many others which he could only imperfectly view, his narrative is both interesting and attractive, having been confirmed in many particulars by the accounts of later travellers, especially Sir Stamford Raffles.

In the strife between the Battas and the Acheens, the latter had decidedly the best of it. Pinto, who was sent by Don Pedro as agent to the Batta court, witnessed the defeat of his allies with no little chagrin. In his account of the country he especially makes mention of the eaquesseitan, a great bird, probably the cassowary. He becomes somewhat imaginative in describing the serpents, some of which he declares to be so venomous "that they can kill people by merely breathing upon them." The great apes and baboons of the island are also mentioned. Speaking of his voyage up a little river which he calls Guateamgrin, he says:—

"Now, while we were navigating with a good wind, we saw through a thicket which was on the bank such a number of bats and other crawling animals not less prodigious by their size than by their singular forms, that I shall not be astonished if those who read this history will not deign to believe what I shall relate concerning them, principally persons who have not travelled, for I am well aware that they who have seen little will believe little, compared with that which will be believed by those who have seen much. Along this river, which, moreover, is not broad, there was a great number of lizards, which may more properly be called serpents, inasmuch as some of them are as large as a little vessel they call Almadia; they have scales on their backs, and their jaws are two feet wide. Those of the country have assured us that these animals are so bold that some of them are to be found who will attack an Almadia, principally when they see only four or five people in it, and that they sink it with their tails in order that they may eat the men, whom they swallow whole, without dismembering them. We also saw in this place a strange animal they call eaquesseitan. They are of the size of a great goose, very black, and scaly on the back, with a row of sharp points on the spine of the length of a writing-pen.

208   THE WORLD'S EXPLORERS.

Furthermore, they have wings like those of the bat, a very long neck, and on the head a little bone, shaped like a cock's comb, with a very

GREAT APES, BABOON, ETC.

long tail marked with green and black spots, like the lizards of this country."

FERNAND MENDEZ PINTO.

In the lizard the reader will not fail to recognise the alligator, though the story concerning the Almadia sunk by the animal's tail, and of the discrimination of the monster, which selects a vessel in which there are "only four or five men," seems very like an attempt of the unscrupulous Battas to impose on their visitor's credulity. The caquesseitan, also, might have puzzled Buffon or Cuvier, so strange a compound of bird and beast does it appear to be. The description goes on to record still greater marvels. Pinto tells us—

"These animals jump and fly together like grasshoppers, and in this manner they chase monkeys and other animals of the kind, which they

GOENONG API—BANDA ISLANDS.

pursue to the tops of the trees, and by this chase they usually subsist. We also noticed hooded serpents as thick as a man's thigh, and so venomous that the negroes of the country told us how, if their breath touched anything living, it immediately died, without there being any remedy or any antidote that could be applied. We saw some others that were not hooded nor so venomous as the preceding, but much larger and longer; moreover, they had heads as big as that of a calf. We were told us that these are accustomed to hunt the others. This serpent mounts the wild trees, of which there are a great number in this country, and twining round some branch with its tail, it lets its body hang down. By the same means, putting its head to the grass at the foot of the tree, it presses one of its ears to the ground, so that in this manner it may hear if anything stirs in the silence of night. If by chance an ox, a wild boar, or any other animal passes by the foot of the tree or near it, they seize it in their jaws; and inasmuch as they

P

have the tail already twisted in the branch of the tree, they catch nothing that they do not draw up on the tree, so that in this manner nothing escapes them. There we also perceived a number of magots (macaques), grey and black, of the size of a great mastiff, of which the negroes of the country are more afraid than of any other animals, because they attack with so much boldness that none can stand against them."

We have made this extract from Figuier's translation, and quote it literally, as showing the style of Pinto and the nature of his inaccuracies. The reader will have no difficulty in recognising the boa-constrictor in the gigantic serpent angling for its prey from the lofty tree ; and the great magots are evidently mandrils and other baboons. It will be seen that what Pinto himself observed he described accurately enough, and that the marvellous particulars with which his narrative is embellished are generally stories with which he has been favoured by the negroes of that country.

Mendez accompanied the King of the Battas as a volunteer in his expedition against the Acheens, and saw some tolerably hard fighting. In the end the latter nation gained the victory, partly by their greater amount of powder and partly by their superior strategy. In the height of the combat they managed to fire a mine and blow three hundred Battas—among whom was the captain who led them—into the air " with so great a noise and so thick a smoke," says the chronicle, " that the place seemed the very picture of hell." This catastrophe decided the victory, and Pinto made the best of his way back to Malacca to his patron Don Pedro, noting, as his manner was, many strange and marvellous things on his way.

II.

Pinto's Mission to the King of Aaru—Hostilities against the Acheens—Pinto's Shipwreck—He is Employed by a Mussulman Merchant—Antonio de Faria turns Pirate, and is Joined by Pinto—Captures and Adventures—Shipwreck—The Chinamen Tricked.

SOON after he had related to his patron the story of the wonderful things to be seen in Sumatra, Pinto was employed on a new and more important mission. The King of Aaru, monarch of another of the five nations of Sumatra, sent an ambassador to Don Pedro de Faria, requesting assistance against the ruler of the Acheens, who was a

Mussulman. This ambassador seems to have been a very Talleyrand of the Eastern seas in his ingenuity of putting a case in the best possible light for his master's purpose. In a long set speech, faithfully recorded in Pinto's travels, he proved to demonstration how " Codlin was the friend—not Short"—how it was the King of Aaru who was "as much a Portuguese and a Christian as if he had been born in Portugal"— how the assistance he craved to prevent the King of the Acheens from taking away his kingdom was a very trifling matter (*fort peu de chose*), being merely the loan of some forty or fifty Portuguese to instruct his majesty's troops in the use of the arquebuss, and the European manner of fighting. Added to this was a request for certain barrels of powder, and a small supply of bullets, for the effectual discomfiture of the tyrant of the Acheens, who would, it was represented, if he succeeded in his nefarious designs against the King of Aaru, decidedly flock up the straits with his men, "and," continued the ambassador, "as his people do not fail to boast aloud, will prevent you from carrying on the commerce of drugs of Banda and the Moluccas, stopping also the commerce and the navigation of the seas of China, Sunda, Borneo, Timor, and Japan. Whereof we are well assured by reason of the treaty he has lately made with the Turks, by the intervention of the Pacha of Grand Cairo, who has made him hope that he would assist him with great forces; and, indeed, you may have learnt this by the letters which I have delivered to you." The moral of all this was, that for their own interest it behoved the Portuguese to give every assistance towards utterly destroying and putting down the tyrant of the Acheens.

Though he let the eloquent ambassador depart "with much discontent, on account of the bad reply he carried back," Don Pedro was soon after moved by various considerations to send some help to the King of Aaru, in the form of a small supply of gunpowder and bullets, together with sundry arquebusses, morions, and other arms offensive and defensive. The duty of conveying these supplies to the king was intrusted to Pinto, who, "for his sins," as he says, "was induced to undertake the commission, and accordingly embarked in a long boat, with his stores, on Tuesday morning, the 5th of October, 1539.

Pinto accomplished his mission successfully and duly delivered his presents to the King of Aaru; but on the homeward voyage his vessel suddenly struck upon a sunken rock on the coast of Sumatra, and out of twenty-eight men who composed her crew, twenty-three were immediately drowned. The others managed to wade ashore through the deep mud, and for a time subsisted miserably upon some shell-fish and the pieces of weed thrown up by the sea. In crossing a small river two of the five were seized by alligators and devoured, and another died of exposure and misery in the arms of his unfortunate leader. Pinto himself, with the sole survivor among his companions, at length hailed the approach of a boat manned by some natives; but these men had no idea of showing kindness to the shipwrecked travellers. They bound them to the mast of their vessel and beat them cruelly to make them discover the whereabout of some gold they supposed them to have hidden; and then, in the supposition that the poor men had swallowed their treasures, proceeded to administer to the companion so abominable an emetic that the poor wretch presently died. As no gold was brought to light by their inhumanity, Pinto's captors did not think it worth while to try the experiment upon him, but contented themselves with carrying him off as a slave. There was no market for him, however, and therefore, to use his own expression, he was "turned out to graze," and lived a miserable life for some months, begging for food from door to door, among a people whose poverty left them very little to give. A Mahometan merchant whom he encountered by chance at length rescued him from his wretched plight, purchasing his freedom for a sum equivalent to less than a pound of our money. The liberator of Pinto, a speculative man, thereupon loaded a vessel with merchandise for Malacca, and departed thither, taking our traveller with him; and thus did Pinto return, the sole survivor of this unfortunate and ill-starred expedition.

After he had recovered his health and strength, Pinto was despatched by Don Pedro de Faria to Pahang, on the Malay peninsula, in charge of a vessel filled with merchandise, and consigned to an agent of Don Pedro's resident there. Again Fernand Mendez arrived in safety at his post; but before his departure a disturbance occurred among the people in consequence of the murder of the King of Pahang; the warehouses were plundered, and Pinto's cargo was carried off by the insurgent populace. Naturally reluctant to return to Malacca without goods or money, Pinto proceeded to Pantani, at the southern extremity of the Malay peninsula. The Portuguese, who had spread themselves pretty generally over this part of the world, had here established a factory, and Fernand Mendez was kindly welcomed by his countrymen. Before he had been long at Pantani there arrived three Chinese junks. It was ascertained (though probably the Portuguese gave themselves the benefit of any doubt which might exist) that these junks belonged to Mohametans from Pahang, and by a rough-

VIEW IN SIAM.

and-ready law of reprisal, Pinto and his companions reconciled it to their consciences to capture these junks and confiscate the cargoes as an indemnification for the merchandise lost at Pahang; and Pinto returned to Pantani rejoicing greatly in his success.

And now an event occurred which was destined to have a great effect on our traveller's future course of life, and to convert him from a sad, sober wayfarer into something suspiciously like a pirate. There arrived in those parts, in charge of a cargo of goods worth 12,000 crowns, a bold man named Don Antonio de Faria, a relative of Don Pedro, the Captain-General of Malacca. Failing a ready market for his Indian stuffs at Pantani, this Don Antonio was informed that at Lugor, in Siam, to the north, on the Peninsula, he could dispose of them to advantage; and accordingly he put the cargo on board a vessel manned by sixteen Portuguese, with Pinto among the number; and in good spirits and full of hope they hoisted sail for Lugor. But "turn and turn about" is said to be fair play; the manœuvre the Portuguese had practised upon the three junks reported to hail from Pahang was successfully practised upon themselves; a great junk, with eighty Mahometan Malays on board, came upon them one day while they were at dinner, and "before they could pick their teeth" twelve out of the sixteen Portuguese were slain. The four others, our hero of course among the number, jumped overboard and swam for the shore, which three of them reached in safety; but one of these died in the woods next day. For the second time in his life Pinto now experienced the kindness of woman. An elderly Siamese lady compassionated his distress, and furnished him and his surviving companion in misfortune with the means of returning to Pantani, where Don Antonio de Faria was waiting anxiously for his return, little anticipating the bad news his plundered deputy would have to impart.

Don Antonio listened to Pinto's miserable tale with feelings of mingled rage and terror. The twelve thousand crowns represented by the cargo of which the Mahometans had possessed themselves, had been borrowed by him at Malacca, and he freely confessed to his countryman, who tried to console him for his loss, that he had not the courage to return empty-handed to Malacca and face his creditors. The course before him was obvious enough to the angry man. He must get back, by whatever means, either his goods or an equivalent for them; and with a curious elasticity of conscience, and a whimsical inconsistency not uncommon in those times, he determined to seek the remedy for having been robbed, in himself turning robber upon the most extended scale. He swore a solemn oath that he would set forth at once in search of the robber, and force him, by fair means or foul, to make restitution a hundredfold for the plunder that had been taken; moreover, he would avenge the death of the Portuguese in the most striking manner, and show these infidels that Christians were not to be massacred with impunity. In short, Don Antonio de Faria resolved to turn pirate. His friends, highly applauding his resolution, joined him to the number of more than fifty, and among the gallant company Fernand Mendez Pinto made one.

The course of life upon which Pinto and his companions now entered was neither more nor less than plain downright piracy. They plundered strange vessels, all of which are scrupulously described as pirates, and occasionally ravaged towns, exercising what among the old Normans would have been called the right of *strandung* in the most effectual manner, and soon their vessels could exhibit a store of wealth far greater than that of which Don Antonio had been originally plundered. The "unkindest cut of all" among their numerous enterprises was, perhaps, the plundering of a bridal party, who were making their way by water "to meet the bridegroom" with songs and rejoicings. The bride and her companions were captured; and shortly afterwards the bridegroom and his friends, meeting Faria's piratical vessel, saluted it with great politeness, little imagining that the ship to which this courtesy was shown held the unlucky bride as a prisoner. Even Pinto, who generally relates these adventures with most edifying gravity, seems to feel some compunction in telling how miserably the poor bridegroom was tricked.

Many a bay and many a coast did these prototypes of the buccaneers explore in their cruisings to and fro in these as yet unknown seas; and steadily did their wealth increase as junk after junk succumbed to their lawless valour. The chief object of their vindictive pursuit, however, was Coja Acem, a Mussulman native of Guzerat, and a great enemy of the Portuguese, and, indeed, it would appear, of all people who had purses in their pockets and goods in their ships. This Coja Acem was a famous rover of the seas. His father and two brothers had followed the same honourable trade and perished in their vocation. Coja it was who had plundered Don Antonio de Faria of his goods; and all the adventurers had sworn to wreak condign vengeance upon the unbeliever. But they themselves were destined to encounter strange mishaps before they should meet their enemy face to face.

Some of the piratical crew now became anxious for a division of the spoil. They had taken three great junks as prizes, and thought it high time for a holiday after so much hard work, especially as there appeared no immediate prospect of falling in with the worthy Coja Acem. Accordingly it was arranged that they should winter in Siam; and the four vessels proceeded in company to the island De los Ladrones, or Thieves' Island, than which they could hardly have chosen a more appropriate port of call. Here arose a great storm, which drove the four vessels against each other, and afterwards flung them on the coast, where they were broken to pieces. "So that," says Pinto, "there died on this occasion five hundred and eighty-six men, among whom were eight Portuguese; and God permitted that the surplus of the crews, fifty-three in all, should be saved, among whom were twenty-three Portuguese, the rest being slaves and mariners. After this dismal shipwreck we went, all naked and wounded, to take refuge in a marsh until the next morning, when, after daybreak, we returned to the margin of the sea, which we found strewn with corpses, a sight so pitiable and so horrible that there was not one among us who thus beheld them that did not fall exhausted on the ground, making a dismal moan over them, accompanied by many blows that each one gave himself; this lasted until the hour of vespers, when Antonio de Faria, who by the grace of God was one of those that remained alive, whereat all of us rejoiced, concealing in his heart the grief that none of us could refrain from manifesting, came where we were, dressed in a scarlet coat that he had taken from one of the corpses, and with a cheerful countenance and dry eyes, made us a short speech."

The harangue delivered on this occasion by Captain Antonio was of the most edifying description. The worthy leader pointed out to his hearers that the goods of this world were very transitory things, a doctrine he had, moreover, very practically impressed upon every owner of a junk with whom he had come in contact. He deprecated all undue lamentation over the losses they had sustained, feelingly pointing out that if in this place they had lost five hundred thousand crowns, there was no reason why they should not gain six hundred thousand elsewhere. Even this cogent argument failed to restore the shipwrecked mariners to cheerfulness and comfort, oppressed as they were with the sense of present misery and ruin. The chapter in which these events are told concludes in the following edifying strain:—

"This brief harangue was heard by all with abundance of tears and of discomfort; then we passed two days and a-half in that place burying our dead who were scattered along the coast. During this time we likewise recovered some victuals and provisions, all wetted, for

BATS.

our subsistence; nevertheless, these did not last us more than five days out of a fortnight that we remained in that place. And, inasmuch as these provisions were wet, they quickly became rotten, and did us no good. This fortnight being past, it pleased God, who never abandons those who really trust in Him, miraculously to send us a remedy wherewith we saved ourselves, all naked and despoiled as we were, as I shall hereafter relate."

The "miraculous remedy" consisted in the arrival, when they were at their wits' end, of a junk full of Chinamen, who landed on the coast while our shipwrecked friends were lurking in the thicket. The unsuspecting Celestials proceeded to enjoy what Jack would call a "run ashore" after their voyage. They brought ashore their linen, and washed it; while some of them were preparing food for the party, others amused themselves with wrestling, leaping, and similar sports until their dinner should be ready. On seeing this, the worthy Antonio de Faria proceeded to demonstrate to his companions that the design of Providence in sending this small junk or lantea to the coast at this exact moment was clearly and manifestly that they, the Portuguese, should seize it suddenly, and, embarking therein, sail away in quest of fresh adventures. If his former harangue had been a comparative failure, the present speech was a brilliant success. The suggestion was acted upon without loss of time. At a given signal the shipwrecked mariners rushed from the wood in a body, made straight towards the junk, and scrambled on board before the bewildered Chinamen clearly knew what they were about. A small cannon fired at them from their own vessel sent the poor deluded fellows scampering into the forest whence their plunderers had just emerged. Pinto tells this with something like a chuckle at the fortune of war. "They ran off into the woods," he says, "where it may be believed that they passed the rest of the day in weeping over their evil fortune, as we until then had bewailed ours." Before carrying off the lantea, the Portuguese added insult to injury by eating up the dinner the Celestials had prepared for themselves; and then these eminently Christian men sailed away, rejoicing in their miraculous preservation, and utterly indifferent as to the fate of the fellow-creatures they had so egregiously duped.

III.

Another Piratical Cruise—Meeting with a Chinese Pirate Junk—Treaty of Alliance—Encounter with Coja Acem—Victory of Antonio de Faria, and Death of Coja Acem and his Crew—Triumphal Reception of the Victors at Ningpo—Further Adventures—Plunder of the Tombs—Disastrous Shipwreck, and Death of Antonio de Faria.

IN the Chinese vessel the adventurers found a cargo valued at four thousand crowns, besides a quantity of good provisions, which latter were exceedingly welcome to them in their starved condition. A part of the lading of the lantea consisted of silks, satins, and damasks, and of these costly materials the captors made themselves suits of clothes, so that they soon appeared bravely apparelled and ready for any new adventures. An unhappy child about twelve years of age, the son of the captain of the lantea, was found on board. Don Antonio de Faria, whose zeal for proselytising seems to have been equally strong with his love of piracy, vehemently urged this young captive to become a Christian; but the boy, says Pinto, "raised his eyes to heaven, and with clasped hands he said, weeping, 'Praised be Thy power, O God, which allows there to be men on earth who speak so well of Thee, though they observe Thy law so badly, as do these miserable blind men, who think that preaching and plundering are things that can satisfy Thee, like the tyrant princes that dwell upon the earth.'"

The next day Faria and his people met with a large junk, and prepared for an attack, which was indeed just about to commence, when a number of red caps, evidently covering Portuguese heads, were noticed on the stranger's deck; and on the principle that "hawks do not pick out hawks' een"—the strange junk being evidently a Chinese pirate vessel—a parley began; and it was ultimately agreed that the two junks should join company and carry on their predatory trade together, the proportion of plunder each crew was to receive being settled by solemn compact and agreement. Soon afterwards a small fishing-boat was seen, wherein were eight Portuguese, sorely wounded and in very evil case. On being taken on board they threw themselves at the feet of Don Antonio de Faria, and with many tears bewailed their piteous case. They had formed part of a large company which had been attacked by Coja Acem, the very pirate of whom Antonio de Faria, that quiet, God-fearing man, was in search; and the said Coja had massacred their companions and taken their vessel, they themselves escaping with the utmost difficulty. Hereupon Don Antonio de Faria took off his bonnet, knelt down on the deck of his ship, and with a fervour which would have been sublime had it not been so whimsical, uttered a long prayer, wherein he invoked the aid of Heaven in his enterprise of seeking out and destroying this wicked pirate. In this extraordinary supplication we find strangely mingled with an allusion to the crimes of Coja Acem, who had killed many Portuguese, a devout aspiration " that he may pay to Thy soldiers and faithful servants what he oweth them for so long a time." Faria seems quite to forget the circumstance that he had recouped himself pretty liberally for the losses he had suffered through Coja Acem.

Soon afterwards the long-desired combat took place. Coja Acem was seen approaching with his vessels in gallant trim, and evidently eager for the fight. Antonio de Faria attacked him with a fury partly inspired by fanaticism and partly due to the remembrance of the ruin Coja Acem had once brought upon him. The Mahometans called upon their Prophet for aid, and the Portuguese invoked the name of the Saviour. The fight was long and desperate. At length Coja Acem fell by the hand of Don Antonio. His death damped the ardour of his followers, and cheered their opponents, who at length achieved a complete victory. Of all the Mahometan pirate's men only five remained alive, and these were bound and flung into the hold of their junk, " in order," observes Pinto very frankly, " that by force of torments they might be made to confess certain things that we wished to ask of them; but," he continues, " they tore each other's throats with their teeth, from fear of the death that they expected, which did not prevent our servants from dismembering them, and afterwards throwing them into the sea, in company with the dog Coja Acem, their captain, grand captain of the King of Bantam, shedder and drinker of the blood of the Portuguese—titles that he ordinarily gave to himself in his letters, and which he vaunted publicly to all the Mahometans; by which cause, and through the superstition of his accursed sect, he was greatly honoured by them."

"The perdition of the enemy," as Fluellen might have expressed it, had in this action been "very reasonable great." With Coja Acem had died nearly four hundred of his people, whilst the Portuguese had lost about forty men. Enriched with many a chest of silver taken from the dog Coja Acem, Antonio de Faria now shaped his course for Chiampoo or Ningpo to repair his ships. The Portuguese merchants resident at that place received him with distinguished honour, escorting him in a kind of triumphal procession; and to the natives, who were anxious to learn what was the rank and dignity of a man thus distinguished by his own countrymen, Antonio replied that he was the man who shod the King of Portugal's horses, with which intelligence the Chinamen were very much impressed. A religious celebration, in which mass was performed, and a sermon preached by an enthusiastic priest, who greatly lauded Antonio and his exploits, gave additional lustre to this triumphal entry. One part of the holy father's exhortation gives a whimsical picture of the theology of those times, and even the grave

JEDDO.

Fernand Mendez can scarcely refrain from a laugh when he describes it. Antonio de Faria himself was heartily ashamed of the extravagant terms in which his praises were sung by the priest, whose robe one of his followers plucked once or twice that he might desist. But he being nettled cried, "I will not stop, but will rather say more, for I speak nothing but what is as true as gospel. In regard whereof let me alone, I pray you; for I have made a vow to God never to desist from praising this noble captain, as he deserves it at my hands, for saving me 7,000 ducats' venture, that Merim Taborda had of mine in his junk, and was taken from him by that dog Acem; for which let the soul of so cursed a rogue and wicked devil be tormented in hell for ever and ever, whereunto say all with me, Amen."

At Ningpo the Portuguese had a strong fort, and it was told to

Faria, whom all treated with great honour and distinction, that there was a great war going on in China, where no less than thirteen princes were contending for the imperial crown. There was nothing to prevent him from taking and plundering the great city of Canton, if he should be so minded, and from what we have seen of Faria it may be supposed that an enterprise of the kind would suit his temper exactly. First, however, he resolved to sail away in search of a certain island, concerning which the Portuguese at Ningpo had given him intelligence, and which was reported to contain the tombs of many Chinese kings, built of gold, and containing many golden idols. Antonio de Faria's navigation was certainly of the boldest, for he ventured into unknown seas and straits and among dangerous rocks and shallows with an intrepidity which did all honour to his courage. It was, indeed, by the additions they made to the stock of maritime knowledge during their semi-piratical, and sometimes wholly piratical, expeditions, that the Portuguese and Spanish rovers of the sixteenth century are entitled to a place among the explorers of the world. On this occasion Captain Antonio was compelled to explore far more than he had intended, for the island of royal tombs seemed to elude his search, and his men were worn out with toil and almost in open mutiny when he at length came in sight of it. But here, as in many other places, the hundred tongues of Rumour had told an exaggerated story, for the gold of popular report on the tombs and images turned out to be burnished copper and brass; but the disappointed mariners broke open the graves, and were consoled by finding a great quantity of silver. They pursued their lawless career among the defenceless islands, plundering without remorse, and sometimes firing the villages near the coasts; and no horde of heathen Danes in the Dark Ages, roaming the seas in search of plunder, the terror of every coast on which they landed, and the avowed enemies of civilisation and industry, could have pursued a course of more unscrupulous rapine than was run by these devout Portuguese, who had a chaplain on board each of their junks to read mass to them, and, sailing with the Cross on their banner, vaunted their Christianity, and looked down with supreme contempt upon the benighted nations they despoiled. Certainly no Northern Viking could have perpetrated a greater act of sacrilege than the breaking open of the graves in the island of Callamplay.

"Mischief shall hunt the violent man," saith the proverb, and the worthy Antonio de Faria's career was destined to be concluded by a sudden and overwhelming calamity. Pinto relates how his commander was in a thoroughly savage humour, and "tore his own beard and scratched his face" with vexation at having by his own indiscretion failed in the finest (piratical) exploit he had ever undertaken. The crews were likewise in very low spirits, "so sad and chagrined," says our chronicler, "that we said nothing at all to any purpose, as if we had been quite beside ourselves." In this humour they were sailing along the Bay of Nanking, when they were caught in one of the violent typhoons which occasionally rage in those seas. Pinto thus relates the catastrophe which then occurred:—"As our boats were for rowing, with low bulwarks, and weak and without mariners, we beheld ourselves reduced to such great extremity, that despairing of saving our lives we let ourselves drift along the coast wherever the current of the water should carry us; for we thought there seemed a much greater prospect of perishing among the rocks than of being swallowed up in the sea, and though we should have chosen this design as the best and the least difficult (that of drifting before the storm), we could not succeed therein; for towards the afternoon the wind came round to the north-east, which caused the waves to rise in such a manner that it was a terrible sight to behold them. The extreme terror in which we were then caused us to throw into the sea everything that we had, even to our chests full of silver. Having done this we cut away both our masts, because our vessels were then quite open. Thus destitute of masts and sails we drifted all the remainder of that day, and towards midnight, at last, we heard from Antonio de Faria's vessel a great noise of people, crying 'Lord God, have mercy on us!' which caused us to think that he was perishing. Then, having replied to them in the same way, we heard them no more, as if they had already been drowned; whereat we were so frightened, and so transported beyond ourselves, that for a full hour no one spoke a word. Having passed all this mournful night in such great affliction, an hour before daybreak our ship's keel opened, so that in an instant we were full of water, eight spans high, and thus we felt ourselves sinking without any hope of remedy. Then we judged that it was the good pleasure of the Lord that our lives and our labours should end here, and in the morning, when day broke and we cast our eyes far abroad over the ocean, we could no longer see Antonio de Faria; and this made us lose all the courage we had left, in such fashion that after that time not one of us had the heart for anything. We continued in this anguish till ten o'clock or thereabouts, with so much apprehension and fear that words would not suffice to express it. At last we struck against the coast, and, almost drowned as we were, the waves of the sea rolled us against a rocky point which jutted out towards us. There we had scarcely arrived when the rolling broke everything to pieces. Then we clung to one another, crying with a loud voice, 'Lord, have mercy upon us!' and of twenty-five Portuguese that were among us there were only fourteen saved, inasmuch as the other eleven were drowned, with eighteen Christian servants and seven Chinese mariners. Such was the great disaster which befell us on Monday, the fifth of August, in the year one thousand five hundred and forty-two, for the which," piously concludes Pinto, "may the Lord be praised for ever!"

IV.

Pinto in Trouble—Kindness of the Bonzes—Retribution—Harsh Captivity—Travels in China—Improved Circumstances—Singular Affray among the Portuguese—Their Punishment—Attack on Pekin by the Tartars—Taking of Quangsay by the Tartars—The Portuguese Enter the Service of the Tartar King.

THUS was Fernand Mendez Pinto, the very Jonah of travellers, once more a shipwrecked, naked man, wandering along a desolate shore with a few companions as miserable as himself. The place swarmed with tigers, and was backed by a dreary swamp. The unhappy mariners dug holes with their nails in the sand, wherein they buried the bodies of their dead companions as the corpses were washed ashore; and passed two dreary nights in that dreadful spot, terrified by the roaring of the tigers and other wild beasts, and miserably contrasting their present forlorn position with their late prosperity. They then set off in the hope of discovering some inhabitants who might succour them in their distress. Their number was quickly reduced to eleven by the death of three, who were drowned in attempting to swim across an estuary; and the survivors were reduced to the extremity of wretchedness when they came upon a company of five Chinamen sitting round a fire. These good people relieved the immediate wants of the shipwrecked mariners, and directed them to a pagoda, inhabited by bonzes, or priests, where poor travellers were hospitably entertained. The bonzes proved themselves worthy of the good character that had been given them. They treated Pinto and his companions in the kindest manner, and passed them on to a second pagoda, whose priests were richer than themselves, and therefore more able to relieve them.

The shipwrecked Portuguese were quite shrewd enough to suspect that the narrative of their late proceedings among the Chinese islands and on the coasts would not constitute a very impressive letter of recommendation. Accordingly they represented themselves as "poor natives of Siam." But it would not do; the Celestials, as Pinto relates with an air of pious injury, insisted on considering them as robbers, and in the course of two months' wandering through the country they received many beatings and little relief. The thoroughly lawless proceedings of the Portuguese in those parts of the world had caused them to be looked upon as the Ishmaelites of the sea; and as their hand had been against every man it was not unnatural that every man's hand should be against them. Thus when they entered the town of Taypor they found Nemesis waiting for them in the shape of a stern mandarin, who, utterly disbelieving their story of being poor Siamese mariners, cast them into a noisome prison, loaded with chains, and with iron collars round their necks. Here they endured such hardships that one of their number died, and Pinto plaintively tells how the twenty-six days he passed in this *carcere duro* seemed to him like twenty-six thousand years, for the amount of suffering compressed into them.

From Taypor they were sent on with a number of Chinese prisoners to Nanking, and here they received such a flogging that two more of them died, and only eight remained to be despatched to Pekin, the capital, where their ultimate fate was to be decided. Thus Pinto had an opportunity of seeing a part of the great Chinese empire under circumstances of great personal discomfort indeed, but such as enabled him to note and observe for himself the condition of the country and its inhabitants. His report is singularly straightforward and accurate, and is in itself sufficient to free him from the imputation of wilful and deliberate falsehood so unjustly attached to his memory. He speaks much of the manners and customs of the Chinese, admires with disinterested approval the manner in which every natural and artificial advantage of the country is utilised, tells us of the hatching of eggs by heat, the singular mode of life among the communities who dwell on the great rivers, the order maintained among the community by the mandarins, the general industry of the inhabitants, and many other particulars. In his numbers, certainly, he sometimes approaches the hyperbolical; but it must be remembered that, like other travellers, while individual objects passed under his immediate notice, and could therefore be accurately described, for others, such as the number of inhabitants and of temples in certain cities, the size of armies, and similar particulars, he had to depend on the reports of natives, and must therefore not be accused of mendacity where these estimates exceed the reality. Thus when Pinto tells us, " *The mandarins assured me* that there are in this city, Nankin, eight hundred thousand hearths, eighty thousand houses of mandarins, sixty-two very large markets, one hundred and thirty shambles, each with eighty shops, and eight thousand streets, whereof six hundred are the greatest and most beautiful;" and again, " *We have been assured* that there are two thousand three hundred pagodas, a thousand whereof are monasteries of men, professed priests of their accursed sect," it will be noticed that he repeats the statements as having been made to him, and does not give them on his own authority. Moreover, it was not until the time of Lord Macartney's embassy in China, at the end of the last century, that any definite or accurate idea was held as to the real extent and population of the Chinese towns; and much that in the time of Cervantes and even of Congreve was considered as gross exaggeration has since been established as sober fact. He gives an accurate account of the great wall of China, and collected many curious particulars concerning the manner in which that gigantic barrier was kept in repair by the work of slaves and criminals.

At last the prisoners arrived at Pekin, the capital, which city they entered bound three and three together, and where their sentence was finally to be pronounced. Thirty lashes apiece were here administered to them as a preliminary taste of Chinese justice, and, as it were, to bring them to a sense of their situation, and to a proper frame of mind for appearing before the high imperial council. To their great satisfaction, their sentence was much lighter than this formidable preparation had led them to expect. They were condemned only to a year's labour on the repairing of the fortifications of Quang-si, and after a stay of two months and a-half in Pekin, were removed to the above-mentioned city, whither they set out on Saturday, the thirteenth of January, 1544. And now we come to perhaps the most characteristic incident of the whole book—an incident which vividly portrays the disposition of these strange, fiery, wonderful vagabonds. The story reads best in the account given by Figuier from the original Portuguese of Fernand Mendez himself, and therefore we present it literally translated from the old French quarto:—

"So soon as we arrived," says Pinto, "the khan caused us to be brought before him, and after he had asked us certain questions he desired that we should be of the number of the eighty halberdiers the king allowed him for his guard. This we took as an exceeding grace of God, inasmuch as the office was not a very hard one, while the entertainment was good and the pay better, added to which we were assured that we should recover our liberty at the expiration of their appointed time." It might have been expected that the travel-worn pilgrims, beaten and abused as they had frequently been, would have made the most of this unexpected and fortunate chance. But their combativeness was too strong, and like the Hibernian hero of a well-known story, they seem after a time to have felt they were "growing mouldy for want of a beating," and accordingly Pinto has the following extraordinary outbreak to chronicle:—

"After we had thus dwelt there for almost a month very peaceably, and much rejoiced that a better fortune had befallen us than we had expected, the Devil, seeing in what union all nine* of us lived together (for all our goods were in common, and when misfortunes overtook us we shared them with each other like good companions), took upon him to sow a discord between two of us, which brought great misfortune upon us all. This quarrel arose from a certain vanity common enough among our Portuguese nation, of which I can render no other reason than that our people are very sensitive concerning everything that touches their honour."

Pinto then tells the story of the quarrel in the following way. He writes:—"Two of the nine of us had a great debate on the pedigree of the Madureyras and the Fonsecas, to determine which of these two houses was held in the greatest honour or esteem at the court of the King of Portugal. This affair was pushed so far that, one word leading to another, they began to exchange opprobrious terms in their harangues, saying one to the other, 'Who are you?' and 'Who are you yourself?' though possibly both of them were not any great things in the king's household. In such manner they let themselves be so violently transported by anger, that one of them gave the other a great box on the ear, which the latter returned by a sword-stroke wherewith he cut off half of his cheek. Then the second, feeling himself wounded, clapped his hand upon a halbert, with which he pierced the arm of the other; whereupon the quarrel was enkindled so hotly among us all, that out of the nine we numbered seven of us were grievously wounded. Meanwhile the khan came running up in person at the noise, with all the officers of justice, who, having seized us, gave us thirty lashes on the spot, which covered us more with blood than our wounds had done. Thereupon they locked us up in a prison underground, where we were kept for the space of forty-six days, with exceedingly heavy collars round our necks, and chains on our wrists

---

* There is a numerical error in Pinto's narrative. He tells of *fourteen* who escaped the wreck, whereof three were drowned in crossing an estuary, one perished in prison, and two died under the flogging they received, which would make only *eight* survivors. There must have been fifteen saved from the wreck to make the numbers tally.

and feet, so that we suffered much, being reduced to this deplorable condition."

CAMELS.

The brawlers were presently brought before an officer of justice, who read them a severe and well-deserved lecture on the folly and wickedness of fighting and bloodthirstiness, and who seems to have been especially severe upon the manifest contradiction between the profession and practice of those Christian prisoners; and to impress the sermon upon their memories the captives received thirty more blows each. They were then removed to another prison less horrible than their underground dungeon; but they still had to endure much from hunger and thirst for a couple of months, at the end of which time the Portuguese were again brought before the "Haute Justice," and a somewhat contemptuous mercy was extended to them, on the ground that, being men naturally depraved and addicted to brawling and all kinds of wickedness, they must be judged by a lower standard than that to which the Chinese were accustomed. Accordingly they were to be pardoned for this once, in consideration of the two whippings they had undergone, and the strictness of their imprisonment; but it was strongly impressed upon them that if any further quarrel occurred, or there was any spilling of blood in public places, they should on that same day be beaten to death. Whereupon the Portuguese, who had expected something worse, congratulated themselves upon escaping so cheaply, and took a solemn and serious pledge that they would thenceforth live in amity and good understanding among themselves, like Christians as they were. They moreover laid down certain rules in writing for the better observance of the new arrangement.

"And in truth," says Pinto, in concluding the chapter, "God gave us grace thenceforth to live in good peace and concord, though we could not live without much labour, and a great lack of those things that are necessary for livelihood."

There are few episodes in the history of travel more whimsical than this strange brawl among men who had endured so much. They must have been strange, hot-headed fellows, who, on the first interval of respite from pain and suffering, could thus come to blows and pike-thrusts on the question of the respective merits of the Madureyras and the Fonsecas.

Stirring times were now approaching, and the valorous Portuguese were soon to have a congenial field for the display of their warlike valour. "We had been eight months and a half in captivity," says Pinto, "wherein we endured many labours and inconveniences, inasmuch as we had for our support only the little alms that we obtained in the town, when at last, on a Wednesday, the third of the month of July, in the year fifteen hundred and forty-four, at a little after midnight, there arose among all the people so great a tumult, that to hear the cries and the noise that resounded on all sides one would have thought the world was being turned upside down." The reason of the commotion was soon imparted to the astonished Portuguese. Certain news had just arrived of an intended attack of the Tartars on the city of Pekin, " with so great an army, that no king from the days of Adam until now had ever levied its like." In describing the numbers of this invading army—which, however, he reproduces from an account given to him—Pinto certainly makes use of very astonishing numbers— —600,000 cavalry and 80,000 rhinoceroses (probably camels) figuring conspicuously in his story among other equally startling items.

Quinsay, or Quangsay, the city where the Portuguese then dwelt, was soon attacked by an immense Tartar horde. According to Pinto's account the enemy advanced " with a terrible aspect." " Their army was divided into seven great battalions, marching with banners displayed, the colours being green and white. In this order, marching to the sound of drums, which they beat after their fashion, they came to a pagoda called Petilau Namegoo, which was very lodgeable in respect of the number of chambers it contained, and not far distant from the walls. In their advanced guard they had a number of light horsemen, who, running confusedly with their lances lowered, careered round the battalions.

"In this order having arrived at the pagoda, they stopped there a good half-hour, and all took up their positions to the sound of warlike instruments, which were continually played, in a great squadron in the form of a half-moon, which encompassed all the city. Then, when they saw themselves near the town wall, within the distance that an arquebuse would carry, they suddenly rushed forward with such a frightful outcry that it seemed as though earth and sky were coming together. Moreover, they set up more than two thousand ladders which they had brought for this purpose, and made an assault on every side where they could attack, mounting the ladders like men of resolute courage and insensible to fear. And although at the outset the besieged made a certain resistance, they were not able to prevent their enemies from fulfilling their purpose; for, through the use of certain batteringrams that they had brought with them, they so completely broke in the four gates of the city as to render themselves masters of it, after having put to death the khan, together with a great number of mandarins and gentlemen who had hastened up to defend the entrance; by this means without any other assistance these barbarians entered this miserable city by eight gates, and put to the edge of the sword as many inhabitants as they found therein, not sparing the life of one of them; and it is calculated that the number of the slain amounts to sixty thousand persons, among whom were many women and girls grandly beautiful, who belonged to the richest lords of the city. After the bloody massacre of so many people, and after the city had been set on fire, the private houses demolished, and the most sumptuous temples razed to the ground, without there being anything that remained standing in this disorder, they remained there for a week, at the end of which time they returned to the city of Pekin, where dwelt their king, and whence they had been sent out on this expedition."

The Portuguese managed to escape the massacre; but they were carried away as captives by the conquering Tartars. In spite of all they had suffered, these indomitable rovers were still full of courage and energy. It was not in the power of stripes, imprisonment, and wounds to cool their fighting blood; and one of them, George Mendez, so effectually recommended himself and his companions to the notice of the Tartar general by his courage and skill at the taking of a castle, that the barbarous leader, who seems to have had a Napoleonic aptitude for discovering merit, rewarded the stranger with the present of a beautiful horse, and began to treat him and his fellow-countrymen with great honour and distinction, as men who were likely to be very valuable to him. They tried to get away to Hainan with the hope of ultimately making their way to Malacca, but their "resignations" were not accepted.

V.

Portuguese Boasting—Raising of the Siege of Pekin—Magniloquent Descriptions of Pinto—George Mendez and his Talents—Departure of the Portuguese — Renewed Quarrels among them—Piracy and Shipwreck—Events at Tanixumaa—The King of Bungo—Great Reputation of Fernand Mendez Pinto.

THE Portuguese accompanied their new patrons to Pekin, where the Tartar khan had pitched his camp for the siege of the city. The monarch received them graciously, and seemed much impressed with the account they gave of the country whence they came. On hearing that their native land was distant a three years' journey, his Tartar majesty was pleased to observe that there must be great ambition and little justice in the country of those people, that they should come from so far away to conquer other lands. The Portuguese, on their side, were not a little surprised at the splendour and magnificence they saw around them. The khan sat, like the Prince of Darkness in Milton's *Paradise Lost*—

"On a throne of royal state, which far
Outshone the wealth of Ormuz and of Ind;
Or where the gorgeous East, with richest hand,
Showers on her kings barbaric pearl and gold."

Pinto gives a very detailed account of the glories of the Tartar camp and court, and in many particulars he has been corroborated by later travellers.

After some time spent before Pekin in skirmishing and other warlike operations, the khan resolved to raise the siege for that time, and retired from the beleaguered city, taking his faithful Portuguese with him. The breaking up of the great camp is described in language strongly savouring of the use of the figure hyperbole, which, as the intelligent reader is doubtless aware, consists in the employment of words conveying more than the idea to be described. Here it is that mention is made of the khan's three hundred thousand horsemen and eighty thousand rhinoceroses. The account of killed and wounded, too, swells to proportions that dwarf to comparative insignificance even the celebrated Russian disasters of Napoleon in 1812. "After the account had been made of all the dead," says Pinto, "it appeared by the reckoning of the captains that they amounted to four hundred and fifty thousand, the greater number of whom had perished from disease, together with three hundred thousand horses and eighty thousand rhinoceroses, which were eaten in two months and a half of famine; so that of one million eight hundred thousand men with whom the khan had gone forth from his kingdom to besiege the city of Pekin, before which he remained six months and a half, he lost seven hundred and fifty thousand, whereof four hundred and fifty thousand had died by plague, famine, and battle, and three hundred thousand had gone over to the side of the Chinese, being induced thereunto by the great pay given them by the latter, and by other advantages of honour and of presents continually held out to them, whereat we must not be greatly astonished, inasmuch as experience has shown us that these inducements have more power in moving men than all other things in the world."

Ultimately the Portuguese obtained permission to depart; but George Mendez, whose engineering skill had been the cause of their good fortune, and who was by this time looked up to as a very Vauban by the Tartar generals, was induced by the prospect of gain and honour to cast in his lot with the Tartars, and to remain permanently amongst them. He took leave of his friends with many tears, and most handsomely bestowed on them a thousand ducats, "which," says Fernand Mendez Pinto, who does not seem greatly impressed by this act of generosity, "he could easily do, inasmuch as his revenue amounted to six thousand already;" nevertheless, it would seem that two months' pay was not a bad parting gift, though Pinto thinks so lightly of it.

Once more the Portuguese adventurers were "set up in the world," furnished with a ship of their own, and ready to seek fresh cruising grounds. As they sailed away down the great river that flowed from the dominions of the generous Tartar khan, they might have sung in the words of the old sixteenth century sailor's song—

> "All things are ready, and nothing we want,
> To furnish our ship that rideth hereby;
> Victuals and provender they be nothing scant,
> Like worthy mariners ourselves we will try."

For seven days they sailed down the river amid villages and pagodas, which Mendez Pinto describes in truly enthusiastic style. "We saw," he says, "a quantity of great burghs and of very beautiful towns, the which, so far as we could judge by their appearance, could only be inhabited by people grandly rich. The which we might well judge from the sumptuousness displayed in the private houses, but still more from the temples, whose towers were covered with gold, and likewise from the great number of rowing boats which were upon this river, laden in abundance with all sorts of provisions and merchandise."

But however well our worthy mariners might be furnished with all things necessary for their voyage, they "abundantly lacked discretion," and, forgetful of the severe lesson they had received in China, they began to quarrel violently among themselves. "Inasmuch as we Portuguese," observes Master Pinto gravely, "have this of our nation that we abound in firmness, and hold fast to our opinions, there was among us eight so great a contrariety of feeling in a matter in which it was of the first consequence that we should preserve peace and union, that we were almost ready to kill one another." The officer who had been commissioned to accompany them some way on their journey was so disgusted at the quarrelling of these turbulent men, that he quitted them abruptly, refusing to take back any letters or messages from such ill-conditioned strangers, and roundly declaring that he would rather the king should cut off his head than offend God by carrying with him anything that belonged to them.

The quarrel had arisen on the question as to which of two junks, ready to depart in different directions, the travellers should favour; and the result was that both vessels sailed away without them, and they were left for seventeen days on an island, in great distress of mind and pain of body. Assistance came in the congenial form of the Malay pirate Samipocheca, who took refuge on the island with two ships, the only vessels that remained to him of a numerous fleet, and who stayed some time on the island till the wounded men among his crew should recover. "As our present necessity constrained us to take some step, be it what it might," says Pinto deprecatingly, "we were obliged to cast in our lot with him, and to let him carry us where he would until it should please God to put us in a safer ship to go to Malacca." So as these extraordinary travellers were still at loggerheads, and their late quarrel had not been followed by any kind of reconciliation, they divided into two parties, one consisting of three, and the other of five, and embarked respectively in the ship commanded by the corsair in person, and in her consort commanded by his nephew. Happy, in this case, were those who had sided with the minority; for in a piratical combat soon afterwards, the two ships being attacked by a corsair fleet, the nephew's vessel, in which were the five Portuguese, was burnt, and all on board perished.

The adventurous company of Portuguese was now reduced to three, and these were very nearly losing their lives in a terrible tempest, which almost overwhelmed their barque. Running for the Loochoo Islands seemed the best chance of safety. But the pirate commander failed to make his port; and at last the storm-tossed voyagers found shelter in an island called Tanixumaa, belonging to Japan. On being interrogated as to the country of the three foreigners in his crew, the pirate captain replied that "they were from a country called Malacca, whither they had come some years before from another country called Portugal, whose king, according to what he had heard us say at other times, lived at the very end of the great world." The Portuguese themselves, in their accounts, patriotically took care to make their country appear to the best advantage in the report they made of it. The governor of the island had heard of the Portuguese, and had somehow imbibed the impression that Portugal was very much larger than China, that the King of Portugal had conquered the greater part of the earth, and that that wealthy monarch possessed two thousand houses, crammed with gold to the roofs. Questioned on these points, Pinto and his two friends unhesitatingly answered in the affirmative as regarded the power and the warlike character of the Portuguese monarch; the third point they diplomatically evaded, by answering, "that for the number of houses, we did not know for certain, the kingdom of Portugal being so large, so full of treasures, and so populous, as rendered it impossible to specify this." Already favourably impressed by this account of the wealth and consequence of the native land of the Portuguese, the governor or nantaquin was struck dumb with astonishment on witnessing the skill of one of their number, Diego Zeimoto, in shooting with the arquebuse, a weapon entirely new and strange to the islanders. The ease and certainty with which small birds were brought down by this apparently magical weapon threw the nantaquin into transports of admiration; and the fame of the travellers having spread to the neighbouring kingdom of Buogo or Bungo, the monarch desired that these wonderful strangers should be brought before him. Here they were likewise well received, and Pinto, who occasionally practised with the arquebuse, was looked upon by the people with admiration, not unmixed with fear, as a sorcerer who had the thunder and lightning of the skies at his command.

VI.

Accident to the King's Son—The Portuguese Depart for Liampoo—Great Expedition Prepared for Japan—Disastrous Events—Pinto Shipwrecked on the Loochoo Islands—Condemned to Death—Pardoned through the Intercession of the Women—Pinto Advocates the Conquest of the Loochoo Islands—Return to Liampoo and Malacca—Pinto's Embassy to the King of Martaban—Treachery of the Portuguese—Martaban Taken by the Burmese—Procession of the Vanquished—Lamentable Fate of the Royal Family.

BUT the favour of courts is precarious, and he who depends upon the goodwill of a prince may at any time be surprised by that "killing frost" which Wolsey so pathetically describes. An untoward accident almost cost Pinto his popularity and his life at a blow. The young son of the king, Aurichandono, a youth of about sixteen years, was naturally anxious to learn the art of shooting, and one day having obtained possession of Pinto's arquébuse while the owner was asleep, he loaded it to the muzzle and fired it off. As might be expected the gun burst, and poor Aurichandono fell to the ground with a shattered thumb. The populace were ready to slay the "magician" on the spot, but Pinto managed, by vaunting his skill as a physician, to evade the immediate danger; and as he succeeded in curing the young prince by a very simple treatment, he quickly regained the prestige and honour he had lost by this unfortunate occurrence.

The corsair captain had meanwhile been selling his plunder to the inhabitants of Tanixumaa; and this necessary business being concluded, and Pinto and his companions having taken leave of the King of Bungo, they all set sail together for Liampoo (or Ningpo), where they arrived without misadventure, enriched by the bounty of the good-natured monarch, and full of the marvels of Japan, of whose wealth they gave a most glowing account. Then a sudden speculative mania seized the Portuguese dwellers at Ningpo. They felt convinced, one and all, that fortunes were to be rapidly made by trading to Japan; and in a furious hurry began to equip junks for an expedition to this Eldorado, whether piratical or commercial, or both, does not very clearly appear. Such speed was made that in fifteen days nine junks were ready; and in hot haste they all set forth, each endeavouring to be the first in the race for gold. But that Jonah of a Fernand Mendez was on board one of the ships, and his presence was enough to bring bad fortune to the whole fleet. Seven of the nine ships were wrecked, and their crews, to the number of 600, among

CHINESE COMMERCIAL JUNKS.

whom were nearly 150 Portuguese, perished miserably. The two surviving ships were separated in a storm; the one in which Pinto had embarked was, at last, thrown on one of the Loochoo Islands—twenty-four men and some women escaping to the shore.

Bruised and wounded by stones and rocks, wet, famished, and miserable, the unhappy survivors were driven by a number of inhabitants into the presence of the King of Lequios. The story of the cruelties of the Portuguese at the taking of Malacca, when many natives of Loochoo had been put to death by the barbarous conquerors, was well known in the island on which the shipwrecked men had been cast; and they were sternly put upon their defence, on the accusation of being pirates by profession, and enemies to all peaceable and well-disposed people. The Portuguese could make but a lame defence where the case against them was so clear, and they were forthwith sentenced to be decapitated and cut to pieces—their quarters to be sent to different parts of the kingdom, and there hung up as a perpetual warning and terror to evildoers. This sentence would most assuredly have been carried into execution against them but for the benevolent interposition of the women of the island, who, moved with pity, chiefly at the distress of the only surviving Portuguese woman, wrote a petition and presented it to the king's mother, begging her to mediate with her son that the lives of the unfortunate captives might be spared. The influence of his mother was sufficient to induce the king to reverse the sentence, and a general pardon was granted.

Fortune seemed inclined once more to smile upon the travellers. The officer who came to announce their pardon to the captives caused two great baskets of native clothing to be brought, from which each of them might provide himself according to his need. Thus equipped the Portuguese were taken before their generous intercessors to offer their thanks, and to receive the congratulations of the ladies. "They consoled us," says Pinto, "with a great demonstration of pity, the which is an effect of the good disposition of the women of this country, and is common to all of them; with which not yet being content, they entertained us in their houses, one after the other, during all the time we were there and until our departure. For we remained there for the space of forty-six days, during which we were provided with all things necessary for us, and that in such abundance that there was not one of us who did not carry away more than a hundred ducats. As for the Portuguese woman of whom I have already spoken, she had more than a thousand, partly in money, and partly in other presents that were made to her; so much so, that her husband in less than a year recovered all the losses he had incurred. After we had passed these forty-two days in great repose, the season suitable for our voyage having come, the officer procured us a place in the junk of certain Chinese who were going to the port of Liampoo, in the kingdom of China; wherein he fulfilled the exact orders given to him by the king. But first of all the captain of the junk was required to give strict security concerning the safety of our persons, so that he might perpetrate no treason upon us during the voyage. In this fashion we went away from the city of Pungor, the capital of the island of Lequios, of which I shall here give some brief particulars, as I have done concerning the other countries whereof I have hitherto treated; in order that if the day should come when it shall please the Lord to inspire the Portuguese nation, so that in the first place, principally for the exaltation and the spreading of the holy Catholic faith, and, after that, for the great profit that may be thence derived, to undertake the conquest of that island, it may know in the first place where to get a footing, and also the great profits that can be derived from the enterprise, and how easy the conquest of the island would be." And here follow some topographical and nautical details, all tending to assist any enterprising spirits among his countrymen who might wish to undertake the subjugation of the kindly and simple race who had treated the Portuguese with such generous lenity!

It does not appear, however, that Fernand Mendez was at all conscious of anything like deliberate ingratitude or treachery in uttering such sentiments. Among the most curious traits of the fanaticism of those times was the fact that the lawless adventurers of the sixteenth and seventeenth centuries fully believed they were doing a good and laudable work in attacking with fire and sword the territories of any heathen prince; and that all the misfortune and ruin their rapacity brought upon the unfortunate nations on whose coasts they descended were fully counterbalanced by the inestimable benefits of a compulsory conversion to the Catholic faith. Moreover, men so reckless of their own safety as were these pirate adventurers were not likely to be scrupulous in so small a matter as involving a nation in war; and thus it is that Pinto speaks of the island of Lequios, and counsels his countrymen to take possession thereof, with an apparent unconsciousness that his advice is at all cruel or treacherous; he talks of the place as though

FERNAND MENDEZ PINTO.

it were inhabited by dogs or monkeys, creatures too insignificant to be taken into account, and ends a somewhat circumstantial account of the Loochoo Islands by saying, "From this brief relation which I have made concerning the island of Lequios, it may be inferred, as much from the things I have heard tell as from those I have seen, that with no more than two thousand men one might take this island and the others of the Archipelago, from which much greater profit might be drawn than from the Indies, and they might be kept with less expense, both as regards men and other things, for we have here spoken to merchants who assured us that the revenue of three custom-houses alone, and of this island of Lequios, amounts to a million and a half of gold, without reckoning the mass of all the empire, and the mines of silver, copper, iron, steel, lead, and tin, which bring in a much greater revenue than the customs. I will say no more concerning the other particulars of this island which I might here report, for it seems to me that this will be enough to rouse the courage of the Portuguese, and to incite them to an enterprise which is of such great service to our king, and of so great profit for ourselves."

In due time the adventurers arrived safely at Liampoo, or Ningpo, where they were received with much rejoicing.

Whatever we may think of Pinto's morality, there is no doubt of his courage and perseverance. All his misfortunes had not taken the heat out of his rover's blood; and his idea now was to get back to Malacca, and thence endeavour to start afresh, in hopes of better fortune. He succeeded in reaching Malacca, where his old patron Faria was still in power, and as Pinto had by this time gained a knowledge of Eastern languages, and an experience of many things that rendered him a valuable servant, he was employed as a kind of diplomatic agent by Faria, in negotiations and arrangements with neighbouring princes. There was no lack of work of this kind to be done. The armies of Siam, Burmah, Cochin China, Pegu, and various other powers were always at war; and the Portuguese were ever ready to take part with one potentate or against another, according to the chances of profit and plunder. Thus we soon find Pinto accredited to the great city of Martaban, with whose rulers he was to enter into alliance, for at that time the commerce between Martaban and Malacca was of great importance. He was also to keep his eyes open, and make use of any chance that might occur to further the Portuguese interests, and to make alliances offensive and defensive where the safety of his countrymen at Malacca seemed to require it. Furnished with these instructions Pinto once more departed from Malacca, in January, 1545.

A remarkable circumstance occurred to delay the arrival of Pinto at Martaban, which place he did not reach until more than two years after the commencement of his voyage. A number of Portuguese adventurers had taken advantage of the troubled state of the Eastern world to form themselves into a kind of association, nominally to protect the interests of one monarch against his rivals. They had manned a little squadron of well-armed vessels, and sailed nominally as a mercenary navy, while in reality they seem to have plundered friend and foe with a grand impartiality. Pinto fell in by chance with these rovers of the seas, and his meeting seems to have had an effect on him like that which the meeting with Napoleon returned from Elba had on Ney and his followers. All the buccaneering blood in Pinto's veins was on fire. Martaban and his mission were alike postponed to the too-tempting prospect of a piratical cruise; and Pinto and the Mahometan captain of his ship made an agreement to join this notable squadron and share its fortunes.

Of fighting they soon had enough, and more than enough. The

entire trade of those seas had been interrupted and terror spread along every coast by the lawless proceedings of the Portuguese squadron, and great efforts were made to destroy it. The armed vessels gave the crews plenty of work, and their victories brought them plenty of glory; but it seemed fated that Pinto should never become rich; and in March, 1547, he arrived at Martaban, having gained little by his long cruise but experience and scars.

Pinto had come to the famous city in an unhappy hour. The King of Burmah had invested the place with an immense army, and was actively prosecuting the siege. For six months the siege had already been going on, and there was no prospect that the place would hold out much longer. The enormous number of the besiegers (Pinto puts them down at the magnificent total of seven hundred thousand) precluded the idea of bringing any assistance to the beleaguered monarch of Martaban. Pinto heard the true state of affairs from some Portuguese, of whom there were many in the besieging army, and who boarded his ships as he entered the river. Part of his commission was to recall all wandering Portugals to Malacca, as an attack on that place by the Siamese Acheens was apprehended; and he seems to have endeavoured to persuade the Portuguese, as in duty bound, to return with him. But this did not at all suit their plans. Martaban could evidently hold out but a short time longer, and it would be manifestly foolish, after bearing the burden and heat of the day during a six months' siege, to abandon the enterprise just as the reward of their labours was about to be dealt out to them in the plunder of a rich city. Therefore did the worthy Portuguese in the army of the King of Burmah, after many assurances that they would never undertake anything to the dishonour or disadvantage of the King of Portugal, proceed to declare that there was not the slightest danger of any attack on Malacca, or of their services being required in that direction. They then went a step further, and proceeded to demonstrate to Fernand Mendez Pinto that as he certainly could be of no service to the King of Martaban, who was a doomed man, his best course would be to join the besiegers and take his chance of a share of the spoil. It was the line of argument acted upon by Cowper's schoolboy in the well-known poem where his comrades say—

> "You speak very fine, and you look very grave,
> But apples we want, and apples we'll have;
> If you choose to go with us we'll give you a share,
> If not you shall have neither apple nor pear."

And Pinto, acting upon the maxim of the sedate youngster of the poem, "He'll lose none by me, though I get a few," gave ear to the tempting suggestion, and forgetful of his diplomatic mission, and the instructions he had received, resolved to join the besiegers and go in for a share of the King of Martaban's apples.

The account given by Pinto of the final surrender of Martaban to the Burmese, and of the events which followed, is graphic and interesting, and in many particulars bears the impress of accuracy and truth, though to the Europeans of the sixteenth and seventeenth centuries, who had a very vague and inadequate idea of the greatness and splendour of the cities and countries of Eastern Asia, it appeared absurdly exaggerated. Here, as elsewhere, it must be remembered that Pinto had no means of accurately estimating numbers, and that he frequently was obliged to take his details from the reports of men who no doubt employed Eastern hyperbole with great freedom.

It appears that the unfortunate King of Martaban had reckoned greatly upon the assistance of the Portuguese, and had held out in the full hope that they would give him efficient succour. When he found them, to his intense chagrin, ranged on the side of his enemies, he gave up his cause for lost, and entered into negotiations with his assailant, offering to surrender his capital on condition that he should be allowed to retire in safety with his family. The faithless Burmese tyrant, after pledging his word that this condition should be granted, shamefully broke the promise he had given, and the unhappy prince was led forth in triumph with his wives and children, and exposed to great humiliation and ignominy. Pinto gives a very circumstantial account of the procession of guards and captives who marched forth from Martaban, giving the names of many of the princes, the chief priest, &c. He then says—"Immediately after these there came in a litter Nhay Canatoo, daughter of the King of Pegu, whose kingdom the Burmese monarch had taken away, and wife of the Chambainhaa. She had with her four little children, two boys and two girls, the greatest of whom was not more than seven years old, and around her were thirty or forty young women of noble family, and grandly beautiful. They all had their faces bowed down towards the ground, and tears in their eyes, and leaned upon other women. After these marched in order certain Falagrepos, who are among themselves like the Capuchins among us, and who all, barefooted and bareheaded, marched onward praying, and carrying in their hands a kind of chaplets. Moreover, they encouraged these ladies as well as they could, throwing water in their faces to revive them when their hearts failed them, which happened often enough—a lamentable spectacle, which it was impossible to look upon without shedding tears. This unhappy company was followed by a number of foot-guards, and after these came some five hundred Burmese on horseback. Near them was the Chambainhaa, mounted on a small elephant, in token of poverty and of the disregard of the world, conformably to the religion to which he had devoted himself anew. There was no greater pomp about him than this, and he was dressed simply in a long garment of black velvet, in token of mourning, having his beard, his hair, and his eyebrows shaved off; and, moreover, he had caused an old cord to be placed about his neck before he gave himself up to the king. This spectacle, too, was so mournful that none could look upon it and refrain from weeping. With regard to his age, he was about sixty-two years old, of very lofty stature, with a grave and severe countenance, and the look of a very generous prince. When he had come to a place where a confused company of women, children, and old men awaited him, when they saw him in such a lamentable condition, before he had emerged from the city, they all raised, six or seven times, such a loud and terrible cry, that one would have said the earth was crumbling under his feet; and these lamentations and cries were incontinently followed by a multitude of blows that they inflicted on their own faces, striking themselves heavily with stones, with so little pity for themselves that the majority of them were in a short time covered with blood. Moreover, these things so horrible, to see and so terrible to hear, in such measure afflicted all the bystanders, that even the Burmese guards, though they were men of war, and consequently little inclined to compassion, and enemies of the Chambainhaa, could not refrain from weeping like children. It was at this place, also, that the heart of Nhay Canatoo, the wife of the Chambainhaa, twice failed her, and all the other ladies gave way also, insomuch that it was necessary to let him dismount from the elephant on which he was riding, that he might be able to encourage his wife and to console her. Then, seeing her lying on the ground like one dead, and embracing her four little children, he knelt down on the ground and looked up with tears in his eyes."

The severest part of the unfortunate prince's trial was the mortification of meeting the Portuguese, who had behaved very treacherously towards him, and who were now standing to see him pass " all clothed in holiday dresses, with cuirasses of buffalo leather, their hats on their heads ornamented with a great number of plumes, and their arquebuses on their shoulders." Juan Cayeyro, one of the number, especially attracted the notice of the Chambainhaa by flaunting in crimson satin. On seeing him, the fallen monarch bent forward on his elephant's neck, and declared that he would go no farther unless these wicked and treacherous men were removed. The Birmans themselves were irritated at the double-dealing of the Spaniards, and the captain of the guard sarcastically bade them go shave their beards, and no longer deceive people into the belief that they were soldiers; and the Burmese would hire a number of women in their stead, who would serve for money. The Burmese guards, following their commander's lead, thereupon pushed away the Spaniards with great contempt, and Pinto adds pathetically, "Not to tell a lie, nothing ever so sensibly affected me as this, for the honour of my compatriots."

The plunder of the rich city of Martaban was the bait that had attracted the Spaniards to serve the Burmese invader. They made no doubt that their help would be paid for by the abandonment to them of a great part of the spoil. But the Burmese conqueror had all the cunning of an Asiatic and all an Asiatic's disregard of promises and oaths. He caused the gates of the city to be very strictly guarded, that none might enter or go out without his express permission. He took occasion to convey away the Chambainhaa's treasure privately; and so great was this treasure, according to Pinto's assertion, that a thousand men were employed for two days in removing it. When he had thus taken care of his own interests, the tyrant gave up the city to be plundered by his own soldiers, to the great chagrin of the Portuguese, who found themselves cheated of the wages of their treachery. Pinto tells the story of these events in his usual graphic style. He says—

"After these two days were past, the king went very early on a hill called Beiddo, distant a couple of gunshots from thence, and caused the captains who guarded the gates to withdraw. Then the miserable city of Martaban was given up to the mercy of the men of war, and as a last signal a cannon was fired. Immediately all the soldiers rushed pell-mell into the place in such crowds that it is considered more than three hundred were suffocated at the entrance of the gates; for as there was an infinite number of men of different nations, the majority of them without a king, without law, or the fear of God, they all rushed with closed eyes to the spoil, and were so fierce about it, that they made no scruple of killing a hundred men for a crown. In truth, the disorder in the town was so great that the king was obliged to go six or seven times to allay it. The sacking of the city lasted three days and a half, and was carried on with such avarice and cruelty by these barbarous enemies that it was completely pillaged, and nothing remained that could attract the eye of covetousness."

And now come some of Pinto's magnificent figures. He tells us—

"When this was done, the king, with a new ceremony of publications, caused the palaces of the Chambaiuhaa to be destroyed, which were very beautiful and very rich; and with them thirty or forty houses belonging to the principal captains, together with the pagodas and temples of the whole city, insomuch that, according to the opinion of many, it is held that the loss of these magnificent edifices may be estimated at ten millions of gold; with which, not yet content, he caused all the buildings of the city which still remained standing to be set on fire, and by the violence of the wind these kindled so fiercely that on the first night there remained nothing that was not burnt down; and even the walls and the bulwarks were destroyed to their very foundations. The number of the dead was more than sixty thousand persons, and that of the prisoners was no less. There was a hundred and forty thousand houses burnt, and seventeen hundred temples, in which were likewise destroyed sixty thousand statues of idols of different metals. Moreover, during the siege, those of the city had eaten three thousand elephants. There were found there six thousand pieces of artillery of bronze and of iron, a hundred thousand quintals of pepper, and as much more of different drugs—of sandal, benzoin, lac, aloe-wood, camphor, silk, and of divers other kinds of very rich merchandise; but especially an infinity of goods that had come from India in more than a hundred ships of Cambaya, Achem, Melinda, and Ceilam (Ceylon), and from Mecca, the Loochoos, and China. As to the gold, silver, and precious stones which were found there, its amount cannot be truly known, because things are usually concealed; therefore it shall suffice me to say that what the Burman king had for himself of the treasure of the Chambainhaa amounted, so far as I was assured, to more than a hundred millions of gold, whereof, as I have before said, our king (the King of Portugal) lost more than half, as much for our sins as for the weakness and want of courage of men who were cowardly and full of evil inclinations."

The promises of the Burman tyrant were no more kept towards his

248   THE WORLD'S EXPLORERS.

captives than his engagements with the Spaniards had been. Wars in Eastern Asia at that time, and long afterwards, were wars of extermi-

nation. A captured dynasty was generally put to death to the last man, woman, or child, for fear of reprisals; and this course was pursued by the conqueror of Martaban. He caused a number of gibbets to be erected; a great body of horsemen came forth from the king's quarters, proclaiming that no man, " on pain of death, should appear in arms, or say with his mouth what he thought in his heart." Presently the whole army was paraded, and amid a great display of barbaric pomp and splendour of war, the unhappy king and his wives, children, and dependants were hanged *en masse* with circumstances of atrocious cruelty. In concluding the chapter which tells us of these barbarous proceedings, Pinto says—" As for the rearguard, it consisted of a hundred elephants, like those that marched in front. So that the number of warriors who were present at this execution, partly as a guard and partly for the pomp of justice, amounted to ten thousand foot soldiers and two thousand horsemen, and two hundred elephants, not to mention an infinity of other men, natives and foreigners, who had assembled to see the end of this wretched and miserable tragedy."

VII.

Description of Siam and Ava—Former Magnificence of the Cities—Effects of Revolutions—New Calamities of Pinto—A Portuguese Renegade—Another Shipwreck—Dreadful Sufferings and Cannibalism—Father Francis Xavier, the Missionary—Pinto's further Adventures—His final Return to Goa—His Return to Portugal, Disappointment, and Neglect — Conclusion of his Chronicle.

THE charge of exaggeration brought against Pinto seems to have originated in a great measure from the fact that Oriental cities are estimated by their present size, population, and wealth, no regard being taken of the terrible revolutions, wars, and overturning of dynasties which have laid them desolate over and over again, and rendered them but the shadows of what they were. After the Burman war in 1825, general attention was drawn to the almost unknown countries of Ava, Pegu, and Birmah, and the writings of several English officers of known veracity and accuracy have corroborated Pinto's account in many important particulars. One of these officers, quoted by Macfarlane, in his excellent *Romance of Travel*, says, speaking of the expedition in which he himself had a share—

" On approaching Pegu our curiosity became much heightened by the anxiety to behold the capital of this unfortunate but once flourishing country; and setting aside the chance of engaging the enemy, which seemed very problematical, we thought only of the interest attached to the ruins of this ill-fated city. Its sudden downfall from the height of splendour to insignificance, the crimes of which it had been the theatre, and the blood which had been spilt under its walls in the last efforts it made to preserve its independence, all conspired to render the spot exceedingly interesting, and made it quite a classical memento with regard to the history of this country. * * * On entering the precincts of the town, the eye in vain searches for those memorials of former greatness which might indicate days of splendour now gone by; the only striking object within a vast area of four square miles, the limits of which were clearly defined by the line of ramparts, being that far-famed temple the Shoomadoo.

"It stands in the north-east corner of the square on a slightly elevated ground, and is surrounded by a few minor pagodas, kioums, and a miserable collection of huts; the rest of the vast square was cultivated with rice; still, here and there a remnant of brick pointed out where a street had once been; but now all was desolate. There is something very melancholy in contemplating a scene like this, and contrasting the idea of the past and the present. Here, not eighty years since, flourished one of the finest cities of the East, renowned in arms, and governed by a long race of kings, but 'now how fallen, how changed!' In one year Pegu witnessed the downfall of that power and preponderance which ages had been maturing; her sovereign and royal family, the captives of an elated conqueror, were soon exterminated; those temples to which all the empire crowded to offer up its adorations, no longer the resort of multitudes, were neglected, and fell into disrepute, whilst the inhabitants of the city were scattered over the country, and became the despised subjects of that very race whom they had before tyrannised over."

Pinto remained for some time in the service of the Burman monarch, much against his own will, but driven by imperative necessity, for the conqueror of Martaban was not the kind of monarch whose sovereign will and pleasure it was at all safe to dispute. The treacherous and unworthy conduct of one of the Spaniards, Gonzalo Falcan, procured him new trouble and fresh imprisonment and torture. This "traitor Gonzalo," also, was the cause that the junk in which Pinto had come from Malacca was seized by order of the Burman tyrant. Afterwards we find him accompanying an ambassador into Siam, Laos, and part of the Chinese Empire. His account of Siam is as graphic and interesting as the rest of his book. He especially speaks of the "white elephant," and of the superstitious veneration with which it is regarded. He was the first who described this creature, which was long considered in Europe as fabulous as the unicorn, though white buffaloes, monkeys, and other animals (all of them what are called albinos) are not uncommon in those regions.]

Pinto returned to Goa, in the East Indies, after years of peril and adventure, as poor and needy as he had set out. With a spirit still unsubdued in spite of all his misfortunes, he determined upon another voyage to the Loochoo Islands and China in search of better fortune; and once more joining himself to a half, or rather a wholly, piratical crew of Portuguese, he began anew the adventurous life of a sea-rover.

On one occasion they took a somewhat remarkable prisoner. He was a Portuguese named Nuno Rodriguez Taborda, and had been away from his country for nearly forty years. He had fought valiantly in the ranks of the first Portuguese occupants of India, and had been entrusted with the command of a vessel by the great Alphonso Albuquerque, the most famous and perhaps the most cruel of the Portuguese conquerors in the East. "I was present with him at the taking of Goa and of Malacca," says this adventurer, who, by the way, was a renegade, and had lived as a pagan among pagans for many years. "After that I worked at the foundations of Ormuz and of Calicut, without once failing on any occasion to serve that famous captain to whom so many different nations have given the title of 'the Great.' I continued to give similar proofs of my courage during the government of Lopo Juarez, of Diego Lopez de Siqueyra, and of the other governors of the Indies, down to Don Henry de Menesez, who succeeded to this office by the death of the viceroy, Vasco de Gama." The career thus auspiciously begun was, however, soon clouded over by the vicissitudes which seem to have attended all the Portuguese adventurers in the East. Nuno Rodriguez Taborda was shipwrecked, and lost not only his vessel but all his crew excepting three on the island of Lirgan; and to preserve his life among the natives of that intolerant region, he had to renounce his religion. He tries to excuse his apostasy as best he can. "Finding myself frequently pressed by the Gentiles," he says, "to follow their pernicious errors, I refused for a long time. But inasmuch as flesh is weak, seeing myself very poor, distant from my country, and without hope of liberty, my sins made me grant to their prayers what they asked of me with so much importunity, for which reason the king always showed me great favour."

This ancient mariner was afterwards taken to Malacca and received into the Christian communion at that place. His adventures form a type of the life of many of his countrymen in the East.

Again Pinto's adventurous career led him to China, and again this most unfortunate of navigators suffered shipwreck. His crew consisted of forty Chinamen and twenty-eight Portuguese; and the Chinamen, having made a large raft, proposed to save themselves upon it and leave the Portuguese to perish. Whereupon a sanguinary affray took place, which ended with the destruction of the Chinamen, but with terrible loss to the victors, sixteen of whom were killed in the battle, while four more died from their wounds next day. The eight survivors who now took possession of the raft soon suffered all the horrors of famine, and were compelled to resort to the horrible expedient of cannibalism to preserve their wretched lives. For five days they lived upon the body of a Caffre servant who had died. At the end of that time they managed to land on an island, and were presently sold as slaves to a merchant of the island of Celebes. Afterwards they passed into the possession of a native king, who not only set them free but sent them away to Sunda, where Pinto obtained the means for a fresh start in life from some of his countrymen. Again we find him journeying to Siam; and presently he enters into the service of the king, not without profit to himself. But poor Pinto never had the fortune to keep what he made.

In one chapter Fernand Mendez breaks out with enthusiasm in praise of the King of Siam, who certainly had treated his Portuguese auxiliaries very well. Pinto says of this monarch—" When he saw that a Portuguese of the hundred and sixty whom he then had with him had remained a little behind, in a combat in which our people had been engaged, wherein they wrought so valiantly and with such courage that they gained the principal fortress which the enemy had taken in the town of Lantor, he commanded him to return to Siam, inasmuch as he was not like his companions; and that so long as he lived there he was not to go out of his house or to give himself the name of a Portuguese, under penalty of having his beard shaved like the warriors of Banca, since he was as cowardly as they. Whereas, on the contrary, to all the others, who, as I have said, were a hundred and sixty in number, he sent three times, doubling their pay, and exempted them from the dues on their merchandise; and, moreover, he decreed that in every part of his kingdom they might build churches, where the name of the God of the Portuguese should be adored, as it was clear and manifest that this God was more powerful than all others. By these

ELEPHANT.

examples, and by others which I could repeat here in sufficient number, it is manifest how great and laudable were the inclinations of that prince, who, though a Gentile, nevertheless had a very good disposition, and was given to virtuous actions."

But the poor King of Siam, who was so laudably given to the virtuous action of doubling the pay of the Portuguese, was poisoned by his wicked wife, to the great chagrin of Pinto, who had never yet found so generous a patron and master. Then came another war between the Siamese and Burmese. Pinto, ever ready to sell his services to the highest bidder, and with a slight tendency to be, like the Duke of Austria in *King John*, "strong upon the stronger side," entered the army of the King of Burmah, and at last returned to Malacca, having gone through many stirring adventures, taken part in many combats, and slightly improved his fortunes.

Lawless, and even piratical, as much of Pinto's career had been, there was in the character of this singular rover a strong element of enthusiasm; and his religious feeling, though tinctured with all the superstition of the age in which he lived, and marred by the life he led, was doubtless sincere. It was now his fortune to meet, at Malacca, one of the most remarkable missionaries the world has ever seen, the Jesuit who was afterwards canonised by the Roman Catholic Church as Saint Francis de Xavier. All the reverence and capacity for hero-worship in Pinto's character was called into action by the conversation and acts of Father Francis. Pinto attached himself to the missionary, with whom he made several journeys, and to whose sayings and doings the latter part of his book is almost entirely devoted. This thorough sinking of his own personality in his admiration for the genius and virtues of another, is alone sufficient to prove that Fernand Pinto was no vulgar boaster. Indeed, throughout the whole of his remarkable book he speaks of himself with a certain grave modesty as a man who has seen affliction, and whose path in life has been strewn with thorns from beginning to end.

After a career of practical usefulness and piety, Father Francis Xavier died at Shan-shan, not far from Macao, on the Canton river, in December, 1552. Pinto was not present at his death, but deplored that event with real and unaffected sorrow, and it is remarkable that the chapter in which he records the holy father's death is by far the longest in the book. Xavier was buried in the first instance at Shan-shan, but soon his remains were removed to Malacca, and finally to Goa, the capital of the Portuguese possessions in the East. After the death of his great patron and hero, Pinto attached himself to the service of Father Belquior, another zealous missionary of the Jesuits, and again we find him pursuing his adventurous journeys. But age was creeping upon him, and the various hardships and privations he had undergone must have made him older in constitution than in years.

And now the wayworn wanderer began to yearn for the country he had left, full of hope and courage, many years before. Indeed, his native land seems never to have been out of his thoughts during his weary pilgrimage, if we may judge by the constant allusions he makes to Portugal and its king in his work. And as his energies began to fail, the impulse to return home came upon him with renewed strength. With Goldsmith he might have said—

> "In all my wanderings round this world of care,
> In all my griefs—and God has given my share—
> I still had hopes, my latest hours to crown,
> Amidst these humble bowers to lay me down—
> To husband out life's taper at the close,
> And keep the flame from wasting, by repose,"

Accordingly, for the last time, he turned his face towards Hindostan, and arrived at Goa on the 17th of February, 1558. He had brought a present of arms and toys of various kinds to the governor, Don Francis Barreto, from the King of Japan, and Barreto received these gifts very graciously, and in return furnished the homeward-bound traveller with a letter to the King of Portugal, wherein were duly set forth the perils and adventures through which Pinto had passed, the imprisonments, shipwrecks, and other disasters he had endured, and the claims he had upon the favourable consideration of the government. Armed with this document, in which he fondly fancied he possessed a guarantee that his long toils and disasters would at last find some reward, Pinto departed from Goa, and arrived at Lisbon on the 28th of September in the same year.

But the evil fortune that had dogged the footsteps of the unfortunate traveller was destined to follow him to the end. Joam III., King of Portugal, to whom the viceroy's letter of recommendation was addressed, had been dead almost a year when Fernand Mendez Pinto landed at Lisbon. The regency had devolved upon Catherine of Austria, his widow, during the minority of his little son Sebastian; and though Catherine granted an audience to Pinto, and heard from the traveller's own lips the story of his perils and adventures, she does not seem to have considered it incumbent upon her to do anything for him. Yet he had done much towards increasing the knowledge of his century concerning the remote lands of the East. He had penetrated to regions which few Europeans had yet visited, and which none had described; and some years of his adventurous life had been spent in the task of spreading the Roman Catholic faith among pagans. Yet all this was disregarded. Catherine, indeed, after hearing his story, handed him over to a minister of state, and this functionary made him live on "the chameleon's diet, promise-crammed," for several years, at the end of which time he left him to his poverty.

What became of Pinto ultimately has never been ascertained. It is certain that he married, and that his wife and a daughter survived him a considerable time; but where and when his eventful life terminated is not known. The last passage in his interesting work breathes a spirit of mingled disappointment and resignation. He says—

"To conclude: These are the services which I have rendered during a space of twenty-one years, in which time I have been thirteen times a slave, and sold sixteen times, in consequence of the unfortunate events whereof I have treated sufficiently at large in this book of long and laborious travel; but although it has been thus, I cannot refrain from thinking that the fact of my being left without the reward which I might expect after so many services and labours, has proceeded rather from Divine Providence, which for my sins has permitted it to be thus, than from the neglect or the fault of him whom the duty of his office seemed to oblige to do me right; for it is true that in all the kings of this country, which is like a live source whence proceed rewards, though they flow sometimes into channels in which partiality is more at work than reason, there has always been a holy and grateful zeal, accompanied by a very ample and large desire, not only to recompense those who serve them, but even to give very great advantages to those who have done them no service at all. It is evident from this, that if I and others have not been satisfied, it has come to pass only by the fault of the channels and not of the source; or rather, it is the doing of Divine justice, which cannot err, and which orders everything for the best, and according to what is necessary for us; wherefore I render abundant thanks to the King of Heaven, who has deigned to accomplish His holy will; nor do I complain of the kings of the earth, inasmuch as my sins have rendered me undeserving of anything more."

And thus ends the chronicle of Pinto's voyages.

SOUTH SEA WHALE FISHERY.

THE VOYAGE OF LA PÉROUSE.

I.

La Pérouse and his Merits—Importance of his Voyage—Its Origin—Its Political Intention—Early Life of La Pérouse—His Gallantry and Humanity—His Conduct towards the English—Plan of his Voyage—Its Exaggerated Extent—Departure from Brest—Remarkable Appearance of St. Elmo's Lights.

THE expedition undertaken, towards the close of the last century, by the unfortunate La Pérouse, occupies an important place in the annals of discovery and exploration. The courage and perseverance of the commander, the singleness of purpose with which, in the face of many difficulties and dangers, he pursued the object of his voyage, his fortitude under reverses, and his loyal and undeviating respect for the memory of the great Cook, in whose steps he followed, entitle La Pérouse to more than "honourable mention" among the navigators of the last century; and the interest excited by the journals he sent home from time to time to Europe was increased by the suspense and expectation that arose when these journals ceased to be followed by others, and the story of his voyage was suddenly broken off. Not till a long time had elapsed was the mystery which hung over the conclusion of La Pérouse's adventures finally dispelled, and the fate of the expedition ascertained—a fate which has stamped this expedition as one of the most unfortunate in its issue, as it was one of the most elaborate in preparation and design among modern voyages of discovery.

Towards the end of the last century the French prestige, in maritime and colonial affairs, suffered very considerably. The loss of the Carnatic in India, and of Canada in America, had been heavy blows alike to the national power and the national pride. In the field of geographical and maritime discovery, also, the French had been distanced by the English, and the successes of Cook and other navigators roused in the minds of the French government a not ignoble spirit of emulation. Inasmuch, also, as the discoveries of Cook, great and important as they doubtless were, had been left incomplete by the lamented death of that eminent navigator at Owyhee, it was obvious that a supplementary voyage that should clear up the points left unascertained, and complete the work that Cook had left unfinished, might be expected to bring both scientific fame and material profit to those who should project, and to those who should carry it out ; and thus originated the idea of a new voyage round the world.

There was another reason, moreover, which had much to do with the fitting out of La Pérouse's expedition—one that whimsically illustrates the frivolous policy of the French government in the period that preceded the great Revolution, and the time-serving and inadequate expedients employed by a ministry, who thoroughly mistook the national spirit, to check or divert the discontent that was already heralding the overthrow of the whole fabric of the State. The expedient of "throwing a tub to a whale" has become proverbial. In this instance the French people was the whale, and the tub that was to divert its attention from the government, the object of its fury, was an expedition to the South Seas. In a singular memorial on the subject presented by a minister to Louis XVI. in 1784, occurs the following strange passage:—" If you wish, Sire, to turn aside the attention of your subjects from this dangerous Anglomania, this passion for liberty, so destructive of good order and of peace, amuse them with new ideas, beguile their leisure by images the bewitching variety of which may feed their frivolity. It is better that they should employ themselves in contemplating the waggish tricks of Chinese monkeys than in following the present fashion which leads them to admire the horses and philosophers of England." What a specimen of statesmanship! A nation groaning under an intolerable burden of taxation, tyranny, and injustice, looking eagerly at the free institutions of a neighbouring country, and gradually working itself up to a stern, unalterable determination that these things should no longer be; and a ministry persuading the king that the relentless march of events could be arrested by diverting the attention of the country to the "bewitching variety" of the incidents in a voyage of discovery. How could such a measure be otherwise than a failure in its effects? The French people had for some considerable time employed itself in contemplating the waggish tricks, not "of Chinese monkeys," but of the ministers of state; and was very much engrossed, but not in the least amused, by that edifying spectacle.

However, the voyage was determined upon. It produced considerable benefit to scientific knowledge, though it failed to prevent the

French Revolution; and the results achieved are mainly owing to the personal qualities of the commander to whom it was entrusted.

Jean François Galoup de la Pérouse, born at Albi in 1741, had already distinguished himself as an active, prudent, and vigilant naval officer. He had been employed in the war between France and England, which broke out in 1778. When the French government formed the project of taking and destroying the English settlements in Hudson's Bay, the carrying out of this difficult design was entrusted to him; and La Pérouse showed on the occasion a courage and resolution which obtained the high approbation of his own government, and a humanity and forbearance that won the respect and admiration even of his foes. Thus, when on several occasions he had been obliged to destroy the settlements of the English, he left provisions and arms for the captives who had taken refuge in the woods, lest they should fall defenceless into the hands of the savages, or perish with hunger. "We ought," says an English navigator, writing an account of a voyage to Botany Bay, "to call to mind with gratitude, in England especially, this humane and generous man, for his conduct when ordered to destroy our establishment in Hudson's Bay in the course of the last war." La Pérouse possessed in a high degree that spirit of chivalry which displayed itself in the wars of the last century, on such occasions as in the battle of Fontenoy, where the "gentlemen of the French guard" were offered the privilege of firing first—and which inculcated respect for the vanquished, and generosity towards every foe, as a chief part of a soldier's duty.

The instructions given to La Pérouse were very definite and elaborate, and the scheme of the voyage itself only too comprehensive. Two fine frigates, La Boussole and L'Astrolabe, were prepared for the voyage, and furnished with every article that experience or forethought could suggest as likely to be useful to the crews, or beneficial to the nations they were to visit. The Boussole was to be commanded by La Pérouse himself, and the Astrolabe by Captain de Langle, an officer of courage and experience. The most elaborate directions were given regarding the policy to be pursued during the voyage, with instructions for the conduct to be observed towards the natives of the countries where the two frigates might touch. Many precautions, evidently suggested by a diligent perusal of Cook's voyages, were ordered for preserving the health of the crews, and a long and detailed plan of the voyage was laid out. This latter had the defect of being too comprehensive; it contained much more than could be possibly comprised within the limits of one expedition. The sanguine projectors of the voyage seem to have expected that La Pérouse could at once supply every hiatus that had been left in the accounts of former navigators, and complete the map of the world in the course of a few

THE COAST OF TRINIDAD.

years. The "plan of the voyage" instructed La Pérouse to sail from Brest as soon as the preparations for the voyage should be completed. He was to make for Funchal in Madeira, to sail thence to Praya, in the island of St. Jago, then to cross the line and successively examine Pennedo de San Pedro, Trinidad, Isle Grande de la Roche, and Cook's island of Georgia. Then he was to try and find Sandwich Land, and, if he succeeded, to examine the coasts, next to double Cape Horn, and anchor in Christmas Sound, on the south-west coast of Tierra del

Fuego, and, after looking out for Drake's Land, to strike across the Pacific Ocean towards Easter Island; then to cruise in the Pacific, to ascertain particulars concerning various islands said to have been seen by the Spaniards, but of whose position no definite knowledge had been obtained. The two frigates were then to part-company, the Boussole to proceed to Otaheite in the expectation of meeting with new islands in her course, the Astrolabe to look out for Pitcairn's Island, and thence to proceed by a circuitous route to join her consort at Otaheite. After a month's stay the rest of the Society Islands were to be visited, and plants, vegetables, seeds, &c., to be left there. Then

FUNCHAL, MADEIRA.

the island of St. Bernard was to be visited, and the part of the Pacific north of the Friendly Islands to be explored, likewise the island of the Bella Nacion, of Quinas and Bougainville's Navigators' Islands; thence to sail to New Caledonia, to run down its south-west coast, and endeavour to make Queen Charlotte's Islands, and try and reconnoitre the island of Santa Cruz of Mendana.

This was only the preliminary task imposed upon the commander. La Pérouse's further instructions comprised a survey of the north-western coast of America, an examination of the Aleutian Islands, and a further cruise to Japan, Manilla, and China. Then the eastern coast of Tartary was to be explored, the island of Yeddo surveyed, and the north-west coast of America visited for a second time. Then the dispersed islands near the Ladrones were to be examined, and Tinian visited if possible. On quitting the isle of Tinian, the instructions said "he may run down and examine the New Carolinas, situate south-west of the island of Guaham, one of the Mariannes, and to the east of Mindanao, one of the Philippines." The Isle of France, or Mauritius, was to be the eighth rendezvous of the ships in case of separation; and La Pérouse was especially enjoined to stay there no longer than might be absolutely necessary to put himself into a condition to return to Europe. Then he was to look out for Cape Circumcision, discovered by Lozier Bouvet in 1739, and thence make sail for the Cape of Good Hope; "if at this period he judge the ships to be not sufficiently furnished with provision, to make their return to Europe;" in any case, however, he was, on his return to Europe, to endeavour to examine the islands of Tristan d'Acunha, Picos, and several others, to dispel some uncertainty which prevailed concerning their position. "He will return to the port of Brest," the instructions concluded, "where it is probable he may arrive in July or August, 1789."

A commander would have required the eyes of Argus and the hands of Briareus to get through such a task as this. But things were destined to take a very different turn, and the July and August of 1789 brought events that distracted the general attention very effectually from the enterprising navigator and the chances of his return.

It was on the 4th of July, 1785, that La Pérouse arrived at Brest to take the command of the expedition, which sailed a month afterwards on the 1st of August. Among the precautions taken against accidents and losses on the voyage had been the providing a completely decked boat about twenty tons burden, which had been stowed in pieces on board the Boussole. A spare mainmast, capstan, and other similar things had also been provided; and the Astrolabe was furnished with equal completeness. The voyagers had a pleasant run to Madeira, and La Pérouse, in his journal, mentions with enthusiasm the warm and cordial reception given him by several English residents there, but deplores the dearness of the wine, of which he had intended to lay in a stock, but which he found more than twice as expensive as the vintage of Teneriffe. In this latter island, where the voyagers made a short stay, an observatory was erected, and some interesting observations were taken relative to the variation of chronometer clocks, as caused by temperature. Here also sixty pipes of wine were bought.

Adverse winds prevented the commander from making the island Pennedo de San Pedro, as he had wished to do; and La Pérouse, who was always exceedingly anxious to carry out his orders to the letter, takes care to note in his journal—"The making of this island was not

THE VOYAGE OF LA PÉROUSE. 263

enjoined in my instructions, but merely indicated, in case it should oblige me to turn only a little or not at all out of my way." Like other

SEAFOWL.

voyagers in the tropics, he notices the great numbers of man-of-war birds and other seafowl that follow ships from 8 degrees north latitude to near the line.

On the 15th of October, during a violent thunderstorm, the Boussole and Astrolabe were both visited by the singular electric phenomenon known to sailors since the Middle Ages under the name of Corpo Santo, or St. Elmo's lights. This phenomenon consists of a vivid blue light dancing at the masthead, and the superstition of the sailors pronounced it to be St. Elmo, their patron saint, who thus appeared to the faithful during a storm to show them by his visible presence that he took them under his protection. In ancient times already these lights had been observed, and both Seneca and Pliny mention them as having flickered about the masts of the Roman galleys during storms. Fernando Columbus, a brother of the great discoverer of America, records how, during the voyage of 1493—the second that Columbus made—the crews of his ships were one night in great peril among the West India Islands from a sudden gusty storm of wind; and how the crew were comforted by the appearance of the phenomenon. "On the same Saturday," he says, "in the night was seen St. Elmo, with seven lighted tapers, at the topmast. There was much rain and great thunder. I mean to say that those lights were seen which mariners affirm to be the body of St. Elmo, on beholding which they chanted many litanies and orisons, holding it for certain that in the tempest in which he appears no one is in danger." In the record of Magellan's voyage a similar circumstance is mentioned. In the superstitious imagination of the sailors the light fashioned itself into St. Elmo, holding sometimes one taper, sometimes two; whereupon the sailors "shed tears of joy and received much consolation."

TAHITIAN NOSE-FLUTE.

II.

Successful Precautions against Disease on the Boussole and Astrolabe—Congregation of Whales in Strait Lemaire—Easter Island—Remarkable Monuments—State of Cultivation—Pilfering Propensities of the Natives—Run to the North—Port des Français—Its Capabilities as a Trading Settlement—Lamentable Accident and Loss of Twenty Lives—Climate of Port des Français compared with that of Labrador—Voyage to Monterey.

NOTHING of importance happened during the time occupied by the voyagers in rounding Cape Horn and entering the Great Pacific. La Pérouse, laudably concerned for the health of his crews, followed out the measures originally adopted by Cook, frequently fumigating the ships, enforcing personally all matters connected with ventilation and cleanliness, and paying especial attention to the diet of the ships' companies. The result, as in Cook's case, was that the ordinary scourges of seamen on long voyages did not appear on the Boussole or Astrolabe. In Lemaire Strait, at half a league distance, they were surrounded by whales. "It was easy to see," says La Perouse, "that they had never been molested. They took no alarm at our ships, swam majestically along within pistol-shot of us, and will no doubt remain sovereigns of these seas till the fishermen go to make war upon them as at Spitzbergen or Greenland. I doubt," he continues, "whether there be a better place in the world for the whale fishery. The ships might be at anchor in good bays, within reach of water, wood, anti-scorbutic herbs, and seafowl; while their boats, without going a league, might kill as many whales as would make them a good cargo. The only inconvenience would be the length of the voyage, which would require near five months for each run; and I should imagine that these latitudes can only be frequented in the months of December, January, and February."

The days of immunity for the whales in the Southern Ocean have long passed away. Increasing competition has brought an increased energy and boldness into whale-fishing as into every other branch of commerce; and the traveller passing through Strait Lemaire would now be told that the whales—rendered timid and distrustful by increasing persecution—have retired to higher latitudes to take refuge from their numerous enemies in the icy regions around the pole.

Early in April, 1786, the voyagers reached Easter Island, in the

South Pacific. Cook had already visited this singular land, but La Pérouse had a better opportunity than the English navigator of examining it, and gives us many interesting particulars concerning the country and its inhabitants. He speaks highly of the ingenuity and friendliness of the people, who welcomed their visitors with every appearance of cordiality ; but they were great thieves, and had a bad habit of stealing the hats and handkerchiefs of the French during the friendliest of interviews. The colossal images found in their burial-places, or morais—monuments of which Cook had made mention—proved on examination to be made of a kind of lava, very pliable, and consequently easily worked. They had evident notions of a future state, and one of them explained that a heap of stones surmounted by one of these statues was a tomb, by laying himself flat on the earth and pointing downward, to indicate that a man lay buried beneath. He then pointed towards the sky, endeavouring to explain to the strangers that the spirit of him whose body was interred there had travelled beyond the clouds.

M. Duché, a scientific gentleman attached to the expedition, sent home a very graphic illustration of a morai of this kind; and with a touch of true French humour he has introduced into his drawing the figure of a native peeping from behind a statue, the dimensions of which two Frenchmen are busily engaged in measuring, and by means of a long stick stealing the hat of one of the scientific investigators. The statues themselves were nearly fifteen feet high. The numerous fields and plantations, of rectangular shape, and evidently cultivated with great care and assiduity, showed that these people had attained some degree of civilisation. There appeared to be no chief of real authority among them. Trees were scarce, and, as a consequence, good supplies of fresh water were not to be procured; for in these regions the amount of rainfall depends in a great measure on the nature and abundance of the vegetation. The presence of the sugar-cane gave evidence of the natural fertility of the soil. The islanders are described as a stout, handsome race, with tawny skins and black hair. Their garments—with which, however, they were very scantily supplied—were made chiefly from the bark of the paper mulberry. They also made hats and baskets of rushes, and were adepts at carving in wood. They had a custom of depositing the bodies of their dead in caverns.

The ships now sailed to the Sandwich Islands, on one of which, Moanee, La Pérouse made a considerable stay; but as this group had already been accurately described by Cook, this part of the French

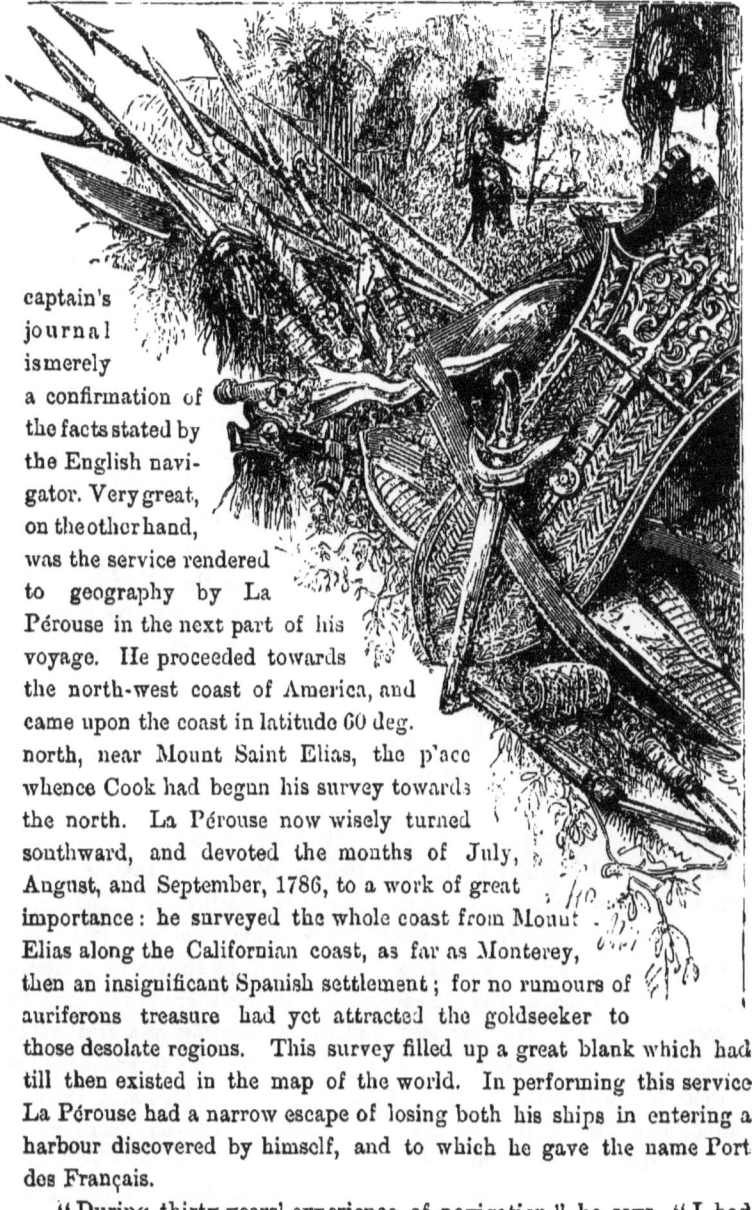

captain's journal is merely a confirmation of the facts stated by the English navigator. Very great, on the other hand, was the service rendered to geography by La Pérouse in the next part of his voyage. He proceeded towards the north-west coast of America, and came upon the coast in latitude 60 deg. north, near Mount Saint Elias, the p'ace whence Cook had begun his survey towards the north. La Pérouse now wisely turned southward, and devoted the months of July, August, and September, 1786, to a work of great importance: he surveyed the whole coast from Mount Elias along the Californian coast, as far as Monterey, then an insignificant Spanish settlement; for no rumours of auriferous treasure had yet attracted the goldseeker to those desolate regions. This survey filled up a great blank which had till then existed in the map of the world. In performing this service La Pérouse had a narrow escape of losing both his ships in entering a harbour discovered by himself, and to which he gave the name Port des Français.

"During thirty years' experience of navigation," he says, "I had never before seen two ships so near being lost; the occurrence of such an event at the extremity of the world would have rendered our calamity still greater."

Port des Français, according to the map published in the account of La Pérouse's voyage, and the description given by the commander in his journal, is indeed a singular place. The entrance is very narrow, and obstructed by a large sandbank and by rocks, many of which are marked as not always visible. Within the dangerous entrance, a long and broad sheet of water extends into the country for some miles, ending in two basins, one on each side, so that the whole has something the form of the letter T. These basins are fed by huge glaciers, of which there are five, pouring their streams into the broad channel. La Pérouse describes this harbour in the following manner :—

"We had already visited the bottom of the bay, which is perhaps the most extraordinary place in the world. To form an idea of it let us suppose a basin of water of unfathomable depth in the middle, bordered by peaked mountains of exceeding height, covered with snow, without a blade of grass upon this immense collection of rocks, condemned by Nature to perpetual sterility. I never saw a breath of air ruffle the surface of this water; it is never disturbed but by the fall of enormous pieces of ice, which continually detach themselves from five different glaciers, and which in falling make a noise that resounds from the mountains. The air is in this place so very calm, and the silence so profound, that the mere voice of a man may be heard half a league off, as well as the noise of some seabirds which lay their eggs in the cavities of these rocks. At the extremity of this bay we were in hopes of finding channels by which we might penetrate into the interior of America. We imagined that it might terminate in a great river, the course of which might be between two mountains, and that this river might have its source in the great lakes to the northward of Canada."

The natives here had an exceedingly good notion of bargaining, and understood the art of regulating their demands by the stocks of goods they had on hand, and by the eagerness of their visitors to purchase, as completely as the most civilised traders. They attached a great value to iron, and at last would hardly take anything else in exchange for their furs and other wares. Of course they were ingenious thieves, and, like the South Sea Islanders, seemed to feel no shame when detected in systematic larceny.

An observatory was erected at Port des Français, on a small island, which La Pérouse purchased of a native chief; though the French commander shrewdly expresses his fears that the purchase might be set aside in any court of law, inasmuch as it appeared doubtful whether

POLAR BEARS.

the chief had any property in the land, or any right to alienate it. "We had no proof," says La Pérouse, "that the chief was the real proprietor, and the witnesses his representatives. Be that as it may, I gave him several ells of red cloth, hatchets, knives, bar-iron, and nails. I also made presents to all his suite."

La Pérouse considered Port des Français would be a spot excellently adapted for a trading settlement, and that a very profitable traffic in furs might be established without interfering with either the Russian or the English interests. That he was right in his conjecture as to the trade, subsequent events sufficiently proved; but the dangers arising from the rocks at the entrance of the bay, and the consequent difficulty of bringing ships up to the anchorage, would have been a very serious, if not a fatal, drawback. Of the extent of this danger, the crews of the Boussole and Astrolabe soon had a lamentable proof in a calamity which befell them just before their departure from Port des Français, and which appeared to them the more unfortunate, as, until then, chiefly by the vigilant care and judicious management of the commander, the crews had enjoyed almost uninterrupted good health, and they had not lost a single man by any casualty.

The calamity happened in the following manner:—La Pérouse wished to have the entrance of the bay accurately sounded, and its breadth determined by measurement. He determined to entrust this duty to M. d'Escures, a lieutenant of the navy, and to despatch the two pinnaces belonging to the Boussole and Astrolabe, and a smaller boat, to perform the task. As the tide sometimes ran violently in and out of the channel, and the entrance was rendered dangerous by breakers, the commander-in-chief had given written instructions to M. d'Escures enjoining him to be very cautious, and not to attempt the passage of the channel if he noticed any indications of danger. So definite and circumstantial were these instructions that the pride of the young officer was somewhat touched, and he remonstrated with his commander upon being "treated like a child," and reminded La Pérouse that he had already commanded ships; whereupon La Pérouse mildly and judiciously pointed out to his zealous subordinate that caution and prudence were equally essential with courage in an officer.

Early on the morning of the 14th of July, the three boats set out. The crews and officers were in the highest spirits, and no one apprehended danger. At ten o'clock the small boat was seen returning alone. M. Boutin, who commanded her, had a terrible report to make. Some unusual circumstances of wind and tide must have made the channel more dangerous than usual on that fatal day. The boats had suddenly been drawn into a current which carried them out to sea at a tremendous rate, while the breakers were rushing into the bay in a direction exactly opposite to the tide, which was rushing out. The small boat—strongly built, and so buoyant that she floated even when full of water—had managed to struggle back against the current, and after great labour, directed by unusual skill, had been brought back by M. Boutin into the bay; but the heavier pinnaces had been seen to founder, and there was little doubt that every soul on board them had perished.

This indeed proved to be the case. La Pérouse remained for some days longer in the bay, in the vain hope that one or other of his unfortunate sailors might have drifted out to sea on a piece of wreck, and be thrown upon the coast. Large rewards were offered to the Indians, some of whom had witnessed the catastrophe, and who seemed sincerely to pity the victims, to induce them to explore the coasts, in search of any survivors. But not even a corpse was recovered. By this calamity twenty brave sailors perished. That it was partly to be ascribed to the rashness of M. d'Escures there is no doubt. That officer evidently miscalculated the strength of the current, and underestimated the difficulties of the duty with which he had been entrusted. M. Boutin, the commander of the small boat, generously tried, in his official report of the disaster, to bear as lightly as possible upon a gallant comrade whose own life had paid the forfeit of his rashness; but it is impossible to misunderstand the meaning of his words. He says—"I think it necessary to explain the motive of M. d'Escures' conduct. It is impossible that he ever should have thought of going into the channel. He wished only to approach it, and imagined the distance he was from it was more than sufficient to keep him out of all danger. Of this distance he, as well as I, and the eighteen persons who were in the two boats, had formed a wrong judgment." The fate of M. de Marchanville, a promising young officer in command of the second pinnace, who perished in the attempt to succour his companions, was especially deplored by his comrades. La Pérouse, after vainly waiting for some days in the hope of finding some relics of his unfortunate shipmates, erected a monument with an inscription to their memory, and sailed away from the fatal harbour.

The fact that climate is influenced by other circumstances besides latitude was strongly illustrated by the experiences of the mariners during their stay on this coast, and by the facts they noted during their excursions into the country. Port des Français is situated between the 58th and 59th parallels of north latitude in a region corresponding in position with icebound Labrador on the opposite coast of the continent; but of its climate and productions the commander gives the following account in his journal. He says—"The climate of this coast seemed to me infinitely milder than that of Hudson's Bay, in the same latitude. We measured pines of six feet diameter, and a hundred and forty feet high. Those of the same species at Prince of Wales's Fort and Fort York (in Labrador) are of dimensions scarcely large enough to serve for studding-sail-booms. I should not be in the least surprised to see Russian corn and a great many common plants thrive there exceedingly. We found great abundance of celery, round-leaved sorrel, lupine, the wild pea, and endive. Every day and at every meal the copper of our ship's company was filled with them; we ate them in soups, ragouts, and salads; and these herbs did not a little contribute to keep us in our good state of health." The woods are described as abounding in gooseberries, raspberries, and strawberries, with splendid forest trees fit to make masts for the largest vessels. The streams abounded in trout, salmon, and other fish. The hunters encountered in the woods many bears, martens, and squirrels; and the Indians had many skins of the black and brown bear to offer for sale. Tanned elk-skins were also noticed among the possessions of the natives. Of birds, we are told, there was no great variety in species, but the individuals were very numerous. The familiar birds of Europe, sparrows, blackbirds, nightingales, and yellow-hammers abounded in the thickets; and their songs appeared delightful to the mariners, hearing, as they did in each note, some echo of home. In the air were seen hovering the white-headed eagle and the large species of raven; we surprised and killed a kingfisher, and we saw a very beautiful white jay, with some humming-birds." In this last particular there must be some mistake. Humming-birds fifty-seven degrees north of the line would be an entirely new phenomenon in natural history. The swallow and martin and the black oyster-catcher are described as building their nests in the clefts of the rocks; and cormorants, gulls, red-footed guillemots, and wild geese appeared among the sea-birds. Among the natives the women had a curious custom of distending the mouth by fixing a piece of wood of elliptical form, and about half an inch thick, firmly in the under-lip. This ornament, which caused the lower part of the face to project in an especially hideous manner, was exceedingly valued by the natives, and those only

THE VOYAGE OF LA PÉROUSE. 273

were entitled to wear it who belonged to families of some distinction. Captain Dixon, in his voyages, notices this strange custom, and tells

SONG BIRDS.

how, when he wished to purchase one of these singular ornaments of an old lady who owned it, his offer of a hatchet was refused with contempt, so highly did the proprietor value her strange decoration; but at last, when almost everything the captain had to give had been offered to the old dame in vain, she was captivated by the glitter of some bright brass buttons, in return for which she surrendered her beloved treasure. The lip-piece measured nearly four inches in length, and was more than two and a-half inches broad at the widest part; it was inlaid with a small pearly shell, and had a rim of copper.

From Fort des Français the ships proceeded along the coast to Monterey. The measurements and observations of the longitude and latitude of the coast are very accurate, and reflect great credit on the energy and industry of the commander. Monterey Bay La Pérouse found full of whales. "It is impossible to conceive the number with which we were surrounded," says the captain, "or their familiarity; they every half-minute spouted within half a pistol shot of our ships, and made a prodigious stench in the air. . . . . The sea was covered with pelicans. These birds, it seems, never go more than five or six leagues from the land; and navigators, who shall hereafter meet with them during a fog, may rest assured that they are within that distance of it. The first time we saw any of them was in Monterey Bay, and I have since learned that they are very common over the whole coast of California; the Spaniards call them alkatræ." There is something whimsical in this idea: "a pelican in a fog" would be rather an unusual landmark.

A number of Roman Catholic missions had already been founded in California. In the presidency of Loretto, on the east coast of the peninsula of Old California, there were no less than fifteen of them. The object of their establishment was to convert the Indians; and the exertions of the missionaries seem here, as elsewhere, to have been untiring and constant. La Pérouse speaks of the Spanish missions in terms of undisguised admiration. Of the character of the Indians of California he seems to have made a very just estimate. He describes them as men totally devoid of the higher impulses of humanity, without emulation or self-control, to be governed rather by the fear of punishment than by the hope of reward, without gratitude to appreciate kindness, or spirit to resent an injury. The monks and priests attached to the missions appeared to rule them as if they had been children, exercising over them an authority sufficiently mild, but entirely arbitrary.

RUSSIAN PEASANTS.

III.

The Portuguese Settlement of Macao—The Philippine Islands—Manilla—The Coast of Tartary—Bay of Castries—The Tartar Inhabitants—Their Honesty and Friendliness—Survey of the Coasts of Sagalien—Kamtschatka—The Russians and their Government.

BEYOND a narrow escape of running on a sunken rock, nothing remarkable occurred in the passage from Monterey to Macao, the Portuguese settlement in China. In 1786 the population was estimated at twenty thousand inhabitants, of whom only a hundred were Portuguese. At Macao, also, an observatory was erected, in an Augustine convent, for astronomical and nautical observations. Some Chinese sailors were shipped to take the places of the men so unfortunately lost at Port des Français; and La Pérouse observes, that though by the laws of the country any one leaving the Empire of China was liable to the punishment of death, the condition of the inhabitants was so wretched, that had the ships required two hundred men they could have enrolled them in a week. From February to April, 1787, was occupied in the run to Manilla in the Philippine Islands, and in making the necessary preparations for an important part of the voyage—the exploration of the east coast of Tartary. The Philippine Islands are described by La Pérouse as a splendid country, capable of producing any amount of revenue, and of maintaining an enormous population, but utterly spoiled by the ignorance and bigotry of the government. In his account of the inhabitants he alludes to the practice of smoking; and it is amusing to observe that his French editor has considered it necessary to append a foot-note to explain in a few words what is meant by "a cigar."

The course of the ships was now to the north-east, past the island of Formosa and the peninsula of Corea, into the sea which lies between the coast of Chinese Tartary and the islands that constitute the Empire of Japan. The navigators were now in regions which had not, like the Pacific, been explored by former navigators. La Pérouse was the first who gave accurate information respecting the coast of Tartary on the one, and the Japanese islands on the other, side of the deep channel up which his ships were running. After touching at various parts of the coast, the ships came to an anchor in the Baie de Castries, on the coast of Tartary, in latitude 51 deg. 29 min. north. The inhabitants of the bay were a mild tribe of Tartars, diminutive and ugly in appearance, but gentle and obliging in their manners. They lived almost exclusively on fish, and seemed to enjoy a quiet, unlaborious existence, being able to supply their wants without much trouble or exertion. They held their women in much greater estimation than any tribes which had been yet encountered—consulting them before making any bargains, and providing for their comfort with unusual solicitude. They differed radically from the nations with whom the travellers had before come in contact in being scrupulously honest; so that the articles of barter they most valued could be left in their cabins unguarded, save by the probity of these simple people. They had a very ingenious method of smoking salmon, but horrified their visitors by devouring raw the gills, small bones, and sometimes the whole skin of the fish, which they could strip off in one piece with much dexterity. They had subterraneous houses for the winter like the Kamtschadales.

PELICANS.

They were accustomed to deposit bows, arrows, fishing-lines, and other articles they considered valuable with the bodies of their dead, in the tombs erected outside their villages; and testified no jealousy or fear when they saw the crews of the ships enter these tombs, not doubting that the feeling of respect for the dead that prevented themselves from plundering these sanctuaries of the departed would influence their visitors also.

When the French began writing down the particulars they obtained by signs from these simple people, the Orotchys, as they were called, became very uneasy, evidently looking upon their questioners as magicians possessed of occult and dangerous powers. La Pérouse tells us the following anecdote in his journal:—

"It was only by the greatest patience and difficulty that M. Lavaux, surgeon of the Astrolabe, attained the formation of the vocabulary of the Orotchys and the Botchys. In this respect our presents could not vanquish their prejudices; they even received them with repugnance, and frequently refused them with obstinacy. I imagined I could perceive that they were, perhaps, desirous of more delicacy in the manner of offering them; and to try if this suspicion was well founded, I sat down in one of their houses, and after having drawn towards me two little children, of three or four years old, and made them some trifling caresses, I gave them a piece of rose-coloured nankeen, which I had brought in my pocket. The most lively satisfaction was visibly testified in the countenances of the whole family; and I am certain they would have refused this present had it been offered directly to themselves. The husband then went out of his cabin, and soon afterwards returning with his most beautiful dog, he entreated me to accept of it. I refused it, at the same time trying to make him understand that it was more useful to him than to me; but he insisted, and perceiving that it was without success, he caused the two children who had received the nankeen to approach, and placing their little hands on the back of the dog, he gave me to understand that I ought not to refuse his children." These friendly Tartars gave their visitors some valuable geographical information. The French officers made a sketch of the Tartar coast so far as they had explored it; whereupon the natives took the pencil from their hands, and indicated by a few strokes the position of the Japanese island of Sagalien, and the fact that that island was separated from the mainland of Asia, merely by a strait almost filled up by the sand and detritus brought down by the Sagalien river, the stream now called the Amour. This island they called Tchoka. "They took the pencil from our hands," says La Pérouse, "and by a touch of it joined the island to the continent; then afterwards pushing their canoe upon the sand, they gave us to understand that, having departed from the river, they had thus pushed their canoe upon the bank of sand which joins the island to the continent, and which they had just sketched; then, plucking up from the bottom of the sea the weed with which I have already said the bottom of this gulf was filled, they placed it upon the shore to signify that there was also this seaweed upon the bank which they had traversed."

Acting upon the information derived from the friendly Tartars, La Pérouse crossed the strait, and made a survey of the coasts of Sagalien, and passed through the strait that separates that island from Jesso, and to which his name has been given. His explorations here threw considerable light upon a part of geography of which little had till then been accurately ascertained. It is a gratifying fact that the name of an enterprising and meritorious navigator should have been preserved to perpetuate the memory of a voyage which, in the sequel, proved very disastrous to all engaged in it.

Some time was now passed by the travellers in Kamtschatka, where the officials of the Russian settlement, in the Bay of Avatscha, and Lieutenant Kaboroff, the Russian officer in command, gave them not only permission to erect an observatory, but valuable assistance. It fortunately happened, moreover, that M. Kasloff Ougrenin, the Governor of Okhotsk, was making a tour through his province at the time, and was expected to arrive very shortly at the neighbouring harbour of St. Peter and St. Paul. A somewhat perilous adventure was here undertaken by the zealous naturalists attached to the expedition, Messieurs Bernizet, Mongès, and Reseveur, who accomplished the ascent of a volcano under circumstances of great difficulty. They found that even Kamtschatka was not destitute of natural productions suitable for the food of man. In those regions,

"Where, tumbling in their sealskin boat,
Fearless the hungry fishers float,
And from their teeming fields supply
The food their niggard plains deny,"

the "niggard plains" and barren hills themselves are not entirely destitute of food. From the stunted pine the Kamtschadale can select one species the cones of which contain nuts or seeds good to eat. From the bark of the birch, which grows even in these northern regions until it is at last found trailing along the ground like the ivy, the people extract an agreeable beverage; and berries of many kinds, black and red, and of acid but not disagreeable taste, are found on the mountain side. Fish could be procured along the coast in such abundance that we are assured a single cast of the net close alongside the frigates would have brought up a haul sufficient to feast the crews of half-a-dozen ships; small cod, herrings, plaice, and salmon forming the chief species of the finny prey.

Monsieur Karsloff, at the settlement of St. Peter and St. Paul, rivalled his subordinate at Avatscha in politeness. He supplied the travellers with oxen, for which he resolutely refused payment; and, moreover, gave a ball in their honour, to which all the women in the settlement, both Kamtschadales and Russians, were invited. The female part of the community were not numerous, but peculiar. They numbered only thirteen, ten of whom were Kamtschadales, with flat faces and little eyes, decked out in silks, and demurely seated on benches round the ball-room. These ladies favoured the travellers with the exhibition of several Kamtschadale dances, which are described as the reverse of graceful or exhilarating in character, though the ladies exerted themselves with thorough good-will, dancing until they fell exhausted to the ground. "As the dances of all these nations have ever been imitative," writes our commander, "and in fact nothing but a sort of pantomime, I asked what two of the women who had just taken such violent exercise had meant to express; I was told that they had represented a bear-hunt. The woman who rolled on the ground acted the animal, and the other, who kept turning round her, the hunter; but if the bears could speak, and were to see such a pantomime, they would certainly complain of being so awkwardly imitated." The ball was interrupted by the arrival of a courier from Okhotsk with despatches for the travellers [from Europe; and La Pérouse was much gratified by finding that his government, anxious to mark its approbation of his zeal and success, had raised him to the rank of commodore. Monsieur Karsloff, the governor, seems to have been especially anxious to make a favourable impression on his visitors, both personally for himself, and as the representative of the Russian Government. The promotion of La Pérouse was celebrated by a discharge of artillery; the congratulations of the governor were accompanied by a number of presents, and every effort was made to exhibit the Russian power as a generous and enlightened one, favourable to progress and science, and desirous of the progress and happiness of humanity.

Unfortunately, however, there was in the suite of the governor a living representative of the other and the darker side of Russian rule. Following the governor from place to place with a humble dog-like affection, which M. Karsloff repaid with indulgent kindness, was an aged, downcast, broken-spirited exile, named Ivaschkin. This man's history was an illustration of the tyranny of despotism, and of the system by which the Russian rule was carried on. Fifty years before, Ivaschkin, a youth not twenty years old, was an officer in the Imperial Guard at St. Petersburg, in the service of the Czarina Elizabeth. The dissolute character of the empress was well known; and in the heat of wine, at the breaking up of a convivial party, Ivaschkin was rash enough to utter a foolish jest reflecting on his imperial mistress. A spy reported the indiscreet expressions, and for this tipsy outburst of petulance the stripling was condemned to the horrible punishment of the knout; his nostrils were slit to stamp him with lifelong infamy, and he was banished to the interior of Kamtschatka. After many years the Empress Catherine granted the unfortunate man a pardon. But his spirit had been thoroughly broken by the cruelties he had endured. The ex-officer of the Guard had no desire to parade his degradation and exhibit his slit nostrils in St. Petersburg; the one fixed purpose that survived in him was the determination to hide his disgrace, and end his days in Siberia. It was with the greatest difficulty that the officers, whose sympathies were strongly excited, could prevail on the unfortunate exile, who had been educated at Paris, and still preserved something of the manners and feelings of a gentleman, to accept the presents of tobacco, powder, shot, and other articles they pressed upon him, for which he stammered out some words of gratitude in the language he still remembered. His first impulse, on hearing of the arrival of the strangers, had been to hide himself from them, and a week had elapsed before they found out his whereabout, by means of M. Lesseps, one of their number.

282   THE WORLD'S EXPLORERS.

KAMTSCHADALE SLEDGE.

IV.

La Pérouse's Memorial to Captain Clerke—The Kamtschadale Nation—Ravages of Small-Pox—Intermarriages with the Russians—De Lesseps Travels to Europe Overland—His Account of his Travels—Return to the Southern Hemisphere—The Island of Maouna—Architectural Pretensions of Native Buildings—Appearance of the Natives—Death of M. de Langle.

LA PÉROUSE did a good work during his stay at St. Peter and St. Paul by erecting a tablet to the memory of M. de la Croyère, an earlier explorer, who had died there in 1741, on his return from an expedition to explore the coast of America, undertaken by command of the czar. With singularly graceful courtesy he erected a similar tablet over the grave of Captain Clerke, Cook's second in command during that celebrated navigator's third voyage, and who had here closed his arduous and eventful career only a few years before. La Pérouse also verified the survey of the Bay of Avatshka, taken by the British in Cook's third voyage, and pronounces their work exceedingly correct. The Kamtschadale nation had been greatly reduced in number about sixteen years before the French commander's visit by that scourge of civilised and savage communities, the smallpox, which had swept away three-fourths of the native population, and the survivors were rapidly losing their distinctive character by constant intermarriage with the Russians. This mingling with the Russians had doubtless improved the position and habits of the Kamtschadales. The filthy yourts, or underground dwellings, in which they had been accustomed to burrow during the winter, had been abandoned for the more civilised isbas, or wooden houses of the Russian peasants, with the large brick stove, whose fierce heat renders these peasant dwellings a pandemonium to the stranger. The women were also beginning to dress their hair in imitation of the Russians, whose costume and language they were likewise adopting. The taxes imposed upon them by the government are described as merely nominal, the produce of half-a-day's hunting being frequently found sufficient to defray the imposts of a year, and altogether the Kamtschadales seem to have been in every way benefited by the Russian occupation of their territory. In character they are greatly preferable to the Esquimaux. "They ought no more to be  compared to the Esquimaux Indians," says our traveller, "than the sables of Kamtschatka to the martens of Canada." He tells us further concerning them—"Ere long the primitive character that distinguished them so strongly from the Russians will be entirely effaced. Their population does not at present exceed four thousand souls, scattered over the whole peninsula, which extends from the fifty-first to the sixty-third degree of latitude, and occupies several degrees of longitude. Hence it appears that there are several square leagues for each individual. They cultivate no one production of the earth; and the preference they give to dogs over reindeer in drawing their sledges, prevents their breeding either hogs, sheep, reindeer, horses, or oxen, because these animals would be devoured before they could acquire sufficient strength to defend themselves. Fish is the principal food of their draught dogs, which go, notwithstanding, as much as twenty-four leagues a day. They are never fed till they come to their journey's end."

M. Lesseps, who had accompanied the expedition as Russian interpreter, here quitted his companions, with the sanction of La Pérouse, as it was his intention to return to Europe overland, with a view of giving a more detailed scientific account of the great Asiatic-Russian territory than had yet appeared. He accomplished his intention, and his book, which contained much interesting information, was afterwards published and translated into English under the title of *Travels from Kamtschatka to France.*

Again the prows of the ships were turned southward, and La Pérouse, after some further exploration of the Pacific, which disproved the alleged existence of land laid down in the old Spanish maps, crossed the line once more into the southern hemisphere, and brought his ships to anchor at Maouna, one of the group called the Navigator's Isles. Maouna was a beautiful island, and seemed to promise a liberal supply of the fresh provisions and water of which the mariners now began to stand in need. The natives, a vigorous and handsome race, many of the men being above six feet in height, who crowded round the strangers with every demonstration of friendship, brought a plentiful supply of cocoa-nuts, guavas, and other fruits, and offered fowls and hogs for sale, with pigeons, paroquets, and other birds, disdaining the iron and cloth that were offered in exchange, and coveting only beads wherewith to deck themselves out. Their houses and furniture showed a considerable degree of skill. "I went into the handsomest of these huts," says the commander, "which probably belonged to a chief; and great was my surprise to see a large cabinet of lattice-work, as well executed as any of those in the environs of Paris. The best architect could not have given a more elegant curve to the extremities of the ellipses that terminated the building; while a row of pillars at five feet distance from each other formed a complete colonnade round the whole. The pillars were made of boughs of trees very neatly wrought, and between them were five mats, laid over one another with great art, like the scales of a fish, and drawing up and down with cords like our Venetian blinds. The rest of the house was covered with leaves of the cocoa-palm."

A certain expression of ferocity in the faces of these architectural savages, who, moreover, like most of the nations inhabiting the South

Sea Islands, were great thieves, pilfering everything on which they could lay their felonious hands, warned the commander to abridge his stay among them. He noticed that although they made no display of offensive weapons, the men were in many cases covered with scars that told of former contests, and plainly indicated their warlike character. They also seemed inclined to become insolent on the strength of their own superior stature, and evidently looked upon their visitors as a curious race of pigmies. There were also disagreeable incidents indicative of hostility. Stones had been thrown at M. Rollin, the surgeon-major, and an attempt had been made to snatch a sword from another officer, M. de Monernon.

All these indications made La Pérouse resolve to abridge his stay at Maouna as much as possible, and he had made every preparation for departure on the following morning, when M. de Langle, who commanded the Astrolabe, returned from an excursion he had made along the coast with the intelligence that he had discovered a magnificent harbour for boats, situated near a pleasant village, and, what was of more consequence, in immediate proximity to a splendid cascade of pure fresh water. Though the ships were all ready to sail, M. de Langle strongly urged that such an opportunity of obtaining a few longboat cargoes of excellent water ought not to be neglected, and suggested that the ships could easily be kept standing off and on outside the harbour while the boats' crews were employed upon this duty. Some of his men were beginning to suffer from scurvy; and Captain de Langle quoted Cook's opinion that water recently shipped was in such cases infinitely preferable to any that had been some time on board. La Pérouse for a long time held out against every representation. He had been seriously alarmed by the turbulent behaviour of the islanders, and was anxious to sail at once; but when De Langle at length offered to head the watering-party himself, and promised to be on board in three hours with all the boats under his command full of water, the commodore allowed himself to be persuaded, and intrusted the command of the expedition to his friend, though with a presentiment of evil which the event fatally realised.

Accordingly the longboats and barges of the two ships were prepared and manned by a party of sixty-one men, fully armed with muskets and cutlasses; and six swivel guns were shipped in the longboats as an additional measure of precaution. It was soon found that M. de Langle, in his eagerness to procure fresh water for his men, had somewhat overstated the case with regard to the magnificent harbour. On examination the harbour proved to be a shallow basin, approached by a winding channel only twenty-five feet wide, and so nearly empty at low tide that the long-boats were presently aground. M. de Langle had examined the bay at high water, and had not calculated for the difference of six feet made by the ebb. The peaceful attitude of the natives, who had their women and children with them, and of whom only about two hundred were present, made De Langle determine to remain in the creek and fill his boats with water. By the time this operation was finished the inflow of the tide would give him plenty of depth to take his boats out of the harbour. The business of shipping the water was, therefore, commenced; but the captain, now thoroughly anxious, could not fail to observe that the crowd of natives was steadily increasing, until it swelled to about a thousand men. Canoes, which had been trading with the ships in the offing, now continually arrived in the bay, where they landed their crews to swell the crowds on shore. Meanwhile, the operation of watering was completed; but the long-boats were still aground, and the cunning islanders seemed fully aware that something was wrong with the French, who had taken post in their boats, and were waiting, with what patience they might, for the rising of the tide. The natives now began to wade into the water around the boats, and to pelt the crews with stones. Like Cook at Owyhee, M. de Langle was unwilling to order his men to fire while there was a chance of avoiding bloodshed; and, like Captain Cook, he lost his life through his humanity.

When at length he began to retaliate, it was too late. The Indians, rendered bold by impunity, had waded into the water quite close to the boats. M. de Langle, struck by a stone, fell over the side of the boat into the water, and was immediately killed by the savages with clubs and stones. The two long-boats were quickly cleared of their occupants, some of whom were massacred in the water by the natives, while others managed to swim to the barges, which lay at a little distance, and very fortunately had been kept afloat. Had those barges grounded, like the long-boats, it is hardly probable that a single man would have escaped. It was lucky also that the savages, having obtained possession of the long-boats, began to tear up the seats and break their prizes in pieces in search of plunder; for the fugitives in the barges, who by their numbers had greatly embarrassed the movements of the crew, gained time to establish some kind of order. The officers behaved with great gallantry under these trying circumstances. M. de Gobien, who commanded the long-boat of the Astrolabe, under the orders of M. de Langle, was the last man to quit the boat and take refuge on board one of the barges; nor did he retreat until he had fired his last charge of powder and ball at his assailants. So deeply laden were the two barges, now encumbered with wounded men who had crawled or had been dragged on board, that one of them grounded. The savages, perceiving this, made an attempt to cut off the retreat of their foes; but by the prudence and coolness of the officers and the courage of the men, the survivors at length effected their escape. At five o'clock the two barges reached the place where the Boussole was riding at anchor, surrounded by a number of canoes, whose crews were busily engaged in trading with the French. The anger and dismay of captain and men on hearing what had occurred was extreme. The sailors and soldiers seized their muskets, and began to cast loose the guns to revenge upon the crowd of natives who surrounded them the outrage perpetrated on their friends. But La Pérouse, whose just indignation did not obscure his reason, peremptorily forbade any attack; pointing out with great ustice that the outrage must have been unpremeditated, and that the fact that these islanders had remained around the ship all day was a proof of their ignorance of what was going on in the bay. A single charge of powder, fired from a cannon, warned them to depart from the ship; and when one of their own canoes shortly after joined them, the news was evidently brought, and they paddled away in great haste.

In this miserable affair twelve persons lost their lives. The mistake made by De Langle seems to have consisted chiefly in his taking counsel rather with his own eagerness than with his judgment, in attempting a landing in a creek where he was separated from the ships, and left to encounter single-handed a great horde of savages, of whose treachery and fickleness he had already received proofs. La Pérouse intended to revenge the deaths of his men by destroying the villages of the treacherous natives; but, on examination, this plan was seen to be fraught with such danger that it was given up. There was no secure anchorage for the ships outside the reef, and to get into the creek was impossible. Had the remaining boats been allowed to proceed alone, they might have grounded, in which case the destruction of their crews would have been a matter of certainty. The natives, with remarkable impudence, put off in their canoes, and laying-to at some distance from the ships, made signs to the crews that they were willing to trade as if nothing had happened; but a round shot that came bounding over the bay towards them, and sent the water splashing into their boats, made them scuttle away; and, with rage and mortification burning in their breasts, the French sailed away from Maouna without even the mournful satisfaction of recovering and committing to the deep the corpses of their murdered comrades.

BARBADOES FROM THE SEA.

V.

Voyage Across the Pacific—Vavao, in the Friendly Islands—Norfolk Island—Run to Botany Bay—La Pérouse's Last Letters—Departure from Australia—Long Doubt concerning the Fate of the Expedition—Voyage of Admiral D'Entrecasteaux in Search of La Pérouse—Unfortunate Issue of D'Entrecasteaux's Voyage—Rumours concerning Relics of the Expedition—Voyage of Captain Dillon, and its Results.

THE voyagers now took their way across the Pacific, and touched at several islands, which had been seen and noticed, but not explored, by Cook. After visiting the Navigators' group, they proceeded to the Friendly Islands, and visited that of Vavao, of the existence of which Cook had been informed by report, though he never visited it himself. Vavao is described as larger than Tongataboo, and as possessing several advantages over that island, such as greater elevation, and a constant supply of fresh water. Near Vavao was another island named Magoura. The caution inculcated by the massacre is seen in an extract of the commander's journal. He says, speaking of the island of Vavao—"Towards noon, I was at the entrance of the port in which Maurelle (a Spanish navigator) had anchored. It is formed by small islands of some elevation, which have narrow but very deep passages between them, and which afford complete shelter against the winds from the offing. This harbour, infinitely superior to that of Tongataboo, would have suited me perfectly well for a stay of a few days; but the anchorage is within two cables' length of the shore, and in that position a long-boat is often necessary to carry out an anchor in order to get off the coast. Every instant I was tempted to lay aside the plan I had formed on leaving Maouna, of putting into no port till I should reach Botany Bay; but reason and prudence made me resume it. I was desirous, however, of making some acquaintance with the islanders, and brought-to at a small distance from the land; but not a single canoe came near the ships."

On the 13th of January, 1788, the expedition, after encountering very heavy and tempestuous weather, came in sight of Norfolk Island, a spot which afterwards acquired a dismal celebrity in the annals of transportation. The attempts made to land here failed; and La Pérouse, who seems to have been doubly cautious after the lamentable catastrophe of Maouna, had strictly enjoined the commander of the boats to run no risk. They were enabled, however, to observe and admire the gigantic Norfolk Island pine; and the verdant appearance of the island, as noticed from the sea, appeared to indicate the presence of many plants, a circumstance which aggravated the disappointment of the naturalists, who had promised themselves a rich scientific harvest. But the commander's orders were too explicit and peremptory to be disregarded. Reluctantly, the boats were put about, and the Boussole and Astrolabe crowded all sail for Botany Bay. The travellers sighted the bay on the 23rd of January, and to their great astonishment found a British fleet at anchor there. Captain Hunter, of the Sirius, sent officers on board the Boussole to pay the captain's compliments, and offer his services to the new comers, "adding, however," says La Pérouse, with what appears to be quiet satire, "that as he was on the point of getting under way, in order to run to the northward, circumstances would not permit him to furnish us either with provisions, ammunition, or sails; so that his services were confined to wishes for the further success of our voyage." The French commander was not to be outdone in politeness. "Sent an officer," says La Pérouse, "to return my thanks to Captain Hunter, who already had his anchor apeak, and his topsails hoisted. Intimated to him that my wants did not extend beyond wood and water, of which we should find plenty in the bay; and that I was sensible that ships destined to establish a colony at so great a distance from Europe could afford no succour to navigators."

The English were, in fact, occupied in forming a settlement at the harbour of Port Jackson, a few miles to the northward of Botany Bay. An amicable intercourse was soon established between the French and English; and La Pérouse took advantage of the departure of an English ship to send to Europe the charts and maps, the records of his discoveries and observations since the time he left Kamtschatka, and also his journal from Kamtschatka to Botany Bay. Already in the preceding September, in a letter dated from Avatscha, he had laid down a plan for his future course. "From Queen Charlotte's Sound," he says, "I shall make a run to the Friendly Islands, and shall do everything I am enjoined to do by my instructions with regard to the southern part of New Caledonia, to the island of Santa Cruz of Mendava, on the south coast of the Terre del Arsacides, and to Bourgainville's Louisiade, by determining whether it be a part of New Guinea, or separated from it. At the end of July, I shall pass between New Guinea and New Holland by a different channel from that of the

Endeavour, provided such a one exists. During the months of August, September, and part of October, I shall visit the Gulf of Carpentaria and the coast of New Holland, but in such a way that it may be possible for me to get to the northward, and to reach the Isle of France at the beginning of December, 1788. I shall sail thence very speedily, to reconnoitre Bonnet's pretended Cape Circumcision, and shall arrive in France, after having put in or not, according to circumstances, at the Cape of Good Hope, in June, 1789, forty-six months after my departure." The latter part of this plan is repeated *verbatim* in a letter written by La Pérouse at Botany Bay, and dated February 5th, 1788. Two days later, on February 7th, he wrote a long letter to a friend; he again speaks of his intentions. "In my letters from Kamtschatka," he says, "I communicated to you the plan for the remainder of the voyage, upon which I was obliged to determine, in order to arrive in France in June, 1789. Neither our provisions, nor our rigging, nor even our ships would permit me to prolong the period of my voyage, which, I imagine, will be the most considerable ever made by any navigator, at least as to length of route."

The concluding paragraph of this, the last letter of La Pérouse, refers in a touching manner to the second great calamity that befell the expedition, and the loss of M. de Langle and his companions in the bay at Maouna—a misfortune that evidently weighed deeply on the humane commander's mind. He ends his letter thus :—"M. de Clonard now commands the Astrolabe, and M. de Monti has taken his place on board the Boussole. They are both officers of the greatest talent. In M. de Langle we have lost a man of great merit. He was endowed with excellent qualities, and I could never discover any fault in him but that of being obstinate, and so inflexible in his opinion, that there was no refusing to follow it without quarrelling with him. He rather extorted from me than obtained the permission which was the cause of his death. I should never have yielded if his report of the bay where he perished had been exact; nor can I conceive how it was possible for so prudent and enlightened a man to be so grossly deceived. You see, my dear friend, that I am still much afflicted by that event. In spite of myself I return to it incessantly."

These words, in which a tinge of self-reproach seems to mingle not ungracefully with the natural regret for a lost friend, are almost the last penned by the hand of the enterprising navigator. A few days afterwards the Boussole and the Astrolabe sailed from Botany Bay, and for a long time nothing more was heard of them or of their crews.

THE TAPIR.

When two years had passed, and no word of news reached Europe, public anxiety began to be aroused in France respecting the fate of

THE VOYAGE OF LA PÉROUSE.

La Pérouse's expedition. The stirring events then convulsing the French kingdom had indeed drawn off public attention from scientific subjects; but when, in the beginning of 1791, the Parisian society of natural history called the attention of the National Assembly to the fact that nothing had been heard of the expedition for two years, and that though there was every reason to fear the ships had been wrecked, it was very probable that part of the crews might still survive among the islands in the Pacific, the government at once determined to fit out two

SCENE IN THE FRIENDLY ISLANDS.

new ships, whose mission should be partly to ascertain the fate of the missing voyagers, and partly to complete the task of exploration La Pérouse had so well begun. The vessels were appropriately named the Recherche and Espérance, and were placed under the command of Admiral Bruny D'Entrecasteaux and Captain Huon Kermadec. The expedition sailed from Brest Roads on the 28th September, 1791.

At the Cape of Good Hope, Admiral D'Entrecasteaux received some intelligence bearing in a very important manner upon the object of his voyage. Captain Hunter, of the Sirius, who had so liberally offered his services to La Pérouse at Botany Bay, had lost his ship at Norfolk Island, and was compelled to return home with his ship's company in a Dutch vessel. Near the Admiralty Islands, in the South Pacific, the commander and crew of the wrecked Sirius had seen several people clothed in European costume, and some of them, especially, appeared to be wearing French uniforms. Captain Hunter, who had frequently seen La Pérouse and his companions, at once declared his belief that these uniforms had been worn by men of the crews of the Boussole and the Astrolabe. Captain Hunter reported this circumstance at Batavia, and hence the report was carried to the Cape. The statements made by the two captains, which were taken down in writing and duly signed by them, were too circumstantial to be disregarded. Though the Admiralty Islands were a long distance out of the intended route of La Pérouse, it was thought necessary that they should be explored; and some time was spent by D'Entrecasteaux in this task. No traces of the lost crews could be found, and the admiral accordingly sailed partly round New Holland, and then followed the route which La Pérouse had mentioned in his letter of February, 1788, as his intended course. The naturalist La Billardière, who, with other scientific men, was attached to the expedition, and who afterwards published a well-written and interesting narrative of the voyage, did good service by a careful examination of the productions of the various countries at which the Espérance and the Recherche touched in their cruise; and thus the voyage of D'Entrecasteaux had a practical result in the advancement of natural history, as well as of geographical science. But so far as its main object was concerned, the expedition failed utterly. In spite of the minutest inquiries and the most diligent researches in the Friendly Islands, not one scrap of information could be gathered concerning the Boussole or the Astrolabe; and at length D'Entrecasteaux felt convinced that La Pérouse had never visited that group at all. Sickness now broke out among the crews to an alarming extent, and D'Entrecasteaux resolved to return home. In his course he passed near the Queen Charlotte Islands, one of which he named, after his own ship, Isle de Recherche. By this time, however, he was convinced that La Pérouse's ships must have foundered far from land, and accordingly he did not explore Isle de Recherche so minutely as he would have done had it been encountered earlier in the voyage. Soon afterwards Admiral D'Entrecasteaux and his colleague, Captain Huon Kermadec, died. The pestiferous climate of Java proved fatal to a great many of the sailors, ninety-nine out of two hundred and nineteen perishing, the great majority in Java itself; and at last, as war had broken out, in 1792, between the French and Dutch, the ships were

THE VOYAGE OF LA PÉROUSE.

seized as prizes by the authorities, and the unfortunate officers lost their commissions. Thus ended the voyage of D'Entrecasteaux; and for many years the adventures and the doubtful fate of La Pérouse were forgotten in the tempest of war that swept over Europe during the period of the first French Republic, Consulate, and Empire.

By a strange chance, when all prospect that the question of La Pérouse's fate would ever be settled had long been abandoned, the mystery in which the end of his voyage had been shrouded was dispelled. The Feejee Islands were then, as now, inhabited by a degraded race, savage, brutal, and treacherous. Nevertheless, European vessels used not unfrequently to touch at those far-off nooks for cargoes of sandal-wood; and sometimes parties of the natives were induced, by presents of arms and ammunition, to give their assistance in loading the ship. Occasionally, also, a sailor would run from a ship and hide himself on shore till his vessel had sailed, preferring the rude liberty of savage life on shore to the treatment too frequently endured by "the dog before the mast" at sea. These settlers, many of whom were very doubtful characters, frequently took part in the wars of the natives; and more than once the natives of an island have risen against the white strangers and massacred them every one. Something of this kind happened in 1813, when the ship Hunter, Captain Robson, was lying at one of the Feejee Islands, loading with sandal-wood. One day a Prussian named Martin Buschart, and a Lascar named Achowha, the former accompanied by a Feejee wife, came in great dismay to take refuge on board Captain Robson's vessel. They were the sole survivors of a general massacre organised by the natives, who had killed and devoured every other foreign resident in the island. The fugitives begged to be put on shore on the first habitable land the Hunter should pass; and they were left among the natives of Tucopia, one of the Queen Charlotte group.

Thirteen years later, Captain Dillon, of the St. Patrick, who had been on board the Hunter in 1813, happened to come in sight of Tucopia on a voyage to Pondicherry, in the East Indies. A feeling of natural curiosity to ascertain whether the old Prussian and his companion survived, prompted him to bring the ship to; and presently, among the swarms of canoes that put off from the shore to trade with the strangers, Captain Dillon saw one rowed by the identical Martin Buschart and his Lascar friend. The latter sold to the gunner of the St. Patrick a silver sword-hilt; and on inquiry, Martin Buschart told

how at his first arrival he had seen on the island many articles of
French manufacture, such as cups, knives, axes, and iron bolts. These
articles, he had afterwards ascertained, came from Manicolo, an island
two days' sail to the west. The story told him concerning them was
to the effect that two ships had come to Manicolo—the very Recherche
Island which D'Entrecasteaux had neglected to explore. One of these
ships, said the islanders, had been wrecked in deep water, and all her
crew perished; the other had been thrown on a coral reef, and her
people had lived for some time on shore, employed in constructing a new
ship from the wreck of the old one. At last they had sailed away,
leaving several of their number behind on the island. Now it happened that Captain Dillon had heard of the voyage and disappearance
of La Pérouse, whose initials he, moreover, fancied he recognised on
the silver sword-hilt. The story of the islanders also seemed to point
to La Pérouse's expedition; and Captain Dillon determined to examine
Manicolo for himself, and set the matter at rest. But baffling winds
and scarcity of provisions forbade him to linger on his voyage, and
he was obliged, in the interest of his owners, to make the best of his
way to Pondicherry, the port of his destination.

Captain Dillon did not fail, on his arrival, to make known what he
had seen and heard, and strongly represented to the government the
desirableness of sending a ship to Manicolo, and, if possible, to ascertain the fate of La Pérouse. He offered to conduct the inquiry himself,
and, indeed, his long experience in the Pacific and among the Society
Islands rendered him peculiarly fit for the duty. He was duly provided
with a ship, and in 1827 started on his mission. At Tucopia he
procured an interpreter, and proceeded to Manicolo, where the natives
told him a story of whose truth he obtained abundant proofs. That
two ships had been wrecked upon the coral reef that surrounded their
island, as reported by Martin Buschart and the Lascar, they declared
to be true. One ship, the smaller, no doubt the Astrolabe, had sunk
in deep water with all her crew, at a place called Whannow; while
the other and larger vessel ran on the coral reef at some distance from
Whannow, and remained fixed in the rock, so that her crew could get
ashore. For five months they remained on the island, occupied in
building a two-masted ship from the wreck of their own. The people
had an idea that they were magicians, inasmuch as they conversed with
the sun and stars through a long stick—the "long stick" in question
being, of course, the telescope used in astronomical observations.

THE VOYAGE OF LA PÉROUSE. 297

Some of these men, said the natives, used to stand on one leg, and hold a bar of iron in their hands—these must have been the sentries.

A more astounding assertion was the one that the strangers had noses a yard long; but the ingenious reader will conjecture that these "long noses" were the cocked hats to which Frenchmen have in all ages been greatly addicted. The Lascar had seen two Frenchmen

REPUBLICANS ESCORTING LOUIS XVI. TO PARIS.

on the island. One of them had died three years before Captain Dillon's visit; the other had departed from the island in the suite of a fugitive chief, who had been compelled to retreat from Manicolo after being worsted in battle.

Captain Dillon now set himself to the task of collecting relics in corroboration of this account, and he found sufficient to set all doubts at rest. The natives came forward with a number of articles, some of which were easily identified. Among these were a piece of a ship's back-board displaying a fleur-de-lis, a part of a theodolite, a ship's bell with a French inscription, a number of bolts and bars, fragments of china, and pieces of philosophical instruments. On examining the reef on which the larger ship was reported to have sunk, the captain raised several brass guns. With these practical proofs of his success he returned to Calcutta, and thence went to Paris, where the king, Charles X., liberally rewarded him for his exertions. Complete certainty was attained when an expert English genealogist identified the arms engraved on a candlestick—one of the relics brought home by Captain Dillon—as those of Colignon, one of the scientific men on board the Boussole.

Thus the fate of the two ships and of one of the crews was ascertained beyond a doubt. What became of the survivors and of the unfortunate commander himself after their departure from Manicolo will ever remain a mystery. That the two vessels should have been lost as they were is somewhat remarkable, when we consider that the natural prudence of the commander had been further stimulated by the unfortunate occurrence at Maouna; but, on the other hand, it must be remembered that so cautious and experienced a navigator as Cook himself barely escaped shipwreck on a coast where coral reefs rose suddenly out of the deep water as at Manicolo. The strangest part of the whole story is that an expedition sent out with the avowed purpose of ascertaining the navigator's fate, should, by an unlucky chance, have failed in its mission, while an English captain, turning out of his course to satisfy an impulse of curiosity in quite another direction, should stumble on the answer to the question that had been a mystery for nearly half-a-hundred years.

Of the importance of La Perousé's voyage, and of the merits of this commander as a navigator and explorer, there can be no doubt. Like Cook, whose example he quoted and followed on every important occasion, he was distinguished by continual vigilance and anxiety for the well-being of his crews, who enjoyed almost as complete an immunity from sickness as those of the Adventure and Discovery. A conscientious, painstaking man, he took care to perform his nautical duties with an honest thoroughness that has rendered his observations especially valuable. His examination of the coast of America to Monterez, and his investigations on the Tartar shore opposite Sagalin, supplied pages that had been wanting in the geography of the world.

Never, perhaps, did an explorer start with fairer prospects of success, or a more thorough determination to achieve it; never did voyage, begun under prosperous auspices, end more unhappily for those who

THE VOYAGE OF LA PÉROUSE. 299

undertook it. Still, though the lives of the brave commander and his followers were sacrificed in the cause, their efforts were not in vain; and the names of La Pérouse and of the voyages of the Boussole and Astrolabe are worthily inscribed on the glorious roll of the heroes of maritime discovery.

ALEXANDER VON HUMBOLDT AND HIS TRAVELS.

I.

Humboldt's Long and Arduous Career — His First Work — His Pursuit of Geology—His Appointment as Inspector of Mines—He Resolves to Travel—Verifies the Experiments of Galvani—Designs to Join Captain Baudin's Expedition to the Southern Hemisphere—On the Failure of that Expedition Resolves to Pass the Winter in Spain.

IN the year 1790, when the project of sending Admiral D'Entrecasteaux into the Pacific to search for La Pérouse was being mooted, there appeared a book on a subject then in its infancy, and very little understood even by scientific men. It was entitled *Observations on the Basalts of the Rhine*, and was published at Brunswick; it treated of certain geological facts, and was in many respects beyond the intellectual grasp of most readers of the day. It excited some attention, however, and the young Baron Humboldt, its author, was already spoken of as a man who had a great future before him. More than sixty years afterwards, in the year 1854, was completed a work of stupendous learning, research, and industry, entitled *Cosmos*. This book contained a great and exhaustive inquiry into the physical nature of the universe, comprising within itself deepest questions in astronomy, geology, distribution of climate, and, in fact, every department of science connected with the nature and operations of our planetary system. This book was by the same hand which in 1790 had indited the work on the basalts of the Rhine. Alexander von Humboldt, more than eighty years of age, was still hard at work, diligently and faithfully delving in the inexhaustible field of science. For more than sixty years had he been investigator, traveller, philosopher, and author; and though past the "fourscore years," the Scriptural limitation of the life of strong men, he still laboured day by day in his study, earnestly and patiently investigating those secrets which Nature only reveals as a reward for diligent and devoted toil.

LA GUAYRA, NEAR CARACCAS.

No scientific investigator has had such a career as Humboldt, no name has been more widely spread, more generally honoured, than his. Goethe, the poet, was called by his admirers "der Allseitige," the all-sided, for the wonderful diversity of knowledge he displayed; the term might with even greater aptness be applied to the great Prussian traveller and philosopher. No department of science was unfamiliar ohim, whether the subject under consideration was the physiognomy

of plants, the relative height of continents, the movements and magnitude of particular stars, the barometric measurement of the height of mountains, the habits of wild animals on the banks of the great South American rivers, the customs, languages, and manners of the still more savage human inhabitants of those regions, the structure and action of volcanoes, the direction of isothermal lines, or any other of the thousand and one branches into which physical science in its widest sense may be divided. Alexander von Humboldt could discourse upon each question as if it had been the one study of his life; and not the least remarkable point in his manner of treating every subject was the total absence of dogmatising self-assertion. In writing of matters which have been with him the peculiar study of years, and to the consideration of which he has brought all the stores of his vast intellect and varied experience, it is touching to observe him writing as if under correction; bringing forward his views as suggestions rather than as assertions, and showing in every line that he considers himself, after all his years of intense study, but a beginner in the mighty task of investigating the secrets and explaining the workings of Nature. No man has achieved more as a traveller, philosopher, or writer; no man has arrogated to himself less, or has been so willing to supplement and to correct his own views by a due and impartial consideration of the labours of others.

The travels of Humboldt occupy a separate and peculiar place in the history of scientific exploration. In maritime voyages the necessity of pursuing the path sketched out, the danger of going far from the ships, and, in many cases, the want of scientific apparatus, and, still more frequently, of leisure for making journeys into the interior of the countries visited, confined the area of investigation to the coasts, and prevented the commander at the head of the enterprise, or the scientific men acting under his directions, however active their zeal might be, from obtaining more than a "coast and island" knowledge of distant regions. Thus one after another, Cook, La Pérouse, and several other navigators, filled in strip by strip the chart of the coast of America from Behring Straits to Cape Horn. But of the wonders hidden in the pathless wilds of the vast regions bordering on the Amazon, the Essequibo, and the Orinoko, in South America—of the marvels of the Andes, and of the records of a past age hidden deep in the forests of Mexico and Peru—of these and a thousand other questions connected with the unexplored tracts alike of the New and of the Old World, of Asia and of America, the scientific world knew nothing until Humboldt, boldly penetrating into those regions, raised the veil which had hung over the climes where Nature is grandest in her manifestations, and returned from his travels to tell his countrymen and the world what things he had seen in wildernesses where the foot of civilised man had never passed till he startled their solitudes by his approach. Let those who would learn to appreciate the flood of light the researches of this greatest of scientific travellers has cast upon Central America and Asia read the admirable *Views of Nature*, in which some of the results of the travels of Humboldt have been epitomised. The vastness of his merits appears nowhere in more shining array than in that wonderful book, in which the veteran traveller has told in plain and simple language, which, however, here and there warms up into natural eloquence, what things he has seen and noted in his wanderings; and modestly, and with a certain graceful reticence infinitely pleasing in a man of such vast attainments, indicates rather than asserts the convictions to which he has been led by a long course of study and experiment.

Frederick Henry Alexander von Humboldt was born at Berlin in 1769, a year which gave to the world such great men as Napoleon, Wellington, and Cuvier. After studying at Göttingen and at Frankfort-on-the-Oder, where the bent of his mind towards investigations in natural science was sufficiently shown, he began his travels by a scientific journey through Germany, and a visit to England and Holland. Geology and botany, in the widest sense, were the studies to which he principally devoted his attention at this time. In 1791, soon after the publication of his work on the basalts of the Rhine, he proceeded to Freyberg, in Saxony, where at that time resided, as inspector of the royal mines, the celebrated Gottlieb Werner, who has been called the father of modern geology. Like several other men who afterwards became distinguished geologists, the young Baron Humboldt respectfully received the instructions of Werner; and, like many of his fellow-students, he found it necessary, at a subsequent period of his career, to forget, or at any rate greatly to modify, much that Werner had taught him. Werner, forming his conclusions from observations restricted to the mountain chains of Saxony, had started what was called the Neptunian theory, which ascribed an aqueous origin to all rocks; and this had not yet been opposed by the theory advanced at a later period by James Hutton, of Glasgow, a theory which very rightly pointed to the evident traces of fire on certain rocks, and declared the aqueous rocks to be the *débris* of earlier formations. The great contest between Neptunians and Plutonians had not yet commenced, and not till afterwards did "Stratum Smith" arise to point out that "both were right and both were wrong," and to put geology on a firm basis. Humboldt's mind was of too original and reflective a cast to be entirely swayed by the assertions of another; and in his works there is abundant proof that while he profited by Werner's instructions, he was not led away by the incorrect generalisation which introduced so much error into the Neptunian theories.

The geological acumen of Humboldt soon attracted attention, and between 1792 and 1795 he was first appointed assessor of the Council of Mines at Berlin, and afterwards director-general of the mines of the principalities of Anspach and Bayreuth, in Franconia. Fortunately for the interests of science, Humboldt was possessed of such ample private means that the emoluments of office were indifferent to him, and in 1795 he resigned his appointment, having resolved to travel. At this time he turned his attention to electrical science, and especially to the discoveries of Galvani, which were at that time looked upon with the scepticism in which ignorance loves to take refuge. Alexander von Humboldt not only repeated the experiments of Galvani, but corrected

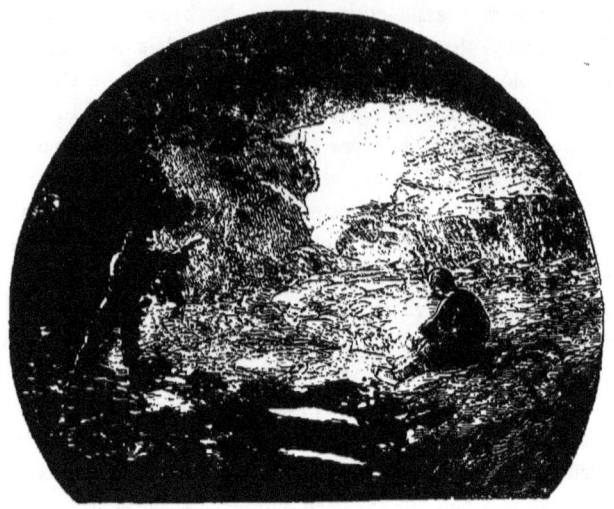

A SILVER MINE.

them in many important particulars. At this period it was that he also made the acquaintance of the celebrated naturalist Leopold von Buch, and of the French botanist Aimé Bonpland, who afterwards accompanied him in his travels. It was Humboldt's first intention to associate himself with an expedition of discovery that was to have been despatched to the southern hemisphere under Captain Baudin, a French man of science of considerable attainments. But France was at that time the Ishmaelite of nations. Her hand was against every man, as every man's hand was against her. The greatest efforts were necessary, the most heroic sacrifices had to be day by day repeated, to insure her national existence. The generals who won her battles on the frontiers had given up the very bullion on their epaulettes and on the facings of their uniforms to provide for the exigencies of the moment, and the government could not grant for scientific purposes the funds that were but too urgently required for powder and iron. The scheme of the voyage to the southern hemisphere was abandoned, and Humboldt and Bonpland now purposing to visit Northern Africa and investigate the flora and the geology of the Atlas range, waited at Marseilles for two months for the arrival of the frigate which was to convey the Swedish consul, who had promised them a passage. News came at last that the vessel had been injured by a storm, and would not sail for some time; accordingly Humboldt and Bonpland parted, and the former determined to pass the winter in Spain.

II.

Humboldt Receives Permission to Visit the Spanish Colonies in South America—Resolves to Travel to New Spain—Writes to Ask his Friend Bonpland to Join Him—Embarks for the West Indies on a Spanish Frigate—Visits the Peak of Teneriffe—The Dragon-Tree at Orotava—Humboldt's Interesting Views and Researches regarding the Age of Trees.

CIRCUMSTANCES now gave a new and far more important direction to our travellers' scheme than had been included in their first plan. Humboldt, who had already become a marked man in the scientific world, was everywhere received with great distinction; and the king, struck by the energy and enthusiasm of the young German stranger, no less than by his undoubted attainments, offered his guest permission to visit, under the government protection, each and every part of the Spanish colonial territory in America, and to make whatever scientific explorations and experiments he should think fit. This was a very valuable concession; for at that time the Spaniards, and indeed almost every nation, looked with suspicion and mistrust upon any stranger who visited their colonial dependencies. The sapient colonial governor had wondered how Cook and his companions could want " to see the north star go through the south pole;" and there was a tendency, both before and after that time, to attribute all exploring voyages and travels to political rather than to scientific motives. Humboldt himself felt the importance of the point he had gained. In his *Personal Narrative* he says—

"Never had so extensive a permission been granted to any traveller, and never had any traveller been honoured with more confidence on the part of the Spanish Government. To dissipate every doubt which the viceroys, or captains-general representing the royal authority in America, might entertain with respect to the nature of my labours, the passport of the *primera secretaria de estado* stated that I was authorised to make free use of my instruments of physic and geognosy, that I might make astronomical observations through the whole of the Spanish dominions, measure the height of mountains, examine the productions of the soil, and execute all operations which I might judge useful for the progress of the sciences. These orders of the court were strictly followed, even after the events which obliged M. d'Urquijo to quit the ministry. I endeavoured, on my part, to justify by my conduct these marks of unceasing attention. During my abode in America I presented the governors of the provinces with a duplicate of the materials which I had collected, and which might interest the mother country by throwing some light on the geography and the statistics of the colonies. Agreeably to the offer I had made before my departure, I addressed several geological collections to the cabinet of natural history of Madrid. The purpose of our journey being merely scientific, we succeeded in conciliating the friendship of the natives, and that of the Europeans entrusted with the administration of these vast countries. During the five years in which we travelled throughout the new continent we did not perceive the slightest mark of distrust; and we remember with pleasure that amidst the most painful privations, and whilst we were struggling against the obstacles which arose from the savage state of those regions, we never had to complain of the injustice of men."

Humboldt immediately wrote the good news to his friend Bonpland, at Paris, and enjoined him to make the best of his way to Spain. Bonpland obeyed the summons; and on the 5th of June the two travellers embarked at Corunna, on board the Spanish frigate Pizarro, on one of the most remarkable voyages of exploration ever undertaken for purely scientific purposes. From beginning to end, during the five years the expedition lasted, the mind of Humboldt was continually at work, and his notebooks soon became a storehouse of scientific wealth, as valuable for the facts they contained as for the new theories they suggested. Nothing seems to have disturbed the equanimity or damped the energy of the ardent inquirer, who found a congenial spirit in his young companion. Spain and England were at war at that time, the Pizarro was not in fighting condition, so a stringent regulation forbade the use of lights in the evening, even in the great cabin, lest the ship should be discovered and chased by the enemy's cruisers. This regulation was extremely irksome to the two investigators during the passages they made in their five years' travels; but Humboldt found out a way, by the use of dark lanterns, to satisfy the requirements of safety and yet to pursue his investigations in examining the nocturnal temperature of the water, and reading the numbers on astronomical instruments. During the run across the Atlantic his attention was especially turned to a question which till then had been only partially investigated, and to the elucidation of which Humboldt offered many new and important facts—the direction and velocity of ocean currents.

308   THE WORLD'S EXPLORERS.

His account of the Gulf Stream is especially interesting. Humboldt mentions how a branch of this stream every year deposits on the western

THE CAPYBARA, OR CAVY.

coasts of Iceland and Norway the fruit of trees which belong to the torrid zone of America, how on the shores of the Hebrides the reeds of the Mimosa scandens and many other plants of Jamaica, Cuba, and the mainland of America are collected; and how barrels of French wines, the remains of cargoes of ships wrecked in the West Indian seas, have found their way, in good preservation, to the western shores of Europe. Still more remarkable instances of the method in which ocean currents have become the means of communication between the Old World and the New are adduced in the *Personal Narrative.* "The wreck of an English vessel," he says, "the Tilbury, burnt near Jamaica, was found on the coasts of Scotland. On those same coasts various kinds of tortoises are sometimes found that inhabit the waters of the Antilles. When the western winds are of long duration, a current is formed in the high latitudes which runs directly towards the east-south-east, from the coasts of Greenland and Labrador as far as the north of Scotland. Wallace relates that twice, in 1682 and 1684, American savages of the race of the Esquimaux, driven out to sea in their leathern canoes during a storm, and left to the guidance of the currents, reached the Orcades. This last example is so much the more worthy of attention as it proves at the same time how, at a period when the art of navigation was yet in its infancy, the motion of the waters of the ocean would contribute to disseminate the different races of men over the face of the globe."

Subsequent travellers and men of science have pursued the investigations begun by Humboldt respecting the effects and the cause of the Gulf Stream; and Lieutenant Maury, of the United States navy, one of the foremost investigators of the natural phenomena of the ocean, has, in his valuable work, the *Physical Geography of the Sea,* advanced a theory which has superseded all former conjectures. Arguing on the well-known phenomena of tropical seas, he ascribes this great "river in the sea," like other ocean currents, to the disturbing influences of change of temperature expanding and contracting the water, and thus altering its relative density or weight.

At Teneriffe the travellers ascended the celebrated Peak, a volcano of very peculiar construction. Humboldt declares that its crater bears no resemblance to those of the majority of volcanoes he visited; for instance, those of Vesuvius, Jorullo in Mexico, or Pichincha in Peru, in which the crater is in the form of a cone, sloping gradually down from the apex to the base at about the same angle, and covered with a layer of small particles of pumice-stone. The Peak of Teneriffe, like Cotopaxi in Peru, has a wall surrounding the crater, "looking at a short distance like a cylinder on a truncated cone." The size of the crater of a volcano, Humboldt observes, is not directly proportioned to the height of the mountain or the intensity of its volcanic action. Thus Vesuvius, which, compared to the Peak of Teneriffe, is but a hill, has a much larger and wider crater than the latter mountain. The usual notion of a volcano presents to the mind the picture of a mountain of moderate height, of conical form, and having a circular opening or crater at the summit. This idea has arisen from the fact that Etna and Vesuvius have generally been considered as the models of all volcanoes. Humboldt, however, points out that the forms of volcanoes and of their craters are as various as are the manifestations of volcanic action themselves; that many of the highest volcanoes in the world, such as those in the lofty Andes range, have extremely small craters; and that the summit of a volcano is by no means the only outlet by which the volcanic force expends itself, lateral outlets or fissures in the side of the volcano often serving as passages for eruptive force. Here, as throughout the whole of his work, the author warns his readers and all scientific students against the mistake continually made in his day, and, as recent experiences would seem to indicate, equally rife in ours—namely, the error of forming general conclusions from a few restricted phenomena. "In order to raise ourselves to geological conceptions worthy of the greatness of Nature," he concludes a paragraph, " we must set aside the idea that all volcanoes are formed after the models of Vesuvius, Stromboli, and Etna."

The toil of climbing the Peak was amply repaid by the splendid view spread out before the travellers when they had reached the summit. The clearness of the air in this semi-tropical climate enabled the travellers to see much farther than they could have done in a higher latitude. Before them lay spread a glorious panorama of the whole Archipelago of the Canaries, the Fortunate Isles of the ancients, where the great myth placed the "Islands of the Blessed." The Peak has now been for many centuries in an inactive state, and its crater is what we call a solfatara; but Humboldt points out that a volcano, from whose fissures exude gases that raise a thermometer to 160 deg., cannot be considered extinct; and mentions the fact that in 1611 the crater of Vesuvius was in the condition of a solfatara, overgrown with shrubs and plants, as a proof that the Peak, like Vesuvius, may some day resume its activity, and burst out afresh into flame.

Near the small town of Orotava, the ancient Taoro, the travellers saw one of the most remarkable historical trees in the world. It was a dracœna, or dragon-tree, of colossal proportions, and was considered "as sacred in the eyes of the inhabitants of the Canaries as the olive-tree in the citadel of Athens, or the elm of Ephesus." This tree had been mentioned by the Norman adventurers De Béthencourt, who, at the beginning of the fifteenth century, conquered the Canary Islands, and was even then remarkable for its great age. In his *Views of Nature*, Humboldt, speaking of the age of trees, has inserted a very interesting note respecting the dragon-tree of Orotava. It appears he and Bonpland measured it several feet above the root, and found the circumference of the tree to be nearly 48 English feet. Lower down and nearer to the root, Le Dru, another naturalist, made it nearly 79 English feet, while Sir George Staunton found the diameter as much as 12 feet at the height of 10 feet above the ground. This dragon-tree was remarkable rather for its thickness than for its height, which latter did not exceed 69 English feet. "According to tradition," says Humboldt in the note, "this tree was worshipped by the Guanches" (the native inhabitants of the Canary Islands) "as the ash-tree of Ephesus was by the Greeks, or the Lydian plane-tree which Xerxes decked with ornaments, and the sacred banyan-tree of Ceylon, and at the time of the first expedition of the De Béthencourts, in 1402, it was already as thick and as hollow as it is now." Remembering that the dracœna grows extremely slowly, we are led to infer the high antiquity of the tree of Orotava. Berthollet, in his description of Teneriffe, says, "When we compare the young dragon-trees that stand around with the gigantic tree, the estimate we are compelled to make of the age of the latter becomes tremendous. The dragon-tree has been cultivated in the Canaries, and in Madeira, and Porto Santo, from the earliest times; and an accurate observer, Leopold von Buch, has even found it wild in Teneriffe, near Igneste. Its original country, therefore, is not India, as has long been believed; nor does its appearance in the Canaries contradict the opinion of those who regard the Guanches as having been an isolated Atlantic nation, without intercourse with African or Asiatic nations. . . . . It is affirmed that in the early times of the Norman and Spanish conquests in the fifteenth century, mass was said at a small altar erected in the hollow trunk of the tree. Unfortunately, the dragon-tree of Orotava lost one side of its top in the storm of the 21st July, 1819."

That some trees have a prodigious antiquity there is no doubt. It is told by Navarete that in 1503, when the ship of Gonzalo Coelho, a

Portuguese navigator, was wrecked on an island near the Gulf of Guinea (probably San Fernando Noronha) inscriptions were found in the bark of trees, of crosses and mottoes, left by navigators employed almost a century before by the Infante Don Henrique, surnamed the Discoverer, one of the first of those enlightened men whose efforts drew attention to the probable existence of a new world beyond the Atlantic. On one tree was the date 1435, and the motto of Don Henrique, "Talent de bien faire." On another appeared an inscription with a date ninety years before. Decandolle, the French naturalist, writing on the longevity of trees, assigns to a yew he saw at Braborne, in Kent,

an age of three thousand years, making his estimate from the annual rings formed under the bark, and the ratio of time between the thickness of the wood and the period of growth. Similar calculations have assigned to the Scotch yew of Fortingal an age of from twenty-five to twenty-six centuries; to those of Crowhurst, in Surrey, and of Ripon, in Yorkshire, fourteen and twelve centuries. At Hildesheim, in Germany, there is a wild rose-tree in the crypt of the cathedral, the root of which is certainly proved to be a thousand years old. The cathedral itself dates from the time of Louis the Pious, the son and successor of Charlemagne, who died in 840, and founded the cathedral some twenty years before his death. In the archives of Hildesheim there is an original document of the eleventh century, two centuries only after the foundation of the cathedral, which tells us that when Bishop Hezilo rebuilt the cathedral, which had been destroyed by fire, he inclosed the roots of the rose-tree of Louis, the founder, with a vault (which still exists), and built upon this vault the crypt, which was reconsecrated in 1061, and spread abroad the branches of the rose-tree upon the walls. The stem, $26\frac{1}{2}$ feet high and 2 inches in diameter, and the spreading branches covering part of the wall of the crypt, are still full of life and vigour; and the tree is justly celebrated as a veteran whose age has been verified by documentary evidence.

314   THE WORLD'S EXPLORERS.

III.

Various Zones of Vegetation in the Island of Teneriffe—Passage to the West Indies—Observations on Atlantic and other Ocean Currents—Great Beds of Seaweed—The Sargasso Sea—Arrival in the West Indies—A Doctor Sangrado—Earthquakes and Eruptions of Volcanoes—Connection of the Phenomena—Humboldt's Views on Volcanic Action.

THE island of Teneriffe was a mine of botanical wealth to our travellers. As Humboldt had afterwards occasion to remark concerning Peru, some countries offer in themselves the productions of various climes and regions, the different productions being arranged in zones or belts, according to the height above the sea level of the places where they flourish. Thus in Teneriffe the productions of tropical countries, the bread-fruit-tree, cinnamon-tree, and others, grow and flourish. The zone of laurels is the next; and this comprises the woody part of Teneriffe. Four species of laurel, an oak species resembling that of Thibet, a native olive, and many myrtles, form, with the chestnut-tree, the staple vegetation of this zone. The third zone, beginning between five and six thousand feet above the level of the sea, offers a great forest of pines, with some cedars interspersed. The fourth and fifth zones, occupying heights equal to the most inaccessible summits of the Pyrenees, and generally volcanic in character, offered flowering-plants of Alpine broom, "that form oases amidst a vast sea of ashes." Two herbaceous plants, the Scrofularia glabrata and the Viola cheiranthifolia, are also found there; and almost to the summit of the Peak lichens are found among the scorified matter, the evidence of the former action of fiery forces. "By this unceasing action of organic forces," says Humboldt, "the empire of Flora extends itself over islands ravaged by volcanoes."

The run from Teneriffe to the West Indies was not marked by any stirring incidents; but Humboldt, whose active mind was easily roused to speculation and theory, made the floating seaweed that was passed in great quantities during part of their passage the occasion of a very valuable treatise on the position of banks of seaweed, as caused and modified by the position and direction of ocean currents. Already in the ancient writers mention is made of a part of the sea where the ships of the Phœnicians, pushing out westward into the great Atlantic, were checked in their course by great masses of weed, forming sea meadows, or connected masses of weed. Some part of these rumours spread by the Phœnicians Humboldt ascribes with great probability to Punic artifice. A great trading nation, having in its own hands the profitable maritime commerce of the Atlantic, would naturally seek to deter other nations from entering into rivalry and competition by an exaggerated account of the dangers and difficulties to be encountered in the navigation of the seas. Some record of the enormous banks of fucus or seaweed to be found in a particular region of the Atlantic had been handed down from ancient times; and the Sargasso Sea, as it is called, is, in fact, the part of the great ocean to which currents from various quarters drift the waifs and strays of marine vegetation. There they accumulate, and are tossed up and down on the long swell of the Atlantic. Fernando Columbus, the son of the great discoverer of America, graphically describes how the fears of the sailors in his father's ships were excited by the immense masses of weed, in which they feared the vessels would be entangled. In the three centuries which have elapsed since the time of Columbus, the position of the great fucus banks has remained the same.

With respect to the appearance of these masses of weed on the surface, Humboldt says, "Though a species of seaweed has been seen with stems 800 feet long" (he is here alluding to the Fucus giganteus of Forster), " the growth of these marine cryptogamia being extremely rapid, it is not less certain that, in the latitude we have just described, the fuci, far from being fixed to the bottom, float in separate masses on the surface of the water. In this state the vegetation can hardly con-

SCENE IN THE ANDES.

tinue a longer time than it would do in a branch of a tree torn from its trunk; and, in order to explain how moving masses are found for ages in the same position, we must admit that they owe their origin to submarine rocks, which, situated at forty or sixty fathoms depth, continually supply what has been carried away by the equinoctial currents."

A malignant fever broke out on board the Pizarro during the passage to Cumana, and a poor young Spaniard, the son of a widow, who had quitted his native land hoping to make his fortune in the New World, fell a victim to the disease after an illness of a couple of days. The fever was ascribed by Humboldt, no doubt correctly, to the incumbered state of the ship, and to the total neglect of ventilation and of ordinary sanitary measures. The working of the ship and the quickness of the passage seemed the two points upon which the attention of those in authority was concentrated; and even after the

JAGUAR, PUMA, AND LYNX

fever had broken out, no measures were taken to confine its ravages. The ignorant Gallician surgeon, a very Doctor Sangrado, ordered copious bleeding of the patients, on the convenient ground that the fever arose from corruption and heat of the blood; of the ordinary fever-bark there was not a single ounce on board. No wonder, therefore, that besides the poor young Spaniard a sailor was speedily at the point of death. The astute surgeon had given up his case as hopeless, and announced that the time had come when the last sacraments of the Roman Catholic Church should be administered to the dying man. The custom on board Spanish ships prescribes that the sacrament should be solemnly borne in procession, preceded by lighted tapers, to he bedside of the sufferer; and as the unhappy sailor was lying in a hammock, with a space of barely ten inches between his face and the deck, it became necessary to remove him to a more convenient spot for receiving the last rites. A berth was accordingly prepared, *in an airy situation*, near the hatchway; and the shipmates of the sick sailor saw with intense astonishment that their unfortunate comrade, who had been slowly suffocating in his miserable den, began to recover so soon as he was placed in a position where he could breathe freely. From the day when he quitted the middle deck the sailor's condition began to amend; whereupon the Gallician Sangrado, imperturbable in his stupidity, and strong in prejudice, insisted on seeing in this wonderful recovery an additional proof of the efficacy of bleeding and purging, and was more than ever confirmed in his own method of practice. "We soon felt the fatal effects of this treatment," says Humboldt. "and wished more than ever to reach the coast of America."

The city of Cumana, at the time when the travellers arrived, was only recovering from the effects of a tremendous earthquake that had almost destroyed it eighteen months before. Indeed, the frequency and violence of the earthquakes forbade the erection of any great or important buildings; unlike Quito, where earthquakes frequently occur, but where lofty and sumptuous churches have, nevertheless, been erected. Humboldt points out this difference, and attributes the greater violence of the earthquakes at such places as Cumana and Lima to the fact of their being distant from any great volcano; and thus their earthquakes are not merely oscillations of the ground, but in their phenomena and effects resemble the bursting of subterranean mines. In an excellent chapter in another of his works he gives an admirably lucid theory of the structure and action of volcanoes in various parts of the earth, pointing out the evident and close analogy between eruptions of burning mountains and the action of earthquakes, as manifestations of the subterranean powers called "volcanic force." He shows that volcanoes are evidently natural vents for the escape of volcanic matter, and adduces facts to show that there are subterranean communications, not only between volcanoes situated at great distances from each other, but even between countries in which there are no volcanoes. Where volcanoes occur, either in a line or scattered over an area, the subterranean fire breaks out sometimes from one summit, sometimes from another. When these forces can no longer find a vent through the craters of active volcanoes, solfataras or extinct craters sometimes are restored to renewed activity. In other cases new craters are formed, frequently in the shape of great rifts or clefts on the sides of mountains; or the force, acting in a horizontal instead of in a perpendicular direction, causes the surface of the earth to heave and swell, and occasionally to burst, and then there is an earthquake. In the above-mentioned dissertation, "On the Structure and Mode of Action of Volcanoes," read by him in the Academy at Berlin, in 1823, Humboldt says—"Even the earthquakes which occasion such dreadful ravages in this part of the world afford remarkable proofs of the existence of subterranean communications, not only between countries where there are no volcanoes (a fact which had long been known), but also between fire-emitting openings situated at great distances asunder. Thus in 1797 the volcano of Pasto, east of the Guaytara River, emitted uninterruptedly for three months a lofty column of smoke, which column disappeared at the instant when, at a distance of 240 geographical miles, the great earthquake of Riobamba and the immense mud-eruption called 'Moya' took place, which caused the death of between thirty and forty thousand persons. The sudden appearance of the island of Sabrina, near the Azores, on the 30th of January, 1811, was the precursor of the terrible earthquake movements which, much farther to the west, shook almost incessantly, from the month of May, 1811, to June, 1813, first the West India Islands, then the plain of the Ohio and Mississippi, and, lastly, the opposite coast of Venezuela or Caranas.

"Thirty days after the destruction of the principal city of that province the volcano of the island of St. Vincent, which had long been quiescent, burst out into eruption. A remarkable phenomenon accompanied this outburst. At the moment when the explosion took place, on the 30th of April, 1811, a loud subterranean noise was heard in South America, which spread terror and dismay over a district of

35,200 geographical square miles. The dwellers on the banks of the Apure, near the junction of the river Nula, and the inhabitants of the most distant part of the seacoast of Venezuela, alike compared the sound to that of the discharge of great pieces of ordnance. Now, from the confluence of the Nula with the Apure to the volcano of St. Vincent is a distance in a straight line of 628 English geographical square miles. The sound, which certainly was not propagated through the air, must have proceeded from a deep-seated subterranean cause, for its intensity was scarcely greater on the seacoast nearest to the volcano where the eruption was taking place than in the interior of the country, in the basin of the Apure and the Orinoko."

The well-known fact that at the time of the great earthquake of November 1st, 1755, at Lisbon, the sea in the north of Europe rose suddenly many feet above its ordinary level on the Swedish coast, and that the Swiss cities were violently agitated as if by a storm, may be cited in support of the theory of the widespread action of subterranean volcanic forces. Even among the Eastern islands of the West India group, such as Martinique, Antigua, and Barbadoes, where the tide never exceeds thirty inches, the sea suddenly rose more than twenty feet.

"All these phenomena," says the great philosopher, "show the operation of subterranean forces, acting either dynamically in earthquakes, in the tension and agitation of the crust, or in volcanoes, in the production and the chemical alteration of substances. They also show that these forces do not act superficially in the thin outermost crust of the globe, but from great depths in the interior of our planet, through crevices or unfilled veins, affecting at one and the same time points of the earth's surface at a great distance from each other."

IV.

Treatment of Slaves—The Marshes of Araya—Salt Works—A Castilian Shoemaker—Cheap Immortality—Manners and Customs of the Natives of Araya—Effect of the Dominion of the Priests—The Capuchins of Caripe—Cavern of the Guacharo—Nocturnal Birds—Singular Method of Procuring Oil—Abundant and Varied Flora of Caripe—The Vultures of Cumana—Their Lazy Habits.

BY astronomical measurement Humboldt ascertained the real longitude and latitude of Cumana, and of many other places, which had been erroneously stated in the maps. The greater part of his time at Cumana was occupied in astronomical labours which furnished data for his subsequent works. The travellers were struck by the wretched condition of the slaves, and wondered at the indifference with which cruelties were inflicted upon these unfortunate people, who were not more considered or protected than if they had been so many head of cattle. The practice of branding them with a hot iron on the arms or the forehead that they might be known in case of an attempted escape was universal; and they were sold in open market without any restriction, the age of the slave being ascertained, like that of a horse, by forcing open his mouth and examining his teeth. In reference to the slaves and their condition, Humboldt quotes the noble passage of La Bruyère :—" We find (under the torrid zone) certain wild animals, male and female, scattered through the country, black, livid, and scorched all over by the sun, bent to the earth, which they dig and turn up with indefatigable perseverance. They have something like an articulate voice, and when they stand up on their feet they exhibit a human face, and, in fact, these creatures are men."

The great salt marshes of Araya, worked by the Spanish government and a source of considerable profit, constitute one of the sights in the neighbourhood of Cumana. A calculation of the amount of salt consumed by the inhabitants of the two provinces of Cumana and Barcelona in 1799 and 1800 gave the astonishing quantity of sixty pounds for each person, while in France, where a few years previously a similar calculation had been made to assess the value of the *gabelle*, or salt-tax, only twelve to fourteen pounds were reckoned by M. Necker, the minister of finance, as consumed by each individual. The difference is partly attributed to the quantity of salt employed in curing meat.

Y

The inhabitants of the peninsula of Araya were a harmless set of black men, living chiefly on the fish they caught, and as shiftless and idle as negroes almost invariably are. When their visitors expressed surprise that they did not cultivate gardens, in which with little trouble they might raise abundance of vegetables and fruit, they replied that their gardens were beyond the gulf, meaning that they could bring back vegetables and fruit from Cumana, whither they carried their fish for sale. They had a very fine breed of goats, which roamed in wild freedom among the mountains, each, however, bearing the mark of its owner. It is recorded as a trait of unusual generosity among these people that when a hunter kills a goat bearing one of these marks, he immediately carries it to the family whose property the mark indicates it to be, and any wrongful appropriation of a goat is extremely rare.

"Dans le pays des aveugles les borgnes sont rois," says the old French proverb. An illustration of this truth was found at Araya, where the travellers encountered one of these one-eyed kings of the blind. The following account is given of him:—"Among the mulattoes, whose huts surround the salt lake, we found a shoemaker of Castilian descent. He received us with the air of gravity and self-sufficiency which in those climes characterises almost all who are conscious of possessing some peculiar talent. He was employed in stretching the string of his bow, and sharpening his arrows to kill birds. His trade of a shoemaker could not be very lucrative in a country where the majority of the inhabitants go barefoot; but he only complained that, on account of the dearness of European gunpowder, a man of his quality was reduced to employ the weapons used by the Indians. He was the wise man of the plain; he knew how the salt was formed by the influence of the sun and the full moon, could tell the symptoms of earthquakes, distinguish the marks by which mines of gold and silver are discovered, and select medicinal plants, which, like all other colonists from Chili to California, he divided into two classes, hot and cold (exciting and debilitating). Having collected the traditions of the country, he gave us some curious accounts of the pearls of Cubagna, articles of luxury for which he expressed the profoundest contempt. To show us how familiar the sacred writings were to him, he took a pride in quoting to us the patriarch Job, who preferred wisdom to all the pearls of the Indies. His philosophy was circumscribed by the narrow range of his daily wants. A very strong ass, which should be able to carry a heavy load of vegetables to the *embarcadere*, was the only possession he coveted." This sage with a great flourish presented a few very small and opaque pearls to his visitors, but the philosophic contemner of this world's goods had sufficient vanity to beg that the travellers would note in their tablets for future publication the fact that a poor shoemaker of Araya, but a white man, and of noble Castilian race, had been able to give away what on the other side of the great sea (a figurative expression among the colonists for Europe) was sought for as a very precious thing. Humboldt promised to make a note of it, and was as good as his word; and thus the philosophic cobbler of Cumana purchased immortality at the price of a few pearls, "small in size and opaque in colour." A shrewd sage, with no small share of the wisdom of the serpent in his composition.

The narrative mentions that in crossing the barren hills of Cape Cirial, the strong smell of petroleum was perceived by the travellers. The first historians of these regions, including Oviedo, had mentioned the petroleum springs as fountains of "a resinous, aromatic, and medicinal liquor," but neither they nor the later explorers had any idea what an important part petroleum was destined in future days to play in commerce. A great marvel was shown to the travellers in the shape of the eye-stone, or *piedra de las ojos*. This production was described by the colonists as one of the marvels of nature, being at once a stone or an animal. Motionless when found in the sand, they declared that when placed on a polished surface, such as a metal or earthenware plate, and excited by lemon-juice, it showed signs of life and moved. Placed in the eye, it turned about and expelled any foreign substance that might accidentally or otherwise be there. At the salt-works and at the village of Maniquarez, where a great many of these eye-stones were offered to the strangers, the natives were especially anxious to show their visitors the efficacy of this wonderful substance, and obligingly offered to put sand in the travellers' eyes, and afterwards show them how easily the eye-stone would expel every particle. A very simple explanation of the marvel is offered by our author. The wonderful stones are nothing more than little convex slabs of a small univalve shell of a chalky nature. When brought into contact with an acid, this chalk or lime effervesces and moves by the action which disengages the carbonic acid. Introduced into the eye, especially with the addition of lemon-juice, the stones naturally increase the flow of tears, and thus every foreign substance is expelled. The inhabitants of Araya, however, utterly refused to believe in the correctness of this explanation, and greatly preferred believing in the supernatural virtues of their eye-stone.

A journey to the interior, to the missions of the Chayma Indians and the mountains of New Andalusia, opened new and wondrous scenes. It was the 4th of September when they set out. The morning was deliciously cool, and the road along the bank of the Manzanares, the river which flows through Cumana, was fragrant with rich vegetation, and presently led through forests of palm-trees and arborescent ferns. The great traveller discusses in a liberal and kindly spirit the nature and effect of the Roman Catholic missions established among the Indians. While fully recognising the benefits of the security afforded to the Indians, and the mildness of the rule established over them, he is far too clear-sighted and too honest to overlook the weak points of the system. The Indians appear, like the Tahitians and other nations among whom missions have been established, to have been denationalised and reduced to a state of helpless dependence, which has rendered them utterly childish. On some swarthy countenances, indeed, the travellers read a lurking expression of defiance which seemed to indicate that the control in which the Indians were kept was anything but welcome; but in general the people appeared thoroughly helpless, pliant, and submissive, anxious to please those in authority over them, with no intellect or judgment of their own, and ready to acquiesce in any proposition or assertion advanced by a white man. Thus the author especially warns those travellers who may come after him to be cautious of valuing "information" received from Indians at more than its worth, for they will frequently fill in details and narrate stories that have no foundation in truth, merely to please their audience. The system of the missions also kept them isolated and apart from each other, so that there was little chance of their development, either intellectually or nationally.

In descending the mountains, occasions frequently occurred to show the admirable sure-footedness of the mules used among the passes. "We found this passage difficult," says Humboldt, "because at that time we had not climbed the Cordilleras; but it is by no means so perilous as they are fond of representing it at Cumana. The path is indeed in several places only fourteen or fifteen inches broad, and the ridge of the mountain, along which the road runs, is covered with a short and exceedingly slippery turf; the slopes on each side are steep, and the traveller, if he should stumble, might slide down on the grass to the depth of seven or eight hundred feet." But the mules were fully equal to the occasion whenever a dangerous spot occurred. They fully understood the nature of the ground they had to traverse; and when they felt there was danger, always stopped, turning their heads uneasily to right and left. They seem to be considering the course they shall pursue, and if left to themselves, and not hurried or forced forward by the traveller, will always bring him safely out of the

MOUNTAIN REGION.

difficulty. They seem to exert a reasoning power beyond and above mere instinct; and this power is fully recognised and valued by their owners. "It is on the frightful roads of the Andes," says the *Personal Narrative*, "during journeys of six or seven months across mountains furrowed by torrents, that the intelligence of horses and beasts of burden displays itself in an astonishing manner. Thus the mountaineers are heard to say, 'I will not give you the mule whose step is easiest, but him who reasons best (*la mas racional*).' This popular saying, dictated by long experience, combats the system that makes animals animated machines, better, perhaps, than all the arguments of speculative philosophy."

A considerable stay was made at a convent of Arragonese Capuchins, at Caripe. The convent itself was built in front of an enormous wall of perpendicular rock, of resplendent whiteness, and the scenery reminded the travellers of a Derbyshire valley. The monks received their visitors with great hospitality, and offered them every facility for carrying on their scientific labours. The fraternity possessed a tolerable library, in which their visitors noticed with surprise the *Lettres Edifiantes*, the *Teatro Critico* of Feijo, and Nollet's *Traité d'Electricité*. It is recorded as greatly to their credit, that though they knew Humboldt to be a Protestant, they never showed a symptom of intolerance or any disposition to meddle with him on religious matters. He tells us that "No mark of distrust, no indiscreet question, no attempt at controversy ever diminished the value of the hospitality they exercised with so much liberality and frankness." The travellers were, indeed, in a kind of scientific paradise. The flora that surrounded them, the geological formations, the various animals that ranged the forests, the very stars in the sky above them, all were as books requiring to be read and studied; and not a day passed that did not bring an accession to their store of information, and to the splendid collection of plants, minerals, and insects they were diligently bringing together.

The chief object of attraction to scientific visitors in the valley of Caripe is undoubtedly the Great Cueva, or cavern of the Guacharo. The name means the cavern of noise or lamentations, and has its origin in the fact that this cavern is the haunt of thousands of nocturnal birds, who are very noisy, and fill their subterranean dwelling with their wailing cries. Humboldt and Bonpland, accompanied by the alcaids, or Indian magistrates, and by a number of monks from the mission, paid a visit to this remarkable cavern. The entrance of the cave is described as "majestic even to the eye of a traveller accustomed to the picturesque scenes of the higher Alps." Humboldt, who had already seen the caverns of the Derbyshire Peak, of the Carpathian and Hartz mountains, and the vast stone caverns of Franconia, with their petrified remains of tigers, hyenas, and bears, was singularly impressed with the magnitude and grandeur of this Caripe cavern. The entrance itself was eighty feet broad and seventy-two feet high, and formed an enormous archway in a vertical rock, festooned to its summit with magnificent flowering plants—bignonias of violet blue, the purple dolichos, and magnificent solandras of orange hue, with fleshy tubes more than four inches long. Not only the outside, but the inside also of the cavern was magnificent with luxuriant tropical vegetation. Plantain-leaved heliconias eighteen feet high, the praga palm tree, and arborescent arums flourished in the semi-darkness of what may be called the vestibule of the cavern of Caripe, to between thirty and forty feet from the entrance. As the travellers penetrated into the darkness, the shrill voices of the nocturnal birds were heard, growing louder and more menacing as the intruders advanced into the gloom. Four hundred and thirty feet from the entrance, it became necessary to light the torches. The guacharo is about the size of a hen; it has a plumage of dark bluish grey, tinged with small streaks or specks of black, and with white heart-shaped spots on the head, wings, and tail. Its cry is something like the croak of the crow. These strange nocturnal birds are hunted once a year, at midsummer, by the Indians, who enter the cavern armed with long poles, with which they destroy many nests, and kill some thousands of the birds. The guacharo would have become as extinct as the dodo but for the superstition of the natives, who are exceedingly averse from entering the cavern, except in large companies on the occasion of their annual hunt. The birds are exceedingly fat; the inert nature of their lives, and the darkness in which they sit cowering month after month, give them the appearance of having been fattened by some artificial process, instead of being lean and skinny like the nocturnal birds of Europe, who live on the scanty prey they hunt with much muscular exertion and toil; while the frugivorous guacharo finds his meal upon every shrub and tree. The abundant fat, called guacharo oil or butter, is melted out of the dead birds. It has the property of keeping fresh and pure for more than a year. Thus this "oil harvest" is a very important time for the Indians. The monks also make extensive use of the guacharo oil; and a family of Indians, who dwell near the cavern and assume to be the original proprietors of this singular preserve, are compelled to furnish a certain quantity of oil for the use of the convent lamps and the convent kitchen. The good monks asserted, indeed, that only for the church lamps was the oil supplied gratis, and that they paid for all the rest; but Humboldt seems to have shrewdly doubted this statement, and there is an under-current of polished irony in the sentences in which he describes the relations between the Morocoymas Indians and their monkish neighbours. "We shall not decide," he says, "either on the legitimacy of the rights of the Morocoymas, or on the origin of the obligation imposed on the natives by the monks. It would seem natural that the produce of the chase should belong to those who hunt; but in the forests of the New World, as in the centre of European cultivation, public right is modified according to the relations which are established between the strong and the weak, the victors and the vanquished." Was there ever a more polite and euphuistic method of proclaiming the hard truth that "might is right, all the world over?"

For the space of 1,458 feet the grotto of Caripe preserves its original form, dimensions, and direction. A small river flows through it, and about fifteen hundred feet from the entrance forms a cascade. The natives were superstitiously reluctant to advance far into the cavern, whose darkness and solitude had for them the terrors with which these attributes are associated in the minds of all uneducated nations. Man should avoid places, they declared, where neither the sun nor the moon gives light. To go and join the guacháros would he to go and seek their fathers—namely, to die. Magicians and poisoners performed their incantations at the entrance of the cavern, to conjure the chief of the evil spirits. After penetrating for some distance farther into the cavern the Indians definitively "struck;" and all the persuasions and authority of the monks could not overcome their superstitious terrors, or induce them to advance one step farther into what was to them the Cavern of Cocytus, peopled with the spirits of the dead. Strangely universal is the tendency in man to associate darkness with ideas of death, while light everywhere typifies life and joy. The travellers were accordingly obliged to retrace their steps, and grope their way out of the cavern; and even Humboldt confesses he was glad to emerge from a region whose darkness was not even accompanied by the peace associated with solitude and silence. From the report of the monks, it appeared that a certain bishop of St. Thomas in Guyana had penetrated farther than our travellers had proceeded into the gloomy cavern. Provided with good waxen torches, which give much light without the suffocating smoke inseparable from those made of bark and resin, he had worked his way for a distance of 2,500 feet into the cave without finding any indication of its ending. At the entrance the monks had prepared a little feast for our travellers in honour of the occasion, and Humboldt and Bonpland sat down on the bank of the river, at the entrance of the cavern, to a repast spread on leaves of banana and heliconia large enough to serve as tablecloths.

On their return to Cumana, the travellers noticed large flocks of a species of vulture perched on the cocoa trees, and roosting in rows like fowls. They appeared of a very lazy disposition, going to roost long before sunset, and slumbering on until long after the sun had risen.

The same tendency to close before sundown and not to unfold their leaves until some time after sunrise was noticed in many of the plants of these regions.

MADRID.

V.

Adventure with a "Zambo"—Narrow Escape of Bonpland—Eclipse of the Sun —Earthquake Shocks from the Volcano of Pichincha—Phosphorescence of the Sea—The Hangman of Cumana—La Guayra—A Zealous Physician— Ascent of the Saddle Mountain—The Difference between Promise and Performance—Harmless Bees.

THE next stage of the adventurous journey was a canoe expedition on the great rivers Orinoko and Rio Negro, and naturally required much preparation of instruments, and many and complicated arrangements. Humboldt was, moreover, very anxious to observe an eclipse of the sun; and the bright, clear climate of Cumana was particularly favourable for astronomical observations. Accordingly the departure from Cumana was deferred till the end of October. A very few days before that appointed for the start, an adventure happened to our travellers which might easily have had fatal results. The two friends had gone out as usual to the margin of the gulf, in the evening, to observe the exact time of high-water. They were walking along the beach, when suddenly Baron Humboldt became aware that some one was creeping stealthily behind him. Turning hastily, he beheld a negro, or "Zambo," armed with a macana, a formidable cudgel of palm wood, thick as a club at one end, and which Zambo flourished menacingly over the head of the astonished explorer. The next moment the macana descended heavily; but Humboldt managed, by a quick spring aside, to avoid the tremendous blow aimed at him. But Bonpland was less fortunate. The Zambo, who appeared as drunk with fury as a Malay running a muck, aimed another blow, which alighted on Bonpland's head just above the temple, and stretched him on the sand stunned and senseless for a few seconds. Humboldt bent over his companion in alarm; both were unarmed, and half a league from any habitation. Fortunately their aggressor did not follow up his attack, but moved slowly away to pick up Bonpland's hat, which had been knocked off by the blow he had given him. Meanwhile the wounded man had regained his senses, and both he and Humboldt started in pursuit of the Zambo, who ran off towards a neighbouring thicket. In spite of his broken head, Bonpland outran the black, who presently stumbled and fell. Bonpland threw himself upon him to secure him; but the Zambo's knife was out in an instant, and he would certainly have done more serious mischief but for the opportune arrival of some Biscayan merchants, who had seen the fray at a distance, and now came hastening to the rescue. The Zambo again took to his heels, but was captured, and submitted quietly to be led away to prison. It afterwards appeared that the poor wretch had been driven almost mad by ill-treatment received on board a privateer belonging to St. Domingo. He had heard Humboldt and Bonpland talking French, and in his poor muddled brain had in some way associated them with his oppressors, and thus resolved on revenge. In those days the course of justice was so tardy that prisoners often remained in durance for six or seven years before they were tried. Accordingly our author expresses his satisfaction when he heard, sometime after his departure from Cumana, that the culprit had escaped from his prison in the castle of San Antonio. Bonpland had a narrow escape. The blow he had received was so severe that he felt its effects for three months afterwards, and at one time his fellow-traveller seriously feared that an internal abscess was forming, but gradually the bad symptoms passed away.

The observation of the eclipse was successfully carried out. A few days afterwards the travellers for the first time felt the shock of an earthquake—a startling and novel experience which naturally made a deep impression on both of them. Humboldt says, concerning this phenomenon:—

"It was a real lifting up, and not a shock by undulations. I did not then imagine that after a long abode on the table-lands of Quito and the coasts of Peru, I should become almost as familiar with the abrupt movements of the ground as we are in Europe with the noise of thunder. We did not think of rising at night, in the city of Quito, when subterraneous rumblings (*bramidos*), which seem always to come from the volcano of Pichincha, announced a shock two or three, and sometimes seven or eight, minutes beforehand, the force of which shock is seldom in proportion to the intensity of the noise. The carelessness of the inhabitants, who recollect that for three centuries past their city has not been overwhelmed, easily communicates itself to the least intrepid traveller. In general, it is not so much the fear of the danger as the novelty of the sensation that strikes so forcibly when the effect of the slightest earthquake is felt for the first time. . . . When a shock is felt, when the earth is shaken on its old foundations, which we had deemed so stable, one instant is sufficient to destroy long illusions. It is like awakening from a dream, but it is a painful awakening. We feel that we have been deceived by the apparent calm of nature; we listen for the least noise; for the first time we mistrust a soil on which we had long placed our feet with confidence. If the shocks are repeated, if they become frequent during several successive days, this uncertainty quickly disappears. In 1784, the inhabitants of Mexico were accustomed to hear the thunder roll beneath their feet, as it is heard by us in the region of the clouds. Confidence easily springs up in the human breast; and at last, on the coast of Peru, we became accustomed to the undulations of the ground, as the sailor becomes accustomed to the tossing of his ship on the waves."

The plan of the travellers was now to pass by sea from Cumana to the town of La Guayra, an important seaport of Venezuela, and the seat of the chief export trade. Thence they were to make their way to New Barcelona and Caraccas, in which latter place they would remain till the end of the rainy season. Then a very important part of their enterprise was to begin—namely, the journey across the marvellous *llanos*, or plains that extend from the valleys of Caraccas to the banks of the Orinoko. This mighty river they then proposed to ascend from the Spanish missions in its lower part to the cataracts near the Rio

Negro, on the frontier of Brazil, and thence to make their way back to Cumana by the capital of Spanish Guyana, Angostura.

Near Cape Arenas the phosphorescence of the sea became especially remarkable. Great porpoises followed the ship, as many as sixteen appearing together on one occasion. Tumbling about after the manner of their kind, they now and then struck the water with their broad tails, whereupon flames would seem to flash up from the depths of the ocean. In swimming through the water, moreover, each band of

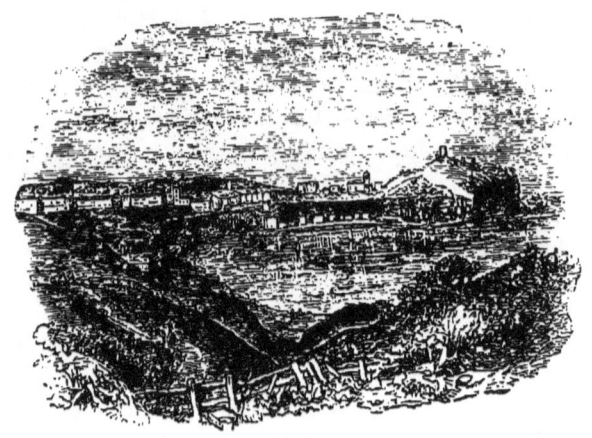

SCARBOROUGH.

porpoises left behind it a track of bluish light, while the rest of the sea showed no phosphorescence. This circumstance induced Humboldt to conjecture that the porpoises, in striking the water with their tails, or rushing along its surface, detached from their own bodies phosphorescent gelatinous substance. Near the group of islands which are named, like the celebrated city Caraccas, from a tribe of Indians long since passed away, a number of flamingoes were seen fishing in creeks where a narrow beach bordered the chalky rocks. On one of the islands, which were then quite uninhabited, a white man had settled about thirty years before with his family. He survived them all, and became rich enough to purchase two slaves, by whom he was eventually murdered. For a long time there was no evidence against the two slaves; but at length one of them, induced by the offer of a pardon if he would turn hangman and execute a number of men who had been condemned to death, but were kept waiting for a Jack Ketch, betrayed

ALEXANDER VON HUMBOLDT.

his accomplice, and in due time hanged him. At the time of Humboldt's visit this wretch was the hangman at Cumana.

At La Guayra the heat was exceedingly great; and as yellow fever frequently rages there, the population, and especially strangers from Europe, are very careful not to expose themselves to the rays of the noonday sun. Humboldt, too much engrossed by scientific pursuits to be nervously sensitive about his health, was one day busily occupied in the balcony of his house at noon, making observations on the difference of temperature as shown by the thermometer in the sun and in the shade. Suddenly he was surprised on finding himself addressed by a stranger, who offered him a potion which he conjured him to swallow. This obliging gentleman was a physician. Having observed that Humboldt had been for half-an-hour exposing himself to the full rays of the noonday sun, he considered the philosopher in " a parlous case,' only to be met by prompt and vigorous treatment; accordingly he conjured Humboldt to drink the potion, or yellow fever would infallibly ensue before night.

" I was not alarmed by this prediction, however serious," says our traveller, " believing myself to have been long seasoned; but how could I avoid yielding to entreaties that had so benevolent a motive? I swallowed the dose, and the physician perhaps reckoned me among the number of the sick whose lives he had saved in the course of the year."

At Caraccas the adventurous voyagers made a considerable stay, and Humboldt speaks enthusiastically of the " noble hospitality" extended to him and his fellow-traveller by the Captain-General of Venezuela, who resided there. The city of Caraccas reminded him more of a European city than any place he had seen in South America. He says they seemed to be nearer Cadiz and the United States at Caraccas and the Havannah than in any other part of the New World. It appeared that no one at Caraccas had ascended to the summit of the Silla, or Saddle Mountain, in the neighbourhood of the city. The two friends accordingly determined to undertake the feat. The enterprise was somewhat arduous, and it speaks well for the energy of our travellers, and their physical endurance, that they passed all the previous night in watching three occultations of the satellites of Jupiter.

At five in the morning they set out, accompanied by Indians and negroes, to serve as guides and carry the instruments. Some of the people from the town likewise came out from Caraccas to take part in the expedition; but a very short trial of mountain-climbing sufficed to cool their ardour, and they returned whence they came, after causing the travellers to lose much valuable time. A young Capuchin monk belonging to the convent had been especially outspoken on the occasion, vaunting the superiority of European Spaniards over those born in America, and promising to fire off some rockets for the edification of his brethren at the convent when he should have reached the summit of the Silla. Whether it was that the reverend friar had miscalculated his strength, or that his monkish garments were ill adapted for climbing, certain it is that he gave in at a very early period of the enterprise, and passed the day in a plantation near the foot of the hill, engaged in the laborious process of watching through a spyglass the progress of the climbing party. Unfortunately he had undertaken the conduct of the commissariat department, and detained the slaves who carried the provisions and water so long that the travellers were ten hours without refreshment of any kind. The chief danger of the ascent arose from the mist which often surrounded the mountain, and hid the landmarks, while it rendered the ground very slippery. Palm-trees and tropical plants were found growing for a considerable distance up the Silla, and at higher elevations appeared European forms of vegetation. Though the elevation of the Silla was not very great, the summit being somewhat lower than that of the European Canigou, the view it offered was magnificent, and the mountain was moreover distinguished by presenting an enormous precipice of six thousand feet on the side next the sea. Not even Mont Blanc could be compared with it in this magnificent feature. A kind of hairy bee, smaller in size than the honey-bee of Europe, was found haunting the summit of the Silla. These bees make their nests in the ground, and seldom fly, seeming benumbed by the cold of the mountains. They were called *angelitos*, or little angels, by the natives, because they hardly ever sting. Humboldt confesses that several times, when numbers of them settled on his hands and face, while he was making observations, he felt a sensation of nervous fear, and was almost tempted to drop his instruments, in spite of the angelic character attributed to these insects by popular consent.

VI.

Journey across the Llanos, or Great Plains—Aspect of the Llanos—Steppes in Various Parts of the World—Animal Life in the Llanos—The Horse and Ox Tribe and Cereal Plants—The Dry Season and the Rainy Season—The Gymnotus, or Electric Eel—Method of Capture—The Apure and Orinoko—Canoe Voyage—Nocturnal Life of Animals—Savage Tribes of America.

HUMBOLDT and Bonpland now began perhaps the most interesting part of their travels. They were to cross the vast stretch of unexplored land lying between Caraccas and the mighty system of rivers that, pouring from the snows of the Andes, flow towards the east through the broadest part of South America. First they had to cross a mountain range running east and west; then they came upon the great *llanos*, or treeless plains stretching from the coast chain of Caraccas to the left bank of the Orinoko, and then to navigate and explore such great and unknown rivers as the Apure, the Rio Negro, and the vast Orinoko itself. Among the mountain valleys of Caraccas appeared the full luxuriance of tropical vegetation. Vast groves of the cacao-tree alternating with the bright and tender green of the Tahitian sugar-cane, spreading tracts of plantain and banana, flourishing plantations of indigo and cotton, render this region one of the most delightful of those favoured climes described by so many writers as terrestrial paradises. The island-studded lake of Tacarigua, 1,470 feet above the level of the sea, appears the most beautiful region in a land of beauty. Then suddenly all is changed, and the traveller sees before him vast treeless plains, stretching to the horizon, as he enters the great llanos, or steppes.

These vast treeless plains form one of the most wonderful of natural phenomena. Their enormous size, the absence of vegetation over their great expanse, the violent and almost sudden changes of temperature and climate to which they are at certain periods subjected, cause these steppes to excite as much astonishment and admiration in the traveller as might be aroused by the mighty Andes range itself.

The account given by Humboldt himself in his *Personal Narrative*, and afterwards in his charming *Views of Nature*, is singularly graphic. He describes the astonished traveller turning suddenly from the view of the rich fullness of organic life to find himself on the dreary margin of a treeless waste. Nor hill nor cliff rears its head, like an island in the ocean, above the boundless plain; only here and there broken strata of flœtz, extending over a surface of more than three thousand English square miles, appear sensibly higher than the surrounding district. The natives term them *banks*, as if the spirit of language would convey some record of that ancient condition of the world when these elevations formed the shoals, and the steppes themselves the bottom, of some vast inland sea. The resemblance between the steppe and the sea is sometimes heightened when at night a sheet of vapour covers the ground, giving the scene the appearance of a shoreless ocean, in whose waters the light of the stars is reflected. But our author justly observes that "the ocean in its continual change is the emblem of life, while the steppes lie stretched before us, cold and monotonous, like the naked stony crust of some desolate planet."

As great steppes or plains elevated far above the level of the sea occur in all parts of the world, so in the various quarters they are distinguished by special characteristics. In Europe they are comparatively small in extent and covered with heath and furze. The great plains of Central Asia, whence the Huns or the Hiognu found their way into Europe, are distinguished by a growth of alkaline grasses, flourishing so luxuriantly that the traveller journeying in the low waggons of the Tartars is often completely hidden by a vegetation five or six feet high. The African desert is characterised by intense heat, arising chiefly from the sandy nature of the ground. But the great llanos of South America present alternately the appearance of a sandy desert, and of a verdant plain. Twice in every year they change their whole aspect, appearing, during one half of it, waste and barren like the Libyan Desert, and during the other covered with verdure, like many of the elevated plains of Central Asia.

The great rivers which, pouring from the Andes range, roll their majestic volume through the breadth of South America towards the ocean, the presence in many parts of dense forests of great extent, and the immense body of water by which the South American continent is almost surrounded, all tend to lower the temperature, and render the climate less burning than that of Africa. But in the position of the continent, which lies between the tropics, the sun has sufficient power during a certain season of the year to dry up almost every trace of vegetation on the parched earth. Almost uninhabited, except by scattered communities living in little towns at long distances from each other on the banks of the mighty rivers, the llanos have been for centuries the dwelling-place of very numerous wild animals. Among the creatures which roam over the treeless plain Humboldt enumerates "agoutis, small spotted antelopes, the shielded armadillo, which, rat-

ARMADILLOS AND PANGOLINS.

like, terrifies the hare in its subterranean retreat, beautifully-striped viverræ, or bats, whose pestilential odour infects the air, the great maneless lion and the variegated jaguar, commonly known as the tiger, whose strength enables it to drag to the summit of a hill the body of a young bull it has slain." But the most remarkable creatures that roam over the great steppes are undoubtedly the wild herds of horses, horned cattle, and mules. Few things in the economy of Nature are more remarkable than the adaptability given to certain species of animals and plants to suit themselves to almost every vicissitude of climate in every variety of circumstances. Thus the cereals or corn-plants, from the hardy rye that flourishes far into the high Northern latitudes to the lordly maize of tropical regions, are found successively distributed over the earth, each zone of climate having its indigenous and representative species. Thus, also, the ox and ass tribe seem to have followed man in all his migrations over the earth, and minister to his comfort and well-being alike in the valleys among the Black Scandinavian hills, and in the burning plains that glow beneath the Indian sky. These animals, which seem indispensable to the comfort of man in certain stages of his social development, are gifted with a wonderful tenacity of life and strength of constitution; and nowhere are these qualities more strikingly displayed than in the llanos of South America.

At almost all the settlements formed on the great rivers that skirt the great plains of Venezuela, the inhabitants have begun to rear cattle. The herds roam across the steppe in a wild state, and have increased prodigiously in numbers. At the time of Humboldt's visit the number of horses, oxen, and mules in the steppe was estimated at a million and a-half. These animals roam over the steppe in perfect freedom; and, in spite of the perils by which they are surrounded, their numbers increase in a marvellous manner.

First there are the sufferings of the dry season. As the intense glare of the sun is poured upon the plain week after week, the streams become dry water-courses, the pools are dried up, and the herds roam wildly over the arid plain seeking for water to allay their burning thirst. The earth cracks and bursts with the intense heat; the palm-trees, whose broad leaves have protected the pools, shrivel amd shrink, and vegetation perishes almost entirely upon the soil. The hot, dry wind, sweeping across the arid waste, raises thick clouds of stifling dust that impede respiration, and shroud the heavens in a copper-coloured haze, and the wind itself glows with the radiated heat. The wretched horses and oxen rush frantically over the plain, tortured alike by hunger and thirst, and oppressed by the hot, dust-laden atmosphere, bellowing and snuffing the air, and seeking for some pool whose waters are not yet entirely exhausted.

The cunning mule resorts to a stratagem to quench his thirst. He cautiously breaks open with his hoofs the thorny rind of the melocactus; for he knows that a watery pulp is contained inside which he greedily sucks. Sometimes, however, he is lamed by the thorns of the plant, which are peculiarly hard and sharp. With the horses and oxen he has to endure the stings of myriads of insects, whose number increases with the intensity of the heat; and Humboldt asserts that huge bats attack the unhappy quadrupeds at night, and, "vampire-like, suck their blood." But this last particular has been disputed by modern naturalists, who declare that all bats are strictly insectivorous. While the horse, mule, and ox are dragging on this wretched existence, crocodiles, alligators, and huge serpents—rendered torpid by the heat—lie in a sleep similar to that of hybernation produced in other regions by the winter cold.

But now the dry season draws to an end. A cloud no bigger than a man's hand appears on the southern horizon—rising gradually towards the zenith, and spreading as it advances until the whole sky is blackened. The muttering of distant thunder is heard, and then follows the ripple of rain, gradually increasing in intensity until it pours down in unbroken sheets amid the lurid flashing of the lightning and the crash of a tropical tempest. The parched ground speedily drinks in the moisture, and as it becomes thoroughly saturated the surface heaves and moves here and there. The affrighted beasts fly from these moving spots with redoubled terror, for they know that a great water-snake or a scaly crocodile is ready to dart from the subterranean lair where it has lain hidden through the dry season. And now the lower parts of the steppe are covered with water, while grasses of various kinds—shooting forth with almost magical rapidity—peer above the liquid surface. The animals can now slake their thirst; but they are obliged to lead the life of amphibious creatures, and swim about in the turbid water, anxious to reach the higher strata, which appear like islands above the watery waste. The crocodile lurks for them in the water and devours many of them; the jaguar springs forth from among the high grass and reeds, fastening with deadly bound on the backs of others; and the rapid current drowns many calves and foals as they try vainly to make head against its impetuous course. Far up among the trunks of the palm-trees spread the rising waters; and as a crowning danger the gymnotus, or electric eel, lies in the deeper pools, benumbing the victims on whom it fastens with the deadly force of its electric discharge.

The gymnotus is one of the most remarkable of the creatures that swarm in the great rivers of South America. It grows to a length of five or six feet. The strange power of imparting an electric shock can be used by the animal at will, and this voluntary power can be exerted with sufficient strength to kill a large quadruped. At one time it was necessary to alter the route by which the caravans crossed the steppe, in order to avoid a certain rivulet infested by the gymnoti; for a great

CAPTURING WILD CATTLE IN THE LLANOS.

number of horses and mules perished every year, in fording this water, from the attacks of the electric eels. At Calabozo, in the llanos, Humboldt and Bonpland witnessed a gymnotus hunt conducted by natives, and in the *Views of Nature* the former gives the following account of what he saw:—

"The mode of capturing the gymnotus," he says, "affords a picturesque spectacle. A number of mules and horses are driven into a swamp, which is closely surrounded by Indians, until the unusual noise excites the daring fish to venture on an attack. Serpent-like they are seen swimming along the surface of the water, striving cunningly to glide under the bellies of the horses. By the force of their invisible blows numbers of the poor animals are suddenly prostrated; others, snorting and panting, their manes erect, their eyes wildly flashing with terror, rush madly from the raging storm; but the Indians, armed with long bamboo staves, drive them back into the midst of the pool. By degrees the fury of this unequal contest begins to slacken. Like clouds that have discharged their electricity the wearied eels disperse. They require long rest and nourishing food to repair the galvanic force which they have so lavishly expended. Their shocks become gradually weaker and weaker. Terrified by the noise of the trampling horses, they timidly approach the brink of the morass, where they are wounded by harpoons and drawn on shore by non-conducting poles of dry wood."

Humboldt himself was on one occasion injured by incautiously putting his foot on a gymnotus, which immediately communicated to him a shock like that of a powerful Leyden jar. Even the anglers in the tributaries of the Orinoko are occasionally benumbed by shocks conveyed along the moistened fishing-line from the enemy that lurks below the surface of the water.

From the llanos the travellers made their way to the Apure and thence to the Orinoko. These are the regions where tropical vegetation appears in all its exuberant vastness and magnificence. The huge forest trees were festooned to a great height with climbing plants hanging like cordage from their gigantic limbs or stretched from bough to bough. By the water's edge the trailing plants and bushes formed a fence four feet in height, through which the wild beasts of the forest— the peccary, cavy, and jaguar—had broken paths that they might come and slake their thirst in the flowing water. As the canoes floated down the river the hedge of sauso grew so thick as to resemble a regularly-trimmed garden-fence, with gate-like openings here and there through which the wild animals gained access to the river. When disturbed, these creatures were often obliged to run for some hundreds of yards along the bank of the river till they came to an opening in the hedge through which they might escape into the woods; thus the voyagers had good opportunities of observing them. The flamingoes and other water-fowl, frightened by the unusual advent of boats in their solitudes, rose up into the air in clouds that darkened the sky. Daybreak and sunset were the times at which the wild beasts resorted most frequently to the river side with their young. "There came to drink, bathe, and fish," says Humboldt, "groups of creatures belonging to the most opposite species of animals; the larger mammalia, with many-coloured herons, palamedeas, with the proudly-strutting curassow. 'It is here as in Paradise' (*es como en el Paradiso*), remarked with pious air our steersman—an old Indian who had been brought up in the house of an ecclesiastic. But the gentle peace of the primitive golden age does not reign in the paradise of these American animals. They stand apart, watch and avoid each other. The capybara—a cavy, or river-hog three or four feet long, a colossal repetition of the common Brazilian cavy (*Cavia aguti*)—is devoured in the river by the crocodile and on the shore by the tiger. They run so badly that we were frequently able to overtake and capture several from among the numerous herds."

This part of the travels of the two friends was especially full of results for the enrichment of natural science. With unwearied zeal and perseverance they formed collections of plants and insects, and of stuffed specimens of such smaller animals as they could carry with them. During seventy-four days they traversed in their canoe more than fifteen hundred miles of the course of the mighty Orinoko, which they explored almost to its sources, and along the Cassiquiari and Rio Negro. The picture of the nocturnal life of animals on the banks of these great rivers is exceedingly graphic. In the *Views of Nature* it is thus given:—

"Below the mission of Santa Barbara de Arichuna we passed the night, as usual, in the open air, on a sandy flat on the bank of the Apure, skirted by the impenetrable forest. We had some difficulty in finding dry wood to kindle the fires with which it is here customary to surround the bivouac as a safeguard against the attacks of the jaguar. The air was bland and soft, and the moon shone brightly. Several crocodiles approached the bank ; and I have observed that fire attracts these creatures as it does our crabs and other aquatic animals. The oars of our boats were fixed in the ground to support our hammocks. Deep stillness prevailed, only broken at intervals by the blowing of the fresh-water dolphins, which are peculiar to the river network of the Orinoko, as, according to Colebrooke, they are also to the Ganges, as high up the river as Benares; they followed each other in long rows.

"After eleven o'clock, such a noise began in the adjacent forest, that for the remainder of the night sleep was impossible. The wild cries of animals resounded through the woods. Among the many voices which echoed together, the Indians could only recognise those which, after short pauses, were heard singly. There was the plaintive, monotonous cry of the howling monkeys, the whining flexible notes of the little sapagous, the grunting murmur of the striped nocturnal ape, the fitful roar of the great tiger (jaguar), the cougar, or maneless

American lion, the peccary, the sloth, and a host of parrots, parraquas, and other birds of the pheasant kind. Whenever the tigers approached the edge of the forest, our dog, which before had barked incessantly, came howling to seek protection under the hammocks. Sometimes the cry of the tiger resounded from the branches of a tree, and it was then always accompanied by the plaintive piping tones of the apes, which were endeavouring to escape from the unwonted pursuit.

"If the Indians are asked why such a continuous noise is heard on certain nights, they answer with a smile that the animals are rejoicing in the beautiful moonlight and celebrating the return of the full moon. To me the scene seemed rather to be owing to an accidental, long-continued, and gradually-increasing conflict among the animals. Thus, for instance, the jaguar will pursue the peccaries and the tapirs, which, densely crowded together, burst through the barrier of tree-like shrubs which opposes their flight. Terrified at the confusion, the monkeys at the tops of the trees join their cries to those of the larger animals. This arouses the tribes of birds that build their nests in communities, and suddenly the whole animal world is in a state of commotion. Further experience taught us that it was by no means always the festival of moonlight that disturbed the stillness of the forest; for we observed that the voices were loudest during violent storms of rain, or when the thunder echoed and the lightning flashed through the depths of the woods. The good-natured Franciscan monk, who, notwithstanding the fever from which he had been suffering from many months, accompanied us through the cataracts of Atures and Maypures to San Carlos, on the Rio Negro, and to the Brazilian coast, used to say, when apprehensive of a storm at night, 'May Heaven grant a quiet night both to us and to the wild beasts of the forest!'"

Few achievements in the history of travel have been more remarkable in their results and incidents than this boat voyage on the great South American rivers. Proceeding onward, amid toil and difficulty and frequent danger—tormented in the daytime by musquitoes, and snatching what repose they might at night amid the howlings of the wild animals of the forest—the travellers pushed their way towards the sources of the Orinoko, undeterred by peril or labour, and having for their one great object the advancement of science and the furthering of knowledge among men concerning that marvellous creation whose wonders reveal themselves to the patient, persevering investigator—that Nature whose voice speaks aloud to him who, with singleness of

344   THE WORLD'S EXPLORERS.

purpose and chivalrous devotion to the cause, seeks to be initiated into her manifold secrets. No trifler, no *dilettante* loiterer in the pleasant

HUMMING-BIRDS.

paths of science, must hope to be rewarded with the discovery of new truths and marvels; for him such knowledge is too high—he cannot attain to it. The true natural philosopher, who may hope to forge a new link in the wondrous chain of physical truth, must be a hard-

SAPAGOUS AND VIVERRÆ.

working, zealous, cool-headed man; a man who can forego sleep for many nights, and live on scanty food for many days; who can endure the heat of the midday sun, and the damp unhealthiness of the night dew—whose one absorbing interest is in the science he has taken in hand to elucidate, and who, offering everything he has, is content to grope his way slowly and unweariedly from truth to truth. And such a man was Humboldt.

The determined hostility of the Indian tribes, especially of the warlike Guaicas and the cannibal Guajaribes, prevented Humboldt and Bonpland from tracing the Orinoko completely to its source, and compelled them to turn their boat's head down the river. It was well remarked by our great traveller that the ferocity and cruelty of barbarous nations is often in inverse proportion to their numbers. Thus the thinly-scattered tribes who traverse the immense wilds bordering on the great rivers are animated by a malignant enmity towards each other which appears unaccountable, when we take into consideration how ample is the territory over which they can roam at will. Parties of savages slink to and fro among the vast solitudes, more suspicious and fierce than the beasts of prey with which they share the shelter of the woods. Whatever ingenuity they possess is devoted to the task of destroying their fellow-men. Some of them extract from the fangs of serpents a poison wherewith they anoint the points of the arrows which they shoot at their foes from behind trees; others smear the wourali or snake poison upon their thumbnail, and thus inflict deadly wounds. Many tribes, when they traverse the wilderness, take care to walk in each other's footsteps as they hasten onward in single line, and the last man of the party carefully effaces the footprints, lest a hostile tribe should become aware of their proximity and pursue them to the death. The strange habit of earth-eating is prevalent among some of these tribes; the Otomacs, who dwelt on the banks of the Orinoko, were accustomed to devour lumps of an unctuous yellow clay. They kneaded this strange comestible into balls of from four to six inches in diameter, which they baked before a slow fire to harden the outer surface. Humboldt found great pyramidal piles of these earth-balls stored up in the Otomac huts, as a provision for the rainy season, during which time earth constitutes the chief food of this extraordinary people. The clay of which these balls are made is selected with some care; it is found on the banks of the Orinoko and the Meta, and is of a yellowish-grey colour, and almost tasteless. It is not entirely from necessity that the Otomacs adopt this strange diet. Although in the rainy season scarcity of provision compels them to have recourse to their piles of clay dumplings, yet in the dry season, when they can procure fish in plenty, they are accustomed to devour an earth-ball or two as a second course, or, as Humboldt expresses it, "as a *bonne-bouche* after their regular meals." The languages of these tribes are very various. Their continual distrust of each other, resulting in a state of chronic strife, has kept them entirely apart and isolated; and wherever there is a want of intercourse between nations, diversity of tongues and dialects must prevail. Thus, in the vast regions of the Orinoko and the Cassiquiari, there are almost as many languages as tribes.

Thus the first part of Humboldt's travels had been devoted to the exploration of the great river system of Western South America, and science had been enriched with a host of new and interesting facts. The second part of our traveller's investigations was to comprise a journey through the mountain chains or Cordilleras of the mighty Andes, and to produce results of equal scientific value and importance.

348   THE WORLD'S EXPLORERS.

VII.

Land Journey across the Cordilleras—Disappointment of Humboldt—Volcanic Agency—Singular Method of Travelling—The Great Volcanic Peaks of the Andes—Their Height, &c.—Public Works of the Old Peruvians—Roads and Palaces—Conquest of Peru, &c.

AFTER a stay of some months in several of the West India islands, Humboldt and Bonpland proceeded to Cartagena, whence they designed to make their way overland to Santa Fé de Bogota, the capital of New Granada, and from thence across the Cordilleras to Quito in Peru. The French scientific expedition, under Captain Baudin, which had been several times "advertised to sail," was now again reported to have actually set out, and to be proceeding to Peru. Humboldt had promised Baudin that he would join him, and accordingly set out for the Peruvian coast, and it was not until some time afterwards that our friends were finally undeceived by the intelligence that the long-projected expedition was to circumnavigate the globe from west to east, and they determined to make their plans in future entirely independent of Baudin and his instructions.

The cheerfulness with which the great traveller was accustomed to bear disappointment, and his happy faculty of extracting the "soul of goodness in things evil," are exemplified in the way in which he notices the arrival of this intelligence, and its effect upon his plans. "American papers circulated in the Antilles," he says, "announced that the two French corvettes, Le Géographe and Le Naturaliste, were to sail round Cape Horn and to touch at Callao de Lima. This information, which I received when in the Havannah, after having completed my Orinoko journey, caused me to relinquish my original plan of proceeding through Mexico to the Philippines. I lost no time in engaging a ship to convey me from Cuba to Cartagena de Indias. But Captain Baudin's expedition took quite a different course from that which had been expected and announced. Instead of proceeding by way of Cape Horn, as had been intended at the time when it was agreed that Bonpland and I should join it, the expedition sailed round the Cape of Good Hope. One of the objects of my visit to Peru and of my last journey across the chain of the Andes was thus thwarted; but I had the singular good fortune, at a very unfavourable season of the year, in the misty regions of Lower Peru, to enjoy a clear bright day. In Callao I observed the passage of Mercury over the sun's disc, an observation of sound importance in aiding the accurate determination of the longitude of Lima, and of the south-western part of the new continent. Thus, amidst the serious troubles and disappointments of life, there may be found a grain of consolation."

On their way from Cartagena to Santa Fé de Bogota, the travellers visited the remarkable *volcanitos*, or little volcanoes, of Turbaco. The natives of Peru and the adjacent countries divide volcanoes into two classes—" de aqua" and " da fuego," or fire and water volcanoes, and those at Turbaco are of the latter kind. They consisted of about eighteen or twenty mounds about five-and-twenty feet in height, and when in eruption discharged great quantities of air with a hollow rumbling sound. The tradition among the Indians regarding them told that they had originally been fiery volcanoes; but, on being sprinkled with holy water by some personage of great sanctity, they immediately lost their dangerous tendencies; the subterranean fire within them was extinguished, and in future eruptions they discharged only harmless gases and water.

With the visit to these *volcanitos* began a long and elaborate series of observations on the nature and characteristics of volcanic action in the vast volcanic hearth that extends along the western seaboard of South America. Singularly patient and persevering as an investigator of Nature's wonders, ever anxious to fortify every

assertion he made by earnest and repeated experiment, Humboldt deprecates, with great justice, the hasty and imperfect conclusions drawn by previous travellers and men of science as to the nature of the structure and action of volcanoes in various parts of the world. He points out how general conclusions can only be justified by widely-extended and oft-repeated investigations; but at the same time he fully acknowledges the difficulties with which the subject had for a long time been surrounded. In a discourse on volcanic action he says—
"Although our geological knowledge may be extensively augmented by researches over vast regions, we can hardly be surprised that the class of phenomena constituting the principal subject of this address should have been so long examined in an imperfect manner, since the means of comparison were difficult and laborious of access. Until towards the close of the eighteenth century all that was known of the form of volcanoes and of the action of their subterranean forces was derived from observations made on two volcanic mountains of Southern Italy, Vesuvius and Etna. As the former of these was more accessible, and, like all volcanoes of slight elevation, had frequent eruptions, a hill became to a certain degree the type according to which a whole world—including the mighty volcanoes of Mexico, South America, and the Asiatic Islands—was supposed to be formed. Such a mode of reasoning involuntarily reminds us of Virgil's shepherd, who fancied in his own humble cot he saw the image of the Eternal City, Imperial Rome."

The natural bridges of Icononzo, since Humboldt's time repeatedly described by travellers, excited the admiring wonder of the friends. These bridges are situated in a region where the volcanic forces have wrought on a tremendous scale of magnitude. Masses of rock have been rent asunder, and deep valleys, or rather fissures, many hundred feet in depth, continually intersect the Cordilleras. In one of these fissures, through which thunders the vast torrent of La Suma Paz, the sandstone rock has not been completely rent asunder. A portion of the rock, fifty feet long and from thirty to forty wide, spans the torrent in the form of a natural bridge; and fifty or sixty feet below this bridge, which towers four hundred feet above the foaming waters, there is a second of still more marvellous construction. Three vast blocks of rock have been tumbled from the precipice above, and have fallen in such a manner as mutually to prevent each other's further descent, the centre mass forming the keystone of the natural arch; and in this second bridge is an aperture through which the torrent may distinctly be seen holding its course through a cavern haunted by nocturnal birds, who, safe in their inaccessible retreat from the pursuit of man, fill the air with their discordant cries. These natural bridges of the Cordilleras are at an elevation of more than three thousand feet above the level of the sea.

A very whimsical method of transit among the valleys of the Andes, as national as the palkee or palanquin in India, was the employment of the carqueros, or porters. These functionaries, generally the strongest men of the valleys, earned a laborious living by carrying travellers in chairs on their backs up and down the mountain ridges. The traveller who uses this extraordinary conveyance is seated with his back to that of the porter who carries him, and whose stooping position compels the passenger somewhat inconveniently to exemplify what Ovid describes as the characteristic of man's superiority over the animal creation, for he is obliged "*erectos ad sidera tollere vultus*"—he must contemplate the heavens, for the angle at which he travels almost precludes him from turning his glance towards the earth. Declining this eccentric method of progression, Humboldt and Bonpland were obliged to embrace the alternative of travelling barefoot, at the risk of frost-bite, among the snow-covered passes. The dangers and difficulties of the route did not, however, deter them from crossing the lofty mountain of Quindiu, on a road or track which sometimes narrowed till only a foot of space separated them from a precipice. Sudden and violent rains that swelled the mountain brooks into torrents difficult and dangerous to ford, increased the labours of the journey; but, on the other hand, the valley of Boquia displayed a wealth of botanical treasures that enriched their collections with many new and valuable specimens, and their journal with many novel scientific facts. Here it was that they found the curious species of palm-tree whose trunk supplies a wax-like substance from which the natives manufacture very tolerable candles; and the forests of Quindin furnished numerous specimens of the vigao, a plant of the banana kind, whose large broad leaves, two feet long by eighteen inches in breadth, are sufficiently strong and tough to resist the drenching rains for a considerable time, and are accordingly used by the natives for roofing their huts. The Indians who accompanied Humboldt and Bonpland several times made tents, the framework of branches of trees, the covering of the highly-varnished vigao leaves; and though the rain poured in torrents in the valley of Boquia, the dwellers beneath these extemporised huts were dry and well sheltered. After a four months' travel, every day of which added to their store of information, they arrived at Quito in the beginning of 1802.

A series of ascents of the chief volcanic mountains, and researches into the antiquities and historical relics of the country, occupied many useful months. Cotopaxi, Chimborazo, Pichincha, Antisama, and Tunguragua were amongst the volcanoes ascended by the indefatigable travellers. The ascent of Chimborazo—the extreme summit of which a fissure prevented them from reaching—was effected by Humboldt, Bonpland, and an energetic and friendly companion, the young Marquis Carlos Montufar, on the 23rd of June, 1802. They ascended the eastern slope of the mountain to a height of 19,286 feet. At an elevation of 18,225 feet, nearly 2,260 feet higher than the summit of Mont Blanc, winged insects were buzzing around, and at more than 16,500 feet above the line of perpetual snow, yellow butterflies were fluttering about. A kind of saxifrage was also found growing among the snow at a height of 15,770 feet, a striking proof of the diffusion of animal and vegetable life in regions where it might be supposed the conditions of climate would forbid its existence. The vertical height of this great mountain was estimated, after careful barometrical measurement, at 21,422 feet.

The derivation of the name Chimborazo, which was explained by several natives as meaning simply "the snow of Chimbo" (a name given to the district in which the mountain is situated), is considered a matter of doubt by Humboldt, who inclines to think the name may be totally independent of the Inca language, and have come down from an earlier and forgotten age. He points out that the names of other mountains, such as Cotopaxi, Pichincha, and Ilinissa, are totally devoid of meaning in the language of the Incas, and conceives that the name Chimborazo, like these, may have been derived from some tongue whose meaning has perished from the face of the earth. At any rate, he observes, the word ought to be written Chimporazo, as there is no *b* in the Peruvian language. The towering Chimborazo is, however, not the highest of mountains. This honour belongs to another range, and our author observes that if we could suppose the pass of St. Gothard, Mount Athos, or the Rigi, piled on the summit of Chimborazo, we should have the elevation ascribed to Dhawalagiri, in the Himalayan range.

TOUCANS.

VIII.

Nature of Volcanic Agencies in the Andes—Cotopaxi—The Quina, or Cinchona Bark—Architectural Remains in Peru—The Inca Roads—Aqueducts and Fortifications—Destruction of Public Works in Peru by Spanish Conquerors—Caxamarca—Remains of the Palace—"Baths of the Inca"—Pizarro and Atahuallpa—The Descendants of Atahuallpa—A Peruvian Aladdin's Garden.

THE tremendous nature of the volcanic agencies which have contributed to the formation of the Andes range will appear as described by Humboldt in the *Views of Nature*, a work in which a very great amount of physical science is concentrated and popularised in a very agreeable manner. The author says—

"From the granitic rocks of Diego Ramirez and the deeply-intersected district of Terra del Fuego—which in the east contains Silurian schist, and in the west the same schist metamorphosed into granite by the action of subterranean fire—to the Polar Sea, the Cordilleras extend over a distance of more than 8,000 miles. Although not the loftiest they are the longest mountain chain in the world, *being upheaved from one fissure which runs in the direction of a meridian from pole to pole*, and exceeding in linear extent the distance which, in the old continent, separates the Pillars of Hercules (Gibraltar) from the icy cape of the Tschuktches in the north-east of Asia. Where the Andes are divided into several parallel chains, those lying nearest the sea are found to be the seat of the most active volcanoes; and it has moreover been repeatedly observed that when the phenomenon of an eruption of subterranean fire ceases in one mountain chain it breaks forth in some other parallel range. The cones of eruption generally follow the direction of the axis of the chain, but in the Mexican table-land the active volcanoes are situated on a transverse fissure, running from sea to sea, in an east and west direction. Wherever the upheaving of mountain masses in the ancient crust of the earth has opened a communication with the fused interior, volcanic activity continued to be exhibited in the mass which had been upheaved like a wall by means of the ramification of fissures. That which we call a mountain chain has not been raised to its present elevation, or manifested as it now appears, at one definite period; for we find that rocks, varying considerably in age, have been superposed on one another and have penetrated towards the surface through fissures formed at an earlier period."

The imagination fails in the attempt to portray the extent of volcanic force necessary to upheave a range of granitic mountains through a distance of 8,000 miles.

Cotopaxi, which the travellers ascended on the 5th of May, though not the most lofty, is at once the most beautiful in shape and the most terrible in its destructive power of the numerous volcanoes in the Andes range. The valleys around it are shown to a great depth, with the ashes and scoriæ which this giant of 18,000 feet has at various periods cast forth. In the great eruption of 1724 the roaring of the volcano is said to have been heard at a distance of 200 leagues. Humboldt and Bonpland distinctly heard it at Guayaquil—more than fifty leagues distant—and its noise is compared to the sound of salvoes of heavy artillery. The dazzling snow-covered cone—six times higher than that surmounting the Peak of Teneriffe—which towers above Cotopaxi, is pronounced inaccessible by Humboldt, who moreover observes that ascents of mountains beyond the line of perpetual snow are rarely productive of any definite scientific result.

One of the most tremendous volcanic outbursts that ever changed the face of these regions happened in February, 1797. The so-called mud eruption of the Moya caused the death of forty thousand Indians in the torrents that swept suddenly from the mountains upon the plains. At Riobamba the travellers had an opportunity of noting the effects of this fearful event. At Loxa their attention was drawn to the tree whence the quina, or cinchona bark, known in Europe as the Peruvian bark, used in cases of fever, is obtained. Humboldt describes the pleasure they felt, after a year's residence in the higher regions of the Andes at an elevation of from 8,000 to 13,000 feet above the level of the sea, in descending to a more genial tract, rich in new and beautiful forms of tropical vegetation. The quina, or cinchona bark, first became known in Europe in the middle of the seventeenth century. According to the assertion of Sebastian Badus, the year 1632 is given as the date of its introduction; but other accounts speak of its being brought to Madrid in 1640 by Juan del Vego, physician to the Countess of Chinchon, wife of the Viceroy of Peru. This lady had been cured of a fever at Lima by the use of this valuable remedy. The following account is given of the quina tree:—

"The trees which yield this bark grow on mica, slate, and gneiss, at the moderate elevations of 5,755 and 7,675 feet above the level of the sea, nearly corresponding respectively with the heights of the hospice on the Grimsel and the pass of the Great St. Bernard. The cinchona woods in these parts are bounded by the little rivulets Zamoob and Cachyacu. The tree is felled in its first flowering season, or about the fourth or seventh year of its growth, according as it may have been reared from a strong shoot or from seed. At the time of my journey in Peru we learned with surprise that the quantity of the cinchona condeminca annually obtained at Loxa by the cascarilla gatherers, or quina hunters (cascarilleros and cascadores de quina), amounted only to 110 cwt. At that time none of this valuable product found its way into commerce; all that was obtained was shipped at Payta, a post on the Pacific, and conveyed round Cape Horn to Cadiz for the use of the Spanish court. To procure the small supply of 11,000 Spanish pounds no less than 800 or 900 cinchona trees were cut down every year. The older and thicker stems are becoming more and more scarce; but such is the luxuriance of growth that the younger trees—which now supply the demand though measuring only six inches in diameter—frequently attain a height of from fifty-three to sixty-four feet. This beautiful tree, which is adorned with leaves five inches long and two broad, seems, when growing in the thick woods, as if striving to rise above its neighbours. The upper branches spread out, and when agitated by the wind the leaves have a peculiar reddish colour and glistening appearance, which is distinguishable at a great distance." A story was extensively circulated to the effect that the lion (puma) chewed the bark and leaves of the quina tree when tormented by fever; but there is no foundation for the "traveller's tale."

Throughout their wanderings in Peru, the travellers were continually astonished at the stupendous remains of great public works erected in the time of the Incas. It is curious to notice what erroneous impressions prevailed in Europe, even long after the return of Humboldt, respecting the civilisation and power of the Peruvians, whom the Pizarros combated so bravely and oppressed so ruthlessly. Lord Macaulay, writing in 1842, draws the comparison, in his masterly essay on Clive, between the natives of Hindostan in the last century, and the Peruvians and Americans of the sixteenth, in which he greatly underrates the importance of the enemies against whom Cortez and Pizarro had to contend, presenting the civilisation of the natives of India as a contrast with the barbarism of Spanish America. "They had not broken in a single animal to labour," he says, speaking of the native

American races, while "the natives of Hindostan had built cities larger and richer than Saragossa or Toledo;" and in an elaborate passage he designates the Mexicans and Peruvians as "savages." But when Humboldt and Bonpland travelled among the relics of the ancient Peruvian dominions, they found the remains of a stupendous road, constructed of slabs of hard black stone, twenty feet in breadth, and extending the whole way between Cuzco and Quito, the two ancient capitals of Peru. Now the distance in a direct line between these two cities is no less than 1,000 miles; and as the road necessarily follows the windings of the mountains, some idea may be formed of the magnitude of this stupendous work and of the co-operation necessary to accomplish it. Some of the old Inca roads are covered with a coating of cemented gravel, and have the appearance of being macadamized. Others, which traverse regions where the mountains are unusually steep, are cut out into broad steps, impracticable indeed for the passage of cavalry, but perfectly adapted to the passage of llamas, the Peruvian beasts of burden, which had only light loads to carry. The great road between Cuzco and Quito traverses the mountains at an elevation considerably higher than the summit of the Peak of Teneriffe. Aqueducts and fortifications, on an equally magnificent scale, were also constantly found. "The early Spanish *Conquistadores*," says Humboldt, "were filled with admiration at the first sight of the roads and aqueducts of the Peruvians; yet not only did they neglect to preserve those great works, but they even wantonly destroyed them. As a natural consequence of the destruction of the aqueducts, the soil was rendered unfertile for want of irrigation. Nevertheless, those works, as well as the roads, were demolished for the sake of obtaining stones, ready hewn, for the erection of new buildings; and the traces of this devastation are more observable near the sea coast than on the ridges of the Andes, or in the deeply-cleft valleys with which that mountain chain is intersected. During our long day's journey from the syenitic rocks of Zaulac to the valley of San Felipe, we had no less than twenty-seven times to ford the Rio de Guancabamba, which falls into the Amazon. We were compelled to do this on account of the numerous sinuosities of the stream; whilst on the brow of a steep precipice near us we had continually within our sight the vestiges of the rectilinear Inca road. The little mountain stream, the Rio de Guancabamba, is not more than from 120 to 150 feet broad; but so strong is the current, that our heavily-laden mules were in continual danger of being swept away by it. The mules carried our manuscripts, our dried plants, and all the other articles

LLAMAS.

which we had been engaged a whole year in collecting; therefore, every time we crossed the stream, we stood on one of the banks in a state of anxious suspense, until the long train of our beasts of burden, eighteen or twenty in number, were fairly out of danger."

The most interesting memorials of the Incas were found in the elevated plain on which is situated the city of Caxamarca, "the Snow city," which in ancient times was the capital of Atahuallpa, the last of the Incas who really reigned in Peru. The remains of the ancient palace of the Peruvian monarchs are still to be seen here. The neighbourhood of Caxamarca is remarkably fertile. In spite of its elevation it enjoys a sheltered position; and its fields are bright with the red, yellow, and white flowers of the datura, with mimosas, and with beautiful rosaceous trees. In the distance, but plainly to be seen from Caxamarca, columns of vapour rise into the air from certain hot springs which still bear the name of "Baths of the Inca," where Atahuallpa was accustomed to spend part of each summer. It is impossible to think, without sympathy mingled with a feeling of indignation, on the history of this unfortunate prince, whose unhappy fate threw him into the hands of men equally faithless and cruel alike as friends and enemies. The dealings of the Spaniards with the nations of the New World were tainted throughout with the vicious notion from which the dealings of our own countrymen in the East were not entirely free—the indefensible doctrine that in dealings with "natives" the common restrictions of honour and honesty may be disregarded, that a Clive may cheat an Omichund by a forged document, without damaging his own character as a gentleman. The conduct of Pizarro and his associates towards the poor, plundered, duped Atahuallpa, disgusts alike by its treachery and rapacity. Though the sum of £3,500,000, stated by the historian Prescott to have been divided by the Pizarros and their associate, Almagro, is considered by Humboldt to have been over-estimated, the amount of plunder obtained under the name of ransom was, doubtless, enormous. The treasures brought from the temples at Huaylas, Huama-Chuco, Cuzco, and Pachacamao, are valued by Garcilaso de la Vega at 3,838,000 ducats. The poor Inca seems to have been very anxious to be buried in Quito; and thither, after a mass had been said for the repose of his soul, in the presence of the Pizarros, who attended the ceremony dressed in deep mourning, his body was conveyed for burial.

At Caxamarca, living in poverty amid the ruins of former splendour, dwelt the descendants of the unfortunate Inca. Some traditions of their former greatness survived in the family of Astorpilca the Cacique, who, in Humboldt's time, was the direct representative of the family of Atahuallpa. Among the Caxamarcans stories were diffused concerning subterranean treasures—gardens like that wondrous region in the Arabian tale, into which the magician led the bewildered Aladdin— groves whose trees were solid gold, bearing jewels for fruit, were believed to exist beneath the dust and rubbish of the dead city, and many besides the Cacique's family were firm in their expectation that a day would come when the ancient dominion of the Incas would be restored in all its glory, and the hidden treasures would blaze in the light of day. Humboldt, who had heard of these traditions, one day questioned the son of Astorpilca concerning them, inquiring if the Cacique and his family had never felt a desire to dig for some of these treasures. The young Peruvian's answer, he says, " was so simple, and so expressive of the quiet resignation peculiar to the aboriginal inhabitants of the country, that I noted it down in Spanish in my journal. 'Such a desire (*tal antajo*),' said he, 'never comes to us. My father says that it would be sinful (*que fuese pecado*). If we had the golden branches, with all their golden fruits, our white neighbours would hate us and injure us. We have a little field and good wheat (*buen trigo*).'" Like the Roman country folk described by Goldsmith in the *Traveller*:—

> "In those domes where Cæsars once bore sway,
> Defaced by time, and tott'ring in decay,
> There, in the ruin, heedless of the dead,
> The shelter-seeking peasant hides his head,
> And, wondering man could need the larger pile,
> Exults, and owns his cottage with a smile."

As strange a contrast as the course of time could well bring about —from Atahuallpa, a Peruvian Damocles on his golden throne, to Astorpilca, content in his poverty with a little field and "buen trigo."

The wanderings of Humboldt and Bonpland were protracted to August, 1804, when they reached Europe, after achieving such results for science as had seldom been attained within the limits of one voyage.

CAPTAIN FLINDERS.

I.

Flinders' Only Memorial—His Early Predilections for Exploring—The Tom Thumb: its Crew and First Voyage—Mr. Bass Penetrates as far as Port Philip—Discovery of Bass's Strait—Lieutenant Flinders is Entrusted with the Command of an Exploring Expedition—The Investigator Commences her Great Work—The French Expedition—Grand Preparations—Interview between Captain Flinders and the French Commander—The Two Expeditions Separate—Hospitality to the French at Sydney—The Investigator Proceeds along the North Coast—Departure for England—Wreck of the Porpoise and Cato.

THE traveller who disembarks on "the Wharf" at Melbourne finds himself in Flinders-street: a frontage of bonded warehouses, wool-stores, and shipping-offices, facing the Yarra-Yarra.* It is the only memorial to an English naval officer, distinguished for high abilities, indomitable enterprise, and most undeserved wrong. To Captain Flinders we are indebted for the very name of Australia, and, in all probability, the preservation within the British Empire of its most important colonies.

In 1788 the first English settlement was formed on the shores of Australia, then known as New Holland. Some eight years after, Mr. Matthew Flinders was appointed to the post of midshipman on board his Majesty's ship Reliance, sent to protect the infant colony. He was filled with an ardent passion for exploring new countries—and here was a whole continent, scarcely known, to quicken it into activity.

Midshipman Flinders, assisted by Mr. Bass, the surgeon of the vessel, constructed a small boat, seven feet long. To this was given the appropriate name of the Tom Thumb. In the Tom Thumb, Mr. Flinders and Mr. Bass—with a crew consisting of one boy—made various explorations along the shores of Botany Bay,† adjoining the new settlement. They ascended one of the rivers falling into the

---

* In the aboriginal languages of Australia, the repetition of the word intensifies its meaning, thus Yarra means simply "flowing."

† So named previously by Captain Cook, in consequence of the great number of new and valuable botanical specimens which it was found to furnish.

CAPTAIN FLINDERS.
GOVERNOR EYRE.

Bay itself. At length, emboldened by success, they proceeded to fill up some of the great gaps existing on the charts of Captain Cook. The presence of a strong current, coming up from the westward, first suggested to them that the great mass of land on which Tasman had conferred the name of Van Diemen, the Governor of Batavia, did not in reality form part of the mainland of New Holland, as supposed, but an independent island. At this particular period, Mr. Flinders was

AN AUSTRALIAN NATIVE.

temporarily detained on ship duty; but Mr. Bass, having penetrated, in an open whale-boat, as far as the entrance to Port Philip—the future seat of Melbourne—found further evidence to confirm the conjecture. On his return, the two friends obtained the aid of the Norfolk, a colonial sloop placed at their disposal to prosecute their researches. In the Norfolk they actually passed between the south coast of New Holland and Van Diemen's Land, coming out on the great Southern Ocean. With a view to extinguishing all trace of its subsequent penal history, Van Diemen's Land is now known as the Island of Tasmania; the separating strait bears the name of Mr. Bass. On the return of the Reliance to England in 1800, the charts of these new discoveries were published, and reflected great credit on the young midshipman and his friend.

The English Government was at that time becoming alive to the necessity of a more intimate knowledge of the vast regions, on the mere borders of which it had planted its colony of New South Wales; and Mr.—now Lieutenant—Flinders was deemed the most fitting man to take the command of an exploring vessel to be despatched thither. With the first year of the new century, he sailed from Sheerness on board the Investigator, an armed sloop of 334 tons burden. England and France being then at war, the expedition was provided—in accordance with the usages of nations—with the proper passport, furnished by the French Minister of Marine, in which the pacific objects of the Investigator were recited, and her captain, officers, and crew recommended to the hospitality and protection of all foreign possessions of the new Republic. This expedition commands additional interest from the fact that among the midshipmen serving on board—a relative, indeed, of the commander—was John—afterwards Sir John—Franklin.

With the following December, Cape Leeuwin, the extreme southwest point of Australia, was sighted, and the work of marine survey began. The whole of the south coast was carefully examined, and names were affixed to the various bays, capes, islands, and headlands. In April, 1802, the Investigator had advanced as far east as long. 138 deg. 58 min.—nearly opposite where the city of Adelaide now stands—when a circumstance occurred deeply affecting the results of the expedition, and which clouded the future years of its commander with most cruel disappointment, and injustice unparalleled in the history of international rights.

That success in maritime discovery which had early distinguished the Spanish, Portuguese, and Dutch, had been, of late, becoming the possession of England. It was not without envy that her rival, France, saw her occupying shore after shore with new colonies, taking firm root, and giving every promise of holding possession of the soil. Most especially was it judged expedient to anticipate her labours in the "Great South Land." For this purpose, an exploring expedition had been fitted out by the French Government on more than an ordinary scale of grandeur and preparation. In the somewhat inflated language of M. Péron, who accompanied the expedition as naturalist, "The magazines of Havre were placed at the disposal of our commander; considerable sums were granted him for the purchase of choice wines, liquors, syrups, sweetmeats of various kinds, Italian cakes, soup-cakes, acid of lemon in crystals, &c. Filtering machines invented by Schmidt, stoves with ventilators, hand-mills, and different apparatus for distilling were put on board each vessel; while instructions of great value were issued by M. Kerandrum, first physician to the navy, for the preservation of health. Our numerous instruments of astronomy, physical instruments, and those requisite for the meteorological and geographical departments, were the work of the most eminent artists of the capital; the *materiæ* of the chemists, painters, draughtsmen, were of the first quality; a numerous library, composed of the best works relating to the sea, to astronomy, geography, physics, natural history, and voyages was prepared for each vessel; for the instructions necessary for scientific researches, it will be sufficient to notice, in order to ascertain how precise and complete they were, that they were the compilation of a Commission of the Institute, formed of MM. Flerieu, Lacépède, Laplace, Bougainville, Cuvier, Jussieu, Lelièvre, Camus, and Langles; M. Degerands, a member of the same learned society, digested for us an interesting work on the method to be followed in our observations on uncivilised people; a national medal was struck to commemorate this grand enterprise; the most flattering passports were furnished by all the Governments of Europe; an unlimited credit was opened for us with the principal colonies of Africa and Asia; in one word, the august chief, under the auspices of whom this important voyage was about to be undertaken, had given directions that nothing should be omitted which might tend to the preservation of the men, facilitate our labours, or guarantee our independence." It is difficult to refrain from a smile when comparing these elaborate preparations with those which the real discoverers and explorers of Australia brought with them to their task. Mr. Bass, we have just seen, made the most important marine discovery affecting those regions in an open whale-boat; and the hitherto impregnable interior has at length yielded to Mr. Stuart, accompanied by two men only. In truth, in matters of exploration, the British Government has mainly left its people free to exercise their own discretion. In general, the most important and successful results have been accomplished by the colonies themselves—indeed, not seldom by private and unassisted individuals.

Towards the close of 1800, this expedition had sailed from France, in the ships Le Géographe and Le Naturaliste. It was not until the spring of 1802 that they arrived at the scene of their proposed labours. What they had been doing during much of the intervening time will be found sufficiently explained by the remark of one of the officers, at a subsequent interview with the commander of the Investigator. "Captain," said M. Bonnefoy, "if we had not been kept so long picking up shells and catching butterfles at Van Diemen's Land, you would not have discovered the south coast before us." No conversation, however, of such a nature took place at this first meeting of the two

AUSTRALIAN FISHERMEN.

expeditions. Captain Flinders went on board Le Géographe, and requested to see Captain Baudin's passport from the English Admiralty. "And when it was found," run Captain Flinders' own words, "and I had perused it, I offered mine from the French Marine Minister; but he put it back without inspection." The commander of Le Géographe made hardly any allusion to the scenes around them, confining his remarks to Van Diemen's Land, and also criticising a certain English chart of Bass Strait in his possession, published immediately before his departure from Europe. He found fault with the north side of the strait, but commended the form given to the south side and to the small islands near it. On Captain Flinders pointing out a note upon the chart, explaining that the north side of the strait was seen only in an open boat by Mr. Bass, without adequate means of taking longitude and latitude, he expressed his surprise, and confessed that that fact had previously escaped his notice. "On my asking the name of the captain of Le Naturaliste, he bethought himself to ask mine, and, finding it to be the same as the author of the chart which he had been criticising, expressed not a little surprise, but had the politeness to congratulate himself on meeting me."

On parting with Le Géographe, Captain Flinders proceeded with his examination of the south coast, and, having made an examination of Port Philip Bay—in which the cities of Melbourne and Geelong have since risen—finally arrived at Sydney in the following May. The French ship, Le Naturaliste, had arrived a few days before, and she was soon followed by Le Géographe. Captain Flinders and the whole of the inhabitants of Sydney were unremitting in their attention and hospitality to the members of the French expedition. Though in time of war, the town and its whole neighbourhood were thrown open to their inspection. They were received at a public dinner on board the Investigator, as also, on several occasions, in the town itself. And while, from the great scarcity of live-stock at that period in the new colony, the governor felt unable to victual the English expedition, large supplies were sent on board Le Géographe and Le Naturaliste.

On leaving Sydney, the Investigator proceeded along the north coast of the island-continent, between the mainland and that most extraordinary production of animal life known as the Great Barrier Reef. This reef is wholly the result of the labours of the coral insect, and runs parallel with the coast for the amazing distance of 1,200 miles.

Along the coast now traversed by Captain Flinders, several excellent bays were discovered, and regions disclosed, which have since led to the foundation of the new colony of Queensland. In completing, however, the survey of the Gulf of Carpentaria, the Investigator was found to be in so unseaworthy a condition as to render a return to Sydney indispensable. At Sydney a Government Commission condemned the vessel as unfit to put to sea again. Under these circumstances, it became necessary for Captain Flinders to sail for England, in order to lay his maps and charts before the Admiralty, and to obtain another ship to complete the coast survey of Australia. A store ship, called the Porpoise, was placed at his disposal by the Colonial Government for this purpose, and two ships bound for Batavia—the Bridgewater, under Captain Palmer, and the Cato, under Captain Park—sailed at the same time, being desirous of his company. For the purpose of some further inspection, it was Captain Flinders' wish to proceed homewards by the north coast, necessitating a second voyage between the east coast of the mainland and the Great Barrier Reef, to which we have already referred. Here, however, his usual good fortune deserted him—unfortunately never to return. When opposite the present colony of Queensland, the Porpoise struck on a detached mass of coral reef. Her masts immediately went overboard, and she turned broadside on to the violence of the waves. It being apparent to those on board that their vessel could not long hold together, all eyes were at once turned in the direction of the Cato and Bridgewater as the only means of escape. But there a truly fearful sight met their gaze. Following in the wake of the Porpoise, these two vessels had perceived her mishap, and now suddenly altered their courses in a last effort to avoid the reef. This manœuvre caused the paths of both ships to cross, and they were now bearing down on each other with every appearance of a collision. By a daring and skilful turn, however, the captain of the Cato avoided the impending shock. The anxious spectators of the Porpoise saw the two vessels pass side by side, almost grazing. Presently they opened off from each other, the Cato steering to the northeast, and the Bridgewater going south. The manœuvre, however, of the captain of the Cato cost him his ship. In another moment she struck on the reef; through the gathering darkness her masts were seen to fall overboard by the crew of the Porpoise, and then night entirely closed on the dreadful scene. One solitary ray alone shone through the thick gloom, still lending hope. A light was shown from the masthead of the Bridgewater, indicating that she, at all events, had escaped from these complicated dangers.

II.

Want of Assistance in the Captain of the Bridgewater—The Bridgewater Deserts the Two Wrecks—The Crews of the Porpoise and Cato Reach an Adjacent Sandbank—Captain Flinders Starts for Sydney and Rescues his Companions —Leaves again for England in the Cumberland—Puts in for Repairs at Mauritius—The Governor Accuses him as a Spy—Filthy Lodgings—The French Government's Passport Repudiated—Appearance of the Record of the French Expedition—Public Feeling in France—The Emperor Signs the Order for his Release—De Caen's Behaviour—Flinders Returns to England —His Death.

SELDOM indeed is a writer called on to record any want of prompt and generous assistance on the part of those whose trade is on the deep to their less fortunate brethren, most seldom when the honour of the

English flag is concerned. Our narrative, however, now compels us to mention as dastardly an act of desertion as it is possible to conceive. Captain Palmer, having escaped into smooth water—mainly through the gallant, though ill-fated, manœuvre of the commander of the Cato —waited for the morning's light—" saw," in the language of Mr. Williams, one of his own indignant officers, "the reef on our weather bow, and, from the masthead, the two ships, and to leeward of them a sandbank"—and then proceeded on his course. "The ships," continues this honest fellow, "were very distinctly to be seen from aloft, and also from the deck; but, instead of rendering them any succour, the captain ordered the ship to be put on the other tack, and said it was impossible to send them any relief." The indignation of Mr. Williams did not end here. Wherever the Bridgewater touched, he spread the report of this base desertion of their fellow-voyagers, and, as soon as opportunity permitted, left the vessel, forfeiting his wages, and even his few articles of property. On the contrary, Captain Palmer, on arriving at Calcutta, communicated to the newspapers a circumstantial narrative of the total destruction of the two vessels and their crews. From India he sailed for England, and was heard of no more.

Let us now return to the scene of the wrecks. As soon as it was placed beyond doubt that the Bridgewater had abandoned them to their fate, the crews of the Porpoise and Cato put forth all their energies to rescue themselves from their vessels, now rapidly going to pieces. After great exertions, they at length succeeded in assembling on an adjacent sandbank, about 150 fathoms long, and elevated some four feet above high-water mark. Thither they conveyed all the stores that could be saved from the ships, and, on the second day after their catastrophe, found they numbered 94 souls, with water and provisions for about three months' consumption. They also saved a couple of six-oared cutters. Most fortunately, Captain Flinders' highly-valuable maps and charts were also preserved. They were now about 800 miles from the nearest settlement—namely, Sydney—and Captain Flinders proposed to go thither, in search of aid, in one of these open cutters. This most difficult achievement he accomplished in less than two months, returning to his companions with the Rolla and a most welcome supply of provisions.

On his return to Sydney, Captain Flinders made his second effort to reach England in the Cumberland, a vessel of only 29 tons burden. She proved leaky, and scarcely able to carry sail. When in the vicinity of

Mauritius, it was found necessary to put into Port Louis to refit. And here that storm, whose early warnings we gave intimation of on the arrival of the French exploring expedition on the Australian coast, burst on the devoted head of our commander. Mauritius—then known as the Isle of France—was, at that period, the property of the French Government. Indeed, it was the chief French privateering station in the Napoleon wars, and the injury which it inflicted on the merchant marine of England is well-nigh incalculable. It was now under the governorship of General De Caen, and Le Géographe had recently paid it a visit on her return home, some months before the arrival of Captain Flinders.

On his first interview with De Caen, Flinders became aware how dangerous a step he had taken in entering Port Louis. The governor behaved with excessive rudeness; affected to believe that so great an explorer as Captain Flinders could not possibly be sent home in a leaky vessel of 29 tons burden; and ended by calling him an impostor and a spy. His diaries, charts, and maps were brought on shore. The Cumberland was taken possession of. Captain Flinders; and his companion, Mr. Aken, were conducted to a miserable lodging, to be there confined to an equally miserable room, containing two truckle-beds without curtains, a small table, two rush-bottomed chairs, and whole legions of fleas, and other still more objectionable vermin. To add to these indignities, early the next morning a sentinel burst open the door, and took up his beat between the two truckle-beds. At dinner-hour, an invitation was given to him to go to the governor's table. But the spirit of a British officer was now thoroughly roused within him. He returned for answer, that he could appear as the guest of the governor only when treated in accordance with his rank and the terms of his passport. In all probability, this was the reply which De Caen sought, and which his previous treatment had been fashioned to bring about. His hospitality had been offered—and was refused: without explanation, the onus of this fact would rest upon his prisoner. Certainly, from that hour all intercourse ceased; nor was even the least reply vouchsafed to Captain Flinders' repeated letters and applications. The identity of Captain Flinders with the commander of the late Exploring Expedition being, of course, capable of the clearest proof, a new expedient, to justify this strange detention, became necessary. The passport issued by the French Government was "to the captain, officers, and crew of the Investigator;" and, of necessity, could contain

CAPTAIN FLINDERS.

no reference to the Cumberland. It was now maintained, on the part of the governor, that he was not bound to recognise the passengers of an unknown ship entering one of his ports; that Captain Flinders, in changing from one vessel to another, had forfeited all rights and privileges conferred on him by the French Minister of Marine.

AN AUSTRALIAN DUEL.

In 1806—while Captain Flinders was of course a close prisoner, and his maps and charts in De Caen's possession—appeared the first volume of the results of the French Exploring Expedition in Le Géographe and Le Naturaliste. Had Captain Flinders obtained a sight of it, he would have stared indeed. The scene of his discoveries is there called "Napoleon's Land." For the various bays, capes, islands, &c., named by him and entered on his charts, appeared " Golfe Bonaparte," " Golfe

2 B

Josephine," "Cap Marengo," "Cap Dessaix." In short, scarce a spot was left which did not bear the name of some member of the new Emperor's family, his marshals, or the incidents which had given importance to his career. Even Port Philip, named from the earliest governor of the settlement—and which recent gold discoveries have made so familiar to English ears—now appeared as "Port de Début." To complete the whole, to the map of this imaginary land (for the charts were rudely and very imperfectly copied from the actual surveys of Captain Flinders) was affixed the representation of an *eye*, with an "N" inscribed therein, looking down on the Southern Hemisphere, on which were traced the outlines of New Holland. It is almost unnecessary to remark that to the map of Australia has long since been restored its honest English nomenclature. Had, however, the life of Captain Flinders then yielded to the harsh treatment and cruel suspense to which he was exposed—as, indeed, it did shortly after to their results—it is difficult to say what might have been the ultimate fate of that portion of the globe, both in a political as well as in a geographical sense. "The state of uncertitude," writes Captain Flinders, "in which I remained, brought on a dejection of spirits which might have proved fatal, had I not endeavoured, by constant occupation, to force my mind from a subject so destructive to its repose. Such an end to my detention would have given too much pleasure to the captain-general; and, from a sort of perversity in human nature, the conviction even brought its support."

It is but fair to the great body of the French nation, at home and abroad, to state that the ill-fated English explorer possessed their entire sympathy. In the island, Admiral Linois made repeated applications to the governor on his behalf. M. Laborde, the chief physician of the medical staff, represented that country air and exercise were absolutely necessary for the restoration of his health; for which he received a sharp rebuff from De Caen. Captain Bergeret made solicitation that his maps and charts should be restored to him, in order that he might employ his enforced leisure upon their completion, while the surveys were fresh in his memory. The civilians of Mauritius offered him all the care and hospitality in their power; and a petition, signed by every one of position and influence in the isle, was forwarded to the National Institute in his behalf. In France, the world-renowned geographer, Malte Brun, hastened to restore these discoveries to their rightful owner. The brother of Captain Baudin, of Le Géographe (Captain Baudin himself had died on the voyage) published the kindness and hospitality with which the French Exploring Expedition had been received by the inhabitants of Sydney. Nay, several letters found their way into the French newspapers—not even excepting the official *Moniteur*—setting forth the injustice of detaining Captain Flinders.

It is needless, however, here to repeat the tale of France's position at the time. The will of the Emperor ruled supreme and undisputed. In very charity, we may suppose he was ignorant of the early detention of the English explorer, or that the facts of the case were placed before him in a distorted form—though the action of De Caen strongly savours of previous instruction. But as year succeeded year, and Captain Flinders still remained a prisoner, that plea loses foundation. In 1806, the Emperor made public approval of the decision of the Council of State, "to grant to Captain Flinders his liberty, and the restitution of his vessel." Yet intrigue rested not still. The British Government was informed that this order was despatched in triplicate to Mauritius in three French vessels. De Caen asserted that he received no order; he certainly acted on none. The English Government placed in his hands a fourth copy of the order; but even this the governor dared to disobey—a proof amounting to conviction that he had received strong and explicit countermanding instructions. Year again succeeded year. Finally it was not till 1810 that Captain Flinders was permitted to quit the island and resume his voyage to England. Eventually, most of his maps and charts were restored. Some of his note-books, however, were never returned. Indeed, it is sufficiently clear, from the use made of them, that it had been found impossible to return them. Captain Baudin himself had placed it on record that he had constructed no charts while on the Australian coast.

On Captain Flinders' return to England, he at once set about preparing his papers and surveys for publication. But hope too long deferred, and repeated attacks of illness resulting from the rigour of his confinement, had already undermined his constitution. On the very day that his work saw the light, and that the claims of the French to these vast "South Lands" were scattered to the winds, he breathed his last. His specimens of marine surveying are models for all future explorers, and, perhaps, have never been excelled up to the present moment. The name "Australia" which he affixed to the scene of his labour, at once took the place of the Dutch New Holland. This name has since continued to be held undisputed, and it is high time that the name of Flinders should be raised from the oblivion into which it has fallen.

EYRE: GOVERNOR AND AUSTRALIAN EXPLORER.

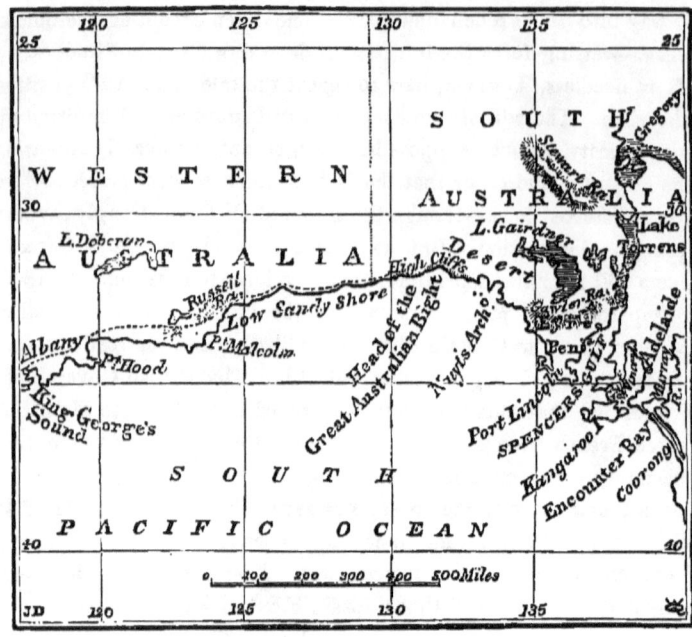

I.

Overlanders—Wealth of the Colonists—Scarcity of Water in the Interior of Australia—The Australian Explorer—Services of the Explorers—Social Position of the Overlanders—Magnitude of their Operations—Demand for New Pastures—Country round Adelaide—Application to Mr. Eyre—He Accepts the Command of the Expedition—Departure of the Explorers— Repeated Failures in Attempting to go Northward—Eyre Determines to go Westward—The Expedition is Sent Back—The Exploring Party—The Coast Line of South Australia—Want of Water.

RECENT affairs in Jamaica having given prominence to the name of Edward James Eyre, we here retrace the previous career of that gentleman in other and even more distant lands. Apart from Jamaica matters, it will be found to furnish incidents of a highly-interesting character ; indeed, in one instance his name is associated with a feat unparalleled in the annals of exploration.

Some quarter of a century ago, Mr. Eyre belonged to a class of Australian colonists on which had been conferred the title of "Overlanders." Up to the time of the Australian discoveries of gold, that great island-continent continued to be solely a pastoral country. The wealth of the colonists consisted entirely in cattle and sheep, and their only concern was to find pasture for them. To a few settlers dwelling on the sea-coast of regions nearly as large as Europe this might not, at first sight, appear a very difficult task, yet it was the great problem which year after year pressed upon the Australian settler. Available pasture lands were found to occur only in isolated positions, and widely remote from each other, while progress into the vast interior presented such insurmountable obstacles, from scarcity of water, that it was only a couple of years ago that the centre of the island was at length reached, after numberless and daring attempts all ending in failure, and then only with the loss of the leaders of the expedition, the gallant Burke and Wills. These peculiarities of Australian settler life brought into existence two classes of colonist, the explorer and the overlander. It was the business of the explorer to discover new pastoral districts; it was the business of the overlander to purchase large herds and flocks in the old district, and to convey them to the new—generally through absolute wilderness—for the purpose of selling them to the eager crowd of settlers who invariably rushed into these newly-opened lands. The Australian explorer battled with the obstacles of nature for honour and glory, but it was an honour and glory somewhat different from that actuating the explorers of other unknown countries. No one in the world would be a penny the richer for the discovery of the sources of the Nile: the geographical problem of centuries would receive its solution, and the name of the discoverer would be handed down to all posterity—that would be his reward. The Australian explorer, on the other hand, conferred immediate wealth on many thousands of his fellow-colonists. The pent-up flocks and herds of the earlier settlements languished for need of new pastures for their superabundant increase : these exploratory expeditions were dismissed into the wilderness with the prayers and God-speed of every colonist, from governor to latest European immigrant, and their return awaited with intense anxiety and eagerness.

With each discovery the whole of the Australian colonies received a solid and permanent accession of material wealth and prosperity; hence the Australian explorer has always been held in peculiar favour among his fellow-colonists as a public benefactor. The overlander, it is true, acted more in accordance with his own private interests and recompense; but the magnitude of his operations, the thousand dangers of the separating desert to which he entrusted his all, his manly bearing, indomitable energy, and evidence of previous culture, all contributed to render him a favourite. He is well described in the words of Sir George Grey, himself governor of an Australian colony,* and an explorer of no mean repute:—

"The overlanders are generally descended from good families, have received a liberal education (Etonians and Oxonians are to be found among them), and, even at their first start in the colonies, were possessed of what is considered an independence. Among them is to be found a degree of polish and frankness rarely to be looked for in such a mode of life, and in the distant desert you unexpectedly stumble on a finished gentleman. The magnitude of the operations of the overlanders would scarcely be credited; a whole fortune is risked—and in the wilderness. The stock of the overlander is the capital which he has invested in a single speculation, and to give an idea of the amount of this, I will show, at a moderate estimate, the value of a herd, the property of an overlander who arrived in Adelaide in the month of March, 1840, from the district of Illawarra, New South Wales:—Horned stock, £8,550; horses, £3,720; wethers, £1,575: total value, £13,845."

As might be naturally expected, the overlander often became the explorer when new lands were more urgently needed—as, indeed, was the case in the instance of the gentleman whose name we have placed at the head of this article. So much for Australian explorers and overlanders—now for the particular exploits of Mr. Eyre.

The progress of Australian settlement had been (and now is) a repetition of the same events, in the same order of succession:—the discovery of a new pastoral region, the rapid and eventually superabundant increase of the flocks and herds which quickly filled it, and then the demand for new lands. Thus New South Wales had found vent in the Adelaide district through the daring achievement of Captain Sturt (a name ever to be remembered in the annals of Australian exploration), who had boldly thrown himself on the grim and unknown interior. And now the

---

* Now Governor of New Zealand.

Adelaide district was threatened with commercial ruin unless a fresh vent could be found. This district—scarcely with propriety known as South Australia—belongs to the eastern corner of the island-continent: the western corner is occupied by King George's Sound and the Swan River settlement, some 1,500 miles distant. This corner was known to consist of good grass lands, and the question arose—long and anxiously debated by the Adelaide colonists—how far these grass lands extended towards them in an eastern direction, and what was the nature of the intervening space? Of this intervening space nothing hitherto had been discovered; up to the moment at which we write it has been trod by one solitary white foot, that of Mr. Eyre himself. All that was known was that all round Adelaide to north and west lay an absolute and most forbidding waste of desert and pools of brackish water, and that necessity obliged them to break through this belt, whatever might be its unknown breadth. Mr. Eyre was appealed to: he had been to King George's Sound by vessel, and his testimony was corroborative of its good pastoral character. His opinion, however, was that the intervening space would be found an inhospitable and unmitigated desert, through which it would be impossible to drive sheep and cattle, and that search in a direct northern course—that is, towards the head of the colony, and in the direction of the centre of the island-continent—would be more likely to lead to available result. On this recommendation, the intended route of a large exploring expedition, already organised, was changed, and the leadership of it offered to Mr. Eyre. It becomes necessary to bear in mind these preliminary details in order to fully appreciate what followed. The command of the expedition was accepted by Mr. Eyre. On the morning of its departure a large entertainment was given at Government House in honour of the undertaking: the ladies of Adelaide had embroidered a Union Jack which Mr. Eyre was to plant in the centre of the continent, and this was now presented to him by Captain Sturt, who at the time held the office of Commissioner of Crown Lands* in the colony which he had helped so materially to found. A gay cavalcade escorted the expedition beyond the city boundaries, and with a parting cheer, and much waving of handkerchiefs by the ladies, sent it on its way into the wilderness. "As we dashed over the bridge," writes Mr. Eyre, "and up the hill in North Adelaide, it was a heart-stirring and inspiriting scene."

---

* All colonial lands not alienated—*i.e.*, sold to private individuals—are known as Crown Lands.

Repeated attempts to advance in a northerly direction all ended in failure. It is not easy to picture the blank desolation which reigns towards the north of the colony of South Australia. The traveller leaves wealthy homesteads, smiling vineyards, and rich golden cornfields, yielding the finest grain in the world, to find himself on the edge of a desert consisting of mud, brine, and patches of water so

HURLING THE SPEAR.

deeply encrusted with salt as to resemble hoar-frost. Later explorers have found a way—more, indeed, by accident than design—through this forbidding belt to more desirable regions. Such accident, however, was denied to Mr. Eyre, and he completed a quadrant of a circle in vain efforts to pierce this treacherous surface, finally arriving at the head of Spencer Gulf, where the belt itself communicates with the Southern Ocean.

An ordinary man would have estimated his defeat at its true value, and returned to Adelaide with his expedition. Such, however—be it to his credit or the contrary—is not Mr. Eyre. He had altered the exploring expedition from its original intention of effecting a junction with the western settlement of Swan River by a direct westerly route. He now determined to take up this westerly route, and live or die in an effort to pass through 1,500 miles of a wholly unknown tract of country. The resolution can scarcely be justified on the grounds of reason or necessity. Mr. Eyre's plan was to risk no European life save his own in the attempt. The expedition was sent back: its officers expostulated with their leader; they pointed out his own previous arguments against a westerly route; finally, they implored permission to accompany him; but Mr. Eyre was firm. One European, who had been for many years his faithful servant, and who now occupied the position of overseer in the expedition, proved as wholly obstinate as its leader; it was his firm resolve to perish with his master, and Mr. Eyre at length yielded to his wishes. Two aborigines who had been brought up on Mr. Eyre's own squatting station were also retained, and a young native black named Wylie, belonging to Swan River settlement. Such was the small force which now set forth on the most hopelessly forbidding region of country which, considering its immense extent, is to be found on the surface of the earth. " We were now alone," writes Mr. Eyre, " myself, my overseer, and the three native boys, with a fearful task before us. The bridge was broken down behind us, and we must succeed in reaching King George's Sound or perish. No middle course remained."

A word as to the peculiar nature of this terrible region may not be inappropriate. Captain Flinders, to whom the world is indebted for the most complete marine surveys of the Australian sea-coast line, had sailed along the whole of this south coast, but had found it impossible to effect a landing: a violent current sweeps round the Great Australian Bight, eating into the coast, while high and perpendicular cliffs were found to tower from 300 to 600 feet above the deck of his vessel. Thus the whole coast-line had remained perfectly abandoned up to the period of Mr. Eyre's visit. He now found the summits of these cliffs to consist of one unbroken level platform, overlooking the lonely ocean, and stretching inland without rise or fall. A thick and perfectly impenetrable screen of "scrub" hid the interior from view; while, occasionally, huge masses of the limestone cliffs became detached, and tumbled into the boiling waves beneath, emitting the only sound which broke the utter desolation of the scene. During the day a fierce sirocco blew from the interior, bearing with it large volumes of fine sand; towards evening this was met by an exceedingly cold blast, coming up from the great Southern Ocean. These two antagonistic atmospheric currents caused a deposition of sand on the edge of this high limestone table-land, on which a few herbs had taken root, barely sufficient to yield a scanty sustenance to the horses and to the few sheep which were to form their food on their journey. Water, however, was the great essential, and the hopes of Mr. Eyre and his man were founded on the supposition that the country would soon become sufficiently open for progress into the interior, or that the elevated table-land on which they trod would become sufficiently depressed for inland streams to find their way to the coast.

II.

The Water-bags Empty—The Horses Give Way—The Sandhills—A Well Made —No Water but at the Various Sandhills—Superior Endurance of Man above Other Animals—Half the Distance Accomplished—Restlessness of the Horses—Mr. Eyre and his Overseer Watch Them—Murder of the Overseer —Escape and Recapture of the Horses—The Adelaide Natives Steal the Provisions—The Horses Killed for Food—A Whaling Vessel Sighted—. Return to Adelaide—Quarrels between the Aborigines and Colonists— Mr. Eyre appointed Black Protector, Governor of Wellington, N.Z.— Lieutenant-Governor of Jamaica—Full Governor—Respect for Mr. Eyre in Australia.

THE first day's march was accomplished without the appearance of any such result—and the second: finally, Mr. Eyre and his small party arrived at the head of the Great Bight without meeting a drop of fresh water, or without possibility of descending to the sea or advancing to any appreciable distance inland. Their water-bags were now quite empty, the sheep in a pitiable state of exhaustion, and the horses—always the first to give in under great drought—strewn along the way which they had traversed. Some distance beyond the Great Bight a few sandhills were seen to raise their insignificant heights, and by digging down to the base of these a little moisture was found to lie concealed between the sand and the limestone table-land. Here they constructed a well, though with considerable difficulty, from the falling nature of the sand, to which the sheep added in their frantic efforts to reach the water. The water-bags were now re-filled, though the water flowed so slowly into the well that the greater portion of the night was consumed in this operation. Loaded with these bags Mr. Eyre and his men retraced their way to the horses, and eventually succeeded in bringing them on to the sandhills. Some days were spent in recruiting, when the party made a fresh start, hoping for better luck.

Extraordinary as it may appear, these groups of sandhills, occurring at distances of 200 and 300 miles from each other, yielded the sole supplies of fresh water which were found along the whole extent of this terrible coast, a circumstance without parallel in the experience of geographical discovery. Mr. Eyre's account of one of these forced marches from sandhill to sandhill well exemplifies the superior endurance of man above all other animals. Generally about the third or fourth day the horses exhibited symptoms of failing. Their light loads, consisting of a few indispensable articles of baggage, were then taken off them and left on the wayside. Relieved of these they managed to struggle on for a day or two more; beyond which, however, no power could get them to advance. Providing themselves with the empty water-bags, Mr. Eyre and his men now pushed forward until a group of sandhills appeared in sight. Here they scooped out a well, slaked their thirst, and took a few hours' rest while the bags were filling. Loaded with these, they returned to the horses, and brought them to the sandhills; occasionally, however, they found one in the agonies of death, and past all assistance. Arrived for the second time at the sandhills, the most laborious portion of these herculean toils commenced. Their baggage, consisting of flour, tea, sugar, guns, and ammunition, still lay strewn along the track, sometimes as much as fifty or sixty miles behind them, and these they were obliged to carry on their backs while the horses regained some little strength at the sandhills. By such means they had advanced so far into these forbidding solitudes as to render a return a matter of extreme uncertainty, and were now led on by hope of some ameliorating change in the character of the country. They had accomplished more than half the distance between Adelaide and King George's Sound when Mr. Eyre's cup of toil and anxiety, already full to overflowing, received a wholly unexpected and most distressing increase.

In addition to the harassing and exhaustive toils we have recorded, Mr. Eyre and the overseer had also taken upon themselves a task of great, and, indeed, vital, importance. The horses—the sheep had long since disappeared—though incapable of the same endurance as themselves, were, nevertheless, of essential service in conveying their few articles from stage to stage as long as the water-bags lasted—that is, during the first three or four days from sandhill to sandhill. At night, however, notwithstanding their weariness, they became extremely restless, especially after the water-bags ran low, seizing every opportunity to return to the last stage. Nor could they be tethered, since, in consequence of the extremely scanty and scattered nature of the few tufts of herbage, they would run the risk of absolute starvation. So responsible a task, therefore, as watching the horses at night, Mr. Eyre and the overseer deemed unsafe to be intrusted to the three aboriginal youths, and up to the present they had taken it in turns between them, Mr. Eyre watching one half the night and his man the other. On one of these occasions, when some two months of their weary journey had been accomplished, the earlier portion of the night watch had fallen to Mr. Eyre's share. The horses—it was now three days since they had passed the last water stage—proved unusually restless, drawing Mr. Eyre to a considerable distance from their temporary camp in their efforts to return. As it approached midnight, when the overseer would relieve him, the chill sea-breeze had risen to a gale, sighing mournfully through the few belts of scrub which alone interrupted the dreary monotony of these desolate wilds. An Australian moon, however, poured its flood of light upon the scene, marking out the alternate wastes of sand and bare limestone surface, the few salsolaceous plants, and the white awning of their nightly dwelling in the distance, with the great Southern Ocean beyond and below. Suddenly the report of a gun was borne on the sea-breeze. Aroused by so startling and unexpected an event, Mr. Eyre hastened towards the camp. About half-way he was met by Wylie, the King George's Sound native, running towards him in great alarm, and exclaiming, "Oh, massa! oh, massa! come here," but unable to afford him any information. On reaching the camp, which he did in about five minutes after the shot was fired, a dreadful sight met his gaze. The scanty stores of flour, tea, and sugar had been broken open, and the contents rifled; the two Adelaide natives had disappeared, and the overseer lay on the ground weltering in his blood, and in the last agonies of death. He had been shot in the left breast by a ball, and in a few moments he expired. The wretched remnant of food had been the incentive to this terrible and most atrocious act, and the Adelaide native youths, the murderers, had also taken with them all the water, and all the arms and ammunition they could lay their hands upon. "The frightful, the appalling truth now burst upon me," writes Mr. Eyre, "that I was alone in the desert. He who had faithfully served me for many years, who had followed my fortunes in adversity and prosperity, who had accompanied me in all my wanderings, and whose attachment to me had been his sole inducement to remain with me in this last, and, to him, alas! fatal journey, was now no more. For an instant I was almost tempted to wish that it had been my own fate instead of his. The horrors of my situation glared upon me with such startling reality as for an instant almost to paralyse the mind. At the dead hour of night, in the wildest and most inhospitable wastes of Australia, with a fierce wind raging in unison with the scene of violence before me, I was left with a single native, whose fidelity I could not rely upon, and who, for aught I knew, might be in league with the other two, who, perhaps, were even now lurking about with a view of taking away my own life, as they had done that of the overseer. Three days had passed

THROWING THE BOOMERANG.

away since we left the last water, and it was very doubtful when we might find any more. Six hundred miles of country had to be traversed before I could hope to obtain the slightest aid or assistance of any kind, whilst I knew not that a single drop of water or an ounce of flour had been left by these murderers from a stock that had previously been so small."

The horses, however, were the first and vital consideration, and, leaving this scene of violence and treachery till the morning's light, Mr. Eyre and Wylie hastened after them. They had already set out on their return to the last stage, and Mr. Eyre and his solitary attendant had considerable difficulty in coming up with them. "Having succeeded in doing so," continues Mr. Eyre, "Wylie and I remained with them, watching them during the remainder of the night; but they were very restless, and gave us a deal of trouble. With an aching heart, and in most painful reflection, I passed this dreadful night; every moment appeared to be protracted to an hour, and it seemed as if the daylight would never appear. About midnight the wind ceased, and it became bitterly cold and frosty. I had nothing on but a shirt and a pair of trousers, and suffered most acutely from the cold. To mental anguish was now added intense bodily pain. Suffering and distress had well-nigh overwhelmed me, and life seemed hardly worth the effort necessary to prolong it. Ages can never efface the horrors of this single night, nor would the wealth of the world tempt me to go through similar ones again." With the morning they returned to the encampment, and proceeded to perform the last sad office to their late companion. So thin, however, was the coating of sand on the surface of the limestone rock, that it was found impossible to bury the body, and, wrapping it in a blanket, they hastened from the dreary and fatal scene. A few pounds of flour was all that their utmost research could discover, and, abandoning everything else, they took their departure. The two Adelaide natives made their appearance as they were starting, and endeavoured to seduce Wylie from his allegiance; but they could not be induced to hold converse with Mr. Eyre. Failing in their attempt, they disappeared again into the wilderness, and were never more heard of. Considering their limited stock of provisions and the absolute desolation of all around, Mr. Eyre is of opinion that they perished.

Mr. Eyre and his dusky companion were now obliged to subsist on their horses, killing one at intervals, curing the flesh in the sun, and carrying on a sufficient stock to last some days. On these occasions the governing instinct of the Australian savage exhibited itself—eating, and eating to satiety. In blackfellow's eyes all human felicity consists in repletion: his mind—and he has an extremely acute one—acknowledges no other incentive to action. When a horse was killed, Wylie devoured several pounds before retiring to rest. Almost hourly during the night, Mr. Eyre heard him getting up to resume his meal. He made sad and dismal moanings, and complained of pain in his throat, the effect, he averred, of having to work too hard. He lay on the ground. He roared in agonies of indigestion. He entreated to be allowed to rest for one day longer—he was ill, very ill, and was curing himself with horseflesh. "I did not find that his indisposition interfered greatly with his appetite, for nearly every time I awoke during the night I found him up and gnawing away at his meat. He was literally fulfilling the promise he had made me during the evening, 'By-and-by, you see, massa, me eat all night.'"* Before resuming their march he loaded himself with choice pieces, and wept over all he was obliged to leave behind him.

At length this immense line of highly-elevated cliff gave indications of depressing, and by-and-by they were enabled to get down to the sea beach, where they occasionally caught a stinging ray. Water, however, was still their great need, and under the wretched and infrequent supplies of it already described, both mind and body threatened to succumb. Indeed, there is little doubt that such would have been the ultimate result but that a whaling barque was at length seen off the coast which had come up from the Antarctic station for the purpose of executing some temporary repairs. "Poor Wylie's joy," writes Mr. Eyre, "now knew no bounds, and he leaped and skipped about with delight as he congratulated me once more upon the prospect of getting plenty to eat. I was no less pleased than he was, and almost as absurd; for although the vessel lay quietly at anchor near us, with no sails loose, and her boats away, I could not help fearing that she might disappear before we could get to her, or attract the notice of those on board." Their signals were perceived, and a boat immediately despatched to them by the commander of the vessel, Captain Rossiter, of the French whaling ship Mississippi. They were received on board with much kindness and hospitality, and being detained until they had fully regained their strength, they were again landed within reach of the small settlement at King George's Sound. They reached the settlement in July, 1841, when twelve months absent from Adelaide. Thus was brought to a termination a forced march which, considering all the circumstances of distance, physical difficulties, and human treachery, stands alone in the history of exploration. After some delay the services of a vessel were procured, and Mr. Eyre returned in safety to the colony of South Australia, long after all hope of him had been abandoned.

About the period of Mr. Eyre's return to Adelaide, the overlanders, in their periodic trips down the banks of the Murray with the cattle of New South Wales, had fallen into very bad relations with the native tribes of the great Australian river. Pilferings of cattle, and bloodshed

---

* Eyre's Journals.

in retaliation, had become the order of the day. Mr. Eyre was now offered the post of black protector and resident magistrate at Menindie, which he continued to fill with satisfaction for the three following years. He supplied the aborigines with food and clothing from Government stores, and succeeded in bringing about a complete footing of friendship between black and white. Mr. Eyre's name is still to be heard uttered with esteem and thankfulness at Menindie. Returning to England, the British Government appointed him Lieutenant-Governor of the province of Wellington, in New Zealand, which position of responsibility he assumed in 1850. In 1854 we find him transferred to the Governorship of the West Indian island of St. Vincent. In 1862 he received the appointment of Lieutenant-Governor of Jamaica, and on the transference of his chief, Sir Charles Darling, to the colony of Victoria, Australia, he was promoted to the post of full governor in 1864. The results of that appointment scarcely lie within the scope of our article, and, indeed, our limits now forbid us to enter upon it. But whatever may be the final and unprejudiced judgment on Mr. Eyre's acts as Governor of Jamaica, we believe our narrative will show him to have been in possession of no ordinary energy, courage, and humanity in the cause of the Australian native, capable of winning the respect and devotion alike of European and aboriginal. As such he is still regarded throughout the whole of the Australian colonies, on whose inhabitants the charges preferred against him have come wholly by surprise.

www.ingramcontent.com/pod-product-compliance
Lightning Source LLC
Chambersburg PA
CBHW030553300426
44111CB00009B/960